VOCATIONAL GUIDANCE AND CAREER DEVELOPMENT IN THE SCHOOLS: TOWARD A SYSTEMS APPROACH

Edwin L. Herr

The Pennsylvania State University

Stanley H. Cramer

State University of New York at Buffalo

HOUGHTON MIFFLIN COMPANY • BOSTON

NEW YORK • ATLANTA • GENEVA, ILLINOIS • DALLAS • PALO ALTO

Printed in the U.S.A.

Library of Congress Catalog Card Number: 72-171425

ISBN: 0-395-12638-X

CONTENTS

EDITOR'S INTRODUCTION   vii

PREFACE   ix

CHAPTER ONE: VOCATIONAL GUIDANCE: PAST, PRESENT, AND FUTURE   3

Definitions • Some Historical Observations • Treatment or Stimulus • Vocational Guidance and Education • Interrelationships Between Education, Vocational Guidance, and Society • A Systems Approach • Plan of the Book • Summary

CHAPTER TWO: THE INGREDIENTS OF CAREER/VOCATIONAL DEVELOPMENT   25

Vocationalization • Approaches to Vocational Development • Reprise • Summary

CHAPTER THREE: THE AMERICAN OCCUPATIONAL STRUCTURE   64

The Changing Scene • Relation of Occupational Structure to Vocational Guidance • Occupation Classification Systems • Summary

CHAPTER FOUR: THE CONSUMERS OF VOCATIONAL GUIDANCE   84

Heterogeneity but Same Basic Needs • Minority Groups • Summary

CHAPTER FIVE: FORMULATING OBJECTIVES FOR VOCATIONAL GUIDANCE   99

Vocational Maturity • Developmental Tasks • Current Research Pertinent to Vocationalization • Approaches to Writing Objectives • A Sample of Program and Behavioral Descriptions Combined • Objectives and Vocational Guidance as Treatment • Summary

CHAPTER SIX: VOCATIONAL GUIDANCE, VOCATIONALIZATION, AND THE ELEMENTARY SCHOOL   143

Principles of Vocational Guidance • Mandates of Vocational Guidance • Strategies of Vocational Guidance • Sequencing Vocational Guidance Experiences • Behavioral Descriptions • Summary

CHAPTER SEVEN: VOCATIONAL GUIDANCE, VOCATIONALIZATION, AND THE
            JUNIOR HIGH SCHOOL   163

Characteristics of Youth in Transition • Sex Differences • Differences in Maturity • A Time for Early School Leaving • Vocational Guidance Strategies • Vocational Guidance Strategies for Decision Making and Problem Solving • Simulation as a Vocational Guidance Strategy • Information Retrieval • Vocational Guidance Strategies and Work • Vocational Education • Staffing for Vocational Guidance • Summary

CHAPTER EIGHT: VOCATIONAL GUIDANCE, VOCATIONALIZATION, AND THE
            SENIOR HIGH SCHOOL   192

Vocationalization, Vocational Guidance, and Vocational Education • Vocational Education and Handicapped Students • Vocational Education for Minority-Group or Disadvantaged Youth • Vocationalization and General Education • Vocational Guidance Strategies to Foster Decision Making • Vocational Resource Centers and Conferences • Placement • Summary

CHAPTER NINE: HELPING STRATEGIES IN VOCATIONAL GUIDANCE   221

Individual Counseling • Group Processes • Environmental Treatment • Summary

CHAPTER TEN: ASSESSMENT AND EVALUATION IN VOCATIONAL GUIDANCE   250

Prediction • Discrimination • Monitoring • Evaluation • Summary

CHAPTER ELEVEN: INFORMATION IN VOCATIONAL GUIDANCE   278

Principles for Using Information Effectively • Types of Delivery Systems • Occupational Information in the Elementary School • Opportunities for Dropout and Terminal Students • Summary

CHAPTER TWELVE: COOPERATIVE EFFORTS IN VOCATIONAL GUIDANCE   308

Some Factors Spurring Cooperative Effort • Planning for Coordination and Cooperation • State-Level Leadership in Vocational Guidance • Teachers • The School Counselor • The Employment Service Counselor • The Rehabilitation Counselor • Business and Industry Personnel • The Guidance Paraprofessional • Summary

CHAPTER THIRTEEN: BRINGING ABOUT CHANGE IN THE SCHOOLS   333

Change from Within Versus Change from Without • General Principles and Strategies of Change • Overcoming Resistance to Change • Inaugurating a Systems Approach

INDEX   347

EDITOR'S INTRODUCTION

At first, there was only day and night, only a small tribe or two of the "first men," only a small food-seeking area, its boundaries limited by rivers and mountains and the fear of possible others. Now one can turn night into day and work or play as he wills. One can travel from one part of the earth to another at 600 miles per hour, to the moon at 24,000 miles per hour. *Systems* of illumination and transportation have transformed the simple "first." Now people exist by the billion in cement cities as well as on the land — all kinds of people with all kinds of cultures and cultural pasts. So *systems* of knowledge develop and *systems* of education to transmit that knowledge and all emerging knowledge. Now nations exist, each having its own political, economic, and defense *systems*. Today each man lives within various *systems* — a national system, a social system, a vocational system, an educational system. We exist by appropriately relating the part to the whole, the individual to the system.

This book deals with vocational development as a *subsystem* within the larger system of education — or of a school. Several systems approaches to the phenomenon of vocational choice have been described within the past decade by such research-oriented writers as Cooley, Loughary, Oettinger, Vriend, Cogswell, Super and his colleagues, Tiedeman and his colleagues. A "system" in the scholarly sense is more precise and exacting than my more colloquial use of the term in the preceding paragraphs suggests. The precise and the colloquial have in common the interrelatedness of the parts that make up the whole and the requirement of cooperative effort. Beyond this, however, a "thinking" system requires (1) establishing the specific and operational objectives to be attained, (2) considering the variables involved and the procedures to be used in achieving the goals, (3) developing a model using these variables and procedures, (4) evaluating the outcomes of the operation of the model against the objectives set at the beginning. The first two steps are the most difficult — stating explicit objectives and recognizing all the variables. One is then ready to develop procedures and test outcomes.

The authors of this book carry the reader through the stages of a systems approach to vocational guidance. They do so with care and explicitness. Their system is clearly within the total context of the school. Vocational development is the objective, and the schools' resources provide the variables and the procedures. Because the authors are mature scholars and well informed in this field beyond normal expectations, they leave no stone unturned in the literature and in their thinking to make the objective explicit and understandable. The school resources they examine are *total* school resources — counselors, teachers, learning methods available, technical equipment available, institutional and community expectations. They apply the systems approach separately to elementary, junior high, and high school levels.

I am pleased that the authors are concerned about the individualization of *each* pupil's objectives and that they analyze programmed learning, individual counseling, and group counseling as varied ways to achieve this individualization. Another strength of the book is that the authors understand vocational education as well as they understand the careful assessment of behavioral outcomes. Few other writers show this knowledge of *total school curricula* combined with *psychological understanding* and assessment.

This is a complete book. All facets of the vocational guidance field are examined, and with care. The reader will leave the book satisfied that he, too, has examined the field thoroughly, led by competent guides.

C. GILBERT WRENN

PREFACE

This book represents as much an attempt to develop a position statement about the potential significance of vocational guidance within the educational context as it does an attempt to survey the approaches to and elements comprising vocational guidance. Some readers of this volume are likely to disagree with the emphasis we have assigned to career/vocational development (or vocationalization) as a significant part of the broad goals to which education should respond. Similarly, other readers may take issue with our analysis of vocational guidance as both a stimulus to vocationalization and a treatment of behavioral deficits resulting from incomplete vocationalization. We view a systems approach to meeting individual and social needs through vocational guidance as having humanizing ends; however, some readers may interpret our stance as mechanistic or fraught with social engineering overtones.

Regardless of how our efforts are perceived, it is clear to us that historically the potential significance of vocational guidance as an integral subsystem of education has not been fully appreciated in the schools of America. In addition, it is apparent that the factors which influence career/vocational development and the elements which comprise it are diverse. Experience, knowledge, attitudes, social values, intellectual prowess, socioeconomic status, chronology, preferences, special aptitudes, race — all these variables and more independently and collectively affect the acquisition of vocational behavior. They also determine the level of the individual's sense of personal competence and the degree to which he is able to approach the future planfully rather than reactively. Hence the diversity of influences, as well as the diversity of individual status based on the behaviors which result, require diversity in vocational guidance.

Although the school counselor is a central figure in career/vocational development, creating the needed conditions and programs, he cannot do the job alone. Many persons in the school and extra-school environment are potentially constructive sources of input to vocational guidance. Many resources, devices, and facilities could provide vocational guidance responses to individual levels of readiness or need.

If we are able to direct the reader's thoughts to what we see as alternative ways of systematically putting into effect vocational guidance programs in the schools, or, more importantly, if we are able to stimulate the reader to reaffirm the importance of such programs to the lives of children and to the ultimate welfare of society, our major purpose will have been achieved.

We are grateful to our colleagues who have performed the research cited in this volume and have thus provided the "science" upon which the "art" of vocational guidance is based. We also appreciate the critical reactions of our colleagues at The Pennsylvania State University and at the State University of New York at Buffalo.

E. L. H.
S. H. C.

DEDICATION

Samuel L. Herr (August 23, 1903 – September 7, 1968),
   weaver, laborer, mechanic, school custodian,
   whose respect for the dignity of work was exceeded
   only by his respect for the dignity of people.

Louis Cramer (March 24, 1903 –   ),
   yankee peddler, retail merchant, jobber,
   who stopped to smell the flowers.

ONE

VOCATIONAL GUIDANCE:
PAST, PRESENT, AND FUTURE

Why vocational guidance? Why the schools? Why a systems approach? These are the questions to which this chapter is addressed. The answers represent the assumptions on which the chapters which follow are based.

DEFINITIONS

Guidance has many roots. It represents the confluence of social pressures, inter-disciplinary insights about human behavior and its dynamics, concerns for maximum use of human resources, and demands for personalization in an increasingly complex and depersonalized society. For these reasons, the term "guidance" is variously used to represent a concept, a philosophy, and a label for the services which implement the philosophy.

Guidance has been defined "as that part of pupil personnel services—and therefore of elementary and secondary education—aimed at maximal development of individual potentialities through devoting school-wide assistance to youth in the personal problems, choices, and decisions each must face as he moves toward maturity" (Hoyt, 1962, p. 692). Guidance has also been seen as the professional use of a science of purposeful action within the specific structure of education (Tiedeman and Field, 1962).

The vocational aspects of guidance, usually called vocational guidance, have a somewhat narrower focus than either of the latter definitions. Vocational guidance is a fusion of educational and vocational concerns for assisting students to locate themselves vocationally in the future and at the same time to make effective use of present educational experiences connected to such further choices. However, it does not preclude the personal. Locating oneself vocationally in the future, however defined, must be predicated upon coming to terms with one's values and life purposes, with one's personal characteristics and orientation toward or away from others—in short, those things about the self that can serve as reference points for sorting and evaluating alternatives made available by society. In one sense, nothing is more personal than choosing the way to spend one's life.

The broad area of vocational guidance is an aspect of every approach to the guidance process (Zaccaria, 1969, p. 38). As such it uses the same tactics—e.g.

counseling, group work, testing, referral, information—used in other types of guidance. Indeed, in practice, it rarely functions apart from a comprehensive program of guidance services designed to meet a complex of student needs. The difference in vocational guidance compared with other kinds lies in its objectives and in the individual performance to be expected.

Vocational guidance has been described as "the process or program of assistance designed to aid the individual in choosing and adjusting to a vocation" (Crites, 1969, p. 23). Thus it is principally concerned with vocational behavior including the antecedents, correlates, and development of such behavior as well as the set of responses ultimately made by individuals to different occupational stimuli. Because of expanding theoretical and research insights into vocational guidance, its historical definitions have been refined. The next section will consider this development.

SOME HISTORICAL OBSERVATIONS

Virtually no present theorist advocates restricting the processes or objectives of a guidance program to vocational guidance. The authors agree that this would be too limiting. Nevertheless, the vocational aspects of a guidance program are sufficiently vital to its overall success to deserve a central place in the perspective of school counselors. It must also be recognized that the objectives of such an emphasis are clearly related to the total aims of education.

Viewed historically, any analysis of the evolution of current guidance services would be incomplete without recognition of the initial stimulus and the continuing pervasive influence of early efforts to provide vocational guidance. Frank Parsons has become the symbol of the founding of the guidance movement, and his posthumously published classic, Choosing a Vocation, encouraged the development of the current methods and concepts of guidance programs. Parsons (1909, p. 5) formulated the following steps for "true reasoning," or vocational guidance:

First, a clear understanding of yourself, aptitude, abilities, interests, resources, limitations, and other qualities.

Second, a knowledge of the requirements and conditions of success, advantages and disadvantages, compensation, opportunities, and prospects in different lines of work.

Third, true reasoning on the relations of these two groups of facts.

Operationally, Parsons' three steps have been interpreted as indicating that an individual can be described as possessing certain traits (e.g. aptitudes, skills, interests), that different occupations can be described as requiring different patterns of these traits, and that fitting the two will result in a meaningful choice. Parsons originally conceived of this process as consisting of the following: surveying the individual's experiences and backgrounds through questionnaires and interviews to determine his abilities and interests, having the individual study occupations through reading and direct observation, and then combining these data through "true reasoning" or counseling to elicit choice.

This approach did not take into account the fact that a choice may be influenced by an individual's perceptions and values. In brief, it assumed that both individual traits and occupational requirements are unchanging anchor points which can define choice for the rest of one's life if "true reasoning" occurs in the first place. Parsons' formulation was, of course, limited by the knowledge then available about human behavior, psychological analysis, and experimental techniques for identifying occupational requirements and for predicting individual success in the tasks.

Parsons' formulation was also a product of the social trends at the beginning of the twentieth century. This was a period of intense immigration along the East Coast, which placed heavy demands upon assimilating the immigrants into an occupational structure that was changing rapidly as a result of the Industrial Revolution. Changes in technology, increasing job specialization, expanding programs of vocational education, acceleration of free public education, the working through of philosophies of individual rights confounded by Social Darwinism, and the rise of urban centers all accented the need for ways to aid the distribution of workers among the various occupations which these factors and forces produced.

Stephens (1970, p. 5) has argued convincingly that in Parsons' view and in that of his contemporaries, vocational guidance and vocational education were complementary responses not only to the slum conditions associated with immigration but also to the need for reforming education. Then, as now, public education was considered to be too college-oriented, too selective in the academic experiences and tasks it provided students, and insufficiently attuned to the needs of the majority of students. While the prime purpose of this book is to explore vocational guidance in the schools, in several chapters the readers will be reminded of the importance of broadening the present area of vocational education to include the total educational process; to create "career education," as it is becoming known, through federal and state legislation (see, for example, Arizona Senate Bill No. 5, 1971). Thus although the emphasis in the present work is on but one of the dimensions of social and educational reform given impetus early in this century, vocational guidance, it is imperative that the other, vocational education, be granted its due in any significant, systematic effort to change American education.

It seems appropriate to apply the statement that every important idea has its historical moment to vocational guidance and to Parsons' formulation of it. A year following the publication of Choosing a Vocation, the Binet tests were brought to the United States. In less than a decade, World War I had stimulated the need for mass psychological screening and for the development of techniques to classify military personnel for the diverse assignments existing in a modern army. In the return to a peacetime economy, the techniques of classification stimulated by military need were translated into methods useful to industry. Evidence about individual differences and their measurement began to accumulate significantly in the 1920's and 1930's, influencing educational processes and developing more responses to individual uniqueness in social institutions. The progressive education movement flourished, and with it an awareness of the importance of mental "hygiene" began to influence studies of individual behavior. The depression years emphasized vocational guidance as a vital force in addressing immediate needs—the problems of unemployment and placement in jobs.

During the depression years, the federal government exerted an increasing influence on shaping and stimulating the provision of vocational guidance. The National Youth Administration (NYA), for example, set up five guidance goals to increase the employment of youth in out-of-school projects (Miller, 1961, p. 160):

1. To help the youth evaluate himself
2. To help him make a vocational choice
3. To help him plan his training program to achieve this choice
4. To place him in the work
5. To follow up on the work assignment to insure good results for him

The NYA also stimulated cooperation among government agencies to provide occupational information and to expand the use of community resources for vocational guidance. The *Dictionary of Occupational Titles* and the Occupational Outlook Service were conceived during this period by the Department of Labor. In 1938, a special unit was established in the United States Office of Education in which responsibilities for guidance were essentially an adjunct of vocational education.

World War II accelerated the application of psychometrics to the selection and classification of personnel, and its conclusion created a strong need to advise veterans about their educational and occupational opportunities in peacetime pursuits. Strong federal support was given to the initiation of vocational guidance programs in schools, colleges, and other community facilities. In 1952, the guidance function in the United States Office of Education was removed from the Division of Vocational Education and placed under a broader designation— Pupil Personnel Services. In 1958, at least partially as a result of the U.S.S.R.'s launching of Sputnik I, the National Defense Education Act appropriated funds which could be used to train secondary school counselors and to reimburse the local development of secondary school guidance programs including the testing of students to identify those with outstanding academic promise. In 1964, this act was amended to extend guidance services to elementary schools and to colleges and universities. Many other pieces of federal legislation at different points in time also influenced the development of guidance programs and the conception of vocational guidance. These will be discussed in various places throughout the book.

This description of some of the historical inputs to vocational guidance, sketchy as it is, does give a sense of the reciprocal effects of societal needs and of the unfolding understandings of behavior and resources which have cast vocational guidance into ever more comprehensive forms. Some support for a cycling of emphases in vocational guidance is apparent in Williamson's contention (1965, p. 77) that although Parsons' focus was on his first step—individual analysis and clarification as it could be accomplished with the techniques available in his day—Parsons' immediate successors concentrated on his second step, which resulted in a fixation on vocational information. However, as vocational information was being developed to describe more precisely occupational requirements in terms of human capabilities, psychologists were applying similar skills to diagnose more adequately individual aptitudes and interests in such terms that vocational information and individual analysis could be used in related ways. On balance, then, Parsons' three-step process provided the underlying structure for vocational guidance efforts even though it underwent refinement and elaboration through most of the period into the 1950's.

By the early 1950's, there had appeared new emphases in psychotherapy, particularly the work of Carl Rogers (1942, 1951), as well as a heightened awareness that neither individual personality characteristics nor occupational/educational requirements are static but are constantly changing. These new trends led Hoppock (1950) to conclude that the foundations of the traditional views of vocational guidance were "beginning to crumble." In 1951, Super recommended revision of the official definition of vocational guidance which had stood since 1937: the "process of assisting the individual to choose an occupation, prepare for it, enter upon and progress in it" (Crites, 1969, p. 21). Super (1951, p. 92) defines vocational guidance as "the process of helping a person to develop and accept an integrated and adequate picture of himself and of his role in the world of work, to test this concept against reality, and to convert it into a reality, with satisfaction to himself and benefit to society."

This definition does not emphasize the provision of occupational information at a particular point in time or a simple matching of man and job. Rather it emphasizes the psychological nature of vocational choice. Indeed, it changes the primary focus from process alone to process and a substantive content. Super's definition effectively blended into a unified whole the personal and vocational dimensions of guidance, which previously had been arbitrarily separated. The resulting, current view of vocational guidance is self-concept oriented. It focuses primarily on self-understanding and self-acceptance, to which can be related the occupational and educational alternatives available to the individual. Finally, Super's definition implies that vocational guidance must rest upon the intent to facilitate accurate self-attitudes and considered value sets, which free the individual to acquire task-relevant skills and permit him to choose with purpose and to pursue with commitment the opportunities available to him (Herr, 1968).

TREATMENT OR STIMULUS

Perhaps the most important point that Super's definition of vocational guidance makes is that it can be conceived of in two different ways: (1) as a treatment condition or (2) as a stimulus variable (Crites, 1968, p. 22). These two conceptions are not mutually exclusive, but they do represent different perceptions of the needs of clients and of the time frame within which vocational guidance operates.

TREATMENT

If vocational guidance is seen as a treatment condition, then it will be seen as problem oriented or, at least, as appropriate primarily at decision points and thus restricted in time. In this sense vocational guidance will be viewed, either directly or indirectly, as responding to taxonomies of vocational problems or to difficulties in choice by applying certain techniques or knowledge to resolve them. The vocational guidance practitioner or vocational counselor is likely to define the vocational difficulties experienced by his clientele in ways similar to those proposed by Williamson, Bordin, Byrne, and more recently Robinson.

Williamson (1939, p. 428) suggested that vocational problems can be described as:

1. *No choice—Individuals cannot discriminate sufficiently among occupations to select one and commit themselves to it.*

2. *Uncertain choice—A choice has been made but the person is uncertain about it.*

3. *Unwise choice—There is a disagreement between the individual's abilities or interests and the occupation which he selects.*

4. *Discrepancy between interests and aptitudes—There is disagreement in the type or amount of these two traits as they interact or should interact in defining choice.*

Bordin (1946, p. 174), commenting upon Williamson's problem categories, suggested that "the assignment of the individual's difficulties to one of this set of classes of difficulties does not provide a basis for predictions of the relative success of different treatments." This observation led him to develop five other problem categories more psychologically oriented than Williamson's:

1. *Dependence*

2. *Lack of information*

3. *Self-conflict*

4. *Choice anxiety and,*

5. *No problem*

Byrne (1958) expressed displeasure at generalizing to high school students from the college samples of vocational problems used by Williamson and Bordin. He suggested that the problems could more adequately be described thus (p. 187):

1. *Immaturity in situation*
2. *Lack of problem-solving skill*
3. *Lack of insight*
4. *Lack of information*
5. *Lack of assurance*
6. *Domination by authority*

Robinson (1963, p. 332) suggested another modification of these diagnostic constructs into the following categories:

1. *Personal maladjustment*
2. *Conflict with significant others*
3. *Discussing plans [instead of Bordin's no-problem category]*
4. *Lack of information about environment*
5. *Immaturity*
6. *Skill deficiency*

In each of these four sets of problem criteria—by Williamson, Bordin, Byrne, and Robinson—symptoms and causes, or some interactions of the two, are confounded. The important point, however, is that they all imply a deficit of some type in the behavioral repertoire of the individual on the basis of which the strategies for vocational guidance treatment will be selected. Further, the assumption of all these criteria is that the problem in any one of the categories will surface at a decision point. Thus vocational guidance will be effective as a *post hoc* response to a problem that is already present and which impedes the individual from progressing to some new phase of life, i.e. entry into the labor force, selection of a specific occupation, etc.

STIMULUS

Conceiving of vocational guidance as a stimulus variable rests on a different set of assumptions than does viewing it as treatment. As a stimulus variable, vocational guidance can be more effectively viewed longitudinally and developmentally. The time frame in which it will operate depends partly upon the setting of the program and partly upon the characteristics of those progressing through the setting.

As a stimulus variable, vocational guidance does not respond to already existing problems. Rather, it aids in acquiring knowledge, attitudes, and skills which individuals can develop the vocational behaviors deemed necessary to cope with decision points, acquire vocational identity, or develop vocational maturity. Whereas in the diagnostic categories previously identified vocational guidance processes were determined by the presenting problem of the person to be assisted, vocational guidance as stimulus is more future oriented and developmental. For example, if the ultimate goal of vocational guidance is to have persons attain "vocational maturity," this rubric must be described and dissected into its behavioral elements. It must then be determined whether individuals can be assisted to acquire those elements on a developmental time line (e.g. preschool, elementary school, junior high school, senior high school). Finally, determinations must be made about both the content and the process to be used in stimulating acquisition of behaviors, knowledge, attitudes, and skills which will interact to build increasingly effective behavior as individuals proceed toward vocational maturity.

Vocational guidance conceived as a stimulus variable seems naturally to cohabit with the process of education. Although the formulation of vocational guidance propositions and the provision of services to implement them began outside of education, no other social institution in Western society has the potential of such intensive, long-term *impact* upon the lives of individuals.

VOCATIONAL GUIDANCE AND EDUCATION

Statements about education have long echoed the importance of preparing young persons to make choices about work and to enter work successfully. For example, the NEA's Commission on the Reorganization of Secondary Education (United States Bureau of Education, 1918) indicated that the seven main objectives of American secondary education were health, command of fundamental processes, worthy home membership, *vocation*, citizenship, worthy use of leisure, and ethical character. This report followed closely the report of the Commission on National Aid to Vocational Education (House of Representatives, 1914), which spoke not only of "actual training for a vocation" but also schooling designed to extend the general "civic or vocational intelligence" of young workers over age fourteen as well as evening schools "to extend the vocational knowledge of mature workers over sixteen years of age." These statements and goals were refined and repronounced throughout the 1920's and 1930's with a resurgence of concern about the fact that secondary schools and colleges were meeting the needs of only a fraction of American youth.

In 1946, under the aegis of the United States Office of Education, a series of regional conferences brought together general and vocational educators from various levels to consider the subject "Vocational Education in the Years Ahead." The consensus of these meetings was (Cremin, 1961, p. 335):

1. Secondary education was "failing to provide adequately and properly for the life adjustment of perhaps a major fraction of the persons of secondary school age."

2. "Functional experiences in the areas of practical arts, home and family life, health and physical fitness, and civic competence" are fundamental to any educational program designed to meet the needs of youth.

3. A supervised program of work experience is essential for most high school youngsters.

4. Those entrusted with the education of teachers need "a broadened viewpoint and a genuine desire to serve all youth."

This persistent concern about the relevance of education to the needs and abilities of youth as they move toward adulthood with its requirement for vocational identity and commitment has not abated. Indeed, the concern of the federal government in particular has accelerated. The importance of work and of preparation for it has been accentuated by the Vocational Education Act of 1963 and more recently by the Vocational Education Act Amendments of 1968. This legislation does not simply provide more vocational education as defined by a narrowly restricted set of manipulative skills (e.g. carpentry, agriculture, machine trades). Rather, in these acts vocational education is increasingly presented as integral to and in partnership with general education and thus of value for large numbers of students, perhaps all. Contemporary legislative proposals, at the federal and state levels, are beginning to use the term "career education" to represent this thrust. These insights are captured in the following recommendations from the General Report of the Advisory Council on Vocational Education, 1968, entitled *Vocational Education: The Bridge Between Man and His Work*. The Advisory Council believes that an adequate system of vocational education should have the following characteristics:

1. *Occupational preparation should begin in the elementary schools with a realistic picture of the world of work. . . .*

2. *In junior high school, economic orientation and occupational preparation should reach a more sophisticated stage with study by all students of the economic and industrial system by which goods and services are produced and distributed. . . .*

3. *Occupational preparation should become more specific in the high school, though preparation should not be limited to a specific occupation. . . .*

4. *Occupational education should be based on a spiral curriculum which treats concepts at higher and higher levels of complexity as the student moves through the program. . . .*

5. *Some formal post-secondary occupational preparation for all should be a goal for the near future. . . .*

6. *Beyond initial preparation for employment, many, out of choice or necessity, will want to bolster an upward occupational climb with part-time and sometimes full-time courses and programs as adults. . . .*

7. *Any occupation which contributes to the good of society is a fit subject for vocational education. . . .*

8. *Occupational preparation need not and should not be limited to the classroom, to the school shop, or to the laboratory. . . .*

9. *Effective occupational preparation is impossible if the school feels that its obligation ends when the student graduates. . . .*

10. *No matter how good the system of initial preparation and the opportunities for up-grading on the job, there will always be need for remedial programs. . . .*

11. *At every level from the elementary school through the post-secondary, adult, and remedial programs, there will be those with special needs. . . .*

12. *Many communities are too small to muster sufficient students for a range of occupational offerings broad enough to provide realistic freedom of occupational choice. . . . An adequate system of occupational preparation will provide residential facilities wherever their absence presents an obstacle to anyone in need of education and training.*

13. *The public system for occupational preparation must be supported by adequate facilities and equipment, buttressed by research and innovation, and by the preparation and upgrading of competent teachers, counselors, and administrators. . . .*

14. *The system of occupational preparation cannot operate in a vacuum. . . .*

The scope of these recommendations cannot be interpreted as speaking only to vocational education as traditionally defined. They strike at the very core of the educational process in the United States. They indicate that as the outcomes of the education of many young persons are appraised, the irrelevance and lack of specific purpose found do not coincide with the philosophical and historical promise of American education. For example, one study published by the United States Office of Education (Grant, 1965) indicates that for every 10 pupils in the fifth grade in 1957–58, 9.4 entered the ninth grade in 1961–62, 8.1 entered the eleventh grade in 1963–64, 7.1 graduated from high school in 1965, 3.8 were expected to enter college in the fall of 1965, and 1.9 would likely earn baccalaureate degrees in 1969. Thus approximately 30 percent of American children leave education before high school graduation. These statistics include young persons with above-average as well as below-average mental ability who find no meaning in school, that is, who perceive that school is not designed for them. The same study also indicates that another 50 percent of the student population at the conclusion of high school enter the labor market directly and must come to terms with vocational choices either purposefully or by chance.

Finally, if college can be viewed as something other than an end in itself, as an intermediate step in vocational development, then those who select this option also need vocational help. Furthermore, students who progress through the public schools labeled as college-bound do not always choose to attend college, and if they do, they do not always stay. Thus that segment of the student population identified as having a prime interest in college needs help in coming to grips with career/vocational development issues just as vitally as do those students going directly from secondary school to work (Herr and Cramer, 1968).

It is not the purpose here to exhaust the documentation supporting the relevance of career/vocational development for preadolescents and adolescents. Studies examining whether career/vocational development and choice making are really of concern to students in elementary and secondary schools demonstrate repeatedly that students assert their interest in these areas. But these studies also indicate that education is not helping students plan the steps leading to their goals, to personal clarification, or to a sense of the vocational and social contexts with which they must cope (Slocum and Bowles, 1967; Campbell, 1968). It seems clear that the central purposes of education—to prepare the young to accept the reality of constructive pathways to adulthood, to help them engage these pathways successfully, and to assist them to find personal relevance in the life options available to them—are not being accomplished for a large number of persons.

To remedy this situation, it must be recognized that career/vocational development is not confined to helping youngsters learn a manipulative skill—the ability to use some set of tools or piece of knowledge to accomplish a specific task. The present dynamics of the occupational structure do not support the generalized importance of such goals.

Rather, the significant elements of career/vocational development are the skills enabling one to use his capabilities—whether limited or great—freely and responsibly in ego-involved activities, activities which contribute both to individual fulfillment and to society's progress. These types of skills precede and transcend task skills. They involve clarification of the personal values and attitudes which motivate one to gain task skills, to want to contribute and be constructive. They are the foundation for goal-directed behavior which is vocationally effective. They involve knowledge not only of specific tasks but of the ways such tasks are combined interdependently in occupations. They involve knowledge of the available opportunities for using oneself to shape personal and social fulfillment. More specifically, vocational guidance is concerned with fostering self-understanding so that the individual can use such understanding to choose better from among available courses of action (Zaccaria,

1969). Such skills and the knowledge on which they rest do not occur spontaneously in a society such as the present one; they must be developed in systematic ways.

In the past, as indicated earlier, the goals of education have reflected a consciousness of the concerns expressed here. However, it has been assumed that these goals and their behavioral correlates would be by-products of general education. Little systematic attention has been given to the need to design experiences to foster the individual attitudes and skills which comprise such goals. In some instances, education has tried to meet the needs of individual groups with emergency programs conceived in gross terms, programs which have not responded to the variance, the heterogeneity, found in any special group—whether it be labeled disadvantaged, rural, pre-dropout, mentally retarded, specialty-oriented, or college-bound. In other instances, education has responded to the "whole child" by allowing the objectives of particular disciplines to define the boundaries within which educational experiences would be conceived. Such practices have too often negated individual possibilities for interrelating, articulating, sequencing, individualizing, differentiating, and integrating the deluge of experiences which constitute growth, learning, and the attainment of personal competence.

INTERRELATIONSHIPS BETWEEN EDUCATION, VOCATIONAL GUIDANCE, AND SOCIETY

This book contends that education and those objectives of vocational guidance designed to aid career/vocational development—or vocationalization as it is termed in later discussions—share a developmental emphasis. It also contends that education and its subsystem vocational guidance are intricately linked with the realities of the larger society. Coombs (1965, p. 102) has stated, "The sad fact is that the accelerated rate of change in American education has been outpaced by an even more accelerated change in the world around it." Such phenomena have more recently been termed "future shock" (Toffler, 1970).

No other term so describes the interdependence of education, vocational guidance, and the surge of change as does *technology*. As a result of technological change, work has clearly become more cognitive in its requirements and in its activities (Venn, 1964). The fundamental interactions of man-machine and machine-machine systems diminish needs for muscle power and expand needs for cognitive skills. Such a shift is evident in the projected future characteristics of the labor force and is already apparent in the nature of the jobs resulting from technological penetrations into space, synthetic materials, ocean exploration, the problems of megalopolises, information packaging and distribution, and pollution abatement.

What has been less clearly evident in the changes wrought by technology is that such changes are interdependent with education. Today more than in any other period of history education is the direct bridge between man and his work. "Technology, in effect, dictates the role that education must play in preparing man for work" (Venn, 1964, p. 1). But education has a reciprocal effect upon the growth of technology. Hollis and Hollis (1969, p. 59) state:

> The rate of change in new jobs and new machines is governed to some extent by the rate that workers can be educated or retrained . . . the educational potential (including training) of individuals is a major determinant of the rapidity of change for each business or industry. Therefore education is becoming more of a determinant of occupations than occupations are of education.

Once the norm was apprenticeships and working *in situ* with a craftsman or a professional to learn the rudiments of work, but such procedures are giving way to the acquiring of intellectual and cognitive capability through extensive education and training. As Chapter 3 points out, the occupational areas which are projected to grow most rapidly are those which require the most training or education. As Venn (1964, p. 18) has asserted, "Technology is demanding workers with a degree of training and related education that can best be offered in a system of education."

Education, then, is becoming to a more intense degree the route to opportunity. It has always been important to the socialization of the young, to social and economic vitality, to the level of academic achievement of children, and as a vehicle for upward social mobility. But never has education been as critical to the conservation of human resources and to the self-fulfillment of a large proportion of the American population as is now true. This challenge to individual integrity as mediated through education is vividly described by Wolfbein (1968, p. 95):

> Anyone who does not measure up educationally is going to be at an in-increasing disadvantage in the competition for employment under this double-barreled challenge: the qualitative dimension represented by the increasing complexity of jobs under the impulsion of advancing technology and the quantitative dimension of the increasing numbers and proportions of workers who do have the requisite educational background.

As the interlocking of education and social need tightens, it is obvious that in the final analysis the student who later will be affected by these conditions is the one whom vocational guidance must aid. Such help is, of course, mediated by the heterogeneous characteristics of students. Put simply, if, as projected, only 5 percent of the jobs in the labor force can be filled by the unskilled (Hollis and Hollis, p. 91), what does this mean to the potential early school leaver? And how do the counselor and the school respond? If lack of interest is the most frequent reason which school dropouts give for leaving school (Venn, 1964, p. 2), how does the counselor help teachers respond to curriculum or motivational changes possible in the educational process? It seems clear that simply keeping the student in school is not the answer unless there are ways other than exposure to more rigorous general and academic studies that will help him capitalize upon his potential and interests.

What of culturally disadvantaged students? How do the counselor and the school help these children build positive self-esteem to counteract feelings of inferiority or of hopelessness? How do the counselor and the school help them develop academic aspirations and achievements as well as develop a plan by which these can be exploited in positive ways? How does the counselor help students fulfill immediate needs and simultaneously locate themselves in the future? How does the counselor help himself and teachers drop attitudes which convey that disadvantaged children are incapable of being educated? As Clark (1963, p. 161) has indicated, "The evidence is now overwhelming that high intellectual potential exists in a larger percentage of individuals from lower status groups than was previously discovered, stimulated, and trained for socially beneficial purposes."

How do the counselor and the school help students for whom college is the prime educational motivation, and their parents, come to terms with the fact that college is not an end in itself but a particular way of meeting certain types of goals if these are first identified and used as a basis of action? How do the counselor and the school help students realize that they may be involved in education, either prior to work or continuing concurrent with it, longer than in work itself? How can individual students be assisted to view education not as an end in itself but as life fulfilling and work enhancing? As McCauley (1965, p. 91) has pointed out, continuing education is important for several reasons:

> First, many workers in the labor force today did not complete high school and need to fill in some of the gaps in their education. Second, technological change is so rapid that even high school graduates who have had excellent preparation for their careers will need additional education during their working lives. Finally, there is some evidence that some persons derive more benefit from educational experiences after they have gone to work than from schooling at the beginning of their careers.

This latter point seems tied to McCauley's observation that students in classes in industry literally sit on the edge of their seats to absorb what is being taught because they may be required to apply that afternoon what they learn in a morning class (ibid.). It is doubtful that this phenomenon is simply a matter of being older or more mature than students in secondary schools. Rather, the more likely reason is that what is being taught is related to something which is to be done and thus is purposeful.

As one views general education, it becomes clear that there is already operating a number of activities which are at least tangentially related to career/vocational development. In fact, all contacts with people, things, and ideas have potential for influencing such development (Roeber, 1965-66) if these contacts are purposefully and systematically addressed to this expectation. The creation of behavioral goals, discussed in Chapter 5 as a way of bringing a conscious vocational focus to the activities and experiences which foster career/vocational development, would be a powerful means of making such activities a central part of vocational guidance at all educational levels.

It is important that general education be seen not just as an opportunity for the *expression* of certain personal characteristics which make up vocational development but rather as a means of *developing* these characteristics. Although this distinction is subtle, it represents the difference between purposeful, sequential development and development by chance and happenstance. Thus a series of career/vocational activities adapted to the developmental level of students or to what is relevant to a particular student at a specific point will have an impact that isolated, compartmentalized experiences can never have.

It is also important to recognize that in providing any such sequential development within general education, the many types and degrees of talent necessary to the world of work must be clearly perceived if the present occupational illiteracy, lack of goals, and nonemployability are to be overcome. If schools are to develop the requisites of career/vocational development, from the elementary school forward emphasis must be given to identifying and fostering the positive elements, strengths, and talents which represent each student's best capital for future success. In addition, vocational guidance and education must attend to the fact—and take it into account in their programs—that students will differ in their approach to vocational orientation and planning. Better, more comprehensive ways must be found to diagnose where students are in their career/vocational development, in academic learning, in interest and value formulations. Equally important is that vocational guidance stimulate in the schools the provision of learning experiences corresponding to the career/vocational development needs and capacities of individual students. In the last analysis, the objectives of vocational guidance must be the development of the individual, the growth of personal competency, not the needs of the labor market. As Riesman has indicated (Coombs, 1965, p. 114), students "need a chance to see what the world is like in the occupational realm. Education must open this realm for them to examine, not just tell them what they are expected to do. They should not act blindly out of an irrational, windmill feeling."

Is it possible within the context of education for the student to achieve a wedding of self-knowledge, knowledge of environmental options, and requisite skills in order to cope with the diverse opportunities which this society affords? The answer is a qualified yes—qualified by the purpose and system which is applied as well as by whether or not a broadening of the lines by which education and the larger society relate takes place. To consider such a challenge rationally requires consideration of a systems approach.

A SYSTEMS APPROACH

A purist in general systems theory, information theory, operations research, cybernetics, or systems engineering may consider the systems approach in this book a corruption. It is generally conceded that these disciplines have contributed to the evolution of systems approaches or defined them since World War II (Thoreson, 1969). Yet the perception of systems entered the world years before in the ecology of the biologist, the Gestalt conceptions of personality, and the anthropological conceptions of culture (Drucker, 1969, p. 38).

Regardless of its true origins, the systems approach "involves the application of the methods of science to problems of the engineering and development of practical programs" (Cooley and Hummel, 1969, p. 252). It suggests that if you wish to end with a product—i.e. a student who possesses vocational maturity—you build toward that goal by taking into consideration the functional relations between parts, elements, and components making up the final product. At least three steps are involved in developing a systems approach (Silvern, 1965, p. 2):

1. *Translate the broad aims of the enterprise into objectives which are explicit and operational.*

2. *Design the procedures which are intended to accomplish these objectives, identify the relevant variables which the procedures are intended to order or change, and construct a model which suggests a priori and consequent relationships among the identified variables.*

3. *Implement the model and evaluate the results of the innovation in terms of the operationally stated objectives.*

One can view the vocational aspects of guidance, or vocational guidance if you will, as a subsystem of a larger system, i.e. education. This seems of particular consequence when vocational guidance is viewed developmentally as a stimulus variable or as an integral component of education. In this sense, if education and vocational guidance share the goal of developing students who possess the characteristics which collectively result in effective vocational behavior, then one is forced to examine the interdependent effects of vocational guidance and education. One cannot examine or treat vocational guidance as an isolated phenomenon. Nor can one restrict oneself to what counselors alone do to produce effective career/vocational behavior.

At its base, a systems approach to educational problems requires a restatement of ends and means of educational philosophy in terms of the application of resources, or means, to the attainment of systems objectives, or ends (Phillips, 1966). With regard to career/vocational development as a unifying theme, the questions become: Can it be accomplished within existing institutional forms— i.e. elementary, middle, and secondary schools? How? If not, why? What modifications to existing structures are necessary? What is required to arrange the

educational environment of individual students so that particular types of behavioral change can take place? What are the management problems for which
solutions must be found? Within the context of education, any system conceived must respond to the separate as well as the interdependent effects of
at least the following:

1. Learner characteristics
2. Resource characteristics (in school and community)
3. Teacher characteristics
4. Counselor characteristics
5. Utility of teaching methods
6. Administrative characteristics or management requirements
7. Community expectations

The basic question is: Which resources or combination of resources (people,
places, media) are appropriate for fostering what type of development in what
type of learner under what conditions (time, place, size of group, and so on)
to achieve what purposes (Phillips, 1966)? Implicit in this question are the
different tempos by which learners can proceed through the system, the required translations of subject matter or other experiences which will aid their
progress, as well as a step-wise series of goals or competencies to be achieved
at different developmental points. Portions of knowledge and increasingly complex skill acquisition should be built upon one another according to the characteristics by which individual readiness is defined. In addition, it is necessary
to define specifically and measurably the terms of competence that students
must demonstrate upon completion of a set of educational experiences. Abstract
or global concepts are not sufficient. The terms of competence must be broken
into their components in ways which diminish semantic effects and provide
increments that can be programmed or measured.

One of the thorniest evaluation problems is the statement of expectations for
students (Hull, 1967). It necessitates the making of value judgments of what the
pupil ought to be able to achieve, and it requires describing these activities in
behavioral terms. If career/vocational development is to be individualized, each
student must be able to work on information or be exposed to experiences different from those of other students at any given time. This requires an emphasis
both on assessment and on the availability of diverse learning experiences from
which can flow prescriptions for individual progress.

Theoretically, at least, the individuality of students demands a set of expectations for each person taking into account where he is at different points in his
career/vocational development. This is true because of the interaction of such
factors as interest and aptitude development, concepts of occupations, concepts
of self, and experiential deprivation or richness in environmental history. Programmed efforts to foster career/vocational development must begin at the
student's level of development and proceed on the basis of personal variables

defined by experiences, aspirations, values, capacities, and a continuously spiraling series of success experiences within the objectives established.

Programmed instruction, as a technology, has made a valuable contribution to a systems process by defining at the outset the desired behavioral change in the student, then breaking down into a series of minute steps the material to effect this change. Continuous reinforcement and encouragement provide immediate recognition of each increment of knowledge, and the learner is continuously tested to determine whether or not the specific behavioral changes have occurred. If they have not, one of the most important elements in programmed instruction is implemented—the system is redesigned until the desired results are obtained.

The intent here is not to foster the use of teaching machines but rather to emphasize the importance of the philosophy of programmed instruction to a systematic approach to career/vocational development. In such an approach neither vocational guidance nor education can afford saturation with just one technique at a time. Instead, available media and personnel must be orchestrated in ways which respond to particular learner characteristics, and they must be recombined in ways related to the characteristics of different learners.

Goodlad (1964), Guba (1965), and Krathwohl (1965) have variously identified other factors which must be incorporated into curricular design and by analogy a systems approach to career/vocational development, among them the needs for an explicit theoretical framework; analysis of objectives at increasing levels of specificity; sequences of experience which move from the bottom up—the elementary school forward; the development and testing of materials with children and youth from divergent cultural groups; the testing of advantages and disadvantages of various learning styles; and the implications of each of these for new styles of preparing teachers and counselors to implement such systematic efforts to individualize development.

Career/vocational development offers the content and the objectives within which a system can be conceived. It requires the ingenuity of teachers and counselors working in tandem and separately to carry such a program through successfully. The remainder of this book attempts to offer some guidelines for such a goal. There is no expectation that all the questions raised in this chapter will be answered in the chapters that follow. Rather it is hoped that an overview of some of the conceptual models and strategies for systematically fostering career/vocational development will stir more application and evaluation of what now is often speculative.

PLAN OF THE BOOK

There are several emphases in this book. The first is the differentiation between vocational guidance as a stimulus and vocational guidance as treatment. Chapter 1 has outlined the implications of such differentiation. Basically, vocational guidance as a stimulus variable in education has as its focus the development of career/vocational behavior and the provision of experiences causing a spiraling of individual possibilities. Implicit in such a goal is the question of criteria to judge the outcomes of vocational guidance as these are reflected in current research. Chapter 2 provides an overview of current research and theory on career/vocational development.

Chapter 3 discusses the current occupational structure in the United States as it offers opportunities for diverse characteristics and talents. It examines the importance of student perceptions of occupations and lines of access to them as influences in decision making. These factors are then related to views of occupations in terms of field and level classifications, clusters of technological processes, and as outlets for combinations of interests, aptitudes, and abilities.

Chapter 4 describes the characteristics of the consumers of vocational guidance. It deals with the arbitrary nature of labels such as the college-bound and the non-college-bound. It explores the importance to all students of such factors as vocational identification, vocational goal direction, and effective vocational behavior as these relate to mental health, decision making, and performance in educational contexts. It discusses the importance of taking into account heterogeneity in the characteristics of those to whom vocational guidance is offered. It also considers specific implications for making effective the provision of vocational guidance to minority-group youth. Chapter 5 considers ways of formulating the goals of vocational guidance whether the focus is stimulus or treatment.

Chapters 6, 7, and 8 examine the application of a systems approach to the interaction of different resources, different student characteristics, and different guidance strategies at different educational levels. Chapter 6 deals with the elementary school, Chapter 7 with the junior high or middle school, and Chapter 8 with the senior high school.

Chapter 9 gives specific attention to vocational guidance as treatment. It focuses on conceptual views of individual and group counseling which see the individual as a product of inner-limiting, inner-directing, outer-limiting, and outer-directing factors. It discusses counselor behaviors as these are oriented to development, choice, and placement.

Chapters 10 and 11 deal with measurement and information respectively as these support counseling and group work as well as the vocational aspects of education considered in Chapters 6, 7, and 8. The chapter on measurement considers particular instruments and techniques for assessing individual status on the developmental tasks and behavioral goals developed in earlier chapters. It also presents an overview of instruments currently used in counseling, e.g. aptitudes, interests. The chapter on information discusses resources as well as continuing educational opportunities for school dropouts and those completing high school but not entering college.

Chapter 12 discusses cooperative links between educational agencies at different governmental levels and manpower agencies such as the Employment Service and rehabilitation services. Also discussed are the implications of federal legislation in support of comprehensive manpower policies and interagency cooperation.

Finally, Chapter 13 deals with factors and strategies influencing or related to change.

SUMMARY

This chapter has briefly placed the rationale for this book into perspective. It has indicated the essential interdependence of vocational guidance and education both from a historical viewpoint and from a future orientation. It has emphasized the importance of viewing each through the lens of a systems approach. It has discussed the evolving emphases on vocational guidance as stimulus and as treatment. Underlying all these observations has been a stress on the importance of developing personal competency in children and youth in order to help them clarify their self-characteristics. Such knowledge would enable them to develop criteria for deciding how to shape their lives vocationally.

REFERENCES

Advisory Council on Vocational Education. *The bridge between man and his work: Highlights and recommendations from the general report.* Washington, D. C.: U. S. Office of Education, 1968.

Bordin, E. S. Diagnosis in counseling and psychotherapy. *Education and Psychological Measurement,* 1946, 6, 169–184.

Byrne, R. H. Proposed revisions of the Bordin-Pepinsky diagnostic constructs. *Journal of Counseling Psychology,* 1958, 5, 184–187.

Campbell, R. E. Vocational guidance in secondary education: Selected findings of a national survey which have implications for state program development. Paper presented at the National Conference on Vocational Guidance, Development of State Programs, U. S. Office of Education, Washington, D. C., Jan., 1968.

Clark, K. B. Educational stimulation of racially disadvantaged children. In A. H. Passow (ed.) *Education in depressed areas.* New York: Teachers College, Columbia University, 1963, pp. 142–162.

*Cooley, W. W., and Hummel, R. C. Systems approaches in guidance. *Review of Educational Research* 1969, 30, 251–262.

Cremin, L. A. *The transformation of the school.* New York: Alfred A. Knopf, 1961.

* Recommended for additional reading.

*Crites, J. O.   *Vocational psychology.*   New York: McGraw-Hill, 1969.

Drucker, P.   *The age of discontinuity.*   New York: Harper & Row, 1969.

Goodlad, J. I.   *School curriculum reform in the United States.*   New York: Fund for the Advancement of Education, 1964.

Grant, V. W.   Statistic of the month.   *American Education,* July-August, 1965, back cover.

Guba, E. G.   Methodological strategies for educational change.   Paper presented at the Conference on Strategies for Educational Change, U. S. Office of Education, Washington, D. C., November, 1965.

Herr, E. L.   Uniquely qualified to divert the dropout.   *American Vocational Journal,* 1968, 43, 14–15.

*Herr, E. L., and Cramer, S. H.   *Guidance of the college-bound: Problems, practices, perspectives.*   New York: Appleton-Century-Crofts, 1968.

Hollis, J. W., and Hollis, Lucille V.   *Personalizing information processes: Educational, occupational, and personal-social.*   New York: Macmillan, 1969.

Hoppock, R.   Presidential Address, 1950.   *Occupations,* 1950, 28, 497–499.

House of Representatives.   *Report of the Commission on National Aid to Vocational Education.*   63rd Congress, 2nd Session, Document No. 1004, 1914.

Hoyt, D. B.   Guidance: A constellation of services.   *Personnel and Guidance Journal,* 1962, 40, 690–697.

Hull, W. L.   Evaluating pupil attainment of vocational tasks.   *American Vocational Journal,* 1967, 42, 15–16.

Krathwohl, D. R.   Stating objectives appropriately for program, for curriculum, and for instructional materials development.   *Journal of Teacher Education,* 1965, 16, 83–92.

McCauley, J. S.   Education for manpower development.   In S. E. Harris, K. M. Deitch, and A. Levensohn (ed.)   *Challenge and change in American education.*   Berkeley, California: McCutchan, 1965, pp. 91–102.

Miller, C. H.   *Foundations of guidance.*   New York: Harper & Brothers, 1961.

Parsons, E.   *Choosing a vocation.*   Boston: Houghton Mifflin, 1909.

Phillips, M. G.   Learning materials and their implementation.   *Review of Educational Research,* 1966, 36, 373–379.

Robinson, F. P.   Modern approaches to counseling diagnosis.   *Journal of Consulting Psychology,* 1963, 10, 325–333.

Roeber, E. C.   The school curriculum and vocational development.   *Vocational Guidance Quarterly,* 1965-66, 14, 87–91.

Rogers, C. R.   *Counseling and psychotherapy.*   Boston: Houghton Mifflin, 1942.

Rogers, C. R.   *Client-centered therapy.*   Boston: Houghton Mifflin, 1951.

Silvern, L. C.   Systems analysis and synthesis in training and education.   *Automated Education Letter,* November, 1965, pp. IC1–IC25.

*Stephens, W. R.   *Social reform and the origins of vocational guidance.*   Washington, D. C.: National Vocational Guidance Association, 1970.

Super, D. E.   Vocational adjustment: Implementing a self-concept.   *Occupations,* 1951, 30, 88–92.

Thoresen, C. E.   The systems approach and counselor education: Basic features and implications.   *Counselor Education and Supervision,* 1969, 9, 3–18.

Tiedeman, D. V., and Field, F. L.   Guidance: The science of purposeful action.   *Harvard Educational Review,* 1962, 32, 483–501.

*Toffler, A.   *Future shock.*   New York: Bantam Books, 1970.

U. S. Bureau of Education.   *Cardinal principles of secondary education.*   Washington: The Bureau, 1918.

Venn, G.   *Man, education, and work.*   Washington, D. C.: American Council on Education, 1964.

Williamson, E. G.   *How to counsel students.*   New York: McGraw-Hill, 1939.

*Williamson, E. G.   *Vocational counseling: Some historical, philosophical, and theoretical perspectives.*   New York: McGraw-Hill, 1965.

Wolfbein, S. L.   *Occupational information.*   New York: Random House, 1968.

*Zaccaria, J. S.   *Approaches to guidance in contemporary education.*   Scranton, Pa.: International Textbook, 1969 (a).

Zaccaria, J. S.   Some aspects of developmental guidance within an existential context.   *Personnel and Guidance Journal,* 1969, 47, 440–445 (b).

TWO

THE INGREDIENTS OF
CAREER/VOCATIONAL DEVELOPMENT

Work has always had the potential of meeting more than the economic needs of man. It also can meet broad social and psychological needs, among which are social interaction, a sense of personal dignity, identification, and human relationships. The current restiveness in American society suggests that the latter potentialities of work are not recognized by large numbers of people. In view of the apparent alienation among the young and the not so young, it seems reasonable to conclude that many individuals have not been assisted to view work as having personal relevance, as being critical to their way of life, or as being a consistent vehicle for self-fulfillment (Childs, 1965).

The fact of the matter seems to be that some types of work do not gratify many of the needs cited above while other types potentially gratify all. In part, this distinction occurs when work tasks are routine and repetitive, seen only partially by their participants as contributing to a final product; or when they offer only limited possibility for personal achievement as contrasted with other types of work which tap greater depths of conceptualization and provide opportunity for personal mastery of work elements and higher personal achievement. Regardless of which of these conditions prevails, even in cases where workers report boredom and monotony (e.g. Morse and Weiss, 1962, p. 30), work is a prime source of personal definition or identity (Stefflre, 1966).

Indeed, the rationale for vocational guidance and for continuing research into career/vocational development implies that work is fundamental to feelings about one's self which are positive rather than negative. In addition, virtually any analysis of human development indicates that access to work, particularly access in ways which maximize freedom of choice, is critical to the ability to move effectively from adolescence to adulthood. Such a concern has particular vitality in those nations with highly developed technology and great affluence, both of which descriptions fit the United States.

For example, Tyler, Sundberg, Rohila, and Greene (1968) found in an extensive cross-cultural study of vocational choice patterns of adolescents that the more complex and affluent a society becomes, the freer one is from choice constraints and thus the more the choice process becomes internalized. Hence at the societal levels of development current in America, it is likely that the direction each individual's life takes is determined more by his own choices than by external social conditions. Finally, the premise upon which this book rests is that vocational behavior and development as well as access to work are based on knowledge, skills, and attitudes which can be fostered rather than left to chance.

To take the above positions is not to be unaware that Utopian forecasts have repeatedly been made that the United States is becoming a leisure society; that work will be replaced by free time in which individual tastes and cultural pursuits will abound unimpeded by the need, or perhaps even the opportunity, to pursue a livelihood as historically defined. Those who predict such a social condition assume that present definitions of work will become obsolescent and that work will need to be redefined as machines become capable of performing most of the tasks in producing goods (Cunningham, 1965).

It is true that since 1945 our society has largely replaced the words "stability" and "scarcity" as characteristics of our economy with the words "change" and "abundance." It is also true that this reversal has occurred largely because of man's fantastic abilities to harness energy and to translate this energy into man-machine systems. It is further true that no occupational group is unaffected by the explosion of knowledge, changing social values, movement to corporate hierarchies, occupational and geographic mobility, new housing patterns, and similar phenomena which attend the fundamental realignment of our occupational structure and our economic base.

To assume, however, that work is disappearing, that automation is displacing huge blocks of labor and causing widespread unemployment, or that a society which has leisure as its principal characteristic has emerged is still premature (McMahon, 1970). Rather, it appears more accurate to suggest that many new types of work are appearing and that the work to be done is changing so much with respect to required levels of personal commitment and capability that the availability of employees in many sectors of the economy is in very short supply. Indeed, President Johnson in his State of the Union Message in 1968 indicated that in the preceding three years, seven and a half million new jobs—jobs which had not previously existed as defined by their activity or industrial classification—had been created as a result of basic changes in the vehicles of productivity and service. To emphasize this latter point, one has but to read the classified help-wanted ads of any metropolitan newspaper and attempt to compare them with similar ads of twenty or twenty-five years ago. It becomes clear that the nomenclature and the complexity of job titles alone reflect significant changes in the type of work being done now and the number of job choices possible. As Drucker (1969, p. 274) has emphatically asserted:

The problem today is not the lack of choice, but the abundance thereof. There are so many choices, so many opportunities, so many directions that they bewilder and distract the young people. No sooner have they shown a passing interest in this or that area than they are encouraged to make it their life's career. There is simply not enough of anything—whether metallurgists or specialists in Oriental languages, whether sta-

tisticians or biologists, whether systems engineers or botanists; all are chronically in short supply.

The main point is that with all the changes in work, work itself is not disappearing from the American scene. In the future work may lose some of its attraction as a necessity to insure economic survival because of growing welfare benefits or the possibilities of guaranteed income; it may occupy a fewer number of hours each week even though it occupies a more central place in one's life due to the continuing education necessary to perform it; or it may occupy a longer period in one's total life because of longer life expectancy. But there is no evidence that work will not be an important corollary defining individual life styles for a long period into the future.

The implications for vocational guidance which result from this sketchy introduction to the present and future character of work and its significance were largely forecast almost a decade ago. For example, Wrenn (1964, p. 41) observed:

The planning for which the vocational counselor can be held responsible is planning for work satisfactions from both employed and non-employed activity . . . to suggest the new emphasis is to say the counselor helps the student to define goals, not merely to inventory capacities. And it is clear that these must be life goals, not occupational goals only. There must be a dove-tailing of work in employed and non-employed settings if life is to be meaningful to the majority of people. . . . It is imperative that vocational counselors accept responsibility for helping students see their life whole.

Drucker (1969, p. 123) seems to support such goals for vocational guidance as he observes in a different context: "What is needed in this world today is not primarily wealth. It is vision. It is the individual's conviction that there is opportunity, energy, purpose to his society, rather than problems, inertia, and hopelessness."

To the degree that the goals just cited are accurate, this book contends that youth must be assisted in systematic ways to develop career/vocational behavior and a personal vision of life goals instead of assuming that these will be obtained at random. In order to develop a "systems approach" to vocational development as a continuing theme in education and also as a rationale for vocational guidance both as treatment and more particularly as stimulus, it is necessary to synthesize the present knowledge about the processes and factors inherent in career/vocational development.

While career/vocational development theory is as yet fragmented and incompletely addressed to women and to the disadvantaged segments of society, what is presently known provides a beginning basis for programmatic efforts to spur the development of effective vocational behavior. If one views the confluence of approaches, theory, and research with objectivity and minimum timidity, one finds tentative sets of constructs and propositions to explain differential vocational behavior and decision making as well as to provide guidelines for aiding such processes. Before surveying these approaches, however, let us consider briefly how the term "vocational development" is used in the discussions that follow.

THE TERMS "CAREER DEVELOPMENT" AND "VOCATIONAL DEVELOPMENT"

Up to this point, the combined term "career/vocational development" has been used. This has been done in part for emphasis and in part because career development and vocational development are the same. However, while the term "career development" has a more favorable connotation for some persons than the term "vocational development," "career development" does not lend itself to use in summarizing the behavioral development that parallels socialization. The term "vocational development," on the other hand, does. Recent theories view vocational behavior as a continuing, fluid process of growth and learning, and they attach considerable importance to individual self-concept(s), developmental experiences, personal history, and the psycho-social environment of the individual as major determinants of the process. *From this perspective, vocationalization is considered the refined corollary of socialization, and the term "vocational development" is preferred to the term "career development." However, in this book wherever the two terms are interchanged or combined, they mean the same.*

Theory and research to explain vocational development are, in reality, a "search for the psychological meaning of vocationally relevant acts (including the exploratory vocational behavior of youth) and of work itself in the human experience" (Borow, 1961, p. 23). Vocational development is concerned with broader phenomena than those represented by the term "occupations." The emphases in the psychological or sociological study of careers (vocational development in this context) are on the continuities and discontinuities in the lives of individuals and on the similar patterns in the lives of groups (Super, 1954). The psychology and sociology of occupations, on the other hand, stress characteristics of single or categorized occupations (Super, 1969b).

The occupational model is primarily concerned with prediction from one point in time to another point in time. "It takes prediction data at an early stage of the career and uses regression methods to predict success to one occupation, or uses discriminant analyses as a means of assessing the likelihood of being found, later, in each of several possible occupations." On the other hand, the career model "is one in which the individual is conceived of moving along one of a number of possible pathways through the educational system and on into and through the work system" (Super, 1969a, p. 3). Both these models are important for different reasons. To make an arbitrary distinction, the occupational model, which stresses matching or acturial relationships of man and job, is central in vocational guidance as treatment, while the career model undergirds vocational guidance as a stimulus.

Vocational development is intimately related to the factors which motivate or impede decisions. But as Tiedeman (1961, p. 18) has pointed out, "Vocational development not only occurs within the context of a single decision; vocational development ordinarily occurs within the context of several decisions. . . . Each decision is also to be considered in relation with a wider context of past and future decisions leading to the presentation of career. . . ." Further, Hershenson and Roth (1966, p. 368) contend, "Vocational development may be conceived of as a decision-making process which creates two trends: (a) narrowing the range of possibilities, and (b) strengthening the possibilities which remain. Through the successive refinement of these trends, events are experienced, construed and acted upon until a career choice is arrived at."

VOCATIONALIZATION

Each of these interpretations of vocational development will be used in this book. However, perhaps the most appropriate label for vocational development as it will be used is "vocationalization" (Crites, 1968, p. 88). Vocationalization, or vocational development, can be considered as analogous to the more familiar term "socialization." The socialization process, if it is successful, "ensures that the maturing child will accept and internalize the system of beliefs and norms governing relationships among people. These beliefs and norms become the basic frame of reference within which the adult experiences his world" (Bradburn, 1963, p. 334). "The socialization process, then, speaks to the articulation of the motivational system of the personality with the structure of the social system" (Parsons, 1951, p. 32).

Similarly, the process of vocationalization, or vocational development, speaks to the various inputs—psychological, sociological, cultural, economic—which across time results in such outcomes as effective vocational behavior, decision-making ability, and vocational maturity. Vocationalization, in sum, has to do with those processes and factors which aid or impede young people's acquisition of the values, knowledge, and skills which lead to effective vocational behavior.

APPROACHES TO VOCATIONAL DEVELOPMENT[1]

The approaches which describe vocational development or some aspect of it have been classified in a number of ways. Hilton (1962) has labeled them the attribute matching model, the need reduction model, the economic man model,

[1] Parts of the material discussed in the following sections have previously appeared in Edwin L. Herr, *Decision-making in vocational development.* Boston: Houghton Mifflin, 1970.

the social man model, and the complex information processing model. Osipow (1968, pp. 10–11) has classified vocational development theory in four ways: trait-factor approaches, sociology and career choice, self-concept theory, and vocational choice and personality theories. Herr (1970) has described them in the following manner: trait-factor or actuarial, economic, social structure, complex-information processing, need, and self-concept. Crites (1968) discussed the nonpsychological theories (e.g. accident, economic, cultural and sociological) and the psychological theories (e.g. trait-and-factor, psychodynamic, developmental, and decision).

These attempts at classification highlight the factors or emphases which distinguish one theory or research effort from another. The various categories are not mutually exclusive or independent but combine to explain the patterns of human existence which result in differential vocational behavior and choices. The remainder of this chapter will place these classifications and their proponents in perspective, considering them in the following sequence: trait-and-factor, or actuarial, approaches; decision theory; sociological emphases; psychological emphases; and, developmental emphases.

TRAIT-AND-FACTOR, OR ACTUARIAL, APPROACHES

Trait-and-factor approaches, coupled with actuarial methods, constitute a venerable theme in vocational guidance. Rooted in the psychology of individual differences, applied psychology, and differential psychology, these approaches conceive of man as an organization of capacities and other properties which can be measured and related to the requirements of training programs or occupations.

A trait-and-factor approach regards the individual as a pattern of traits— e.g. interests, aptitudes, achievements, personality characteristics—which can be identified through objective means, usually psychological tests or inventories, and then profiled to represent the individual's potential. Trait-and-factor approaches consider occupations similarly—that is, as susceptible to being profiled according to the "amounts" of individual traits they require. When one prolfie is overlaid on the other, the degree of fit between man and job can be identified.

Such an approach represents the essence of the occupational model previously identified in this chapter. As Super (1969b) has noted, vocational psychology from its beginnings until shortly after 1950 was essentially a psychology of occupations. The occupation was the subject, and the persons in it were the sources of data on the occupation. Thus, from an actuarial standpoint, predictions can be made using individual traits as predictors and the degree to which these traits are possessed by successful persons in different occupations as criteria. Further, the techniques and results of the numerous studies combining different traits and different occupational requirements also provide a means of appraising an individual's possibilities.

Historically, trait-and-factor studies have provided the technical foundation for elaborating the three-step process of vocational guidance laid down by Parsons (1909, p. 5). As psychological instruments to assess individual traits have been developed, and as knowledge about differences in occupational and educational requirements including aptitudes, interests, and personality factors has accumulated, vocational guidance processes have become an increasing scientific aid to choice. This approach stands in contrast to pre-Parsonian assumptions that subjective descriptions of occupational or training requirements were a sufficient basis for choice.

The assumptions upon which trait-and-factor approaches rest, while contributing significantly to the current character of vocational guidance, can lead to a narrow perspective on vocational development. Trait-and-factor approaches have been primarily oriented to specific occupations or tasks as the criteria toward which predictor variables such as aptitudes, mental ability, socioeconomic characteristics, interests, values, personality manifestations, and other variables are directed. However, vocational development is not concerned solely with the choice of an occupation but also with the process by which such choices can be purposefully integrated within a patterning of decisions, thereby maximizing freedom of choice and implementing the personal meaning of the ways one conceives his traits.

Yet there is no indication that the classical trait-and-factor approaches will not expand. O'Hara (1969, p. 29), for one, has asserted that all vocational counseling must be set in the context of career development (vocational development as we have defined it) but that "persons at any stage are chiefly concerned with the immediate decision to be made, and only remotely concerned with prediction of career development." Thus trait-and-factor approaches and vocational development models are complementary and yet useful singly for different purposes. Indeed, the acceleration of multivariate designs and computer availability will undoubtedly add increased insights to this approach. As Cooley (1964) has indicated, the trait-and-factor problem today is not simply the task of relating a test score (a predictor) to some final occupation but the consideration of patterns of attributes and their relationship to the sequence of decisions a young person must make in establishing himself in the world of work. If such a procedure becomes available, it will diminish a major weakness of trait-and-factor approaches—the view of individual traits and environmental requirements as relatively static rather than dynamic.

A persistent finding in trait-and-factor, or actuarial, approaches has been that the typical measures used predict training success more effectively than job success (Super and Crites, 1962). Roe (1956) reported that many studies have examined trainability but few deal with job proficiency following the training period. After analyzing 127 studies, Brown and Ghiselli (1952) concluded that there is no certainty that a test which perdicts a worker's ability to learn to perform a task also predicts how well he will perform following training. Thorndike (1963) observed that prediction of performance in school- and work-training programs may be the most one can expect of our current test batteries.

Thus despite all that the trait-and-factor approach has to commend it—statistical sophistication, testing refinement, and technological application—the resulting predictions of individuals' success in specific occupations has been discouragingly imprecise. For example, Tiedeman (1958, p. 9) in a review of trait-and-factor studies on predictions of vocational success concluded: "In every study, the choice and successful pursuit of a goal has proven to be a function of one's aptitudes, *but* in every instance the most striking feature of the distributions of aptitudes for the people making the various choices was their *overlap.*" And as a result of a massive actuarial study examining the traits of 10,000 men and the careers in which they were found a decade or so later, Thorndike and Hagen (1959, p. 350) wrote: "We should view the long-range prediction of occupational success by aptitude tests with a good deal of skepticism and take a very restrained view as to how much can be accomplished." The point seems to be that aptitudes and other predictors of occupational success are important but so are other manifestations of personality such as values, energy levels, perseverance, and so on.

If one were to subscribe to the trait-and-factor approach as the sole description of vocational development and decision making, one would have to assume that people have a much greater degree of self-insight than most of them seem to have—self-insight not simply of the measurable aspects of the self but of the self as a wholly functioning organism, and the relationships between self and the personally important components of the options among which one can choose (Hilton, 1962). In addition, if one considers the counselor as the major source of information about self-characteristics and occupational factors, one must face the possibility that the counselee is accepting such information on the basis of faith in an authority figure. Consequently, his choices are not made as affirmations of identity developed from insights into himself, his feelings, and his view of the world. Rather they are made because it is expedient to assume that he will find success in an occupation on the basis of statistical findings that he resembles certain occupational populations.

Trait-and-factor approaches thus maintain that choice is primarily conscious and cognitive. Such a premise seems more hopeful than valid, as succeeding approaches to vocational development in this chapter will demonstrate. Choice occurs not only as a function of relating an individual's traits to the characteristics of alternatives but also as a function of complex interactions between his developmental history and his environment. In fact, the richness or impoverishment of his reservoir of experience, the accuracy and relevance of the information he has, the distortion in his appraisal of self-characteristics or possibilities of reaching his aspirations, the scope and nature of his self-concept system, as well as many other combinations of factors, also enter into choice, frequently making it more psychological than logical.

Before leaving trait-and-factor approaches, a review will be made of selected research which discusses the interrelationships or the interaction between specific traits and different criteria particularly appropriate to adolescents or preadolescents.

Abilities. To turn briefly to abilities, it is obvious that a person's intelligence or his aptitudes play a significant part in the vocational level he is likely to attain, the training he is likely to be admitted to or succeed in, and the work he is able to perform. Intelligence and aptitudes do not relate in the same fashion to each of these possibilities. As noted earlier, intelligence and/or specific aptitudes typically correlate more highly with success in training than with success in work performance—principally because the latter is based upon a wider range of expectations and criteria than is the former. There are differences between learning to do something and applying one's knowledge in a work setting in which one's work skills must be integrated with those of others, performed under rigid deadlines, or conditioned by other dimensions eliciting personality traits. The evidence continues to support this conclusion of Super and Crites (1962, p. 99): "Given intelligence above the minimum required for learning the occupation, be it executive work, teaching, packing or light assembly work, additional increments of intelligence appear to have no special effect on an individual's success in that occupation."

As proposed by several theorists considered in subsequent sections of this chapter—e.g. Roe, Holland—there is a relationship between ability and the levels attained within career fields. For example, Elton (1967) has reported a finding regarding field (engineering) and the career role within that field (researcher, teacher, administrator, salesman, or practitioner). His data suggest that personality plays a part in the vocational choice of engineering but ability influences the career role within a specific field.

Needs and Interests. Other traits which are relevant here are needs and vocational interests, which have been found to be closely related (Thorndike, Weiss, and Darvis, 1968). Suziedelis and Steimel (1963) also found a number of significant relationships between specific predominant needs and particular interest patterns. Correspondence between needs, vocational interests, and curricula areas was found in a study which showed that personality identifications of students (following Holland's model) were related to their initial vocational choices (Osipow, Ashby, and Wall, 1966).

This relationship between needs, occupational interests, and personality identifications has also been demonstrated when typologies other than that of Holland were used. Riesman's characterization of inner-directed and outer-directed personalities was employed by Kassarjian and Kassarjian (1965) to examine the potential relationships between these two personality types, occupational interests, and social values. It was found that inner-directed and outer-directed personalities did differ in their occupational interests and that inner-directed persons scored higher on the theoretical and aesthetic value scales and lower on the economic, social, and political scales than their outer-directed contemporaries. Bohn (1966) has reported similar findings.

It is not just typological characteristics in general that relate to occupational interests or values or achievement but specific individual manifestations within typologies. For example, it has been found that undecided students in college are more dependent than more decided students but are equal in achievement to them (Ashby, Wall, and Osipow, 1966). And Hummel and Sprinthall (1965) found that when mental ability and social status variables are held constant, underachievers are less adaptive in ego functioning than achievers. It also seems apparent that racial, ethnic, and cultural background affects choice. For example, one study comparing the vocational interests of Negro and white ninth-grade students in North Carolina (Chansky, 1965) found that Negroes are more interested in occupations requiring interpersonal relations while whites prefer thing-oriented work.

Educational and vocational interests are also related. In one study Miller and Thomas (1966) found that an educational interest tends to be subsequently related to several vocational interests, some of which do not directly correspond to the academic area being examined. They explain that a liking for *being* a functioning member of an occupational group does not, of necessity, indicate that the student will like the training or the courses involved in reaching that occupation. The fact that there is a close relationship between some school subjects and some occupations is obvious (Hatch, Parmenter, and Stefflre, 1962). What has yet to be achieved is an understanding of the *instrumental* relationships between those subjects and specific occupations which are not *directly* related, particularly in terms of attitudes and other elements constituting psychological readiness, to which such subjects may contribute.

The relative importance of interests to vocational decisions has been rather clearly established (Bordin, Nachmann, and Segal, 1963). Certain occupations evidently satisfy specific needs, and these needs, as has just been demonstrated, are related to interests (Kohlan, 1968).

A continuing dilemma concerns the part that interests play in comparison with the part that abilities play in the making of a vocational decision. For example, Holland and Nichols (1964) report that of National Merit Finalists, 50 percent changed college majors because of lack of interest, while only 25 percent indicated lack of aptitude as a reason. Sharf (1970) states that male students report interest as more significant than ability in vocational decision making, although the difference is not so great as the 2:1 ratio reported by Holland and Nichols.

Stereotypes and Expectations.   Expectations and stereotypes also appear to influence vocational decision making. Information which young people have regarding occupations is likely to be indirect and stereotypic. As they go about making a vocational choice, they may search for environments which they perceive will meet their needs and expectations (Holland, 1963), and it seems likely that stereotypes of occupations are held by such searchers and that these are part of a foundation for vocational choice (Hollander and Parker, 1969).

It is also likely that students' vocational decisions are affected by the prestige or status which they assign to various occupations. Typically, high school students express preference for high-status or prestige occupations even though they cannot realistically be expected to enter these occupations (Clack, 1968). The student eventually realizes that his own abilities, interest, and skills are limiting factors and that his choice must be changed.

Significant Others. If educational interests and vocational interests are related either negatively or positively, one can assume that adults other than parents have an influence through identification, support, and encouragement of occupational preferences. Day (1966) found:

1. Some students do choose teachers as vocational models.

2. Teachers also exert influence on the vocational plans of many students whether or not they are a vocational model.

3. Boys are significantly more influenced by teachers than are girls.

4. Teacher influence is generally proportional to the amount of formal training required for an occupation.

That the influence of teachers and counselors upon students' vocational plans, interests, values, preferences, and choices is not more persuasive may be partially explained by Watley's findings (1966) that these adults are selective in the students they advise, encourage, or otherwise influence toward certain occupations and, one can speculate, toward any occupation.

Values. There is considerable evidence that what an individual values both in work itself and in the rewards he perceives work as offering has an effect on his vocational decisions and is internalized fairly easily in development (Super, 1962; Thompson, 1966). Values, however, cannot be viewed in isolation. The values a person holds are the products of his upbringing, his environment, his education, and a host of other variables (Hershenson, 1967). For example, although there are distinctive differences in the occupational value structure of parents and their offspring, there is greater similarity between values of daughter and mother than between those of father and son (Wagman, 1968).

Another complicating factor with regard to values and vocational choice has to do with cause-effect. Do values determine career choice, or does career choice determine values? Underhill's research (1966) suggests that there is substantial variation across careers in this relationship. For example, in the humanities, education, and law, values appear stronger; while in medicine, engineering, physical sciences, and business, the career choice predominates. Whatever the cause-effect or lack of it, it is clear that occupational groups can be differentiated by discriminant analysis in terms of the values and personalities of their membership (Irvin, 1968). This discrimination strongly suggests that work values are at least partially considered in vocational decision making.

Residence. Evidently, the size of the community from which an individual comes is related to the type of vocational choice he makes. For instance, in one study involving almost 10,000 high school seniors, the proportion choosing high-status occupations increased as the size of the community increased. When sex, intelligence, and socioeconomic status were controlled, differences in occupational choice by community were eliminated for girls but maintained for boys (Sewell and Orenstein, 1965). In general, then, boys reared on farms, in rural, nonfarm areas, or in small cities aspire to lower prestige and lower-paid occupations than do youth raised in larger communities. "As the population density of an area increases, aspiration levels and occupational attainment tend to rise (p. 555).

Family. Family influences, including child-rearing patterns and socioeconomic level, also appear to have an effect on vocational choice. Using almost 80,000 college freshmen, Werts (1968) compared fathers' occupations with sons' career choices. His results suggest that certain groups of occupations, such as physical sciences, social sciences, and medicine, are inherited. Although we do not know *why* there is an association between a father's occupation and his son's career choice, this relationship apparently does exist. In some cases, the obverse may hold true—that is, fear of parental competition, generally irrational and unconscious, may affect vocational choice (Malwig, 1967).

Roe's theory of vocational choice, described later in this volume, rests on the hypothesis that child-rearing processes determine subsequent vocational choices. An individual's nurture may thus be more important than his nature in ultimate vocational choice.

Family factors may also influence whether an individual has or has not made a vocational choice. In the Career Pattern Study, apparently those individuals followed up at age twenty-five who had made a choice were more accepting of a father or a father substitute than those who had not made a choice (Marr, 1965), although the choice was not found to be related to parents' occupational level. In a study of sixth-graders, Creason and Schilson (1970) found that children generally express occupational preferences higher than their fathers' occupational levels.

Finally, it may be that family socioeconomic status is related to career choice. In one study, middle-class white boys and lower-class black girls expressed greater preference for white-collar and professional occupations than did lower-class black boys or middle-class white girls (Clark, 1967). However, the race variable tends to complicate class differences.

Adjustment. Factors of adjustment may affect vocational choice. The career development pattern of emotionally disturbed students is not so smooth as that of well adjusted students (Osipow and Gold, 1968), and usually such students tend to have artistic, musical, and literary interests (Stenberg, 1956; Drasgow and Carkhuff, 1964).

In one study, Crites and Semler (1967) followed up 483 fifth-graders seven years later when they were in the twelfth grade. The results indicate that fifth-grade adjustment is related not only to later adjustment and educational achievement but also to vocational maturity. Thus general adjustment does appear to be related to vocational adjustment.

Perhaps it is best not to force vocational exploration and decision making for maladjusted individuals but to wait for the appropriate time. Berdie (1968) suggests that considerable change occurs in the personality of typical students from grades 9 through 13 and that a college freshman is somewhat better adjusted personally than he was as a high school freshman. There is also evidence (Hollander, 1967) that vocational choices become more realistic with advancing age. Hence, especially in the case of the maladjusted individual, delay in vocational decision making may be desirable.

Risk taking.   Another personality variable which may be related to vocational choice is risk taking. Early work by Ziller (1957) found a significant relationship between vocational choice and a propensity for risk taking. Subsequent studies (Burnstein, 1963; Mahone, 1960; and Morris, 1966) also found evidence that risk taking plays a part in vocational decision making. However, a large-scale study by Slakter and Cramer (1969) has demonstrated that while there is some evidence that risk taking is related to vocational choice, the current measures of risk taking are too crude to capitalize on this relation.

All that can be said at this time is that a relationship between risk taking and vocational choice does seem to exist but we do not know the extent or understand the dynamics.

Aspirations.   Level of aspiration appears to contribute to vocational choice. At least in males, level of aspiration seems relatively constant during secondary schooling (Flores and Olsen, 1967). Level of aspiration usually affects curriculum choice and hence vocational choice. It would appear that typical eighth- or ninth-grade boys are, therefore, ready to make such choices. Using the Occupational Level Scale of the Strong Vocational Interest Blank, Elder (1968) concludes that for adolescent males the scale provides a general indication of the prestige level (level of aspiration) of a vocational goal but does not measure personal commitment to a vocational goal.

Summary of Traits and Factors.   It is clear that a great many variables enter into vocational decision-making: work values, occupational stereotypes and expectations, residence, family socioeconomic status and child-rearing practices, general adjustment, personality factors including needs and propensity for risk taking, educational achievement, level of aspiration, and sex. Each of these is influenced by the others. They are in dynamic interrelationship. The preponderance of one or more variables in vocational decision making depends heavily upon the individual making the choice. Some individuals are more influenced by some factors; others lend more weight to other factors (Healy, 1968).

DECISION THEORY

Increasingly apparent in the professional literature are attempts to theorize about vocational choice through the use of decision models. In one sense, these approaches are economic in origin. The assumption, based upon Keynesian economic theory, is that one chooses a career or an occupational goal which will maximize his gain and minimize his loss. The gain or loss is, of course, not necessarily money but anything of value to the particular individual. A given occupational or career pathway might be considered as a means of achieving certain possibilities—e.g. greater prestige, security, social mobility, or a spouse—when compared to another course of action. Implicit in such an approach is the expectation that the individual can be assisted to predict the outcomes of each alternative and the possibility of such outcomes. He will then choose the one which promises the most reward for his investment—e.g. time, tuition, union dues, delayed gratification—with the least probability of failure.

More specifically, the notion is that an individual has several possible "alternatives," or courses of action, among which to choose. In each of them certain events can occur. Each event has a value for the individual, a value which can be estimated through some method of psychological scaling. Also, for each event a probability of its occurrence can be estimated through actuarial prediction. If for each course of action, the value of each event is multiplied by its probability and these products are summed, the sound decision from this point of view would be for the student to choose the alternative in which the sum of the expected "values" is the greatest (Hills, 1964).

Brayfield (Brayfield and Crites, 1964) has stressed the importance of considering choice as occurring under conditions of uncertainty or risk. The individual assigns a reward value (utility) to alternative choices and appraises his chances of being able to realize each of them (subjective probability). As a result, he will attempt to maximize the expected value in making a decision. Thoresen and Mehrens (1967, p. 167) have also addressed this point. They state, "Objective probabilities are not directly involved in the decision-making process, but are only involved insofar as they are related to subjective probabilities. The question that arises is the extent to which certain information (objective probability data) actually influences what the person thinks are his chances (subjective probability) of an outcome occurring." Similarly, Blau, Gustad, Jessor, Parnes and Wilcock (1956, p. 533) contend, "A choice between various possible courses of action can be conceptualized as motivated by two interrelated sets of factors: the individual's valuation of different alternatives and his appraisal of his chances of being able to realize each of the alternatives."

Although formal decision theory conceives of decision making as (1) a process, (2) having an essentially rational base, and (3) involving the selection of a single alternative at a particular point in time (Costello and Zalkind, 1963), when applying such a conception of adolescents or young adults, one must consider the validity of Hansen's (1964–65) position that decisions are frequently more psychological that logical. This point was raised previously in relation to trait-and-factor approaches.

Within the valuation of alternatives, Tillinghast (1964) contends that planning and deciding by the counselee and the counselor inevitably include some combination of choices concerned with (1) the probable, (2) the possible, and (3) the desirable. Concern with the *probable* focuses on alternatives stressing security, stability, and safety, e.g. jobs which are likely to remain relatively unaffected by the changing times, colleges with admission requirements safely within the demonstrated scholastic ability of the counselee, emotional and social expressions of the counselee which are safely within the boundary of "socially sanctioned utterances." This orientation defines what is best for the individual in terms of the numerical advantage for success.

A choice orientation toward the *possible* holds that the rewards of success are more important than the consequences of failure; thus danger, erratic and vague influences, excitement and unpredictable events are not things to be avoided in trying to maximize security. In this context, the counselor is concerned with what the individual *might be* and emphasizes widening the counselee's perceptual field with respect to choices and plans.

Alternatives emphasizing the *desirable* are not what *could be* or even what *might be* but what *must be* or *should be*. This choice orientation gives little attention to statistical reality as it now exists in situations as reasonably projected. Tillinghast suggests that counselees of this orientation are likely to be described as dedicated, single-minded, or even *unrealistic*, but he maintains on their behalf that to consider only those courses of action in which the odds for success are 95 out of 100 (the probable) is to deny a large portion of life's potential.

Several decision theorists (Davidson, Suppes, and Siegel, 1957) describe the process of making a decision between uncertain outcomes as requiring reconciliation of several general factors: the relative valuing of the outcomes, the cost of attaining the outcomes, and the probability that each outcome may occur. This approach, similar to what Hilton (1962) has labeled "probable gain," includes the dimension of investment. It suggests that within any choice or decision the individual must assess his resources and how much of them, tangible or psychological, he wants to commit to a particular alternative in such a manner as to maximize his gain and minimize his loss. Garbin (1967, p. 17) has stated in this regard, "A vital facet of the decision-making process involves a consideration of the requirements, rewards, and duties inherent in the several available alternatives at the point of choice as balanced with considerations of personal capacities, interest, and values."

Katz (1966) has suggested, in a model of guidance for career decision making, that an index of "investment" be developed to represent the substance of what an individual risks or loses in preparing for or electing any career option. This assumes that the person can be helped to determine the "odds," the chances of success in entering or attaining some alternative. More importantly, however, it means that knowing the odds is insufficient for decision making. As Katz has indicated, the person must also assess the importance to himself of success in each option or the seriousness of failure. To make such assessments immediately places one's decisions in a value domain. Thus decision making includes the identifying and the defining of one's values: what they are and what they are not, where they appear and where they do not appear.

Another approach to vocational decision making is based on principles of learning theory. Miller (1968, p. 18) has proposed that a vocational decision is "any behavior that consistently and significantly relates to eventual participation in an occupation." He argues that there are four categories of decision behavior: overt physical activities, overt verbal statements, covert emotional or physiological changes, and covert verbal responses or thoughts.

Finally, any learning theory of vocational decision making should involve accurate prediction, explanation, and control of vocational decision *behaviors*. In order to achieve this prediction, explanation, and control, the learning theorists must first identify those behaviors that constitute the decision. Once this task is accomplished, the environmental stimuli which pertain to the decision would have to be isolated. These stimuli might include positive and negative reinforcers, general learning principles of classical and instrumental conditioning, stimulus-response sequences, convergences and divergencies, and other principles of learning. The primary requirement for a learning theory model of vocational decision making is relatively complete information of an individual's past history. In summary (Miller, 1968, p. 22):

> In order to predict decision behaviors the learning theorist would want to know for an individual the discriminative stimuli that control his overt and covert responses, the relative strengths of his learned and unlearned motives along with effective reinforcers, and the strengths, composition, and relations among S-R mechanisms. Given such information the learning theorist would expect to be able to predict all kinds and combinations of decision behaviors with an extremely high degree of accuracy.

An application of learning theory principles to vocational decision making is offered by Krumboltz and his colleagues (Krumboltz and Thoreson, 1964; Krumboltz and Schroeder, 1965). In this series of studies, students were encouraged to seek vocational information by means of behavioral counseling methods, which, of course, are based on social learning principles. If information-seeking behavior can be considered an aspect of vocational decision making, then the Krumboltz et al. experiments indicate clearly that vocational decision making by means of the application of principles of learning theory can be broadened to include a much wider range of vocational behavior.

Another approach still within the general domain of decision theory—with particular relevance to the outcomes of premature choosing and the resulting restrictions upon full vocational development—is what has been called complex information processing (Hilton, 1962). Within this context, it is contended that "the reduction of dissonance among a person's beliefs about himself and his environments is the major motivation of career decision-making." Although James (1963) has recommended that Hilton substitute conflict for dissonance, the roots of this approach are Festinger's (1957) early Theory of Cognitive Dissonance. The latter, here grossly oversimplified, indicates that the magnitude of information and the number of factors to be considered in decision making are so great that the individual chooses prematurely, without fully considering the implications of the choice, in order to reduce the pressures besieging him as he sorts through the torrents of information relevant to the choice. He then reinforces the choice by rationalization: selective attention to those data which make the choice look good both to himself and to external observers. Although the chooser "knows" there are other options with which he could relate more compatibly particularly over the longer range, it is comforting to make a selection and suppress the costs of its unrealism by a variety of self-deceptive devices.

Hershenson and Roth (1966, p. 369) have suggested that mechanisms operating in ways similar to that described by Hilton may depend upon certainty, or the level of choice-making vulnerability which the individual is experiencing. They state, "Earlier in the decision process, a less significant event may have a greater impact on an individual's career decisional process."

SOCIOLOGICAL EMPHASES

Much floundering in decision making, vocationalization, or vocational development stems from the social structure of which one is a part: both from limited avenues through which one can implement choice and from limited knowledge of opportunities available. Caplow (1954) as well as Miller and Form (1951) among others have discussed the accident theory of vocational choice or development, which stresses the importance of chance as a determinant of personal opportunities for choice.

But the sociological factors bearing upon choice or development are not restricted to chance or intervening variables. The narrowness or the breadth of the individual's culture or social class boundaries has much to do with the choices he can consider, make, and implement. No more vivid an example exists than those raised in poverty. As Moynihan (1964) has pointed out, the circumstances in which poverty flourishes produce a distinctive milieu that conditions the social responses, educational attainment, vocational ambition, and general intellectual level of the overwhelming majority of those raised within it. Certainly, it is important to avoid speaking glibly about social class differences. Leacock (1968, p. 845) reminds us that "unfortunately, lower-class culture is fast becoming a new stereotype behind which the individual is not revealed more fully, but instead is lost." Nevertheless, an important factor in the vocational development of an individual is the impact of the culture and society in which he lives upon the goals he is conditioned to value. Within this context are found such elements as family income levels, social expectations, levels of social mobility, and psychological support for patterns of educational and occupational motivation.

Lipsett (1962) has argued that counselors must understand the implications for a particular individual of the following social factors as they interact with vocational development:

1. Social class membership—e.g. occupation and income of parents, education of parents, place and type of residence, and ethnic background.

2. Home influences—e.g. parental goals for the individual, influence of siblings, family values and counselee's acceptance of them.

3. School—e.g. scholastic achievement, relationships with peers and faculty, values of the school.

4. Community—the "thing to do in the community," group goals and values, special opportunities or influences.

5. Pressure groups—the degree to which an individual or his parents have come under any particular influence that leads him to value one occupation over another.

6. Role perception—the individual's perception of himself as a leader, follower, isolate, etc.; the degree to which his perception of himself is in accord with the way others perceive him.

The important concern here is that the factors identified by Lipsett operate directly or indirectly in the lives of every person. The degree to which they operate as determinants or constraints in development and choice, however, can be assessed only in the individual case. The ways in which social class background shapes vocational development can be seen in the research of Gottlieb (1967). In this study, which used as a sample 1,327 male adolescents (Caucasian and Negro) who were enrolled in the Job Corps, no support was found for the proposition that the lower-class culture has a built-in set of values that discourage social mobility. Rather, it appears that lower-class parents, although wanting their children to succeed, lack the abilities to help them move into more advantageous social positions and "there are few other adults in their lives who have the ability to help the youngster in both the business of goal clarification and goal attainment."

Zito and Bardon (1968) examined a similar phenomenon in terms of achievement imagery. In particular, they attempted to determine how Negro adolescents in an urban area perceive the probabilities of success and failure in both school and work. They found that achievement imagery, or the need to achieve, is equally strong in Negro adolescents from the same urban environment regardless of intelligence and type of program. However, they also found that school-related material tends to threaten Negro adolescents with failure, even though work-related material arouses fantasies of successful achievement of goals. The subjects in this study, discouraged as they were with their present occupation (school), looked forward to a more optimistic future (work).

Stevic and Uhlig (1967) examined the concepts that youth with an Appalachian background have concerning their probable life work. When comparing a group of students remaining in Appalachia with a group of students who had migrated to an Ohio city, they found the following:

1. Appalachian youth who stay in the geographic area have a significantly lower aspirational level than do those students who are native to an urban area.

2. Youth who remain native to Appalachia have different personal role models and characteristics for success than those students who have migrated from it.

3. A major problem in raising the occupational aspirations of Appalachian students appears to be lack of information and opportunity rather than lack of ability.

Williams and Byars (1968) studied the self-esteem of Negro adolescents in southern communities where public facilities and schools were desegregated. Generally, the findings indicated that Negro students are low in self-confidence, defensive in self-descriptions, confused concerning self-identity, and similar in performance to neurotic and psychotic individuals as measured by the Tennessee Self-concept Scale.

Lo Cascio (1967) studied continuity-discontinuity in vocational development among many different populations. He described developmental units as continuous, delayed, and impaired based on differences in behavioral repertoires, learning, and the incorporation of learning. It appears that the vocational development of those labeled as disadvantaged is more likely to be delayed or impaired than that of their more favored contemporaries. Studies by Schmeiding and Jensen (1968) of American Indian students and by Asbury (1968) of rural disadvantaged boys, like those previously cited studies of Negroes and Appalachian youth, support Lo Cascio's conclusions.

Social class factors limit vocational development not only among the poor and the lower classes. The expectations or demands upon middle and upper socioeconomic class youth can be restrictive also. Krippner (1965), in a study of the educational plans and preferences of upper-middle-class junior high pupils, found that most of them were expected to attend college and that neither pupil dislike of school nor poor achievement deterred these students from agreeing with their parents that higher education should be given high priority. He stated (p. 259): "It seems incredible that nine out of ten parents, whose children are the poorest students in their class, should give their sons and daughters the impression that they are to attend college. Many of these boys and girls are working two grades below their present school placement, yet this fact is apparently ignored."

Gribbons and Lohnes (1966, p. 69), in their studies of students in the Boston area, found a similar factor operating: "We may tentatively conclude that students in the lowest aptitude levels expect more education and think that their parents want them to have more education than is realistically possible or even beneficial." In terms of the college mystique that operates in this society, it is frequently observed that middle- and upper-class students are in college because they have not had an opportunity to consider any other option or avenue by which their goals might more effectively be met. It is probably accurate to suggest, however, that if such a choice proves wrong, the middle- or upper-middle-class youth has a greater range of alternatives available to him than have his less advantaged contemporaries.

Perhaps the most important point gleaned from sociological studies of vocational development and choice is that while the vocational preferences of individuals across various social or economic classes are essentially the same, lower-class expectancies are not congruent. In other words, what they would prefer to do is not what they expect to be able to do. Such inconsistency may stem from a recognition of their inability to do what they prefer because of lack of intellect or aptitude (Osipow and Gold, 1967; Clack, 1968). But the more pertinent reason seems to be their recognition of cultural constraints which will prohibit them from access to their preferred choices. Thus it is likely that occupational preferences will reflect the family's occupational level and, therefore, the pupil's socioeconomic milieu. As Super (1969a, p. 3) has asserted, the individual's "starting point is his father's socioeconomic status; he climbs up the educational ladder at a speed fixed both by his psychological and social characteristics and by the resources provided by his family environment."

While the personal aspirations of an individual raised in an environment which does not support planfulness or commitments to long-range goals may be the same as those reared in more favored circumstances, if he does not have the knowledge or the techniques by which he can cope effectively with his environment to realize his aspirations, he is at a considerable disadvantage in achieving the vocational prerequisites for reaching his goals.

PSYCHOLOGICAL EMPHASES

Psychological approaches to vocational choice stress intrinsic individual motivation to a greater degree than the others discussed thus far. Tying the psychoanalytic, need, and self emphases into a single body of psychological approaches, Crites (1969, p. 91) observes: "Each of them proposes that the most significant factor in the making of a vocational choice is a motivational or process variable. For this reason, they contrast sharply with the trait-and-factor theories, which emphasize the observable characteristics of the individual and not the inferred states or conditions which prompt him to behave as he does."

Prominent proponents of psychological approaches include the psychoanalysts, as well as other schools of personality less clearly defined. The major assumption of these approaches is that because of differences in personality structure, individuals develop certain needs and seek satisfaction of them through occupational choices. Thus it is assumed that different occupational or, indeed, curricular areas are populated by persons of different need types or personality types. These approaches rather consistently develop a classification of personality or need, and then relate it to gratifications available in different environments—occupational or educational. In one sense, the distinguishing characteristics of these approaches are the disciplinary lenses through which vocational phenomena are viewed and the emphasis on the antecedents of vocational behavior.

The most comprehensive application of psychoanalysis to vocational choice or development has been made by Bordin, Nachmann, and Segal (1963). While preceded by Brill's (1948) psychoanalytic concepts of guilt and exhibitionism and of the pleasure and reality principles to explain the choice attraction of various vocations, Bordin, Nachmann, and Segal have extended the emphasis on the gratifications which various types of work offer to meet certain individual impulses. Much like Brill, they consider "work as sublimation—but in the broad sense of pregenital impulses turned into artistic activities." For the more commonly described traits such as interests and abilities, they substitute individual modes of impulse gratification, the status of one's psychosexual development, and levels of anxiety. More specifically, they maintain that connections exist between the early development of coping mechanisms and the later development of more complex behaviors, that adult vocations are sought for their instinctual gratifications as need for these is developed in early childhood, and that in terms of personality formation and the needs inherent in the individual structure, the first six years of life are critical.

From analyses of such roles as accountants, creative writers, lawyers, dentists, social workers, clinical psychologists, plumbers, physicists, and engineers, Bordin and his colleagues have conceived an elaborate matrix of the basic need-gratifying activities found in different occupations. They have divided into psychic and body-part classifications those activities important to psychoanalytic persuasions. They have then related these to the potential gratification, the objects from which gratification are available, and the sexual mode of gratification which exists in each of the occupations indicated above.

The theoretical and research efforts of Roe (1956) also apply personality theory to vocational development. Indeed, as Osipow (1968, p. 17) has pointed out, Roe marries two major personality theories: (1) She extends the earlier work of Gardner Murphy (1947)—Murphy's canalization of psychic energy and emphasis on the relationship between early childhood experiences and later vocational choices. (2) She applies Maslow's (1954) theory of prepotent needs to vocational behavior. Roe also accents the importance of genetic factors as these interact with need hierarchies to determine vocational behavior and choice. "In other words, given 'equal' endowments genetically, differences in occupational achievement between two individuals may be inferred to be the result of motivational differences which theoretically, are likely to be the outcome of different childhood experiences" (Osipow, 1968, p. 18).

Roe, from her studies of different types of scientists (1953), concluded that there exist personality differences evolving from child-rearing practices (e.g. rejecting, overprotecting, democratic) and that these differences are related to the kinds of interaction that such persons ultimately establish with other people —toward them or not toward them—and with things. Persons seek such individual interactions in vocational development to satisfy needs. She suggests that there are relationships between the psychic energy, genetic propensities, and childhood experiences which shape individual styles of behavior and that the impulse to acquire opportunities to express these individual styles is inherent in the choices made and the vocational behavior which ensues. Thus the strength of a particular need, the amount of delay between the arousal of the need and its satisfaction, and the value that the satisfaction has in the individual's environment are the conditions—shaped by early childhood experiences—that influence vocational development.

To elaborate the need constructs, Roe has applied Maslow's theory of prepotent needs to vocational behavior. Maslow (1954) arranged human needs into a hierarchy in which he conceived the emergence of higher-order needs as contingent upon the relative satisfaction of lower-order, more primitive needs. The needs in ascending order are:

1. Physiological needs
2. Safety needs
3. Needs for belongingness and love
4. Needs for importance, self-esteem, respect, independence
5. Need for information
6. Need for understanding
7. Need for beauty
8. Need for self-actualization

Roe's concern with specific child-rearing practices, the manner in which the parents interact with the child, the resulting need structure, and the ensuing orientation toward or away from persons have been translated into a useful field and level classification of occupations, which includes the following (Roe, 1956, pp. 143–152):

Fields	*Levels*
I. Service	1. Professional and Managerial (1)
II. Business Contact	2. Professional and Managerial (2)
III. Organizations	3. Semiprofessional, Small business

IV. Technology   4. Skilled

V. Outdoor   5. Semiskilled

VI. Science   6. Unskilled

VII. General Culture

VIII. Arts and Entertainment

An example that integrates Roe's various propositions follows. Persons entering service occupations (Group I), it is assumed, are primarily oriented toward persons and probably come from a home which generated a loving, overprotecting environment. Within a service occupation the level attained—the level being based on work complexity or responsibility—is dependent upon genetic factors manifested in degree of intelligence as well as the style of environmental manipulation.

To a greater degree than any of her other contributions, this field and level classification, which also has been described as a circular array (Roe, 1956) of occupational groups contiguous in their emphasis on people (Groups I, II, III, VII, VIII) or on things (Groups IV, V, VI), describes more validly than any of Roe's other contributions the occupational preferences of high school students (Jones, 1965). Perrone (1964) found that high school boys with similar scores on cognitive measures tend to prefer similar occupational groups as defined by Roe's eight groups. Indeed, when job changes are examined they are found to be nonrandom. That is, people typically move from a job in one group to another in the same group as defined by Roe's field classifications. They do not typically move to a group in which the orientation or activity is in direct opposition to the initial group (Hutchinson and Roe, 1968).

Attempts to test other aspects of Roe's theory, particularly the effects of the family on later vocational behavior, have found much less positive results or at least very ambiguous results (Crites, 1962; Brunkan and Crites, 1964; Brunkan, 1965). However, one study with rather interesting findings is that of Green and Parker (1965). They took a seventh-grade sample of boys and girls living with their parents and administered to them Roe and Siegelman's (1964) Parent-Child Relations Questionnaires. The responses provided data about the current home atmosphere of the children. These data were then examined to see whether the occupational preferences of these children indicated person or nonperson orientation. It was found that for boys the perception of either parent as warm and supporting results in person-oriented occupational choices and that for girls cold parental relationships result in nonperson career choices. But it was also found that boys do not make nonperson-oriented choices in a cold environment nor do girls make person-oriented choices in a warm environment.

Both the personality approach of Bordin, Nachmann, and Segal and that of Roe imply that occupational choices are made as aspects of self-classification, whether the central focus is impulse gratification or need satisfaction. Thus vocational choices are made as affirmations of personal behavioral styles.

Holland's (1966) approach gives explicit attention to behavioral style or personality type as the major influence in vocational choice and development. He assumes that at the time a person chooses his vocation he is a product of his heredity and environment. As a result of early and continuing influences of genetic potentialities and the interaction of the individual with his environment, there develops a hierarchy of habitual or preferred methods for dealing with social and environmental tasks. The most typical way in which an individual responds to his environment is his modal personal orientation, which falls into one of six classifications: realistic, intellectual, social, conventional, enterprising, and artistic. It directs the individual toward an environment that will satisfy his particular orientation. Thus occupational groups provide different gratifications which require different abilities, identifications, values, and attitudes.

To emphasize the person-situation correspondence, Holland has classified work environments into six categories analogous to the six personal orientations. In other words, he describes the person and the working environment in the same terms. Accordingly, Holland makes more explicit than do most of his contemporaries that occupations are ways of life, environments which manifest the characteristics of those inhabiting them as opposed to being simply sets of isolated work functions or skills. In addition, Holland has extended his examination of types of occupational environments to educational environments, particularly collegiate.

Holland also addresses himself to level hierarchies within occupational environments. Somewhat like Roe's conception of field and level, the level hierarchy—or the particular level of responsibility or skill level within an occupational field, which one gravitates to—is dependent upon his intelligence and his self-evaluation. Holland also emphasizes the importance of self-knowledge to his conception of the individual's movement through educational decisions to occupational environments. Self-knowledge refers to the amount and accuracy of information an individual has about himself as contrasted with self-evaluation, which refers to the worth he attributes to himself.

In summary, Holland's theory (1966, pp. 2–14) emphasizes that individual behavior is a function of the interaction between one's personality and environment and that choice behavior is, then, an expression of personality. Thus people seek those settings and occupations, including curricula, which permit expression of their personality styles. Indeed, in our culture, one can discuss personality types and environments in similar ways, classifying them into realistic, intellectual, social, conventional, enterprising, and artistic. Since persons inhabiting particular environments, vocational or educational, have similar personality characteristics, their responses to problems and interpersonal situations are likely to be similar. For these reasons, interest inventories are personality inventories, and vocational stereotypes held by individuals have important psychological and sociological implications.

Finally, Holland (1966, pp. 73–78) alleges that congruent interactions of people and environments belonging to the same type or model, in contrast to incongruent interactions, are conducive to the following:

1. More stable vocational choice
2. Higher vocational achievement
3. Higher academic achievement
4. Better maintenance of personal stability
5. Greater satisfaction

The major point here is that "presumably, congruent interactions produce these outcomes because by definition they involve situations where the tasks and problems presented by the environment are well suited to the person's coping abilities."

DEVELOPMENTAL EMPHASES

Developmental emphases on vocational behavior and decision making differ from the emphases previously discussed—trait-and-factor, decision theory, and psychological—not because they reject the latter but rather because they are typically more inclusive, more concerned with longitudinal expressions of vocational behavior, and more inclined to focus on the individual self-concept.

Ginzberg, Ginsburg, Axelrad, and Herma (1951) were early leaders in speculating about vocational development as a process which culminates in one's early twenties in a vocational choice. In particular, they assert (p. 185): "Occupational choice is a developmental process: it is not a single decision, but a series of decisions made over a period of years. Each step in the process has a meaningful relation to those which precede and follow it." Ginzberg and his colleagues identified four sets of factors, the interplay of which influences the ultimate vocational choice: individual values, emotional factors, the amount and kind of education, and the impact of reality through environmental pressures. More particularly, they gave impetus to a view of the choice process as delimited by life stages in which certain tasks are faced by preadolescents and adolescents. Within the interaction that occurs as these tasks are confronted, compromises between wishes and possibilities contribute to an irreversibility as the process unfolds.

Ginzberg and his associates have labeled the gross phases of the vocational choice process—the periods of development—as fantasy, tentative, and realistic. With the exception of the fantasy, each of these periods is broken into sub-aspects. Thus the tentative period is divided into interest, capacity, value, and transition stages. Following this period, there emerges the realistic period, which is broken into exploration and crystallization substages.

Ginzberg et al. have given credence to the notion that vocational behavior finds its roots in the early life of the child and develops over time. They have indicated that vocational behavior and career choice become increasingly reality-oriented and more specific as one moves toward the choice itself. The following is an impressionistic description of how the theory of Ginzberg et al. might be translated into the action of youngsters in the fantasy, tentative, and realistic period (Herr, 1966, pp. 1–2):

> Young children select any or all careers without regard to the social consequences or the social values attached to their choices. They also change direction very rapidly and without regard to the barriers of an educational nature that stand in their way. They have little awareness of the time span and sequential nature attendant to preparing for and entering a career. Thus, until about age 11 or 12, the factor which is most important in vocational behavior is interest. In other words, youngsters choose those careers which appeal to them because of their relationship to things in which they are immediately interested, which they enjoy doing, and which seem glamorous or adventuresome. They are also influenced by those whom they enjoy being around. It is not surprising that the young child will almost concurrently express desires to be a garbage collector, a milk man, a cowboy, a fireman, an aviator, a teacher, a physician, an astronaut all in the same breath.

> As the child matures, ages 11–15, another factor enters the picture: capacity. The youngster more systematically raises questions about his ability and his adequacy to do particular kinds of things. As reality in the form of needed education, financial needs, social/psychological restrictions, social class limitations begin to intrude upon his fantasy, his choices begin to filter out in terms of those which he believes himself capable of success in accomplishing. He begins to realize that one does not become a medical doctor, nurse, astronaut, or teacher without a long period of training and that along the way certain prerequisites are required. Since the medical doctor or nurse must be "good" in biology and chemistry and mathematics to get to the next step on the educational ladder, he begins to think about his competencies in these areas. He wonders whether his C– in algebra is an indication that he might better consider something else where mathematics or physics are less important. This is not to suggest that young people have just learned about individual differences at age 12, 13, or 14. Their awareness of those differences between themselves and their peers began early in the family and in neighborhood play groups. This simply means that capacities have now been more clearly tied to prerequisites for further training and particular careers.

> As questions of personal capacity become more intense, a further factor intrudes in the reveries of youngsters: values. The adolescent begins to realize that society places different values upon different careers and provides the individual occupying different career roles better or poorer rewards whether these be status, or money, or vacation-time, or security. It also becomes more clear that when one chooses an occupation, one in fact

chooses or adopts a value system. Hence, where one works, the kinds of people with whom one works, the hobbies that he will have, the friend-ship patterns possible, the seasonal or shift nature of the work, the need for geographic mobility are all parts of this value system to which one either adapts or finds himself misplaced and incompatible.

As these three factors—interests, capacities, and values—become sequen-tially prominent, they act as screens by which choices are narrowed. The child starts with fantasy choices. With increasing maturity some of these choices become tentative choices. Finally, he arrives at what for him are realistic choices. As the child matures through pre-adolescence, adoles-cence, and young adulthood, we get a convergence effect moving from the general to be specific. Even realistic choices have stages of converg-ence and greater specificity; the stages of exploration and of crystalliza-tion. Hence, the child after considering his interests, his capacities, his values as well as his family's approval, the reactions of his peers, financial implications and other forces affecting choice, arrives at a point of entry to the Realistic Period and its first stage of Exploration as he enters his first job or the early years of college. The results of the evaluation which occur move him to a more refined and clearer vocational pattern called Crystallization, which concludes with a stage of Specification and Imple-mentation. If this process of 10 or 15 years duration does not work out, he may reinstitute, in condensed fashion, the whole cycle—Fantasy, Tenta-tive, Realistic—as he considers other types of training or jobs to which he might move or transfer.[1]

Probably the developmental approach which has received the most continu-ous attention, stimulated the most research, influenced most pervasively the field of vocational psychology, and is the most comprehensive is the one promulgated by Super and his many colleagues in the Career Pattern Study (Super et al., 1957; Super et al., 1963; Super, 1969a, 1969b). This approach is an integrative one which stresses the interaction of personal and environ-mental variables in vocational behavior.

In a larger sense, Super has made explicit the intimacy of vocational develop-ment and personal development. He has synthesized much of the early work of Buehler (1933) and of Ginzberg, Ginsburg, Axelrad, and Herma (1951) in his longitudinal attempt to focus developmental principles on the staging and the determination of career patterns. He has characterized the vocational de-velopment process as ongoing, continuous, and generally irreversible; as a process of compromise and synthesis within which his primary construct—the development and implementation of the self-concept—operates. The basic theme is that the individual chooses occupations which will allow him to func-

[1] From *Decision-making and vocational development* by Edwin L. Herr (Boston: Houghton Mifflin, 1970), pp. 1-2. Copyright © 1970 by Houghton Mifflin Company. Reprinted by permission of Houghton Mifflin Company.

tion in a role consistent with his self-concept and that the latter conception is a function of his developmental history. Further, because of the range of individual capabilities and the latitude within occupations for different combinations of traits, he has indicated that most people have multi-potentiality.

It may be, however, that occupational choice goes beyond *implementing* a self-concept into the realm of *actualizing;* that is, rather than implementing a self-concept, an individual vocational choice may be an attempt to actualize an *ideal* self-concept (Wheeler and Carnes, 1968).

Although Super's approach has been labeled typically as a developmental self-concept theory (Osipow, 1968, p. 117), Super himself has most recently labeled it differential-developmental-social-phenomonological psychology (Super, 1969b). Such a label indicates the confluence of knowledge bases which this approach has attempted to synthesize and order to explain vocational development.

Super gives prominence to individuals' mastery of increasingly complex vocational developmental tasks at different stages of vocational development. Here he has attempted to synthesize the work of Miller and Form (1951) and of Havighurst (1953) by integrating these two perceptions of life-stage phenomena into a more elaborate set of constructs. Miller and Form, after extensive analysis of the work histories of a sample of men, conceived the following work periods as descriptive of a total life perspective: initial (while in school), trial (early, short-lived, full-time work), stable (normally mature adult), and retirement (after giving up employment). These work periods in concert with those of Buehler (1933)—growth (childhood), exploration (adolescence), establishment (young adulthood), maintenance (maturity), and decline (old age)—provided the broad outlines of Super's concerns, although he has primarily focused on the exploratory and establishment stages.

These two stages are divided into substages. The exploratory stage breaks down into the tentative, transition, and trial (with little commitment) substages; the establishment stage, into the trial (with more commitment), stabilization, and advancement substages (Super, 1969b). He has further formulated gross developmental tasks—crystallization, specification, implementation, stabilization, and consolidation—which rests upon substages and meta-dimensions contributing to increasing vocational maturity (Super, 1963). Within these stages are factors internal as well as external to the individual which influence the choices made. These factors continue to narrow the array of options the individual considers. There is an emphasis, then, on vocational convergence and greater specificity in behavior. A more detailed treatment of research findings from the work of Super and his colleagues will be examined in Chapter 5.

The work of Tiedeman and O'Hara (1963) represents a stream of thought parallel to that of Super's on the staging and development of vocational behavior. In regard to Tiedeman particularly, Super (1969a, p. 4) has stated:

Some men continue to change occupations throughout life, while others have stable periods followed by new periods of trial, which in turn lead to stabilization for a second or third time. Thus, there are stable (direct entry into the life-work), conventional (trial leading to stability), unstable, and multiple-trial careers. The life stage processes continue more or less throughout life, repeating themselves in the sequence: INITIAL—TRIAL—STABLE —DECLINE. *Tiedeman's (1958) use of this concept in theorizing about position choice, each decision concerning the occupancy of a position involving exploration, establishment, and maintenance, is a useful refinement.*

Tiedeman alone, and more recently with O'Hara, views vocational development as part of a continuing process of differentiating ego identity. In these terms, how a person's identity evolves is dependent upon his early childhood experiences with the family unit, the psychological crises—as defined in terms of Erikson's constructs (1963)—encountered at various developmental stages and the agreement between society's meaning system and the individual's meaning system as well as the emotional constants of each.

This view of vocational development as a sequence of developmental life stages or events is also broken into subaspects. For example, the aspect of anticipation of or preoccupation with career goals includes the substages of exploration, crystallization, choice, and clarification. Further, the aspect of implementation or adjustment includes steps such as social induction, reformation, and integration. Pervading these stages are continuing processes of differentiation and integration as outcomes of personality or psychosocial crises.

Finally, Tiedeman and O'Hara suggest further that individual personality is shaped by perceptions of career choices and to some degree by the individual's conformance to the norms and values of those persons already established within the vocational setting. They stress, then, the intimacy of self-concept and career concept as they develop gradually through many small decisions.

At the present time, at least two other longitudinal investigations of vocational development are under way and are worthy of mention. Gribbons and Lohnes (1968) are completing a ten-year study of readiness for vocational planning. Crites (1968, p. 205) is involved in an eight-year study attempting to standardize measures of vocational development through four kinds of interrelated research activity: survey, techniques, theoretical, and applied. Some of the findings of Crites and of Gribbons and Lohnes will be considered in Chapter 5.

APPROACHES TO VOCATIONAL DEVELOPMENT—A REPRISE

In the approaches covered in this chapter, vocational development is described as a process shaped by an interplay of self-references; self-knowledge; knowledge about training; and educational and occupational opportunities; as well as by genetic and early childhood influences; evolving personality styles; and patterns of traits which individuals express cognitively and psychologically in their choice behavior and vocational identity. The collective finding of these descriptions of vocational development is that like all human behavior it is complex and is part of the total fabric of personality development.

Vocational development is characterized by progressive growth and learning operating from infancy through at least young adulthood within a network of impinging forces intrinsic and extrinsic to the individual. Within this context, choice behavior involves a series of interdependent decisions which are to some extent irreversible and which are intimately tied to the individual's personal history, to his personal perceptions of the future, to both his antecedent experiences and future alternatives.

It is important to note that most of the approaches to vocational development discussed are based upon limited samples of rather privileged persons. They are, in general, addressed to those in the middle range of socioeconomic characteristics rather than to those who veer from this classification in either direction. Consequently, these approaches tend to emphasize the continuous, uninterrupted, and progressive aspects of vocational development which seem possible primarily in those whose limits upon choice are minimal, for whom both psychological and economic resources are available to aid purposeful development, and in whom a high correspondence between self-concept and vocational concept is most probable. Such criteria do not fit all the persons about whom guidance practitioners must be concerned.

Responding to these assumptions of continuity in vocational development, Lo Cascio (1967) found that such continuity is not evident in all groups. He described developmental units as continuous, delayed, or impaired, with each class having different effects on adequacy in behavioral repertoire, learning, and the incorporation of learning. He concluded that the vocational development of those typically described as disadvantaged is more likely to be impaired than that of their more favored contemporaries.

Another characteristic of these current approaches to vocational development is that while they predict that individuals with particular need hierarchies or self-concepts will reject occupations and career patterns that do not seem compatible with their personal characteristics, little attention is given to the possibility that work itself is not central to the life styles or aspirations of some persons or that it has connotations that repel rather than attract. As Zytowski (1965, p. 746) has stated, "They assume that all men want to work, that the idea of a vocation has a positive valence as a goal, or that the effect attached to career behavior is positive." For many persons, however, choices are based not on what they want to do but on what they do not want to do. For these people vocational choice seems to be more nearly a matter of moving away from the undesirable rather than moving toward an ideal (Gross, 1967). For other persons, work is not the central commitment for investment of identification or energy that many theories assume. Slocum (1965, p. 862) has observed:

> The work histories of most American men indicate that their work lives have been characterized by lack of commitment to a specific occupation. There is a high probability that most of the pivotal occupational de-

cisions of such men have been made on the basis of expediency and situ-
ational factors rather than on the basis of any long-term life plan.

Another point of concern in present descriptions of vocational development is the age or level of maturity required to make choices. "Most would feel that a certain maturing process must take place before youth (ages 14 to 18) can sensibly make choices—especially vocational ones" (McDaniels, 1968). Mc-Daniels rebuts this assumption by stating that youth "are not too young to choose, only too poorly prepared to make choices." Thus in much of the thinking about vocational development, there is insufficient attention to the heterogeneity in every group within the population whether classified by age, sex, race, social class, or any other basis.

Perhaps the most important point of all in analyzing current approaches to vocational development is that they largely describe what happens if nothing is done to influence the process. Although several longitudinal approaches have emerged—e.g. Super's Career Pattern Study (1957), Crites' Vocational Develop-ment Project (1968), Gribbons and Lohnes' Readiness for Vocational Develop-ment (1968)—their purpose has not been to systematically influence vocational development but only to describe it at different stages of life. It is true that longi-tudinal studies of the effects of different strategies on vocational development are desirable to have. However, the current needs of large numbers of stu-dents for enhanced vocational development precludes waiting another twenty or thirty years until more facts about different strategies are in in order to maxi-mize vocationalization or, indeed, to focus treatment. We must begin now with the knowledge base available.

SUMMARY

This chapter has briefly described the current status of work in American society with particular attention to the effect of technological advances both on work and on educational requirements. The concept of vocational development has been defined and applied to the term "vocationalization," which suggests the possibility of influencing such development rather than leaving it to random events. Finally, five current approaches to describing vocational development—trait-and-factor, decision, sociological, psychological, and developmental em-phases—have been discussed and some of their implications identified.

Whatever the process of vocational decision making, it is clear that vocational choice involves a series of mini-decisions made over a relatively long period of time. If systematic assistance in making these decisions can be provided in the schools, the likelihood seems to be increased that the decisions will be "good" —that is, in terms of outcome or in terms of what appears appropriate for the chooser. The factors that enter into a vocational decision and the process by which that decision is made are highly complex. Content and process are intricately related. What a systematic approach to vocational guidance accomplishes is to bring some order into what is typically a chaotic, haphazard choice.

Finally, it is important to reassert that the present theories of vocational development are incomplete in describing the behavioral development at issue. They have not been formulated as a result of or in conjunction with repeated or longitudinal studies to the degree that one would hope. Neither do they use samples of subjects from female or disadvantaged populations in sufficient magnitude that one can feel confident of the similarities or dissimilarities across subcultures that are implied in some of these theories.

REFERENCES

Asbury, F. A. Vocational development of rural disadvantaged eighth-grade boys. *Vocational Guidance Quarterly,* 1968, 17, 109–113.

Berdie, Ralph F. Personality changes from high school entrance to college matriculation. *Journal of Counseling Psychology,* 1968, 15, 376–380.

*Blau, P. M.; Gustad, J. W.; Jessor, R.; Parnes, H. S.; and Wilcock, R. C. Occupational choice: A conceptual framework. *Industrial Labor Relations.* Rev. 1956, 9, 531–543.

Bohn, M. J., Jr. Vocational maturity and personality. *Vocational Guidance Quarterly,* 1966, 15, 123–126.

*Bordin, E. S.; Nachmann, Barbara; and Segal, S. J. An articulated framework for vocational development. *Journal of Counseling Psychology,* 1963, 10, 107–116.

Borow, H. Vocational development research: Some problems of logical and experimental form. *Personnel and Guidance Journal,* 1961, 40, 21–25.

Bradburn, N. M. The cultural context of personality theory. In J. M. Nepman and R. W. Heine (eds.) *Concepts of personality.* Chicago: Aldine, 1963.

Brayfield, A. H., and Crites, J. O. Research on vocational guidance: Status and prospect. In H. Borow (ed.) *Man in a world of work.* Boston: Houghton Mifflin, 1964, 310–340.

Brill, A. A. *Psychoanalytic psychiatry.* London: John Lehman, 1948.

Brown, C. W., and Ghiselli, E. E. The relationship between the predictive power of aptitude tests for trainability and for job proficiency. *Journal of Applied Psychology,* 1952, 37, 370–372.

Brunkan, R. J. Perceived parental attitudes and parental identification in relation to field of vocational choice. *Journal of Counseling Psychology,* 1965, 12, 39–47.

* Recommended for additional reading.

Brunkan, R. J., and Crites, J. O.   An inventory to measure the parental attitude variable in Roe's theory of vocational choice.   *Journal of Counseling Psychology,* 1964, 11, 3–11.

Buehler, Charlotte. *Der menschliche Lebenslauf als psychologisches Problem.* Leipzig: Hirzel, 1933.

Burnstein, E.   Fear of failure, achievement motivation, and aspiring to prestigeful occupations.   *Journal of Abnormal and Social Psychology,* 1963, 67, 189–193.

Caplow, T.   *The sociology of work.*   Minneapolis: University of Minnesota Press, 1954.

Childs, G. B.   Is the work ethic realistic in an age of automation?   *Phi Delta Kappan,* 1965, 46, 370–375.

Clack, R. J.   Occupational prestige and vocational choice.   *Vocational Guidance Quarterly,* 1968, 16, 282–286.

Clark, Edward T.   Influence of sex and social class on occupational preference and perception.   *Personnel and Guidance Journal,* 1967, 45, 440–444.

Clarke, R.; Gelatt, H. B.; and Levine, L.   A decision-making paradigm for local guidance research.   *Personnel and Guidance Journal,* 1965, 44, 40–51.

Cooley, W. W.   Research frontier: Current research on the career development of scientists.   *Journal of Counseling Psychology,* 1964, 11, 88–93.

Costello, T. W., and Zalkind, S. S. (eds.)   *Psychology in administration: A research orientation.*   Englewood Cliffs, N. J.: Prentice-Hall, 1963.

Creason, Frank, and Schilson, Donald L.   Occupational concerns of sixth-grade children.   *Vocational Guidance Quarterly,* 1970, 18, 219–224.

Crites, J. O.   An interpersonal relations scale for occupational groups.   *Journal of Applied Psychology,* 1962, 46, 87–90.

*Crites, J. O.   *Vocational psychology.*   New York: McGraw-Hill, 1969.

Crites, J. O., and Semler, I. J.   Adjustment, educational achievement, and vocational maturity as dimensions of development in adolescence.   *Journal of Counseling Psychology,* 1967, 14, 489–496.

Cunningham, R. L.   The redefinition of work.   *Modern Age,* 1965, 9, 279–293.

Davidson, D.; Suppes, P.; and Siegel, S.   *Decision-making: An experimental approach.*   Stanford, Calif.: Stanford University Press, 1957.

Day, S. R.   Teacher influence on the occupational preferences of high school students.   *Vocational Guidance Quarterly,* 1966, 14, 215–219.

*Dilley, J. S.   Decision making: A dilemma and a purpose for counseling.   *Personnel and Guidance Journal,* 1967, 45, 547–551.

Drasgow, J., and Carkhuff, R. R.   Kuder neuropsychiatric keys before and after psychotherapy.   *Journal of Counseling Psychology,* 1964, 11, 67–69.

*Drucker, P.   *The age of discontinuity.* New York: Harper & Row, 1969.

Elder, G. H.   Occupational level, achievement, motivation, and social mobility.   *Journal of Counseling Psychology,* 1968, 15, 1–7.

Elton, C. F.   Male career-role and vocational choice: Their prediction with personality and aptitude variable.   *Journal of Counseling Psychology,* 1967, 14, 99–105.

Erikson, E. H.   *Childhood and society.* 2nd ed.   New York: W. W. Norton, 1963.

Festinger, L. A.   *A theory of cognitive dissonance.*   Stanford, Calif.: Stanford University Press, 1957.

Flanagan, J. C., and Cooley, W. W.   *Project talent: One-year follow-up studies.*   Pittsburgh: School of Education, University of Pittsburgh, 1966.

Flores, T. R., and Olsen, L. C.   Stability and realism of occupational aspiration in eighth- and twelfth-grade males.   *Vocational Guidance Quarterly,* 1967, 16, 104–112.

Garbin, A. P.   Occupational choice and the multidimensional rankings of occupations.   *Vocational Guidance Quarterly,* 1967, 16, 17–25.

*Ginzberg, E.; Ginsburg, S. W.; Axelrad, S.; and Herma, J. R.   *Occupational choice: An approach to a general theory.*   New York: Columbia University Press, 1951.

Gottlieb, D.   Poor youth do want to be middle-class but it's not easy.   *Personnel and Guidance Journal,* 1967, 46, 116–122.

Green, L. B., and Parker, H. J.   Parental influences upon adolescent's occupational choice: A test of an aspect of Roe's theory.   *Journal of Counseling Psychology,* 1965, 12, 379–383.

Gribbons, W. D., and Lohnes, P. R.   A five-year study of students' educational aspirations.   *Vocational Guidance Quarterly,* 1966, 14, 66–69.

*Gribbons, W. D., and Lohnes, P. R.   *Emerging careers.*   New York: Teachers College Press, Columbia University, 1968.

Gross, E.   A sociological approach to the analysis of preparation for work life.   *Personnel and Guidance Journal,* 1967, 45, 416–423.

Hansen, Lorraine S.   The art of planmanship.   *Chronicle Guidance Professional Services.*   Moravia, N. Y.: Chronicle Guidance Publications, 1964–65.

Hatch, R. N.; Parmenter, M. D.; and Stefflre, B.   *Planning your life's work.*   Bloomington, Ill.: McKnight and McKnight, 1962.

Havighurst, R. J.   *Human development and education.*   New York: Longmans, Green, 1953.

Healy, C. C.   Relation of occupational choice to the similarity between self-ratings and occupational ratings.   *Journal of Counseling Psychology,* 15, 317–323.

Heath, B. R. G., and Showig, R. W. Predicting occupational status for non-college-bound males. *Personnel and Guidance Journal,* 1967, 46, 144–149.

Herr, E. L. What we know about career selection. *Guidance Keynotes,* 1966, Harrisburg, Pa.: Department of Public Instruction.

Herr, E. L. *Decision-making and vocational development.* Boston: Houghton-Mifflin, 1970.

Hershenson, D. B. Sense of identity, occupational fit, and exculturation in adolescence. *Journal of Counseling Psychology,* 1967, 14, 319–324.

*Hershenson, D. B., and Roth, R. M. A decisional process model of vocational development. *Journal of Counseling Psychology,* 1966, 13, 368–370.

Hills, J. R. Decision theory and college choice. *Personnel and Guidance Journal,* 1964, 43, 17–22.

*Hilton, T. J. Career decision-making. *Journal of Counseling Psychology,* 1959, 9, 291–298.

Holland, J. L. Explanation of a theory of vocational choice: Vocational images and choices. *Vocational Guidance Quarterly,* 1963, 11, 232–239.

*Holland, J. L. *The psychology of vocational choice.* Waltham, Mass.: Blaisdell, 1966.

Holland, J. L., and Nichols, R. C. Explorations of a theory of vocational choice: III. A longitudinal study in change of major field of study. *Personnel and Guidance Journal,* 1964, 43, 235–242.

Hollander, M. A., and Parker, H. J. Occupational stereotypes and needs: Their relationship to vocational choice. *Vocational Guidance Quarterly,* 1969, 18, 91–98.

Hollender, J. W. Development of a realistic vocational choice. *Journal of Counseling Psychology,* 1967, 14, 314–318.

Hummel, R., and Sprinthall, N. Underachievement related to interests, attitudes, and values. *Personnel and Guidance Journal,* 1965, 44, 388–395.

Hutchinson, T., and Roe, Anne. Studies of occupational history: Part II. Attractiveness of occupational groups of the Roe system. *Journal of Counseling Psychology,* 1968, 15, 107–110.

Irvin, F. S. Personality characteristics and vocational identification. *Journal of Counseling Psychology,* 15, 329–333.

James, F., III. Comment on Hilton's model of career decision-making. *Journal of Counseling Psychology,* 1963, 10, 303–304.

Jones, K. J. Occupational preference and social orientation. *Personnel and Guidance Journal,* 1965, 43, 574–579.

Kalder, D. R., and Zytowski, D. G. A maximizing model of occupational decision-making. *Personnel and Guidance Journal,* 1969, 47, 781–788.

Kassarjian, W. M., and Kassarjian, H. H.   Occupational interests, social values, and social character.   *Journal of Counseling Psychology,* 1965, 12, 48–54.

*Katz, M.   *Decisions and values: A rationale for secondary school guidance.*   New York: College Entrance Examination Board, 1963.

*Katz, M.   A model of guidance for career decision-making.   *Vocational Guidance Quarterly,* 1966, 15, 2–10.

Kohlan, R. G.   Relationship between inventoried interests and inventoried needs.   *Personnel and Guidance Journal,* 1968, 46, 592–598.

Krippner, S.   The educational plans and preferences of upper-middle-class junior high school pupils.   *Vocational Guidance Quarterly,* 1965, 13, 257–260.

Krumboltz, J., and Thoresen, C. E.   The effect of behavioral counseling in group and individual settings on information-seeking behavior.   *Journal of Counseling Psychology,* 1964, 11, 324–333.

*Leacock, Eleanor.   The concept of culture and its significance for school counselors.   *Personnel and Guidance Journal,* 1968, 46, 844–851.

Lipsett, L.   Social factors in vocational development.   *Personnel and Guidance Journal,* 1962, 40, 432–437.

*LoCasio, R.   Continuity and discontinuity in vocational development theory.   *Personnel and Guidance Journal,* 1967, 46, 32–36.

*McDaniels, C.   Youth: Too young to choose.   *Vocational Guidance Quarterly,* 1968, 16, 242–249.

McMahon, G. G.   Technical education: A problem of definition.   *American Vocational Journal,* 1970, 44, 22–23.

Mahone, C. H.   Fear of failure and unrealistic vocational aspiration.   *Journal of Abnormal and Social Psychology,* 1960, 60, 253–261.

Malnig, L. R.   Fear of paternal competition: A factor in vocational choice.   *Personnel and Guidance Journal,* 1967, 46, 235–239.

Marr, Evelyn.   Some behaviors and attitudes relating to vocational choice.   *Journal of Counseling Psychology,* 1965, 12, 404–408.

Maslow, A. H.   *Motivation and personality.*   New York: Harper & Row, 1954.

Miller, A. W.   Learning theory and vocational decisions.   *Personnel and Guidance Journal,* 1968, 47, 18–23.

Miller, D. C., and Form, W. H.   *Industrial sociology.*   New York: Harper, 1951.

Miller, D. C., and Thomas, D. L.   Relationships between educational and vocational interests.   *Vocational Guidance Quarterly,* 1966, 15, 113–118.

Morris, J. L.   Propensity for risk taking as a determinant of vocational choice.   *Journal of Personality and Social Psychology,* 1966, 3, 328–355.

Morse, Nancy, and Weiss, R. S.   The function and meaning of work and the job.   In S. Nosow and W. Form (eds.)   *Man, work, and society.*   New York: Basic Books, 1962.

Moynihan, D. P.   Morality of work and immorality of opportunity.   *Vocational Guidance Quarterly,* 1964, 12, 229–236.

Murphy, G.   *Personality: A biosocial approach to origins and structure.*   New York: Harper & Row, 1947.

O'Hara, R. P.   Comment on Super's papers. *The Counseling Psychologist,* 1969, 1, 29–31.

*Osipow, S. H.   *Theories of career development.*   New York: Appleton-Century-Crofts, 1968.

Osipow, S. H.; Ashby, J. D.; and Wall, H. W.   Personality types and vocational choice: A test of Holland's theory.   *Personnel and Guidance Journal,* 1966, 45, 37–42.

Osipow, S. H., and Gold, J. A.   Factors related to inconsistent career preference.   *Personnel and Guidance Journal,* 1967, 46, 346–349.

Osipow, S. H., and Gold, J. A.   Personal adjustment and career development.   *Journal of Counseling Psychology,* 1968, 15, 439–443.

Parsons, T.   *The social system.*   Glencoe, Ill.: Free Press, 1951.

Perrone, P. A.   Factors influencing high school seniors occupational preference.   *Personnel and Guidance Journal,* 1964, 42, 976–979.

Roe, Anne.   A psychological study of eminent psychologists and anthropologists and a comparison with biological and physical scientists.   *Psychological Monographs,* 1953, 67, No. 352.

*Roe, Anne.   The psychology of occupations.   New York: John Wiley & Sons, 1956.

Schmeiding, O. A., and Jensen, Shirley.   American Indian students: vocational development and vocational tenacity.   *Vocational Guidance Quarterly,* 1968, 17, 120–123.

Sewell, W. H., and Orenstein, A. M.   Community of residence and occupational choice.   *American Journal of Sociology,* 1965, 70, 551–563.

Sharf, R.   Relative importance of interest and ability in vocational decision-making.   *Journal of Counseling Psychology,* 1970, 17, 258–262.

Slakter, M. J., and Cramer, S. H.   Risk taking and vocational or curriculum choice.   *Vocational Guidance Quarterly,* 1969, 18, 127–132.

*Slocum, W. L.   Occupational careers in organizations: A sociological perspective.   *Personnel and Guidance Journal,* 1965, 43, 858–866.

*Stefflre, B.   Vocational development: Ten propositions in search of a theory.   *Personnel and Guidance Journal,* 1966, 44, 611–616.

Sternberg, C.   Interests and tendencies toward maladjustment in a normal population. *Personnel and Guidance Journal,* 1956, 35, 94–99.

Stevic, R., and Uhlig, G.   Occupational aspirations of selected Appalachian youth. *Personnel and Guidance Journal,* 1967, 45, 435-439.

*Super, D. E.   Career patterns as a basis for vocational counseling. *Journal of Counseling Psychology,* 1954, 1, 12–20.

Super, D. E.   The natural history of a study of lives and of vocations. *Perspectives on Education,* 1969, 2, 13–22 (b).

*Super, D. E.   *The psychology of careers.*   New York: Harper & Row, 1957.

Super, D. E.   The structure of work values in relation to status, achievement, interest, and adjustment. *Journal of Applied Psychology,* 1962, 46, 227–239.

*Super, D. E.   Vocational development theory: Parsons, positions, and processes. *The Counseling Psychologist,* 1969, 1, 2–9 (a).

*Super, D. E., and Bohn, M. J., Jr.   *Occupational Psychology.*   Belmont, Calif.: Wadsworth, 1970.

*Super, D. E., and Crites, J. O.   *Appraising vocational fitness.*   New York: Harper & Row, 1962.

Super, D. E.; Crites, J. O.; Hummel, R. C.; Moser, H. P.; Overstreet, Phoebe, L.; and Wornath, C. F.   *Vocational development: A framework for research.* New York: Teachers College, Columbia University, 1957.

*Super, D. E.; Starishevsky, R.; Matlin, N.; and Jordaan, J. P.   *Career development: Self-concept theory.*   New York: College Entrance Examination Board, 1963.

Suziedelis, A., and Steimel, R. J.   The relationship of need hierarchies to inventoried interests. *Personnel and Guidance Journal,* 1963, 42, 393–396.

Thompson, O. E.   Occupational values in high school students. *Personnel and Guidance Journal,* 1966, 4, 850–853.

Thoresen, C. E., and Mehrens, W. A.   Decision theory and vocational counseling: Important concepts and questions. *Personnel and Guidance Journal,* 1967, 46, 165–172.

Thorndike, R. L.   The prediction of vocational success. *Vocational Guidance Quarterly,* 1963, 11, 179–187.

Thorndike, R. L., and Hagen, Elizabeth.   *10,000 careers.*   New York: John Wiley & Sons, 1959.

Thorndike, R. L.; Weiss, D. J.; and Darvis, Rene V.   Canonical correlation of vocational interests and vocational needs. *Journal of Counseling Psychology,* 1968, 15, 101–106.

Tiedeman, D. V.   Decision and vocational development: A paradigm and its implications. *Personnel and Guidance Journal,* 1961, 40, 15–20.

Tiedeman, D. V.   The Harvard studies in career development in current perspective.   Dec., 1958. Mimeographed.

*Tiedeman, D. V., and O'Hara, R. P.   *Career development: Choice and adjustment.*   New York: College Entrance Examination Board, 1963.

Tillinghast, B. S., Jr.   Choice orientations of guidance.   *Vocational Guidance Quarterly,* 1964, 13, 18–20.

Tyler, Leona E.; Sundberg, N. D.; Rohila, P. K.; and Greene, M. M.   Patterns of choice in Dutch, American, and Indian adolescents.   *Journal of Counseling Psychology,* 1968, 15, 522–529.

Underhill, R.   Values and postcollege career change.   *American Journal of Sociology,* 1966, 72, 163–172.

Wagman, M.   Perceived similarities in occupational value structure.   *Vocational Guidance Quarterly,* 1968, 16, 275–281.

Watley, D. J.   Student decisions influenced by counselors and teachers.   *Vocational Guidance Quarterly,* 1966, 15, 36–40.

Werts, C. E.   Paternal influence on career choice.   *Journal of Counseling Psychology,* 1968, 15, 48–52.

Wheeler, C. L., and Carnes, E. F.   Relationships among self-concepts, ideal self-concepts, and stereotypes of probable and ideal vocational choices.   *Journal of Counseling Psychology,* 1968, 15, 530–535.

Williams, R. L., and Byars, H.   Negro self-esteem in a transitional society.   *Personnel and Guidance Journal,* 1968, 47, 120–125.

Wrenn, C. G.   Human values and work in American life.   In H. Borow (ed.)   *Man in a world at work.*   Boston: Houghton Mifflin, 1964.

Ziller, R. C.   Vocational choice and utility for risk.   *Journal of Counseling Psychology,* 1957, 4, 61–64.

Zito, R. J., and Bardon, J. I.   Negro adolescents' success and failure imagery concerning work and school.   *Vocational Guidance Quarterly,* 1968, 16, 181–184.

Zytowski, D. G.   Avoidance behavior in vocational motivation.   *Personnel and Guidance Journal,* 1965, 43, 746–750.

THREE

THE AMERICAN OCCUPATIONAL STRUCTURE

This chapter on the American occupational structure discusses its changing nature, its relationship to vocational guidance, and some representative occupational classifications.

THE CHANGING SCENE

Many futurists have attempted to predict what the United States will be like ten, twenty, fifty, or a hundred years from now. All agree on only one point: The future will bring a change. Beyond this simplistic conclusion, however, futurists agree on very little. Whether predictions emanate from historical and qualitative analyses or from more empirical and quantitative bases, conclusions also suggest that the occupational structure of the United States is one of those societal elements that will undergo the greatest upheaval. What precise form this drastic flux will take, however, is moot—at least insofar as one is able to predict long-term changes.

Drucker (1968), for example, predicts a massive shift to what he terms "knowledge work" and the consequent creation of a knowledge society. Historically, the economy of the United States has been concerned with the production of goods; in the future, the production of knowledge will be the focus, he maintains. While it is clear that the manual worker is motivated by pay, that his job is simply a livelihood, and that a "boss" decides what he will do, there are no clear-cut motivations and demands for the knowledge worker. As well as the tangible reward of pay, the knowledge worker will likely require satisfaction in his work activities, achievement motivation or job challenge, and demands on him which stem from knowledge or objectives rather than from bosses or people. In fact, in a knowledge society there are no bosses; knowledge is organized as a team "in which the task decides who is in charge, when, for what, and for how long" (p. 289).

Leisure and a kind of career malaise also are problems to be resolved in a knowledge society, Drucker points out. The manual worker has no great problems with leisure; the separation of his work from his leisure pursuits is usually complete. The knowledge worker, on the other hand, is apparently controlled by the habit-forming nature of knowledge work. He cannot easily separate his leisure-time cultural pursuits from his work; he cannot easily retire.

He escalates quickly to the "top" of his work sphere, and then frequently a general malaise results.

College teachers, for example, often are hurtled from assistant professors to full professors in from six to ten years. Many universities are thus top-heavy with full professors. Contrast this structure with the European university, in which there are very few full professors and an individual spends his entire working life trying to reach that rank. A great many members of the educated middle class are in the same situation. In the Middle Ages, an affliction known as *accidie,* a condition of emotional dissatisfaction and despair, befell the *clerc* at about age 30 when he realized that he would never be a saint or an abbot. Similarly, knowledge workers in contemporary America often become bored and dispirited with their jobs when they reach their forties. Drucker suggests that the cure is to make it possible for the middle-aged knowledge worker to start a second knowledge career and to direct as much energy toward psychological planning for retirement as he now directs toward financial planning for retirement.

At the same time, one can note increasing numbers of educated dropouts from conventional work modes. People who have worked at supposedly productive jobs have left the occupational mainstream apparently because of contempt for the work offered by a technological society. Increasing numbers of young, educated Americans are attempting to return to the agrarian past from which America emerged. They feel that most work in our competitive society is "meaningless, degrading, and inconsistent with self-realization" (Reich, 1970, p. 182). From the viewpoint of this volume, such individuals are victims of arrested vocationalization—victims because education has failed to provide them with the experiences which lead to adequate vocational development.

In a knowledge society, Drucker asserts, the unskilled worker is relegated to a position of social impotence and unimportance, reverting to a position which he held fifty years ago. Because of the upsurge of labor in the first fifty years of this century, the unskilled worker acquired "political power, social cohesion, pride, and leadership" (p. 299). But with the application of knowledge to work, the supply of people available for unskilled, mass production jobs begins to increase faster than the demand, and with the decrease in job availability goes the unskilled worker's social position. Retraining becomes paramount; change, mandatory. At the same time, even skilled work is changing, shifting from craft-based skills to work based in knowledge. This shift demands that individuals have the psychological capacity to relearn. Drucker (1968, p. 305) argues:

> Both transition problems, that of the unskilled mass-production worker and that of craft skill and craft organizations, will be most acute in the United States. For it is here that the new knowledge economy is developing the furthest and the fastest. Above all both are inextricably entwined with our most dangerous, most sensitive, and most urgent problem, the race issue.

The American Negro is the worst sufferer in the decline of the mass production

worker, according to Drucker. While it is important to find immediate mass production and craft jobs for the unskilled Negro, it is more important to find, develop, and place the largest number of Negro knowledge workers as soon as possible. Although Negro knowledge workers have been increasing at twice the rate
of white knowledge workers, they started from almost a zero base, and a great
deal must be done. Drucker (p. 130) states:

> The emergence of knowledge as central to our society has converted into
> dead-end streets the avenues by means of which earlier Negro leaders had
> hoped to reach the goals of Negro equality, Negro dignity, and Negro ful-
> fillment: ownership of the small farm and access to manual work as an
> equal. It has instead opened up knowledge jobs as the greatest opportunity
> the black man has yet had in America.

These are but a few of the ruminations of our futurist regarding the nature of
work and the occupational structure in the years to come. However provocative
and brilliantly developed these ideas are, they are still only educated guesses. But
they do suggest a broad direction in which the occupational structure may go. Certainly the extrapolation of descriptive data which we already have suggests that
Drucker's views are a logical extension of these data.

In looking at the changing occupational structure, it is useful to know the current proportions of workers in the various occupational groups and the changes
which are likely to occur. Wolfbein (1968), utilizing data from the United States
Department of Labor and from the National Commission on Technology, Automation, and Economic Progress, presents the changes in employment by major
occupational groups reflected in Table 1.

Wolfbein's table suggests several interesting changes. First, it is evident that
there will be a large labor-force increase through 1975, an increase proportion-
ally greater than the growth in population. Hence we can look to more young
workers (the post–World War II baby boom), to more women in the labor force,
and to a great many more Black workers as the primary causes of this increase.
The United States Department of Labor estimates a work force of 100 million by
1980, of whom 37 million will be women. This compares with 18 million women
in 1950 and 30 million in 1969. Second, Table 1 indicates that disadvantaged workers are currently employed in those jobs which will have less-than-average growth
to 1975. Obviously, only massive retraining and changed prevocational education
can cope with this situation.

Several other predictions of changes in the occupational structure are possible
either by extrapolation from data or by nonempirically based conjecture. Hall
(1968) echoes previous writings of Kimball and McClellan (1962) when he suggests that work is moving away from individualized settings into organizational
settings. This change requires concomitant changes in the direction of vocationalization, changes that are alluded to in other chapters. It is also evident, as

Table 1   Employment by Major Occupational Group
Actual 1965/Estimated 1975

OCCUPATIONAL GROUP	EMPLOYMENT (000)		CHANGE/1965-75	
	1965	1975	000	%
Total	72,177	88,700	16,523	23
White collar	32,104	42,800	10,696	33
Professional and technical	8,883	13,200	4,317	48
Proprietary and managerial	7,340	9,200	1,860	26
Clerical	11,166	14,600	3,434	31
Sales	4,715	5,800	1,085	23
Blue collar	26,466	29,900	3,434	13
Craftsmen	9,221	11,400	2,179	24
Operatives	13,390	14,800	1,410	10
Laborers	3,855	3,700	−155	−4
Service	9,342	12,500	3,158	34
Farm	4,265	3,500	−765	−18

Source: 1965 data from U. S. Department of Labor, Bureau of Labor Statistics, Employment and Earnings and Monthly Report on the Labor Force; 1975 data from National Commission on Technology, Automation and Economic Progress, *The outlook for technological change and employment,* Appendix Vol. I (Washington, D. C.: Government Printing Office, 1966).

From: S. L. Wolfbein, *Occupational information: A career guidance view* (New York: Random House, 1968), p. 49. By permission.

the previous portion of this chapter has emphasized, that mental skills will be at a premium. For example, the growth of professional and technical occupations will reflect a change from approximately 10.2 million workers in 1968 to a projected 16 million workers by 1980 *(Occupational Outlook Handbook, 1970).* At the same time, Venn (1964) argues that the greatest single need in the future will be for more people in middle-level technical and skilled occupations. In any case, the great needs for manpower in the foreseeable future relate to skilled work, to brain power, and consequently to specialized and extended education and/or training.

Another way to look at the changing occupational structure is to view the changes which are likely to occur, by type of industry rather than by major occupational groups. Figure 1 (page 69) presents such data.

An analysis of Figure 1 indicates that state and local government will experience the most rapid growth, an employment of some 52 percent. This will be followed by services with a 40 percent increase, and construction with a 35 percent increase. While manufacturing will grow only 11 percent, it will still be the largest industry in the United States in 1980. Agricultural employment will continue to decline; by 1980 the nation's food will be grown by only 3 percent of the labor force.

The summary points that can be made regarding the changing occupational structure for at least the next decade are the following:

1. Young adult workers will be the fastest growing group in the labor force.

2. Teen-agers will be added to the labor force far more slowly than in the 1960's.

3. Blacks will continue to make gains in education.

4. Women will continue to enter and re-enter the labor force in increasing numbers.

5. Part-time work opportunities will reach—and are reaching now—major proportions.

6. Employment will continue to shift toward white-collar and service occupations. Professional, technical, and service occupational groups will grow fastest.

7. The 1970's will be a period of strong economic growth accompanied by extensive growth in work force.

8. The largest number of employment opportunities will continue to be in the service-providing industries.

9. State and local governments and service industries will have especially rapid employment gains.

The point that all these changes emphasize is that trends in occupation and industry growth necessitate continued adjustments in career decisions. Using information now available, counselors and students can plan for the future insofar as supply and demand factors affect career decisions. For example, it is likely that reduced teacher openings will cause many college students to major in other fields and to enter other occupations. In the past, two of every three women college graduates entered teaching. Obviously, women will require a broadened outlook on career opportunities.

RELATION OF OCCUPATIONAL STRUCTURE TO VOCATIONAL GUIDANCE

Chapter 2 identified the major ways in which the antecedents and the processes of decision-making behavior are described. Weaving throughout this discussion are the factors which produce the individual differences that shape personal styles of approach to choice and implementation of choice. In the present chapter, perhaps the important point to be made is that such considerations are valid only if a diversity of choices exists and if any given individual has sufficient political and social freedom to choose among opportunities. The fact that these two conditions do exist in the United States has historically impelled the provision of vocational guidance to foster not only freedom of choice but informed choice as well.

Figure 1. Employment by Major Industries: 1969–1980

EMPLOYMENT (MILLIONS)		INDUSTRY
1968	**1980**	
80.8	99.6	ALL INDUSTRIES
9.1	13.8	State and local government
19.1	21.1	Services: personal, professional, business
4.0	5.5	Construction
3.7	4.6	Finance, insurance, and real estate
16.6	20.5	Trade
20.1	22.4	Manufacturing
4.5	4.9	Transportation, communication, and public utilities
2.7	3.0	Federal government
0.6	0.6	Mining
4.2	3.2	Agriculture

From: U.S. Department of Labor, *U.S. manpower in the 1970's* (Washington, D.C.: Superintendent of Documents, 1970.)

Individuals must choose something; in the terms of this book, they must choose an occupation from among the thousands of possibilities which exist. For example, the *Dictionary of Occupational Titles* (DOT) lists over 21,000 jobs. New jobs are created each day; obsolescent jobs are daily phased out of existence.

If, however, as is contended at several points in this volume, personal identity is acquired through such characteristics as commitment, planning, seeing oneself and what one does in the present as affecting the future, then vocational guidance should aid the choice of an occupation within the context of vocation or career. These latter terms connote not simply choice at a point in time but a series of immediate choices made to achieve one's goals at future points in time as well.

In order for an individual to relate himself to the occupational and educational alternatives available to him, he needs some "handles" which will help him see how these alternatives differ. In an effort to bring some order into what can well be a chaotic situation, various schema have been devised to classify in logical ways the thousands of individual jobs and the variety of educational programs. Each scheme emphasizes at least one characteristic for differentiating occupations. As will be indicated in Chapter 5 (vocational guidance objectives), in Chapters 6, 7 and 9 (the application of vocational guidance practices at different grade levels), and in Chapter 11 (information systems), these occupational differences can be used to give substance to efforts at vocationalization; to reality-test one's characteristics against job requirements; and to create filing systems or man-machine interaction systems for providing better access to information.

Since one of the prime differences between occupational alternatives relates to levels and kinds of education, a system for classifying differences in educational opportunities by overt and covert criteria (Herr and Cramer, 1968) will not be elaborated here—except as it is included in the variables for classifying occupational characteristics in the DOT. However, it is important when considering the range of opportunities in the American occupational structure to recognize the relationship between level and kind of education and level and kind of work.

OCCUPATIONAL CLASSIFICATION SYSTEMS

Classifications of occupations have been formulated for various purposes on both a priori and post hoc bases and with their roots in economics, psychology, and sociology. Among the major classification systems are the following (Hatt, 1962):

1. By industry (e.g. 1970 Census Industry Codes)

2. By socioeconomic groups

3. By ability and/or aptitudes

4. By occupation

5. By interests

6. By field and level

7. By field, level, and enterprise

8. By income

9. By type of work

10. By educational or occupational prerequisites

11. By occupational duties performed

12. By life span (e.g. early entry—early leaving, etc.)

13. By rewards (e.g. financial, honorific values, working conditions, or a combi-nation

This chapter describes merely a few of these possibilities in some detail, those which seem most important to the purposes of this book: psychological, socio-logical, census, status, the DOT.

PSYCHOLOGICAL

Many classification schemes are based on the psychological characteristics of workers. One example is the system developed by John Holland and his associates at the Johns Hopkins University (Holland, et al., 1970). In Chapter 2, Holland's theory of vocational development is described; the reader will recall that it is based on a theory of personality types. Evolving out of this theory, Holland and his colleagues have devised six classses of occupations: realistic, investigative, artistic, social, enterprising, and conventional. Each of these has five to sixteen subclasses; within each subclass, occupations are arranged by the years of gen-eral education required. In all, 431 common occupations—comprising about 95 percent of the labor force of the United States—are included. The model upon which classification is based makes clear the interrelationship of the various classes.

All occupations are arranged in a system that uses the six Holland code letters:

Realistic occupations (R) include skilled trades, many technical and some service occupations.

Investigative occupations (I) include scientific and some technical occupa-tions.

Artistic occupations (A) include artistic, musical, and literary occupations.

Social occupations (S) include educational and social welfare occupations.

Enterprising occupations (E) include managerial and sales occupations.

Conventional occupations (C) include office and clerical occupations.

The three classes which persons in a specific occupation most resemble are designated in order by the code letter for those classes Thus counselors, for example, are designated SEA, meaning that they most of all resemble people in social occupations, that they next most resemble people in enterprising occupa-tions, and that they still less resemble people in artistic occupations.

To relate this classification scheme to a more familiar system, Holland further identifies occupations by their DOT numbers. These numbers provide a description of the occupation and estimates of interests and aptitudes associated with it. (The DOT system is more fully described later in this chapter.) Thus the occupation of counselor is now described by the DOT designation, 045.108, and by the three occupational classes, or types, which counselors most resemble, SEA.

Finally, a 1-6 designation describes the level of education development demanded by an occupation. Levels 5 and 6 refer to college training; levels 3 and 4 mean high school and some college, technical, or business training; levels 1 and 2 mean only elementary school or no special training, so we now have the complete Holland classification for the occupation of counselor.

	DOT	ED	CODE
Counselor	045.108	5	SEA

The Holland classification system and the validity of the occupational groupings are too new to permit evaluation of their usefulness in occupational research, vocational guidance, vocational education, and social science. It is, however, a promising development that may well stand the rigors of close empirical verification, and it is an excellent example of an attempt to classify occupations psychologically. Assuming the validity of the typology, it can be converted to a workable vocational guidance delivery system as will be seen in Chapter 11, which discusses Holland's *Self-directed search for educational and vocational planning.* The value to vocational guidance of any classification system is its ability to break down the complex occupational world into manageable categories to which individuals can then relate important self-characteristics.

SOCIOLOGICAL

Various classification systems are based on norms or population data, drawing heavily on sociology. Some of these systems are socioeconomic class, earnings, status, rewards, etc. The most common sociological-type classification system is that utilized by the United States Census. The 1970 Census of Population Occupational Classification is as follows:

General Category	Number of Occupational Categories
Professional, technical, and kindred workers	124
Managers and administrators, except farm	24
Sales workers	15
Clerical and kindred workers	48
Operatives, except transport	54
Craftsmen and kindred workers	96

Transport equipment operatives	12
Laborers, except farm	16
Farm laborers and farm foremen	5
Service workers, except private household	38
Private household workers	6
Workers not classified by occupation	1

The Census further classifies occupational titles into industry codes or type of employment setting. Since the 1940 Census, the number of occupational categories has considerably expanded. The Census classification is valuable because it updates every ten years the distribution of workers into occupational categories and by industry. It thus provides data to a variety of consumers in terms of a standardized classification scheme.

Another sociological classification is based on the status of occupations. Status level is usually determined by the prestige of the occupation, which, in turn, is based on such factors as money earned, power, the type of work involved, the degree of responsibility for social welfare, the amount of education necessary, or other prerequisite factors. That earning power is not the primary criterion of status is evident by the relative ranking of occupations on the various scales. For example, one scale ranked 100 occupations according to prestige (Smith, 1943). Leading the list was the occupation of United States Supreme Court Justice; last was the occupation of professional prostitute. Available data suggest that a "successful" prostitute makes considerably more money annually than does a jurist sitting on the highest court. In fact, there is no linear relationship between occupational roles and social status for a number of reasons (Nosow and Form, 1962, p. 113):

1. The occupational structure itself is not an absolutely or clearly ordered status continuum.

2. The occupational structure is undergoing very rapid change, increasing the ambiguity of occupational roles.

3. There is continuous change in the numbers and types of persons entering the local labor market. . . .

4. Contradictory values also operate in the community to becloud both the occupational and the general community status structures.

The classic prestige scale is the one established by the National Opinion Research Center of the University of Chicago. It is generally referred to as the NORC Scale of Occupational Prestige and presents the following prestige hierarchy of occupations:

> Government officials
> Professional and semiprofessional workers
> Proprietors, managers, and officials (except farm)
> Clerical, sales, and kindred workers
> Craftsmen, foremen, and kindred workers
> Farmers and farm managers
> Protective service workers

Operatives and kindred workers
Farm laborers
Service workers (except domestic and protective)
Laborers (except farm)

The NORC Scale closely parallels another prestige ranking system, Duncan's Sociometric Status Index of 1950. The average status score for all occupations is 30. In relation to that average, the following occupational group scores prevail:

Professional, technical, and kindred workers	75
Managers, officials, and proprietors (except farm)	57
Sales workers	49
Clerical and kindred workers	45
Craftsmen, foremen, and kindred workers	31
Operatives and kindred workers	18
Service workers (except private household)	17
Farmers and farm managers	14
Farm laborers and foremen	9
Private household workers	8
Laborers (except farm and mine)	7

These occupational status rankings have remained relatively stable over a number of years (Hodge, Siegel, and Rossi, 1964), suggesting that American perception of the prestige of various occupational groups remains basically similar to what it was in the first quarter of this century. This finding is supported by Hakel, Hollman, and Dunnette (1968), who found only minor changes in the social status or prestige order ascribed to occupations. They compared the results of a 1925 study by Counts and a 1946 study by Deeg and Paterson with their own 1967 study utilizing perceptions of undergraduates at the University of Minnesota. Although no great differences were found, scientific occupations increased in prestige, culturally oriented occupations dropped, and artisans rose steadily upward. The results are summarized in Table 2.

Of course, what makes these results somewhat suspect is the fact that since 1925, indeed since 1946, a whole new batch of occupations has emerged which could well skew the results. However, there is also evidence that occupational prestige structures do *not* differ greatly from country to country nor from underdeveloped countries to more modern countries—although the latter conclusion may be spurious because of the relatively modern sample of individuals responding (e.g. students) in underdeveloped countries (Armer, 1968). In fact, because so many prestige studies have utilized students as samples and because academic performance and intellectual ability largely determine what a person regards as occupational prestige (Spaeth, 1968), it may be dangerous to generalize the results of occupational status studies.

Table 2   Social Status Ranks of 25 Occupations as Reported in Three Studies over 42 Years

OCCUPATION	RANK ORDER BY COUNTS (1925)	RANK ORDER BY DEEG AND PATERSON (1946)	RANK ORDER BY HAKEL, HOLLMAN, AND DUNNETTE (1967)
Banker	1	2.5	4
Physician	2	1	1
Lawyer	3	2.5	2
Superintendent of schools	4	4	3
Civil engineer	5	5	5
Army captain	6	6	8
Foreign missionary	7	7	7
Elementary school teacher	8	8	6
Farmer	9	12	19
Machinist	10	9	12
Traveling salesman	11	16	13
Grocer	12	13	17
Electrician	13	11	9
Insurance agent	14	10	10
Mail carrier	15	14	18
Carpenter	16	15	11
Soldier	17	19	15
Plumber	18	17	16
Motorman	19	18	20
Barber	20	20	14
Truck driver	21	21.5	21
Coal miner	22	21.5	23
Janitor	23	23	22
Hod carrier	24	24	24
Ditch digger	25	25	25

The correlations between the rank orders (rho) are as follows: 1925 and 1946, .97; 1945 and 1967, .93; and 1925 and 1967, .88.

From: M. D. Hakel, T. D. Hollmann, and M. D. Dunnette, Stability and change in the social status of occupations over 21 and 42 year periods, *Personnel and Guidance Journal*, 1968, 46, 764. Copyright © 1968 by the American Personnel and Guidance Association. By permission.

It is important to realize that as early as the ninth grade, students are acutely aware of occupational prestige values and tend to regard work as desirable for its own sake rather than merely as a means to an end (Slocum, 1966). Yet, while high school students are aware of occupational prestige values, the value of a specific occupation is not a good predictor of their occupational likes and dislikes (Slocum and Bowles, 1968). Contrary to popular belief, high school students find a wide range of occupations attractive, independent of their prestige.

All this is not to say that the occupational structure is unresponsive to genera-
tional changes. A classic example of recent times was the great upsurge of scientific
and engineering careers stimulated by Sputnik and the resulting reactions. More
recently, however, because of cutbacks in federal support, the United States finds
that it has a surplus of scientists and engineers. Accordingly, it is expected that
the numbers of these professionals will diminish. We have also recently witnessed
a reluctance of college graduates to enter large, corporate business structures
either because of the perceived depersonalization of such organizations, because
of a movement away from material goals on the part of this generation, or because
of some other factor.

The point is that the way in which occupations are perceived and consequent
interest in entering them are contingent upon supply and demand, which are
shaped by priorities in the society and by the prevailing work ethic of each generation. Thus Campbell (1969) could survey the vocational interests of Dartmouth
College freshmen from 1947 to 1967 and conclude that interest in scientific occupations had increased while interest in business occupations had decreased. If
such a survey is made ten years hence, it will likely indicate that interest in scientific occupations has decreased, having been replaced by some other occupational
group.

Occupational status classification systems are useful in that they permit youngsters in the process of vocationalization to project into the future in order to discern probable changes in occupational status levels. If young people are to appreciate the dignity which they can bring to all work, they must understand the
bases on which some occupations are perceived as prestigious and others are not.
If occupational prestige is a consideration in vocational decision making, it is
important that youngsters understand the factors that determine prestige.

FIELD, LEVEL, AND ENTERPRISE

Most occupational classification systems are unidimensional—that is, they classify
occupations on the basis of a single factor, or variable. As has been previously
noted, it is possible (and desirable) to classify occupations by combining two or
more variables into a multidimensional scheme. One of the first attempts of this
sort was made by Roe (1954). Her classification system combines eight fields and
six levels. The eight fields, which are based on the work of interest measurement
researchers, such as Strong, are: physical; social and personal service; persuasive
business; government, industry; mathematics, physical science; biological science;
humanities; and arts. Her levels are based on the responsibility, education, and
prestige involved in an occupation. These levels are: professional and managerial
(higher); professional and managerial (regular); semiprofessional and low managerial; skilled support and maintenance; semiskilled support and maintenance;
and unskilled support and maintenance.

It soon became clear that still another dimension was needed to describe
an occupation fully. The concept of enterprise, roughly related to industrial classi-

Figure 2. A Scheme for Classifying Occupations by Level, Field, and Enterprise

LEVEL	I Outdoor-physical	II Social-personal	III Business-contact	IV Administration-control	V Math-physical sciences	VI Biological sciences	VII Humanistic	VIII Arts
1. Professional and managerial, higher		Social scientist		Corporation president	Physicist	Physiologist	Archeologist	Creative artist
2. Professional and managerial, regular	Athletic coach	Social worker	Sales manager	Banker	B. Engineer	Physician	Editor	Music arranger
3. Semiprofessional and managerial, lower	Athlete	Probation officer	Auto salesman	Private secretary	Draftsman	Laboratory technician	Librarian	Interior decorator
4. Skilled	Bricklayer	Barber	Auctioneer	Cashier	Electrician	Embalmer		Dressmaker
5. Semiskilled	Janitor	Waiter	Peddler	Messenger	Truck driver	Gardener		Cook
6. Unskilled	Deckhand	Attendant		Watchman	Helper	Farm hand		Helper

ENTERPRISE

A. Agri-forest
B. Mining
C. Construction
D. Manufacture
E. Trade
F. Finance, etc.
G. Transport
H. Services
I. Government

From: *The psychology of careers* by Donald E. Super (p.48). Copyright © 1957 by Donald E. Super. By permission of Harper & Row, Publishers, Inc.

fication, was added by Super (1957), who drew from the work of Moser, Dubin, and Shelsky (1956) as they modified Roe's original classification. What emerges is a tridimensional classification of occupations that describes them in terms of field, level, and enterprise.

The tridimensional classification system clearly depicts the fact that occupations differ in at least three dimensions: in terms of the field of activity or interest; in terms of level of ability, education and training, autonomy and authority, prestige and rewards; and in terms of the enterprise in which the work is performed. Figure 2 (page 77) presents these differences in graphic form.

The field-level-enterprise classification system is another attempt to bring order into the potential chaos of people's awareness of the thousands of jobs which exist. The assumption is that no single dimension is adequate to do this job and that therefore several dimensions must be combined. If a counselor understands such multidimensional structure and also understands the student, then he can help the student to relate his self-characteristics to the occupational structure. In schools, most vocational guidance has centered on field and level dimensions and has relatively ignored the enterprise dimension.

THE DOT

Perhaps the most widely used occupational classification system is that employed in the *Dictionary of Occupational Titles* (DOT). The DOT was first issued in 1939 with 29,744 job titles, and the second edition in 1949 with 40,023. The third and latest edition was published in 1965 and, with considerable paring, presents 35,550 job titles—although some 6,432 are new listings, reflecting the dynamic nature of the American occupational structure.

All jobs in the DOT are designated by a six-digit number. The first digit refers to an occupational group. There are nine of these groups:

0 and 1   Professional, technical, and managerial occupations
    2   Clerical and sales occupations
    3   Service occupations
    4   Farming, fishery, forestry, and related occupations
    5   Processing occupations
    6   Machine trade occupations
    7   Bench work occupations
    8   Structural work occupations
    9   Miscellaneous occupations

These nine categories are divided into six two-digit divisions, which are then subdivided into 603 three-digit groups. The reader will recall from the discussion of Holland's classification system that the DOT scale number for counselor is 045.108. The first digit—0—indicates that the occupation of counselor is professional level. The next two digits—45—designate that the occupation is in the general field of psychology.

The last three digits refer to worker traits. Thus whereas the first three digits of the code denote the type of job being done, the second trial refers to the worker's relationship to data, people, and things. Each of these three items has a hierarchy of relationship levels, and the code digit refers to the highest level within the hierarchy at which a worker is required to function. Following are the hierarchies for each digit:

Data (4th digit)	People (5th digit)	Things (6th digit)
0 Synthesizing	0 Mentoring	0 Setting up
1 Coordinating	1 Negotiating	1 Precision working
2 Analyzing	2 Instructing	2 Operating-controlling
3 Compiling	3 Supervising	3 Driving-operating
4 Computing	4 Diverting	4 Manipulating
5 Copying	5 Persuading	5 Tending
6 Comparing	6 Speaking-signaling	6 Feeding-offbearing
7 } No significant	7 Serving	7 Handling
8 } relationship	8 No significant relationship	8 No significant relationship

To return to our example of the counselor occupation, the 1 designates counselor as an occupation in which data are largely coordinated—"determining time, place, and sequence of operations or action to be taken on the basis of analysis of data; executing determination and/or reporting on events." The 0 indicates that the counselor's function in relation to people is largely a mentoring one—"dealing with individuals in terms of their total personality in order to advise, counsel, and/or guide them with regard to problems that may be resolved by legal, scientific, clinical, spiritual, and/or other professional principles." Finally, the 8 indicates that the counselor's function has no significant relationship to things. In summary, then, the code number for counselor is read as follows:

Professional	Psychology	Coordinating Data	Mentoring People	No Sig. Relationship to Things
0	45	1	0	8

From these worker trait hierarchies one can see that jobs in many occupational categories involve the same relationships with data, people, and things. For example, some of the jobs that require nothing more complicated than copying data (5) are mail clerk (231.588), sample-tester (579.585), and cigarette inspector (790.587). Some of the jobs that involve nothing above the level of supervising people (3) are manager, display (142.031), news editor (131.038), and machine shop foremen (600.1<u>3</u>1). Occupations having no significant relationship to things (8) include meteorologist (025.08<u>8</u>), hotel clerk (242.36<u>8</u>), and rigger foreman (823.13<u>8</u>).

This section of the DOT (Volume II) is also important because it presents the abilities, personal traits, and individual characteristics a worker must have for average successful job performance. Six components make up these traits: training time, aptitudes, interests, temperaments, physical demands, and working conditions. For any occupation an individual may find data in the DOT under the general headings of: work performed, worker requirements, clues for relating applicants and requirements, training and method of entry, related classifications, and qualifications profile.

In Volume I of the DOT, definitions of job titles are listed alphabetically. Each listing either gives or directs one to the place in the DOT where he will find any or all of the following information:

1. Standard or main job title (most common name by which the job is known) in boldface capital letters

2. Synonyms for the job title (other names by which the job is known)

3. Code number indicating how the job is classified

4. Short definition of the job (i.e. statement of duties)

5. Reference to related jobs listed in the DOT

Continuing with our example of counselor, here is the actual job listing taken from Volume I of the DOT:

COUNSELOR *(profess. & kin.) II. 045.108. guidance counselor; vocational advisor; vocational counselor. Counsels individuals and provides group educational and vocational guidance services; Collects, organizes, and analyzes information about individuals through records, tests, interviews, and professional sources, to appraise their interests, aptitudes, abilities, and personality characteristics for vocational and educational planning. Compiles and studies occupational, educational, and economic information to aid counselees in making and carrying out vocational and educational objectives. Refers students to placement service. Assists individuals to understand and overcome social and emotional problems. Engages in research and follow-up activities to evaluate counseling techniques. May teach classes. may be designated according to area of activity as* COUNSELOR, COLLEGE; COUNSELOR, SCHOOL.

This information combined with the classification of specific requirements found in Volume II constitutes an amazingly comprehensive reservoir of information on some 21,741 separate occupations.

Finally, as a kind of overview of the occupational classification of Volume II, here are some elements of the clerical and sales category.

Occupational Classification	Typical Occupations	General Characteristics and Requirements
2. CLERICAL AND SALES		
20. Stenography, Typing, Filing, and Related Work	Secretary, file clerk, stenographer, duplicating machine operator	Occupations concerned with preparing, transcribing, transferring, systematizing and preserving written communications and records; collecting accounts; distributing information; and influencing customers in favor of a commodity or service. Includes occupations closely identified with sales transactions even though they do not involve actual participation.
21. Computing and Account Recording	Bookkeeper, cashier, bank teller	
22. Material and Production Recording	Shipping clerk, stock clerk, weigher	
23. Information and Message Distribution	Postal employee, telephone operator, receptionist	
24. Miscellaneous Clerical Work	Hotel clerk, claims adjustor, bill collector	
25. Saleswork, Services	Salesmen for real estate, securities, or repair work	
26-28. Saleswork, Commodities	Saleswork in nursery products, textiles or business equipment	
29. Miscellaneous Merchandising Work	Peddler, auctioneer, model, canvasser	

In summary, combining the data in Volumes I and II of the DOT should give the student a detailed picture not only of a job but also of the typical person so employed. Besides its direct value when used in this manner, the DOT provides a framework for putting vocational development theories to practical use (for example, the Holland system's integration with DOT described earlier in this chapter).

SUMMARY

Occupational classification schemes provide ways of examining the American occupational structure, an understanding of which is essential to vocational guidance. Such classification systems are valuable in that they provide a framework for the delivery of guidance services. The occupational system helps us to understand the total social system of our society since it is a society's primary structuring element. Several unidimensional and multidimensional systems have been described. Each, in its own way, provides a means of bringing order into the potential chaos of occupational investigation.

REFERENCES

Armer, J. Michael.   Intersociety and intrasociety correlatives of occupational prestige.   *American Journal of Sociology,* 1968, 74, 28–36.

Bureau of the Census.   *1970 census population: Occupation classification.*   Washington, D. C.: U. S. Department of Commerce, Feb., 1970. Mimeographed.

Campbell, David P.   The vocational interests of Dartmouth College freshmen: 1947-67.   *Personnel and Guidance Journal,* 1969, 47, 521–530.

Counts, G. S.   Social status of occupations.   *School Review,* 1925, 33, 16–27.

Deeg, M. E., and Paterson, D. G.   Changes in social status of occupations. *Occupations,* 1947, 25, 205–208.

*Drucker, Peter F.   *The age of discontinuity.*   New York: Harper & Row, 1968.

Hakel, Milton D.; Hollman, Thomas D.; and Dunnette, Marvin D.   Stability and change in the social status of occupations over 21- and 42-year periods.   *Personnel and Guidance Journal,* 1968, 46, 762–764.

*Hall, Richard H.   *Occupations and the social structure.*   Englewood Cliffs, N. J.: Prentice-Hall, 1969.

Hatt, Paul K.   Occupation and social stratification.   In Sigmund Nosow and William H. Form (eds.) *Man, work, and society.*   New York: Basic Books, 1962. Pp. 238–249.

*Herr, E. L., and Cramer, S. H.   *Guidance of the college bound: Problems, practices and perspectives.*   New York: Appleton-Century-Crofts, 1968.

Hodge, Robert W.; Siegel, Paul M.; and Rossi, Peter H.   Occupational prestige in the United States, 1925-63.   *American Journal of Sociology,* 1964, 70, 286–302.

Holland, John L.; Viernstein, Mary; Kuo, Hao-Mei; Karweit, Nancy; and Blum, Zahava.   *A psychological classification of occupations.*   Report No. 90, Center for the Study of Social Organization of Schools, Johns Hopkins University, 1970.

*Kimball, Solon T., and McClellan, James.   *Education and the new America,* New York: Harper & Row, 1962.

Moser, H. P.; Dubin, W.; and Shelsky I.   A proposed modification of the Roe occupational classification.   *Journal of Counseling Psychology,* 1956, 3, 27–31.

Nosow, S., and Form, W. H., eds.   *Man, work, and society.*   New York: Basic Books, 1962.

Reich, Charles E.   *The greening of America.*   New York: Random House, 1970.

Roe, Anne.   A new classification of occupations.   *Journal of Counseling Psychology,* 1954, 1, 215–220.

* Recommended for additional reading.

Slocum, Walter L.   *Occupational careers.*   Chicago: Aldine, 1966.

Slocum, Walter L., and Bowles, Roy T.   Attractiveness of occupations to high school students.   *Personnel and Guidance Journal,* 1968, 46, 754–761.

Smith, Maphens.   An empirical scale of prestige status occupations.   *American Sociological Review,* 1943, 8, 185–192.

Spaeth, Joe L.   Occupation prestige expectations among male college graduates.   *American Journal of Sociology,* 1968, 73, 548–558.

*Super, Donald E.   *The psychology of careers.*   New York: Harper & Brothers, 1957.

U. S. Department of Labor.   *A supplement to the dictionary of occupational titles.* 3rd ed.   Washington, D. C.: U. S. Government Printing Office, 1966.

U. S. Department of Labor.   *Dictionary of occupational titles,* Vols. I and II. 3rd ed.   Washington, D. C.: U. S. Government Printing Office, 1965.

U. S. Department of Labor.   *Occupational outlook handbook.*   Washington, D. C.: U. S. Government Printing Office, 1970.

U. S. Department of Labor.   *United States manpower in the nineteen-seventies.* Washington, D. C.: U. S. Government Printing Office, 1970.

Venn, Grant.   *Man, education, and work.*   Washington, D. C.: American Council on Education, 1964.

*Wolfbein, Seymour L.   *Occupational information: A career guidance view.* New York: Random House, 1968.

FOUR

THE CONSUMERS OF VOCATIONAL GUIDANCE

HETEROGENEITY BUT SAME BASIC NEEDS

The consumers of vocational guidance in the schools are indeed a heterogeneous group. Their diversity extends along many dimensions. They range from elementary age children to adults. They cut across all races, religions, ethnic groups, and socioeconomic classes. They represent all levels of aptitudes, interests, values, and aspirations, as well as all personality dimensions. In short, they include much more than the white, middle-class prototype to which our educational institutions have traditionally directed their energies.

To speak of today's youth is not necessarily to speak of tomorrow's youth. People change, the labor market changes, and the routes through which one enters vocations also change. But it may be instructive to look at a profile of current American youth in order to realize the diversity that does exist. Perhaps no modern study gives so complete a picture as John C. Flanagan's *The American High School Student* (1964). Using data gathered from approximately 62,000 students, Flanagan and his associates rather clearly demonstrate the heterogeneous nature of the American student. The dispersion of abilities, the great variability in knowledge and values, and the magnitude of these differences are startling. To cite merely one example (p. 14-2): "Twenty to 30 percent of students in grade 9 know more about many subject-matter fields than does the average student in grade 12. Variability *within* grades is greater than variability *between* grades." Similar diversity can be found in the occupational aspirations of these students and in the weightings they assign to determinants of occupational choice, including: personal variables, such as age, physical limitations, sex, ability, and aptitudes; perceived interpersonal relationships; general social and cultural factors; reference group values; work experience; occupational information; economic factors; and school experience.

The variable of educational plans alone illustrates this great diversity (p. 14-4): "About 53 percent of the high school senior boys and 46 percent of the girls expected to enter college immediately after graduation; about 73 percent of the boys and 58 percent of the girls planned to attend college at some time; but only 53 percent of the boys and 33 percent of the girls expected to graduate from a four-year college."

The use of college-bound and non-college-bound labels is, in many ways, an unfortunate practice. Because of these labels, counselors have often assumed that they need to treat these two groups differently—both qualitatively and quantitatively—in fostering vocationalization. The net result is that the treatment of both groups has been less than satisfactory. For example, Betz, Engle, and Mallinson (1969) conducted in-depth interviews with over 300 non-college-bound high school graduates. Two of the conclusions were that employment-bound high school graduates view the school and its personnel as highly partial to the college-bound student and that counselors gave them little help in reaching satisfactory vocational decisions. The investigators affixed the blame for these perceptions in part to the lack of a systematic, developmental guidance approach.

The indictment of the counselor's role with employment-bound youth is harsh indeed, but there is an equally discouraging picture when one looks to the results of guidance of the college-bound. Herr and Cramer (1968), after reviewing studies of the effectiveness of the counselor's help to the college-bound, concluded that they remained largely dissatisfied with the guidance they had received. The authors attributed this dissatisfaction to a piecemeal approach to school guidance. They argued (p. 77), ". . . either through lack of integration of the guidance program, inadequacy in personal-social counseling, or other limitations, an unfortunate trichotomy of counselor functions exists which tends to separate and fragment the interdependence of vocational, educational, and personal dimensions in any given decision. It is difficult to conceive of an educational decision without vocational implications or vice versa."

Given that all students need much the same assistance in vocationalization and that this need transcends rubrics of any sort—especially the labels college-bound and employment-bound—the goal of vocational guidance in the schools must be to provide *all* consumers with data and tools for *total* vocational decision making as based on an intermix of vocational, educational, and personal-social factors.

A specific example may clarify the thesis. This book has repeatedly stressed the idea of vocationalization—of preparation for a life of work. Such preparation has many dimensions, and previous chapters have cited possible specific foci. By way of illustration, however, suppose that we simply use a sociological analysis of what is required in vocationalization. In this context, Gross (1967) has suggested four main types of preparation: (1) for a life in an organization, (2) for a set of role relationships, (3) for a level and kind of consumption (style of life), and (4) for an occupational history. These preparations argue for more than simply job counseling; they demand a consideration of all aspects of human behavior, including needs, values, attitudes, and the like, as these relate to certain immediate decisions which all individuals must make. They are universal requirements for a preparation for work life which are independent of any convenient category schemes. All students require these types of preparation. The differences are not in degree and are very small in kind.

Or let us take another example. Hershenson (1968) has postulated a life-stage vocational development system, which has been alluded to earlier in this book. He advocates that counseling can be meaningful only in relation to the stage at which an individual finds himself (p. 29).

One cannot do vocational counseling until the client has shown the capacity to make choices and engage in goal-directed activities. Likewise, one cannot do occupational counseling (the activity which currently is most frequently performed under the name of "vocational counseling") until the client has demonstrated the capacity to work and has realistic choices to consider. Should the client not have reached that stage, the counselor can only do "pre-occupational counseling" in order to help the client progress to the stage where he can meaningfully deal with occupational issues.

The point is that all students fit into this pattern. Despite their great heterogeneity in terms of aptitude and personality dimensions, their basic needs in vocationalization are the same.

A highlight of their heterogeneity is the fact, already touched on, that youngsters of the same age, in the same grade, and even from similar cultural backgrounds, exhibit great variety in vocational maturity, in the vocational information which they possess, in their decision-making skills, and in their motivations for vocational decision making. Thus diversity extends also to the treatment aspects of vocational guidance. Some students come to the counselor with career choice made and want only some specific piece of information relating to that career. Other students have no idea at all what occupations to choose; they know only what they do not want to be. Still others want immediate job placement. Some have no idea what their self-characteristics are; others have a fairly accurate picture of themselves but have no notion to what these characteristics can be related. Still others have all the educational, occupational, and self data which they require but have no skills for using these data in decision making.

To summarize: vocationalization requires that all students acquire certain fundamental skills, abilities, knowledges, habits, attitudes, and values. The rate at which these vocational essentials are acquired varies greatly from individual to individual, although what they all should consume remains relatively constant. Also, within the general population there are various minority groups about which the counselor should have special knowledge and attitudes. Several of these groups are discussed in the following pages.

MINORITY GROUPS

BLACKS

There are approximately twenty-five million Blacks in the United States, representing about 12 percent of the total population. The working members of this minority group are largely concentrated in unskilled sectors of the labor force, notably as farm workers, urban laborers, and service workers. For over two centuries the Black American has been subjected to the most heinous forms of social and economic oppression and consequent deprivation.

Occupationally, this poverty and prejudice have led to incremental "loadings" at the lower end of the occupational hierarchy. Pettigrew's (1968, p. 159) classic analysis of the Black American has made three points abundantly clear:

1. *"Racial differences" do exist, but they are not a matter of innate group "superiority" or "inferiority";*

2. *persistent patterns of segregation and discrimination help to create and perpetuate these racial disparities; and*

3. *even if discrimination were totally abolished tomorrow, the impoverished social and economic resources of the majority of Negroes would act to maintain these racial disparities.*

This latter view is supported by Lieberson and Fuguitt (1967), who indicate that the absence of racial discrimination in the labor market would not immediately eliminate racial differences in occupations because of the broad societal processes operating to the disadvantage of Blacks. They suggest that racial differences in occupations would decline sharply only after one generation in which discrimination was absent, and that full parity would be reached only after several generations.

These views appear pessimistic and discouraging but probably are nonetheless accurate. Yet society is becoming more open, and the upper levels of the occupational structure are becoming highly permeable for Blacks. While it is perhaps realistic that true occupational equality is a relatively long-range goal, the situation is constantly being ameliorated. A prime change agent can well be the vocational guidance worker who assists Black youth.

To accomplish this task will require, in Pettigrew's terms, "major societal surgery." The need for occupational upgrading of various segments of society currently overrepresented in lower echelon work comes at a time when automation and the knowledge society have upheaved the labor force. Therefore, Blacks need to be encouraged to enter a wide range of jobs in the professional, managerial, service, skilled, and clerical fields.

This goal will not be easily achieved. The current situation, especially in inner cities and the rural South, is such that "Negro youth are abandoned to scramble for a diminished number of unskilled, unfulfilling, and undesirable jobs" (HAR-YOU, 1964, p. 14). Obviously, the situation requires massive intervention. A start has been made; more is required. Enhanced education and training from pre-school to post–high school, special remedial programs, and job training programs have merely touched the top of the iceberg.

The problems are many. The focus of vocational guidance with Black youth may well be attainable goals. The research on aspiration levels of Blacks is inconclusive. Some studies have found that Black families hold high aspiration levels, while other studies have determined that their level of aspiration is low (Weiner and Murray, 1967). Whichever finding has validity, there is reason to believe on a priori grounds that the concept of goals development is central in working with Black youngsters. Bloom, Davis, and Hess (1965, p. 30) point up the need to establish immediate and intermediate goals in the vocational guidance of Blacks:

> *Education and preparing for a skilled job or a profession . . . are long-term goals. One must have some economic security or stability, if one is to hope to finish high school and college . . . Economic deprivation inevitably weakens the interests of most Negro families and children in striving for the long-term goals of education.*

Ausubel (1969, p. 295) suggests a solution to this problem of goals in the development of extrinsic motivation:

> *Intensive counseling can . . . compensate greatly for the absence of appropriate home, community, and peer group support and expectations for the development of long-term vocational ambitions. In a sense counselors must be prepared to act in* loco parentis *in this situation. By identifying with a mature, stable, striving, and successful male adult figure, culturally deprived boys can be encouraged to internalize long-term and realistic aspirations, as well as to develop the mature personality traits necessary for their implementation.*

The Black home, the Black culture, and the Black experience are unique. They must be understood by anyone who seeks to be a significant intervening force in the vocational guidance of young Black people. Black ghetto youth grow up with little knowledge of a father and his occupation and little knowledge of family occupational traditions (Moynihan, 1967). The roles of husband and wife are often reversed, creating a matriarchy. Cultural mores are different from those of the white middle class, and this fact often causes conflict when Black youngsters are thrust into schools that reflect the values of the dominant culture. The most taken-for-granted teaching methods are often inappropriate for Black youth, and the routine use of common guidance tools, such as tests, frequently causes catastrophic results. The nuances of difference are many and are as staggering as the more obvious elements of difference.

Take, for example, the relatively routine recommendations which a counselor makes concerning a course of study for ninth-grade students. He typically utilizes aptitude test data as input into his recommendations. Chansky (1965) has demonstrated that the interests of Black and white ninth-graders with the same aptitude test scores are significantly different. Therefore, vocational guidance in the form of curriculum selection would not be the same for students with the same aptitudes but with different racial backgrounds.

This same point of vocational development differences could be documented in many ways. The point is, however, that the counselor of Black students must understand the cultural backgrounds of those with whom he works. Certainly, a counselor should understand the backgrounds of all students he aids, but a more intensive effort to understand is needed when he is helping students from a minority culture. This task encompasses not only an understanding of how the tools and strategies of guidance affect Black youth but also an attempt to discover such culturally related knowledge as speech and language patterns; aspirations, interests, and self-concepts; peer mores and norms; and various environmental influences. In addition, it is almost axiomatic that counselors need a deep, consuming commitment to involvement with Blacks. Perhaps *respect* is the key requirement (Goldberg, 1964).

The vocational development of Blacks is further influenced by the type of school attended. Wilson (1967) has demonstrated that when parents' occupation and education are held constant, the academic preferences and aspirations of Black students are highest when they go to middle-class schools. The crucial nature of the type of school attended is highlighted by Crain's study (1970, p. 593), which found: "American Negroes who attend integrated public schools have better jobs and higher incomes throughout at least the next three decades of their life."

The problem of Black occupations is further complicated by the fact that occupational mobility and occupational gains of Blacks are not uniform throughout the United States (Gibbs, 1965). In fact, despite popular opinion to the contrary, Blacks actually lost occupational ground in the South during the 1950's (Hare, 1964). Again, however, the one variable that stands out as crucial to Black occupational mobility is education. As an integral part of that education, counselors play a vital role in the vocational development of Blacks.

The diagnosis of the problem has been presented. What treatment is appropriate? Bloom, Davis, and Hess (1965, p. 33) suggest a reasonable course to follow, although their proposed point of intervention is probably too late.

> With the very rapid changes in the civil rights movement and its effect on occupational opportunities, Negro students must have up-to-date occupational information. Also, they will need more educational and vocational guidance than other students. It is recommended that beginning with secondary school, Negro students have periodic interviews with capable guidance workers who thoroughly understand the current occupational picture. Such guidance workers should also have job placement functions for these students.

More realistic approaches to the vocational guidance of Blacks in the United States are proposed in a brilliantly perceptive essay by West (1968). He suggests five propositions regarding the vocational function of education of Blacks (pp. 360-362):

1. "Compensatory education is not an adequate answer to the vocational problems of minorities." Rather, improvement of instruction for all pupils is necessary with, of course, the workable features of compensatory programs built into the entire system.

2. "The school should deliberately set out to change the values and attitudes of those whom it instructs." Teaching facts and skills is not enough; personality traits and values must also be changed—while at the same time their source must be recognized and moralizing avoided.

3. "Preparation for the world of work must be accepted as a major objective of schools: it must have a priority fully equal to preparation for academic or professional careers." This proposition represents the objective of this book.

4. "Effective vocational programs of counseling, education, and training must be locked into the real world of work, where all activities are actually performed for which youngsters are being prepared." The chapter in this volume dealing with "cooperative linkages," as well as portions of other chapters, detail this proposition.

5. "Authentic and believable models are essential in the career preparation of minority youth."

In 1789, almost one of every five people in the new United States was a Negro (Bennis, 1965). Today the Black American still constitutes a relatively large proportion of the population. It is a segment of society that until recently has suffered from misuse and abuse of human resources. America can no longer—economically or morally—countenance that loss.

GIRLS

The vocational development of girls entails unique considerations. We have tended to regard the vocational role of females as homemaking. This notion is probably more myth than reality. Rossi (1964, p. 608), for example, has observed, "For the first time in the history of any known society, motherhood has become a full-time occupation for adult women." The implication here is that women have always been a part of the labor force, largely through necessity. If motherhood is a full-time occupation as Rossi claims, it is a short-lived one indeed. More than one in three of the total female labor force of thirty million are mothers (Rosenfeld and Perrella, 1965). These thirty million women are drawn from all socioeconomic strata; 55 percent are married, 24 percent are single, and 21 percent are widowed, divorced, or separated (Baruch, 1966).

Women are obviously a valuable resource in the world of work, a resource that has remained largely untapped or poorly utilized. A variety of reasons can be offered for this gross waste. The prime cause is perhaps traceable to the vocational guidance of girls framed by antiquated vocational stereotypes and obsolescent expectations of the larger culture. A movement is beginning in the United States that foretells the blurring of male and female work roles. Increasing numbers of women are militantly expressing their belief in the right to equal work with men, the right to be "liberated" from the three K's (Kuche, Kinder, and Kirche—kitchen, children, church) via meaningful work (Konopka, 1966). Those who are responsible for the vocational guidance of girls must be aware of and responsive to these trends.

In addition to the social or cultural explanations of the subordinate vocational role of women, other reasons for it include the physiological differences between men and women. The question of innate psychological differences between the sexes is still moot. In any case, the picture typically held of the American girl in terms of career planning is that described by Kovar (1968, pp. 67-68):

> The girl wants to work for a year or two after marriage and in the somewhat distant future, perhaps after children go to school, but such work entails no real involvement in a career. She engaged in little serious speculation about career choices, though she mentions the possibility of the customary service fields appropriated by women: secretary, nurse, or teacher. "Career and marriage somehow don't mix," is a common response. "The husband has to have the more important career. I don't want to get my heart set. My career might conflict with his." "Boys have to earn a living. They're more stable than girls, more interested in their education." The "career" is a job to go back to "if the marriage doesn't work out or something like that," or "if something happens to your husband."

> The rare girl to whom career is more important than marriage says she probably won't marry. "I don't want to get married," affirms one lower-class career-oriented girl. "I think marriage interferes with your career. Once a girl gets married, she just stays home." So too the upper-middle-class careerist who wants to make a name for herself through her writing asserts, "I don't want family and children to stand in the way of my career. I want a completely self-disciplined career."

One can take the stance, as does Ohlsen (1968), that counseling girls is basically the same as counseling any other segment of the general population. Or one can agree with Eyde (1970), who has indicated that the complexities of a woman's role require that she be given special assistance in planning her career. In the case of women the areas of counseling for vocational choice must be widened to include nonwork considerations, such as the number of children they would like to have. In short, what is required is planning based on the total life style of the woman. Too, the new role of women demands that the counselor seriously examine his or her own values and attitudes toward women and his or her conception of women's role as workers. Stereotypes of any sort are dangerous; they are especially noxious if present in the counselor as he seeks to assist girls in their vocational development. In Eyde's words (p. 27), ". . . counselors need to be aware of subtle changes occurring in occupations so as to be preparing women for the future instead of the past."

The unique vocational considerations that apply to women are echoed by Bailyn (1964), who points out that girls must make a choice that boys do not have to make—the choice of whether or not to work at all. What is a generally unquestioned course for men involves considerable choice anxiety for women. Only after a girl has decided that she will include work in her life style can realistic vocational choice commence.

It has become increasingly clear that career development theories which emanate from studies of largely middle-class, male subjects are inadequate to explain the career development of women. Recognizing this fact, Zytowski (1969) has formulated some tentative notions regarding the work life of women, their unique developmental stages, their patterns of vocational participation, and the determinants of the patterns. His nine postulates, described in Chapter 7, focus on what has been rather than what will be. But his thoughts are seminal and can generate much needed research.

How do girls go about making vocational choices? Some current research suggests that changes in vocational choice occur in girls during the secondary school years. Astin (1968a) reports on the career plans of 817 high school senior girls drawn from the Project Talent Data Bank. Using their ninth-grade personal characteristics and certain environmental factors from their high schools, she discovered that senior girls choosing different careers can be differentiated from each other in terms of interests, career plans, and aptitudes as early as the ninth grade. Her findings suggest that occupational preference of women can be predicted at an earlier developmental stage and can thus contribute to earlier systematic vocational guidance.

In a related study of 7,061 Project Talent girls, Astin (1968b) investigated changes in career plans between ninth grade and one year after high school graduation. In this time period, over two-thirds of the students changed their career choices. Astin sought to determine why they changed and what type of changes occurred. Her findings were (p. 966): ". . . the career changes that take place during the high school years result partly from greater self-awareness and recognition by the students of the aptitudes and skills that are necessary to educational and occupational success. As girls mature, their vocational plans tend to become more realistic. Brighter girls tend to raise their occupational aspirations, whereas the scholastically less able aspire to less intellectually demanding careers."

That career choice for girls is partly based on aptitude is evident. However, the same is true of men's career choices. Two other factors may play a significant role in girls' career selection—namely, interest and personality variables that cause some girls to enter pioneer vocations while others go a more traditional route. Rezler's (1967) study is instructive. He found that those girls who wished to be pioneers (e.g. physicians, mathematicians, natural scientists) had significantly higher academic aptitudes and achievements, more intellectual and masculine personalities, and higher scientific and computational interests. The traditional girls were basically social- and status-minded in a feminine way, their primary goal being marriage and a family.

The matter of interests as a factor in occupational choice of women gives rise to the question of whether career-oriented women can be differentiated from noncareer-oriented women. The answer appears to be affirmative. Schissel (1968), using the Strong Vocational Interest Bank, has demonstrated that women can be ordered along a continuum of career orientations on the basis of interests. Specifically, the interests of career women tend to be higher on the bipolar continuum of Things versus People than do the interests of noncareer-oriented women.

The implications for guiding girls in their vocational development within a systems approach are clear:

1. The barriers of occupational sex stereotyping must be overcome in both the counselor and the girls with whom he works. This task requires exposing females to all types of occupations from the early elementary grades on.

2. Vocational guidance intervention in the developmental stages of girls must be accomplished early. Girls must be assisted to think vocationally as well as domestically.

3. Girls must be encouraged to explore a broad area of occupations and to consider a variety of social alternatives and a total life style.

4. Girls' entry and re-entry into the work world must be recognized as an important consideration.

Perhaps the problems in the vocational guidance of women are best summarized by the following statement from the Report of the President's Commission on the Status of Women (1963, p. 13):

> Because of differences in life patterns of women as contrasted with men, the counseling of girls and women is a specialized form of the counseling profession. From infancy, roles held up to girls deflect talents into narrow channels. Among women of all levels of skill there is need for encouragement to develop broader ranges of aptitudes and carry them into higher education. Imaginative counseling can lift aspirations beyond stubbornly persistent assumptions about "women's roles" and "women's interests" and result in choices that have an inner authenticity for their workers.

Almost a decade later, this statement is still appropriate.

APPALACHIAN YOUTH

The people of Appalachia, which includes parts of Alabama, Georgia, Kentucky, Maryland, Mississippi, New York, North Carolina, Ohio, Pennsylvania, South Carolina, Tennessee, Virginia, and all of West Virginia, are distinguished by their poverty-level existence. Appalachian youth, especially those from the southern states, typically migrate to large northern cities in great numbers, and because of their poverty-laden and backwoods background and environment, they present their new schools with special problems.

Part of that background includes a view of work as merely a means of sustenance rather than as an activity that can bring enjoyment. Because of this factor and others, the notion of actually choosing a vocation and training for it is relatively foreign (Hansen and Stevic, 1971). Hence one special task of the counselor who works with Appalachian youngsters is helping them to realize that they can make occupational choices and assisting them to plan for and make these choices.

There is a danger, however, in stereotyping all youth who come from Appalachia and in assuming that their values are greatly disparate from those of other lower-class and lower-middle-class students. Riccio (1965) has demonstrated that migrant adolescents from the Appalachian South do not differ significantly in occupational aspiration, role models, or cultural conformity from lower-middle-class youngsters residing outside of Appalachia. He concludes (p. 29): "To prejudge an individual on the basis of his geographical origin is every bit as undesirable as prejudging him on the basis of race, religion, or ethnic origin—especially when both empirical evidence and moral code counsel against such action."

Those who *stay* in Appalachia, however, may well have different characteristics from those who migrate. Stevic and Uhlig (1967) report that youth who stay in Appalachia have lower levels of aspiration, different personal role models, and different characteristics for success from those who migrate. They conclude by suggesting that a primary problem in raising the occupational aspirations of Appalachian students is simply lack of information and opportunity.

Perhaps this lack will be met as Appalachia continues to become less and less provincial. The mass media, many federally sponsored programs, and ease of transportation are all working to break down the cultural isolation of the Appalachian people. Ultimately, the Appalachian youngster may come to a counselor at the same level of vocational maturity as other children in more advantaged settings, especially if he has been exposed to systematic efforts to advance his vocationalization.

OTHER MINORITY YOUTH

Several other categories of minority youth merit special attention from the counselor and require specialized knowledge. Unfortunately almost nothing is known about the unique aspects of vocational development of these groups. For example, the special factors that should be considered in the vocational guidance of American Indians (native Americans) must be considerable, but they are not manifest in the professional literature. Hence somewhere between a half million and three-quarter million Americans are being offered guidance services primarily on the basis of guidance as an "art" and with very little or no relevant scientific base to inform that art. What is needed is a base resulting from empirical studies of how the vocational development and vocational concerns of American Indians differ from those of the white, middle-class majority.

Similarly, the literature is extremely scant on the unique, vocationally important characteristics of Puerto Ricans, Mexican-Americans, and a variety of other "hyphenated" citizens of the United States. Fink (1970), for example, compared Anglo-American and Mexican-American students in their attitudes and values toward the world of work, occupational preferences, occupational expectations, and perceptions of obstacles to success in the work world and discovered significant differences between the two groups. Knowledge of those differences gives direction to the guidance services that assist vocationalization of Mexican Americans. Too few of these types of studies exist; more such studies relating the environmental and cultural factors of various subgroups to vocationalization are needed.

Another sizable minority in the United States about which we know little in terms of vocational guidance is the Puerto Ricans. As is the case with any conspicuous minority, distinguishing characteristics are present which probably affect vocational development. One characteristic is that the home language is frequently Spanish rather than English. School achievement is thus adversely affected. A second characteristic is the Puerto Rican emphasis on *machismo* (Glazer, 1967), which, in turn, affects the entire concept of work. Puerto Rican families generally have high aspirations for their children. In school, however, Puerto Rican youth often meet overwhelming frustrations.

Currently, Puerto Ricans account for over 16 percent of the population of New York City (Crow, Murray, and Smythe, 1966). They also constitute sizable segments of the population in many other large cities and represent a large proportion of the migrant workers. Invariably, for poverty-level Puerto Ricans education and work have meaning only in terms of future prospects, not in terms of the intrinsic rewards of learning or the satisfaction of work (Sexton, 1965).

Again, however, the professional literature does not provide a great deal of data regarding the vocational development characteristics of minorities other than Blacks and women. A great deal of research needs to be done in these areas; Mexican-Americans, American Indians, Puerto Ricans, and other conspicuous minorities provide fertile ground for such research. In the absence of definitive data, one can only caution counselors about applying to minority populations the findings of studies made of middle-class youth, and urge them to learn as much as they can about the unique cultural, ethnic, and environmental influences shaping the attitudes of such youngsters.

SUMMARY

This chapter has considered the heterogeneity of the consumers of vocational guidance and has emphasized the dangers inherent in using rubrics of one type or another which promote preferential treatment of one group over another. At the same time, this chapter has explored the unique concerns that must be taken into account in providing vocational guidance for certain subgroups in society: women, Blacks, Mexican-Americans, American Indians, Appalachian youth, and

Puerto Ricans. Whatever the group, the ultimate goal of vocational guidance is adequate vocationalization directed toward helping every young person develop the knowledge, skills, and attitudes which make up personal preference, planning, and purposive action. Such requisites to personal action and power are important regardless of whether one's next step is employment or college. The diversity of the consumers of vocational guidance and their common need for vocationalization provides the raison d'être for vocational guidance in the schools.

REFERENCES

Astin, Helen S.   Career development of girls during the high school years. *Journal of Counseling Psychology,* 1968a, 15, 536–540.

Astin, Helen S.   Stability and change in the career plans of ninth-grade girls. *Personnel and Guidance Journal,* 1968b, 46, 961–966.

Ausubel, D. P.   A teaching strategy for culturally deprived pupils.   In Harry L. Miller and Marjorie B. Smiley (eds.) *Education in the metropolis.*   New York: Free Press, 1967, 284–295.

Bailyn, Lotte.   Notes on the role of choice in the psychology of professional women.   *Daedalus,* Spring, 1964 (The woman in America), 700–710, 712.

Baruch, Rhoda.   *The interruption and resumption of women's careers.* Harvard Studies in Career Development No. 50.   Cambridge, Mass.: Center for Research in Careers, 1966. P. 1.

Bennis, W. G.   Changing organizations.   *The Journal of Applied Behavioral Science,* 1965, 1, 247–263.

Betz, R. L.; Engle, K. B.; and Mallinson, G. G.   Perceptions of non-college-bound, vocationally oriented high school graduates.   *Personnel and Guidance Journal,* 1969, 47, 988–994.

Bloom, B. S.; Davis, Allison; and Hess, R.   *Compensatory education for cultural deprivation.*   New York: Holt, Rinehart, and Winston, 1965.

Chansky, N. M.   Race, aptitude, and vocational interests.   *Personnel and Guidance Journal,* 1965, 43, 783–784.

Crain, R. L.   School integration and occupational achievement of Negroes.   *American Journal of Sociology,* 1970, 75, 593–606.

Crow, L. D.; Murray, W. I.; and Smythe, H. H.   *Educating the culturally disadvantaged child.*   New York: David McKay, 1966.

Eyde, Lorraine D.   Eliminating barriers to career development of women.   *Personnel and Guidance Journal,* 1970, 49, 24–28.

Fink, H. O.   The world of work as perceived by Anglo-American and Mexican-American secondary school students in a border community. Unpublished doctoral dissertation, University of Arizona, 1970.

*Flanagan, J. C.   The American high school student.   Pittsburgh, Pa.: Project Talent, 1964.

Gibbs, J. P.   Occupational differentiation of Negroes and whites in the United States.   Social Forces, 1965, 44, 159–165.

Glazer, N.   The Puerto Ricans.   In H. L. Miller and M. B. Smiley (eds.) Education in the metropolis.   New York: Free Press, 1967, 105–123.

Gross, E.   A sociological approach to the analysis of preparation for work life.   Personnel and Guidance Journal, 1967, 45, 416–423.

Goldberg, Miriam L.   Adapting teacher style to pupil differences: Teachers for disadvantaged children.   Merril-Palmer Quarterly, 1964, 10, 161–178.

Hansen, J. C., and Stevic, R. R.   Appalachian students and guidance.   Guidance monograph series.   Boston: Houghton Mifflin, 1971.

Hare, N.   Recent trends in the occupational mobility of Negroes, 1930–1960: An intracohort analysis.   Social Forces, 1965, 44, 166–173.

Harlem Youth Opportunities Unlimited, Inc.   Youth in the ghetto: A study of the consequences of powerlessness and a blueprint for change.   New York: HARYOU, 1964.

Herr, E. L., and Cramer, S. H.   Guidance of the college-bound: Problems, practices, and perspectives.   New York: Appleton-Century-Crofts, 1968.

Hershenson, D. B.   Life-stage vocational development system.   Journal of Counseling Psychology, 1968, 15, 23–30.

Konopka, Gisela.   The adolescent girl in conflict.   Englewood Cliffs, N. J.: Prentice-Hall, 1966.

*Kovar, Lillian C.   Faces of the adolescent girl.   Englewood Cliffs, N. J.: Prentice-Hall, 1968.

Liberson, S., and Fuguitt, G. V.   Negro-white occupational differences in the absence of discrimination.   American Journal of Sociology, 1967, 73, 188–200.

*Moynihan, D.   The Negro family.   In Harry L. Miller and Marjorie B. Smiley (eds.) Education in the metropolis.   New York: Free Press, 1967, 249–269.

Ohlsen, M. M.   Vocational counseling for girls and women.   Vocational Guidance Quarterly, 1968, 17, 124–127.

*Pettigrew, T. F.   A profile of the Negro American.   Princeton, N. J.: Van Nostrand, 1964.

Report of the President's commission on the status of women.   American Women.   Washington, D. C.: Superintendent of Documents, 1963, 13.

Rezler, Agnes J.   Characteristics of high school girls choosing traditional or pioneer vocations.   Personnel and Guidance Journal, 1967, 45, 659–665.

* Recommended for additional reading.

Riccio, A. C.   Occupational aspirations of migrant adolescents from the Appalachian South.   *Vocational Guidance Quarterly,* 1965, 14, 26–30.

Rosenfeld, C., and Perrella, Vera C.   Why women start and stop working: A study in mobility.   *Monthly Labor Review,* Sept., 1965.

*Rossi, Alice S.   Equality between the sexes: An immodest proposal.   *Daedalus,* Spring, 1964 (*The woman in America*), 607–652.

Schissel, R. F.   Development of a career-orientation scale for women.   *Journal of Counseling Psychology,* 1968, 15, 257–262.

Sexton, Patricia C.   *Spanish Harlem.*   New York: Harper & Row, 1965.

Stevic, R. R., and Uhlig, G.   Occupational aspirations of selected Appalachian youth.   *Personnel and Guidance Journal,* 1967, 45, 435–439.

Weiner, M., and Murray, W.   Another look at the culturally deprived and their levels of aspiration. In Joan Roberts (ed.).   *School children in the urban slum.* New York: Free Press, 1967, 295–297.

*West, E. H.   Education and jobs.   *The Journal of Negro Education,* 1968, 37, 359–363.

Wilson, A. B.   Residential segregation of social classes and aspirations of high school boys. In A. H. Passow, Miriam Goldberg, and A. J. Tannebaum (eds.) *Education of the disadvantaged.*   New York: Holt, Rinehart and Winston, 268–283.

Zytowski, D. G.   Toward a theory of career development for women.   *Personnel and Guidance Journal,* 1969, 47, 660–664.

FIVE

FORMULATING OBJECTIVES FOR
VOCATIONAL GUIDANCE

If vocational guidance can be characterized either as treatment or as stimulus in the manner advocated in Chapter 1, then it is necessary to make explicit the objectives of such processes. Frequently no distinction is made between the functions and the objectives of vocational guidance. For example, the dissemination of information and the provision of group guidance are often described as though they are objectives, or goals, rather than functions by which objectives can be achieved. In other words, in describing programs of vocational guidance, the emphasis is often on the *how* of the program rather than on the *why*, on what is done for or to students as opposed to why it is done. Shaw (1968, p. 32) has stated:

> *What we do (functions) should not determine our goals nor should our goals determine the kinds of values and/or assumptions which we are willing to make. It is rather the opposite which holds true. Value systems should dictate the goals or objectives of the program. Objectives in turn should dictate the functions which guidance specialists perform or the roles which they assume.*

In terms of Shaw's perspective, the values or assumptions which form the premises for this book are (1) that vocational identity is an important corollary to progressing from adolescence to adulthood; (2) that development of vocational identity and the ingredients of effective vocational behavior should be fostered through the educational process rather than left to chance; and (3) that a systems approach is the best method of accomplishing this purpose. Both the research and the theoretical approaches which weave throughout this text, as well as the projections regarding the future occupational structure, support these values or assumptions. But they are assumptions. As such, they have little meaning without statements of objectives, for these make possible a practical approach, ultimately providing the outlines for designing the functions needed to accomplish the objectives. This chapter will discuss the formulation of objectives for vocational guidance first as stimulus and second as treatment. The primary emphasis will be on developing objectives for vocational guidance as stimulus rather than as treatment because treatment typically ensues when some aspect of stimulus fails to occur and thus uses only subsets of objectives found in the stimulus.

VOCATIONAL MATURITY

Before one can properly specify objectives for the vocational development, or vocationalization, of students, it is necessary to identify the overall ultimate goal toward which the separate objectives will be directed. That goal which appears most frequently in the literature and which seems to have the most face validity is vocational maturity. This term, while useful as an ultimate goal, is too global to be useful for intermediate purposes unless it can be dissected into its elements. Thus it is necessary to convert the elements of ultimate vocational maturity into unifying themes and behavioral descriptions and place these along a developmental line leading to vocational maturity at some point in life, e.g. high school graduation, tenth grade, etc.

When attempting such a task, however, one must recognize that, just as in other developmental processes, individuals will differ in their readiness for various elements or aspects of vocationalization and in the ways by which they develop such behavior. Not everyone will reach the same point at the same time, nor will all proceed through the elements of vocationalization at the same pace. As previously indicated, the speed of such movement and the readiness for it will depend upon the individual's personal history and many extrinsic as well as intrinsic factors.

The objectives of vocationalization, then, rest upon statements of expectations for students, which in turn necessitate judgments of what individual students ought to be able to achieve and behavioral descriptions of these activities. But it is also important to recognize that for optimum effect, vocationalization should be individualized with each student who is able to work on information or who has been exposed to experiences different from other students at any given time. While the literal realization of such a goal may be too much to expect, any attempt to aid vocationalization systematically requires an emphasis both on diagnosis and on the provision of diverse learning experiences, from which can flow prescriptions for individual progress. The point is that it is not enough simply to say to a student, "Be vocationally mature." If this is what we want him to become, he needs to understand what being vocationally mature means, what the consequences of vocational maturity are, how he becomes vocationally mature, and what opportunities must be available to him to aid such effort.

In essence, a systems approach to vocationalization at its best would represent an unbroken continuum of experiences planned with and for the individual student which takes him wherever he is and moves him progressively toward the goal of vocational maturity by mustering all the resources and persons that are available to help toward such an end. Shane (1970, p. 390) makes an important distinction for this context, although it is directed primarily to curriculum development:

> The personalized curriculum differs from individualized instruction in at least one major respect. Individualized instruction, which has been attempted for many years, was intended to help a child meet group norms or standards, but at his own rate of progress. The personalized curriculum continuum serves as a means of making the school's total resources available to a child so that his teachers can figuratively help him to "create himself" without reference to what his "average" chronological age-mates may be accomplishing.

Mitzel (1970) speaks of this as adaptive education, as a condition which suggests that something unique about the learner has been taken into account in a dynamic way to build an instructional sequence.

Fostering vocationalization seems to require both individualizing and personalizing. As will be shown later in this chapter, there are certain elements of effective behavior which all students need to acquire in their individual way. But there are also points when, as individual goals become clearer, the student needs the opportunity and the assistance to "create himself," that is, to develop the ways by which he can create himself and his life style independently of his fellows.

Before directing further specific attention to the objectives of vocationalization, it is important to consider vocational maturity itself more specifically. Although Carter (1940) and Strong (1943, 1955) each examined the relationship between interest patterning and levels of maturity in adolescents and adults, the meaning of vocational maturity has taken on a greater comprehensiveness since approximately 1950. For example, Ginzberg, Ginsburg, Axelrad, and Herma (1951, p. 60) reported:

> To some degree, the way in which a young person deals with his occupational choice is indicative of his general maturity and, conversely, in assessing the latter, consideration must be given to the way in which he is handling his occupational choice problem.

Extending this definition, Super (1957, p. 186) indicated that in a gross sense vocational maturity can be described as "the place reached on the continuum of vocational development from exploration to decline." Later still, Crites (1961, p. 259) described it as "the maturity of an individual's vocational behavior as indicated by the similarity between his behavior and that of the oldest individuals in his vocational life stage."

A clarification of these two definitions of vocational maturity is provided by Super et al. (1957), who differentiate Vocational Maturity I (VMI) from Vocational Maturity II (VMII). They define VMI as "the life stage in which the individual actually is, as evidenced by the developmental tasks with which he is dealing in relation to the life stage in which he is expected to be, in terms of his age" (p. 132). They define VMII as "maturity of behavior in the actual life stage (regardless of whether it is the expected life stage), as evidenced by the behavior shown in dealing with developmental tasks of the actual life stage compared with the behavior of other individuals who are dealing with the same developmental tasks" (pp. 57, 132).

These definitions of Vocational Maturity I and II raise several other points. One is that vocational maturity differs when defined as the vocational behavior expected of persons at different points in life. What is vocational maturity at age 10 will not be that expected at age 16 or 25 or 35. Second, although in VMI there is an expectation that gross characteristics of vocational development are universally descriptive of broad chronological periods in life, VMII attends to how a particular individual is coping with vocational development in an ideographic sense. In other words, it asks, "Where is he now, and what knowledge, attitudes, or skills does he need to progress to higher levels of vocational development?" Third, VMI and VMII introduce the concept of developmental tasks as means by which vocational development progresses.

Most of the examples of ingredients important to vocational maturity which are reported later in this chapter have evolved from the work of Super and his colleagues in the Career Pattern Study. Some readers may consider this an imbalance. However, as Norton (1970) has noted, whether one examines the concurrent, related work of Vriend (1968), Crites (1965), Gribbons and Lohnes (1968), Nelson (1956), or Westbrook (Westbrook and Cunningham, 1970), the essential signs or criteria of vocational maturity remain relatively constant. What does change, however, across these approaches to vocational maturity are the methods of measuring the presence of specific elements of vocational maturity. Chapter 10 will discuss these measurement strategies and their present availability for counselor use.

It is important to recognize that if vocational maturity is to be used as the goal of vocationalization and if a systems approach to achieving it is to be mounted, measures of vocational maturity are needed in order (1) to assess pupil readiness to make educational-vocational decisions or to participate in particular types of vocational development experiences; (2) to serve as diagnostic instruments for determining treatment, and (3) to evaluate the degree to which strategies for aiding vocationalization are accomplishing their objectives (Westbrook and Cunningham, 1970).

DEVELOPMENTAL TASKS

A number of theorists, including Havighurst (1953), Erikson (1963), Super (1957), Super, Starishevsky, Matlin, and Jordaan (1963), Tiedeman and O'Hara (1963), and Gribbons and Lohnes (1968), either directly or indirectly have wedded particular developmental tasks with stages of increasingly mature vocational behavior. Thus the assumption can be made that the developmental task concept is useful both as a description of the changing demands on individuals as they move through life, as well as a means of organizing those demands—whether knowledge, attitudes, or skills—into a systems approach to vocationalization.

In terms of the first use of developmental tasks just cited, Havighurst (1953, p. 2) has provided the following definition: "A task which arises at or about a certain period in the life of the individual, successful achievement of which leads to happiness and success with later tasks, while failure leads to unhappiness in the individual, disapproval by society, and difficulty with later tasks." This definition has come to be accepted almost universally. As Zaccaria (1965, p. 373) has reported, those who formulate developmental tasks generally agree on the following statements:

1. *Individual growth and development is continuous.*

2. *Individual growth can be divided into periods or life stages for descriptive purposes.*

3. *Individuals in each life stage can be characterized by certain general characteristics that they have in common.*

4. *Most individuals in a given culture pass through similar developmental stages.*

5. *The society makes certain demands upon individuals.*

6. *These demands are relatively uniform for all members of the society.*

7. *The demands differ from stage to stage as the individual goes through the developmental process.*

8. *Developmental crises occur when the individual perceives the demand to alter his present behavior and master new learnings.*

9. *In meeting and mastering developmental crises, the individual moves from one developmental stage of maturity to another developmental stage of maturity.*

10. *The task appears in its purest form at one stage.*

11. *Preparation for meeting the developmental crises or developmental tasks occurs in the life stage prior to the stage in which it must be mastered.*

12. *The developmental task or crisis may arise again during a later phase in somewhat different form.*

13. *The crisis or task must be mastered before the individual can successfully move on to a subsequent developmental stage.*

14. *Meeting the crisis successfully by learning the required task leads to societal approval, happiness, and success with later crises and their correlative tasks.*

15. *Failing in meeting a task or crisis leads to disapproval by society.*[1]

---

[1] Copyright © 1965, by the American Personnel and Guidance Association, Inc.

Table 1 Examples of Conceptions of the Development of Vocationally Related Behavior

TIEDEMAN (1961) IN ZYTOWSKI	GESELL, ILG, and AMES (1956, p. 376-382)	GINZBERG et al (1951)	BUEHLER (1933)
			Birth
		F A N T A S Y Interests	G R O W T H 5-10
Anticipation or Preoccupation	Exploration Crystallization Choice Clarification		10-15
	10: Plans for careers indefinite: careers chosen are varied. Tens make several choices often unrelated		
	11: Very few have no idea of what they want to do. More than tens make single choice, choices become more realistic; occupations chosen become smaller		
	12: Trend toward a single, definite choice continues. Fewer make several choices or express indecision. Boys more likely than girls to be definite and express only one choice	T E N T A T I V E	E X P L O R A T I O N
	13: Marks peak for single definite choices about future work. Tends to assert choice without indecision	Capacities	
	14: Show less certainty in career choice. More individuals make multiple choices and a greater variety of choices than ages 13 or 15. Now recognize the difficulty of a single choice		
Implementation or Adjustment	Induction Reformation Integration		15-25
	15: Many quite indefinite about their choice of future career. Group as a whole names many fewer careers than earlier, but find it difficult to decide on a single choice		

HAVIGHURST (1964, p. 216)	ERIKSON (1965 2d ed.)	SUPER (1969)
	Basic trust (basic mistrust)	
	Autonomy (shame and doubt)	

I. Identification with a worker—father, mother, other significant persons
The concept of working becomes an essential part of the ego-ideal
Principal developmental tasks of middle childhood
1. Developing fundamental skills in reading, writing, and calculating
2. Learning physical skills necessary for ordinary games
3. Learning to get along with age mates
4. Learning an appropriate masculine or feminine social role
5. Developing concepts for everyday life
6. Developing conscience, morality, and a scale of values
7. Achieving personal identity
	Initiative (guilt)
	Industry (inferiority)
	  Fundamentals of technology
	  First sense of division of labor and of differential opportunity
	Outer and inner hindrance	

II. Acquiring the basic habits of industry
Learning to organize time and energy to get a piece of work done (school, work, chores)
Learning to put work ahead of play in appropriate situations
	Identity (role confusion)
	  Ego identity and the tangible promise of career
	Occupational identity
	Sexual identity
		Substages
		  Tentative
		  Transition
		  Trial (with little commitment)
		  Developmental Tasks
		    crystallizing a vocational preference
		    specifying it

III. Acquiring identity as a worker in the occupational structure; choosing and preparing for an occupation
Getting work experience as a
	Intimacy (isolation)
	  The capacity to commit oneself to concrete affiliations and partnerships and to develop the ethi-
		Substages
		  Trial (with more commitment)
		  Stabilization
		  Advancement
		  Developmental Tasks

Table 1   Examples of Conceptions of the Development of Vocationally Related Behavior
(Continued)

TIEDEMAN (1961) IN ZYTOWSKI	GESELL, ILG, and AMES (1956, p. 376-382)	GINZBERG et al (1951)	BUEHLER (1933)
	16: More decisiveness appears. A considerable variety of choices is mentioned. Sex-typed choices predominate for boys and girls		
		R E A L I S T I C Values	
			E S T A B L I S H M E N T 25+
			45
			M A I N T E N A N C E
			60
			D E C L I N E

HAVIGHURST (1964, p. 261)	ERIKSON (1965 2d ed.)	SUPER (1969)
basis for occupational choice and for assurance of economic independence	cal strength to abide by such commitments	stabilizing in the chosen vocation
Principal developmental tasks of adolescence	Ethical sense True genitality	consolidating one chosen status advancing in the occupation

Principal developmental tasks of adolescence

1. Achieving new and more mature relations with age mates of both sexes
2. Achieving a masculine or feminine social role
3. Achieving emotional independence of parents and other adults
4. Achieving assurance of economic independence
5. Selecting and preparing for an occupation
6. Acquiring a set of values and an ethical system as a guide to behavior
7. Preparing for marriage and selecting a mate
8. Starting a family
9. Getting started in an occupation

IV. Becoming a productive person; mastering the skills of an occupation; moving up the ladder within the occupation

Generativity (stagnation)
  productivity
  creativity

Ego integrity (despair)

V. Maintaining a productive society

VI. Contemplating a productive life

The developmental task concept can be used to describe an average set of demands with which the individual must cope, as well as a way of looking at how a given individual is attaining such an expectation, at what points he is having difficulty, what specific experiences or competencies he needs to acquire, and what resources might aid his development. Such a concept makes it possible to provide sequential developmental experiences that will prepare the individual to meet emerging developmental tasks and to prescribe (on an individual basis) alternative methods of coping successfully with developmental task difficulties.

Individual variation in accomplishing developmental tasks can be further considered in the following ways: "A given task has a unique *meaning* to each individual. . . . Secondly, individuals vary with respect to their *general approach* to developmental tasks. . . . The third idiographic dimension of developmental tasks is the patterning of developmental tasks" (Zaccaria, 1965, p. 374). As previously pointed out, Lo Cascio (1964) has identified three basic patterns for mastering developmental tasks: continuous developmental pattern, delayed developmental pattern, and impaired developmental pattern. The individual differences which produce such differential patterns are values, attitudes, need systems, age, sex, temperament, as well as cultural factors such as socioeconomic class.

If one accepts developmental tasks as an organizing structure for thinking about vocationalization, one must then determine what are the developmental tasks relevant to vocational behaviors that move one along a continuum to vocational maturity. There are several conceptualizations from which one can draw. Table 1 (pages 104-107) presents major emphases in these various approaches. It is obvious that the emphases are not parallel in the sense that each discusses developmental tasks as Havighurst defined them. Nor do they agree on the exact time span in which particular development ensues. They do, however, agree that vocational development occurs in a series of critical steps with each systematically related to those which precede it and succeed it. These steps also relate to turning points in each developmental stage, where individuals either progress or fall back as a function of their success in grappling with the central issues of the stage.

In a sense, each of these discussions of development also supports the concept of the movement of the individual first in coming to terms with himself as a creature differentiated from his environment and, then, with the expansion of his social radius, in coming to terms with such relationships as self and institution, self and environment, and self in process (Herr, 1969). Tennyson has talked about this phenomenon as becoming some one before becoming some thing (Tennyson, 1967). Hershenson (1968) has stated it as a series of unfolding vocational questions from birth through adult life such as, Am I? Who am I? What can I do? What will I do? What meaning does what I do have for me?

Although the illustrations in Table 1 are too gross to be directly translated into objectives of vocationalization, other pertinent points are discernible. For example, what does Havighurst's first stage—identification with a worker—suggest for a student who comes from a home and a culture in which there are no

productive workers? If the achievement of later tasks depends upon such identification, education must respond to that lack in the case of this individual. In
accordance with the general rationale of developmental tasks that one must repeat
a missed stage before going on, the question becomes what resources, what role
models, what experiences can the school provide which will help this particular
youngster acquire a concept of work as a part of his orientation to the future?

Another implication in Table 1 stems from the developmental tasks of middle
childhood as described by Havighurst. If, for example, the development of the
fundamental skills of reading, writing, and calculating are critical to later developmental success (and there is no doubt that they are), and if developing a
concept of work as a part of one's future orientation is also essential, cannot
these two tasks be cooperatively accomplished through the use of work-oriented
materials and experiences in teaching children to read, write, and calculate?
The answer seems to be obviously affirmative; the subject will be more fully
discussed in Chapters 6, 7, and 8.

Another example of the longitudinal shaping of tasks relevant to ultimate
vocational behavior is provided by Stratemeyer, Forkner, McKim, and Passow
(1957, pp. 208-214). Table 2 illustrates this approach. In Table 2 the concept

Table 2   Using Effective Methods of Work

	CHILDHOOD	LATER CHILDHOOD	YOUTH
Planning			
Deciding on and clarifying	Identifying immediate purposes in general terms	Determining major issues involved in achieving purposes	Extending ability to identify aspects and long-time implication affecting purposes
Determining sequence of steps to achieve purpose	Planning immediate next steps	Making longer-range plans	Extending range and details of planning
Budgeting time and energy	Planning time allotments with the help of others	Developing the ability to make independent decisions as to use of time	Budgeting time in terms of a greater number of activities and a larger time span
Evaluating steps taken	Deciding on the success of immediate steps	Considering the effectiveness of progress toward longer-range plans	Taking increased responsibility for evaluating progress toward goals

Source: Florence B. Stratemeyer, H. L. Forkner, Margaret McKim, and A. W. Passow, *Developing a curriculum for modern living* (New York: Teachers College, Columbia University, 1957), pp. 208-214.

Using Effective Methods of Work is broken into a constituent element, Planning,
which is in turn subdivided into aspects of planning, i.e. deciding on and clarifying purpose, determining sequence of steps to achieve purpose, budgeting time
and energy, etc. Each aspect is then extended across chronological age periods,
which move from gross to more specific manifestations of the behavior. Such a
procedure permits the elaboration of a conceptual scheme which begins with

the earliest point at which education may intervene and purposefully builds experiences on experiences as these contribute to common denominators judged basic to developing vocational maturity. This scheme also permits a gross profile of the experiential background which an individual is expected to have but which may not be present in his history. Thus, the scheme can be used to show present and future behavioral expectations, as well as to determine what experiences need to be presently acquired and what successes an individual needs to move from a particular developmental plateau to more effective behavior.

Both Tables 1 and 2 provide a frame of reference for formulating specific objectives. In each, the themes presented are more global than objectives should be. As written, they do not provide behavioral descriptions which permit evaluation of the degree to which an individual has accomplished the goals set for him. They also fail to include current findings from vocational development as input to help decide upon objectives. Before turning to the development of specific objectives or the matter of behavioral descriptions, let us consider some current research findings.

CURRENT RESEARCH PERTINENT TO VOCATIONALIZATION

Research of particular relevance to vocational maturing has been accomplished in the Career Pattern Study (Super, 1969a, b); in Super, Starishevsky, Matlin, and Jordaan (1963); and in the Project on Readiness for Vocational Planning (Gribbons and Lohnes, 1968). Each of these research studies has identified the elements of vocational maturity, particularly as these have implications for preadolescents and adolescents.

The Career Pattern Study has focused principally upon the exploratory and establishment steps of vocational development. It has been assumed that these are the stages crucial to education and, in particular, to curriculum development and guidance. As Table 1 illustrates, the developmental tasks which span these two life stages (in the period of approximately age 14 to 25 plus) are as follows:

> Crystallizing a vocational preference
> Specifying it
> Implementing it
> Stabilizing in the chosen vocation
> Consolidating one's status
> Advancing in the occupation

Because the principal focus of this book is on vocationalization during the preadolescent and adolescent periods, the discussion here will be confined to those tasks most appropriately performed within this period. Thus crystallizing, specifying, and implementing a vocational preference are the principal emphases herein because they are tasks expected to be accomplished during the middle and later years of adolescence.

Essentially, *crystallizing* a vocational preference has to do with the individual's "formulating ideas as to fields and levels of work which are appropriate for him, self and occupational concepts which will enable him, if necessary, to make tentative choices, that is, to commit himself to a type of education or training which will lead him toward some partially specified occupation" (Super, Starishevsky, Matlin, and Jordaan, 1963, p. 82). *Specifying* a vocational preference is the "singling out of a specific occupation and the attitude (not the act) of commitment to it" (ibid.). *Implementing* the preference is converting it into a reality. Thus these separate stages are divided between all the factors in *preference*, on the one hand, and those in actual *choice* (acting on one's preference) on the other. Choice in this context can be represented by entering an entry-level job, participating in an apprenticeship, or entering a post-secondary educational program designed to prepare one for his preferred goal.

The implications of this line of reasoning are that the major emphasis in vocationalization to the twelfth-grade level is upon enabling the individual to crystallize and specify preferences or to anticipate the act of choice.

What, then, are the behaviors or attitudes which foster the crystallization or specification of a vocational preference? What are the subelements underlying these behaviors which could be set forth in a chart similar to Table 2? One list is as follows, paraphrased from the work of Super, Starishevsky, Matlin, and Jordaan (1963, pp. 84-87):

1. *Awareness of the need to crystallize*—Fundamentally, this attitude acts as a precursor of those which follow. It has to do with developing an attitude of readiness to involve oneself in the succeeding elements. This is perhaps more adequately described by Jordaan (1963) as becoming oriented to the need to *explore.*

2. *Use of resources*—This element is principally a set of instrumental behaviors by which one copes with exploration whether it is focused on self-understanding or occupational description; this element is present in relationship to a large number of persons or objects: parents, counselors, teachers, materials, part-time jobs.

3. *Awareness of factors to consider in formulating a vocational preference*—This involves knowledge of the possible bases for preferences—whether intellectual requirements, relationship between interests and appropriate outlets, need for alternatives, or availability of outlets for different self-characteristics, i.e. security, prestige.

4. *Awareness of contingencies which may affect vocational goals*—The existing evidence (Super and Overstreet, 1960, p. 51) suggests that this element and items 2 and 3 coexist in the sense that they collectively contribute to narrowing preferences and adding stability to those preferences which remain. Fundamentally, this element concerns the factors which may impede implementation of a particular preference, and the alternative which can be actualized if necessary.

5. *Differentiation of interests and values*—This element is the ability of the

individual to differentiate the personally important from the unimportant and to concentrate his attention on certain objectives and activities rather than others as a basis for decision making and for action.

6. *Awareness of present-future relationship*—This factor is concerned with coming to terms with the interrelationship between present activities and intermediate or ultimate vocational activities: for example, understanding educational avenues and their requirements as these provide access to different fields or levels of occupational activity.

7. *Formulation of a generalized preference*—All the factors described to this point should culminate in the formulation of a generalized preference—or crystallization. This level of preference is less a specific occupation than a general one out of which further specification will ensue. In such cases, the preference represented by a particular occupational title is likely to symbolize related activities that are liked rather than a specific occupation.

8. *Consistency of preference*—Consistency may be primarily verbal, or it may be manifested instrumentally in course selection and in such areas of extracurricular or part-time occupational activities.

9. *Possession of information on the preferred occupation*—This element represents possession of more specific information about the generalized preference. It is characterized by greater variety and accuracy of information and by a higher degree of understanding than is represented by the formulation of a generalized preference.

10. *Planning for the preferred occupation*—The focus here is on decisions as to what to do and when and how to do it. As Super and Overstreet demonstrated in their work in 1960, specificity both of planning and of information are measurable characteristics of vocational maturity in early adolescence.

11. *Wisdom of the vocational preference*—This is in large measure a criterion of the previous elements. Although certain external criteria can be applied, it is generally assumed that wisdom is really more a function of the processes by which a preference is developed than the preference itself.

12. *Specification*—This level of vocationalization represents elaboration of the preference, i.e. more specific information and planning, a greater commitment to the preference, and a refinement of the steps already described, with a sharper focus on the particular preference and the steps preceding implementation.

A recent analysis of the studies (within the Career Pattern Study) concerned with the elements just identified affirmed the presence of planfulness and time perspective at the ninth grade. Second, although ninth-grade boys had not attained an understanding of themselves or of the world of work to ready them for making sound vocational or prevocational decisions, these manifestations of vocational maturity were related to ability, to opportunity for the arousal of interest and the use of abilities, and to the taking advantage of such opportunities.

Further, these studies found that vocational maturity factors common at both the ninth and twelfth grades included occupational information (educational, psychological, and economic) as well as planning, independence, crystallization of interests, and specification and implementation of preferences (Super, 1969a). Super further reported that the available data suggest that the "realism of the late teens is more the reality of the self, of its abilities and interests, than that of opportunities beyond the realm of personal experience." More important, however, is his finding (pp. 5-6):

> Vocational maturity in the ninth grade, judged by occupational information, planning and interest maturity, were significantly related to vocational success in young adulthood. . . . In the twelfth grade vocational maturity, judged by the same measures as in grade 9, proved even more valid. Information about training and education required for the preferred occupation yielded a significant number of anticipated relationships. Those with educational and occupational level attained by age 25 were moderately high, and those with career development and stabilizing-floundering were fair . . . measures of awareness of choices to be made and of information and planning bearing on the choices, which seemed to have some construct validity in ninth grade and twelfth grade have predictive validity for vocational development in young adulthood.

These recent studies have somewhat tempered earlier findings (Super and Overstreet, 1960) that ninth-grade boys are not yet ready to make sound decisions concerning fields or even levels of work. In other words, these later studies show that aspects of vocational maturity at the ninth grade more accurately predict vocational maturity at the twelfth grade and at age 25 than had been earlier found. Further, since these studies demonstrate that some students reach vocational maturity levels at ninth grade which predict vocational maturity at age 25, they support the theory that education can aid vocationalization for a great many students.

Additional support for direct attention to vocationalization as a dimension of general education is implicit in findings reported in another article by Super (1969b, p. 18). He states, "Boys who are given opportunities in school and out-of-school and who use these opportunities during their school years tend also to make good use of their later career opportunities." Thus it has been found that measures of vocational maturity in high school predict career success better than do the conventional predictions based on test scores or grades, and better than occupational success; in other words, how boys deal with developmental tasks at one stage tells something about coping at later stages. It further stresses that in the early growth years the foundations of later careers are laid.

As indicated in Chapter 2, throughout the history of the Career Pattern Study, the role of the self-concept in vocational development has been a key concept, the synthesizing agent. Super (1951, 1953, p. 185) has proposed the following:

*In expressing a vocational preference, a person puts into occupational ter-
minology his ideas of the kind of person he is, in entering an occupation,
he seeks to implement his self-concept, and in stabilizing in an occupation
he attempts to achieve self-actualization. In a chronological sense, three
phases of self-concept evolution occur: formation, translation and implementation. Through growth and learning as well as the constant interaction
of the individual with external influences the self-concept system is modified and adjusted until a synthesis is finally evolved.*

Each of the critical phases of the evolving self-concept has certain emphases and
processes integral to it (Super, 1969b, p. 19):

*1. The formation process includes exploration of the self and of the en-
vironment, the differentiation of the self from others, identification with
others who can serve as models, and the playing of these selected roles
with more or less conscious evaluation of the result (reality testing).*

*2. The translation of self-concepts into occupational terms may take place
through identification with an adult role model ("I am like him" or "I want
to be like him"), experience in a role in which one has been cast, or learning that some of one's attributes should make one fit well into a certain
occupation.*

*3. The implementation process involves action as in obtaining the special-
ized education or training needed for the preferred occupation or finding
employment in it.*

Research has begun to accumulate which supports the importance of the self-
concept in vocational development, in the formulation of occupational preference, and in choice making. For example, studies have demonstrated that individuals have a greater similarity of interests with the occupations they most
prefer than with those they least prefer (Blocher and Schutz, 1961; Oppenheimer,
1966). In addition, it has been demonstrated that sometimes individuals, in this
case college students, distort perceptions of occupations to fit their own characteristics (Gonyea, 1961; Grunes, 1957). Healy (1968) used an index labeled
"incorporation" (defined as the similarity between an individual's rating of himself on significant traits and an occupation on similar dimensions) to examine the
operation of the self-concept in occupational choice. His data supported the
assumption that the greater the similarity of the two elements in incorporation,
the greater the probability that the occupation in question will be chosen.

O'Hara (1966) has demonstrated that the self-concept relates not only to occupational choice but to high school achievement as well and that these relationships increase from ninth to twelfth grades. These relationships apparently function even earlier than the ninth grade. Williams and Cole (1968) report that
measures of self-concept at the sixth grade are significantly and positively related

to the child's conception of school, social status at school, emotional adjustment, mental ability, reading achievement, and mathematical achievement. It has also been demonstrated that the implementation of the self-concept in choice does not always just perpetuate the status quo but in some instances actualizes the self through exposing it to experiences which will cause one's talents, capacities, and interests to be expanded (Pallone and Hosinski, 1967; Wheeler and Carnes, 1968).

To perceive vocational development as either a continuing effort to implement the present self-concept and maintain the status quo or as an attempt to achieve self-actualization and self-enhancement seems tenable if for no other reason than that sociologists have found pervasive connections between an individual's career or occupation and his entire way of life or life style (Cohen, 1964). But vocational development as an expression of personality and as an attempt to implement an evolving self-concept can also be seen as part of the identity search. As Galinsky and Fast (1966, p. 89) have stated, "In our society one of the most clear-cut avenues through which identity concerns are expressed is the process of making a vocational choice. . . . Choosing a vocation involves a kind of public self-definition that forces one to say to the world, 'This is what I am.' "

In sum, theory and research support the self-concept as a dynamic factor in shaping individual behavior. As Herr has noted (1970, p. 67):

> Motivation, perseverance, choice, and generalized behavior each relate to the labels persons apply to the different aspects of the self and to the elements which comprise the contexts or situations with which they do or expect to interact. Self-labels, or self-concepts, represent the pieces making up the composite self-picture, the self-concept system, one uses to trigger or restrain particular modes of behavior under specific contingencies. One's self-concept may be an accurate representation of the self, it may be distorted, or it may be obscure either in general or under specific conditions.

In any of these instances, vocationalization must foster an effective, accurate self-concept as it simultaneously develops other necessary elements of vocational maturity.

In the search for other measures of vocational maturity as input for building vocationalization objectives, it is important to consider the work of Gribbons and Lohnes (1968). They have examined the concept of Readiness for Vocational Planning as a measure of vocational maturity during adolescence. Their research has identified eight variables, which in combination correlate to a high degree with readiness for vocational planning at the eighth grade and at post-secondary school levels. They are (pp. 15-16):

Variable I.   Factors in Curriculum Choice
Awareness of relevant factors, including one's abilities, interests and values and their relation to curriculum choice; curricula choice to occupational choice.

Variable II.   Factors in Occupational Choice
Awareness of relevant factors, including abilities, interests, values; educational requirements for choice; accuracy of description of occupation.

Variable III.   Verbalized strengths and Weaknesses
Ability to verbalize appropriately the relation of personal strengths and weaknesses to educational and vocational choices.

Variable IV.   Accuracy of Self-appraisal
Comparison of subject's estimates of his general scholastic ability, verbal ability, and quantitative ability with his actual attainments on scholastic aptitude tests, English grades and mathematics grades.

Variable V.   Evidence of Self-rating
Quality of evidence cited by subject in defense of his appraisal of his own abilities.

Variable VI.   Interests
Awareness of interests and their relation to occupational choices.

Variable VII.   Values
Awareness of values and their relation to occupational choices.

Variable VIII.   Independence of Choice
Extent of subject's willingness to take personal responsibility for his choices.

Gribbons and Lohnes found that vocational maturity—as measured by the eight Readiness for Vocational Planning scales cited—increased from grades 8 to 10. They also indicated that an overlapping of scores in these two grades showed that some eighth-graders had already achieved considerable vocational maturity while some tenth-graders evidenced a considerable lack of it. More important as a rationale for vocational development is their finding that levels of eighth-grade vocational maturity are predictive of educational and occupational planning, educational aspirations, and level of occupational aspirations in the twelfth grade; of field and level of actual occupation two years after high school; and of two-year, post–high school career adjustment. The RVP scales failed to discriminate among those students manifesting Differential Career Processes—constant maturity, emerging maturity, degeneration, and constant immaturity—but they did demonstrate a trend from idealism in the eighth grade to realism in the twelfth grade, with brighter students (above I.Q. 105) appearing to choose more consistently with their measured intelligence than less bright students.

Two other items of potential input for formulating vocationalization objectives will be considered before a synthesis of the research findings reported is attempted. The first is a sociological perspective on preparation for work life (Gross, 1967). Gross has contended that such preparation involves four emphases:

1. Preparation for life in an organization, involving authority, security quests, impersonality, routine, conflict, mobility, and demotion

2. Preparation for a set of role relationships

3. Preparation for a level of consumption involving a certain style of life

4. Preparation for an occupational career, involving changes in the nature of jobs, and different types of jobs depending on the position in the life cycle

Each of these represents potential themes for organizing vocationalization activities.

The second perspective is on the ingredients of human effectiveness (Blocher, 1966). Blocher contends that basic to an individual's human effectiveness is a knowledge of the social roles which he is likely to play and the implications for him of others' structured expectations about appropriate behavior in these roles. In terms of vocationalization, the analysis of social roles should extend to the opportunities available for the expression of individual characteristics—opportunities such as leadership, creative or original contributions, helping relationships, and unusual levels of accomplishment. Tied to such analysis of social roles is the second emphasis—coping behaviors. Blocher suggests that possession of a range of coping behaviors and knowledge of the consequences of these in relation to social roles enhance personal effectiveness. Finally, he contends that developmental tasks and the discontinuities between social situations and available coping behaviors are additional themes worthy of vocationalization efforts.

For the purposes of this chapter, then, the theory and research emanating from Super's Career Pattern Study, the related work of Gribbons and Lohnes, as well as the sociological and psychological perspectives of Gross and Blocher have been treated as examples of appropriate input for formulating vocational guidance objectives. Before turning to the specific matter of formulating objectives per se, however, some synthesis is necessary.

According to these four positions, in order to attain different aspects of vocational maturity, students need a comprehensive body of information which links what they are doing educationally at particular points in time to future options they will have in both education and work. They need to know what curricula will be available to them, what factors distinguish one curriculum from another, what components make up separate curricular pathways, what personal factors are relevant to success in different curricula, and how the various curricula are linked to different field and level responsibilities in the occupational world.

Students also need self-knowledge. They need to be able to differentiate personal values and personal interests as these are related to personal strengths and weaknesses in abilities—verbal, quantitative, scholastic. They need to be able to assess these elements of the self, incorporate their meaning into the self-concept, and relate this self-information to the choices with which they will be confronted.

Students also need to understand the characteristics of the organizations in which they are likely to work as these determine role relationships, social relations, flexibility of coping behavior, level and kind of consumption, and changes probable throughout the occupational history.

Transcending this necessary base of knowledge is the motivation to use it in purposeful ways; or, as Clarke, Gelatt, and Levine (1965, p. 41) observe, to develop "an effective strategy for analyzing, organizing, and synthesizing information in order to make a choice." In the making of decisions there are skills which can be learned. Once a person has made a plan for some segment of his life with which he is content to live, he is better able to make the next one intelligently and with less hesitation or conflict. But it must be remembered that one cannot make vocational decisions without educational implications and vice versa. Nor can effective planning and choice making occur without one's recognizing and assessing the psychological and emotional implications of various devices.

An inherent finding in the studies of Gribbons and Lohnes and of Super and his colleagues is the need for an attitude of planfulness in students, for recognition of possible alternative actions, and for ways to assess the desirability of outcomes on the basis of personal preferences and values. Students can be helped to evaluate the sequence of outcomes of immediate choice—proximate, intermediate, ultimate—as well as the factors which are personally relevant at experiential branch points, the probabilities associated with these factors, and the personal desirability of the three outcomes in the sequence. The fostering of planfulness and of vocational development, then, involves providing the student not only with knowledge, but also with opportunities to apply the knowledge to his personal characteristics. Vocationalization must, among other things, help students commit to work a sense of value, ego-involvement, personal endeavor, and achievement motivation.

A partnership between education and vocational development rests upon the following assumptions:

1. Students can be equipped with accurate and relevant information translated in terms of their individual developmental level and state of readiness.

2. Students can be assisted to formulate hypotheses about themselves, the choice points which will be in their future, and the environmental options available.

3. Students can be helped to develop appropriate ways of testing these hypotheses against both past and new experiences.

4. Students can be helped to come to terms with the educational and occupational relevance of what they already know, or will learn, about themselves and their futures.

5. Students can be helped to see themselves in process and to acquire the tools and knowledge which will allow them to exploit this process in positive, constructive ways.

Table 3 (page 119) synthesizes in gross terms some of the points of emphasis within the time spans most appropriate to vocationalization, thus providing an organizing framework for developing objectives.

Table 3 Synthesis of Inputs to Vocationalization

Approximate Ages ⟶

	Pre-school	5-9	10-14	15	18	19-25
	Formation of self-concept ⟶		Translation of self-concept into vocational terms ⟶		Implementation of self-concept	
	Developing preference or anticipation ⟶			choice ⟶ induction ⟶ reformation ⟶ integration		
	Fantasy		Tentative		Realistic	
			Trial (with little commitment) ⟶		Trial (more commitment) ⟶ stabilization ⟶ advancement	

Items developing across Pre-school → 10-14 (arrows indicating continuous development):

- Awareness of the need to crystallize (orienting) ⟶
- Formulating interests ⟶
- Developing a vocabulary of self ⟶
- Developing a vocabulary of work ⟶
- Rudiments of basic trust in self and others ⟶
- Rudiments of initiative ⟶
- Rudiments of industry ⟶
- Knowledge of fundamentals of technology ⟶
- Differentiating self from environment ⟶
- Identification with a worker ⟶
- Developing sex social role ⟶
- Learning rudiments of social rules ⟶
- Learning fundamental intellectual, physical and motor skills ⟶

Items at 10-14:

- Use of resources (exploring) ⟶
- Relating interests and capacities
- Awareness of factors to consider in formulating a vocational preference
- Awareness of contingencies which affect vocational goals
- Differentiation of interests and values
- Awareness of present-future relationships
- Accepting oneself as in process
- Relating changes in the self to changes in the world
- Acquiring basic habits of industry
- Learning to organize one's time and energy to get work done
- Learning to defer gratification, to set priorities
- Achieving personal identity

- Acquiring knowledge of life in organizations
- Preparation for role relationships
- Preparation for level and kind of consumption
- Preparation for an occupational career
- Formulation of generalized preference
- Possession of information concerning the preferred occupation
- Planning for the preferred occupation

- Choosing and preparing for occupation
- Achieving more mature relations with peers of both sexes
- Achieving emotional independence of parents and other adults

Items at 15–18:

- Relating interests and capacities to values

Items at 19-25:

- Preparing for marriage
- selecting a mate
- Developing capability for intimacy
- starting a family
- Becoming a productive person
- Mastering the skills of an occupation
- Moving up the ladder within the occupation

Independence of choice (at 18)

Bottom section:

- Developing planfulness
- Developing decision-making strategies
- Role-playing, curricula exposure ⟶ reality testing ⟶ work-study
- Role-playing ⎱ attitudes of others ⟶ identification ⟶ self-appraisal
- Identification ⎰

APPROACHES TO WRITING OBJECTIVES

Terms like "accountability" and "performance contracting" and acronyms like PERT and PPBS have come to be considered synonymous with needs for evaluation, whether related to cost benefit analysis or changes in human behavior. Flanagan (1967) has pointed out that the lack of well-defined teaching objectives and inadequate procedures for determining whether students attain objectives have prevented the use of modern decision making and operational procedures in education. O'Dea and Zeran (1953), Rothney and Farwell (1960), Patterson (1960), Herr (1964), and Cramer, et al. (1970), among others, have discussed the lack of suitable criteria as a major difficulty in evaluating guidance services. Thus if we are going to evaluate a program or if we are going to systematically try to influence human behavior, we must start with objectives.

In order to take a systems approach to vocational development, we must determine the appropriate behaviors or ideas or attitudes or knowledge which students need to gain as they move toward vocational maturity. The most effective approach is to convert the factors that have been found to predict vocational maturity among some students into objectives capable of being achieved by greater numbers of students. Finally, one must determine the form in which such objectives will be cast.

The current emphases in objectives development stress the importance of defining the outcomes of instruction or guidance in terms of observable human performance, citing the conditions under which it should be demonstrated, and determining the standard or criterion of success. Within this context, however, there are several suggested ways of stating objectives based on different purposes.

Tyler (1950, p. 30) asserts: "The most useful form for stating objectives is to express them in terms which identify both the kind of behavior to be developed in the student and the content or area of life in which this behavior is to operate." An objective of vocational guidance stated in Tyler's terms would be as follows: *To write clear and well organized reports of requirements in preferred occupations.* Such an objective does not discuss the procedures for accomplishing the goal, but it does specify the skill—to write clear and well organized reports— and the domain of concern—requirements in preferred occupations—which are important components of the goal.

Goals stated in the terms advocated by Tyler resemble what McAshan (1970) has termed minimum-level behavioral objectives. Goals stated at this level can be used to denote program goals without specifying precise expectations for individuals or the criteria upon which evaluation is based.

Probably the best-known current approach to writing objectives is that advanced by Mager (1962). According to this approach, a statement of objectives is a collection of words or symbols that describe an educational intent. Such a statement should include: (1) what the individual will be doing (terminal behavior) when demonstrating his achievement, (2) the important conditions under which the terminal behavior is to occur, and (3) a criterion of acceptable performance or standard that indicates when the learner has successfully demonstrated his achievement. An objective relevant to vocationalization developed in line with these criteria is as follows: *Given ten occupations, the student must be able to correctly identify, by labeling, the minimum educational requirements of at least nine of them (list of occupations inserted here.)*

The latter format for writing objectives provides to a greater degree than the others, behavioral descriptions which permit evaluation of whether a student has accomplished the goals set for him. Such a format represents, however, the danger of becoming too restrictive either in the criterion of success used, the evaluation activities, or the requirement that all students accomplish goals in the same way.

Gronlund (1970), in reviewing the format proposed by Mager for develop-ing objectives, suggests that such an approach is most useful when the desired outcome is to have all students perform alike at a specified minimum level. In particular, such a format could be used at lower levels of cognitive activity like the acquisition of vocabulary, knowledge, or facts for labeling occupational distinctions, educational characteristics, or self-traits like interests and aptitudes. Levels of knowledge such as these are basic to higher-order activities like analyz-ing, applying, synthesizing, and evaluating, and in Gronlund's perception (1970, p. 33) they are minimum essentials. Gronlund maintains that in addition to stat-ing objectives in terms of minimum essentials, it is necessary to state more com-plex objectives in such form that they encourage each student to progress as far as possible toward predetermined goals. Thus the objective to be attained by students is stated in a general form with samples of representative behaviors at different levels of complexity indicated. An example of this kind of objective appropriate to vocational guidance is as follows:

Objective: Understands the interdependence of the occupational structure.

1. States the principle of interdependence in his own words.

2. Gives an example of the principle.

3. Identifies work orientations—e.g. data, people, things—which contribute to interdependence.

4. Distinguishes between field and level lattices in job families as representative of interdependence.

In Gronlund's approach to stating objectives at a developmental level, he combines a general goal that provides program direction and specific behaviors which contribute to the general goal at different levels of complexity. The specific behaviors provide the rudiments of a scheme for determining how far individual students have progressed in terms of the general goals. Thus each of the specific behaviors could be assessed independently for individual students and judgments made about what additional knowledge or experiences the stu-dent could pursue to aid his achievement of the general goal.

Few applications of these different approaches to stating objectives for student outcomes have appeared in professional literature on vocational guidance. One exception is Hull's (1970) work. Hull coupled Mager's approach with the taxonomic efforts of Bloom et al. (1956), who divided the cognitive domain into six classes: knowledge, comprehension, application, analysis, synthesis, and evaluation. These classes represent a hierarchical arrangement of cognitive complexity. Hull applied this scheme to the evaluation of pupil attainment in six occupational fields. Most important for the purposes here, he defined *behavioral* tasks, the attainment of which can be measured. Table 4 presents his analysis.

Table 4   Hull's Approaches to Stating Behavioral Objectives in
Six Occupational Fields

OCCUPATIONAL FIELD	OBJECTIVE CLASS	OPERATIONALLY DEFINED TASKS IN THE COGNITIVE DOMAIN
Office occupation	Knowledge	To spell a list of fifty "most difficult" words correctly
Carpentry	Comprehension	To lay out a rafter-cutting diagram for a gable roof with a ¼ pitch
Food service	Application	To serve a full-course dinner to a party of eight persons quickly, efficiently, and without disrupting conversations
Distribution	Analysis	To recognize unstated reasons for the customer's initial questions about a sales product
Production agriculture	Synthesis	To plan a schedule of fertilizer application (time of year, type and amount of fertilizer, etc.) for a given crop rotation on a particular farm
Welding	Evaluation	To apply 60,000 pounds of pressure per square inch to a butt weld of ⅜ inch mild steel

Source: W. L. Hull, Evaluating pupil attainment in vocational tasks. *American Vocational Journal,* 1967, 42, 78-79. (Figure 1). Reprinted from the *American Vocational Journal* by permission.

Hull, of course, uses vocational tasks related to the acquisition of occupational skills rather than to the concepts of vocationalization, or vocational development, as we have defined them. His illustration also represents a point-in-time approach rather than a longitudinal, or sequential, process, which would be needed to foster vocational development. The major reason for presenting this illustration, however, is that it meshes a cognitive concept with a specific behavior. The latter can then be used to determine whether the individual has acquired the skill inherent in the concept.

With some juxtaposing of time and space and by ignoring the occupational-field labels in the first column of the table, one can imagine adapting the classes of knowledge, comprehension, application, analysis, synthesis, and evaluation to the developing characteristics of groups of children or particular children in a longitudinal scheme for fitting particular cognitive emphases with developmental tasks.

Although Hull used as a model the analysis of the cognitive domain by Bloom et al., there is a more recent companion piece dealing with the affective domain Krathwohl, Bloom, and Masia, 1964). Stripped of their definitions, the category and subcategory titles which describe the spiraling complexity of each of these two domains is presented in Table 5 (page 124).

Krathwohl has stated (1965, p. 54), "If the analysis of the cognitive and affective areas is correct, then a hierarchy of objectives dealing with the same subject-matter concepts suggests a readiness relationship that exists between those objectives lower in the hierarchy and those higher." Applying this premise to vocationalization, the taxonomies of the cognitive and the affective domains provide models which can be extended longitudinally, which can be used to represent universal expectations, which can be translated into profiles of individual development, and to which can be related experiences for fostering progress in particular categories of development.

There is also in preparation a third taxonomy, which is directed to the psychomotor domain. Since much of the learning in business education, industrial arts, vocational education, and the fine arts presumes student capability or the development of capability in motor skills, categories of simple to complex performance in this domain will extend the usefulness of the present taxonomies for educational or vocational guidance planning. When the taxonomy of the psychomotor domain is completed, it will likely aid analysis of learning outcomes in such areas as assembling, building, creating, fastening, grinding, gripping, mending, mixing, sketching, weighing, manipulating (Gronlund, 1970, p. 24). In some instances these areas are primarily neurophysiological, and in others they include both cognitive and affective elements.

Each of the ways of writing objectives described has validity for charting a system of dimensions along which vocationalization should proceed. Whichever method a particular reader chooses, it will require substantial effort, time, and evaluation. One must constantly keep in mind that the purposes of writing objectives are:

1. To specify clearly what areas of vocationalization in the lives of students a vocational guidance program intends to affect

2. To provide a framework by which resources in the school and in the community can be tied in to the accomplishment of the stated objectives

3. To provide a series of goals for which different evaluation methods can be devised.

Table 5   *Classifications of the Affective and Cognitive Domains by Hierarchy of Complexity*

AFFECTIVE DOMAIN	COGNITIVE DOMAIN

1.0 Receiving (attending)
  1.1 Awareness
  1.2 Willingness to receive
  1.3 Controlled or selected attention
	1.0 Knowledge
	  1.1 Knowledge of specifics
	  1.2 Knowledge of ways and means of dealing with specifics
	  1.3 Knowledge of the universals and abstractions in a field

2.0 Responding
  2.1 Acquiescence in responding
  2.2 Willingness to respond
  2.3 Satisfaction in response
	2.0 Comprehension
	  2.1 Translation
	  2.2 Interpretation
	  2.3 Extrapolation

3.0 Valuing
  3.1 Acceptance of a value
  3.2 Preference for a value
  3.3 Commitment (conviction)
	3.0 Application

4.0 Organization
  4.1 Conceptualization of a value
  4.2 Organization of a value system
	4.0 Analysis
	  4.1 Analysis of elements
	  4.2 Analysis of relationships
	  4.3 Analysis of organizational principles

5.0 Characterization by a value or a value complex
  5.1 Generalized set
  5.2 Characterization
	5.0 Synthesis
	  5.1 Production of a unique communication
	  5.2 Production of a plan, or proposed set of operations
	  5.3 Derivation of a set of abstract relations

	6.0 Evaluation
	  6.1 Judgments in terms of internal evidence
	  6.2 Judgments in terms of external criterion

Source: From *Taxonomy of educational objectives, Handbook I, Cognitive domain* and *Handbook II, Affective domain* by B. S. Bloom, D. R. Krathwohl, and B. B. Masia (New York: David McKay Company, Inc.). Used by permission of the publisher.

The question now becomes, How can the input from current work in vocational development be placed into a model which is longitudinally viable, which lends itself to behavioral description, and for which vocational guidance or educational experiences can be designed? One approximation of such an approach has been designed by the University City Science Center (Weeks, 1967, pp. 53-54) to direct career-development efforts in the Philadelphia public schools. In this report, "career development standards of mastery" have been identified at four educational points: on entering first grade, on entering fifth grade, on entering ninth grade, on graduating from high school. Table 6 presents these standards on two of the several possible dimensions of vocationalization: career awareness and decision making.

Table 6   Selected Examples of Proposed Career-Development Standards of Mastery for Philadelphia Public Schools in the Areas of Career Awareness and Decision Making

CAREER AWARENESS	DECISION MAKING
1. On entering first grade 1. In "playing school," identifies people such as principal, teacher, nurse, janitor secretary, and acts roles.	1. Given a selection of different activities (paint, hear story, or play with blocks) makes choices.

2. On entering fifth grade
  1. Identifies in his neighborhood:
  —who works for himself;
  —who works for others;
  —who does not work for pay.
	1. Having stated an interest (pilot, nurse, soldier) decides whether to learn more by:
	  —reading about it;
	  —role playing;
	  —using tools/paints.

3. On entering ninth grade 1. Given a list of basic career clusters, identifies major hierarchy levels, states basic educational requirements for each level, and major subjects required for entry.	1. Completes subject selection game successfully.

4. On graduating
  1. For selected interest area describes:
  —major continuing educational facilities;
  —major employers;
  —skills required;
  —life style;
  —tools used.
	1. Given three simulated job offers, arrays advantages/disadvantages and makes selection.

The standards proposed by Weeks do not exhaust the possibilities for demonstrating the standards for career-development mastery. But they do represent (1) the type of context expected—e.g. group play, role playing, playing school, use of Career Information System of Learning Resources; (2) the type of condition expected—e.g. a list of basic career clusters, a selection of different activities, three simulated job offers, a profile of a high school graduate; and (3) the type of behavior expected—e.g. describes and expresses, demonstrates, identifies, compares, names, correctly diagnoses, lists, labels, lays out plan. In particular, they plot in ways that can be measured the areas of behavior and the particular kinds of knowledge to be expected of students at various developmental levels. These examples of objectives are unusual in that the words describing what students will be doing are unambiguous, clearly denoting what is expected. They are not vague generalizations such as "to know," "to appreciate," "to understand," "to self-actualize."

Metfessel, Michael, and Kirsner (1969) have proposed a method, using the Bloom et al. and Krathwohl et al. taxonomies previously discussed in Table 5, to use behaviorally oriented infinitives, combined with objects, as a basis for meaningful, cohesive, and operational statements. For example, at the level of knowledge where the objects are terms like "vocabulary," "meanings," "definitions," "categories," they recommend the use of infinitives such as "to define," "to distinguish," "to acquire," "to recall," "to recognize," as ways to be descriptively precise about what students are expected to do. At a more complex level, such as analysis, where appropriate direct objects are statements, assumptions, themes, techniques, points of view, the infinitives might be "to distinguish," to detect," "to identify," "to contrast," "to compare." Such an approach is not confined to the use of the taxonomies cited but emphasizes that descriptions of expectations for student behavior should denote as clearly as possible what skill, knowledge, or attitude is to be achieved so that this is what can be evaluated. Gronlund (1970, pp. 53-55) has proposed, rather than infinitives, a list of verbs which can be related to outcomes in different content or attitudinal areas.

Obviously, each school system will need to develop independently a set of operationally stated objectives to guide its effort to foster vocationalization in the students for whom it has responsibility. The particular objectives developed will reflect the characteristics of the students to be served as well as the resources available. It will also be necessary for each school system to devise or select measures of student performance on these objectives. In schools where there is great variability in the personal histories of the students, it will also be necessary to assess the degree to which individuals or groups can already perform the behavior. Finally, as such a system is implemented, it will be necessary to continuously evaluate whether the guidance and educational activities designed to accomplish the objectives are actually bringing about changes in the behavior of the students.

Table 7 presents some sample objectives which might be used at different educational levels to facilitate particular emphases on vocationalization. They are not exhaustive, nor are they necessarily the right objectives for a given situation. They do blend, however, some of the research inputs contributing to vocational maturity previously discussed in this chapter with strategies for developing objectives. As the key illustrates, separate objectives roughly approximate different levels of the cognitive and affective domains identified by Bloom et al. (1956) and by Krathwohl, Bloom, and Masia (1964).

Table 7   *Sample Objectives to Facilitate Vocationalization at Different Educational Levels*

ELEMENTARY SCHOOL	JUNIOR HIGH SCHOOL	SENIOR HIGH SCHOOL
In an oral exercise, the student can identify at least six of the types of workers who contributed to building his school (C, K)	The student lists correctly the different educational areas both in the immediate and distant future that are available to him, the nature and purpose of each, the possible outcomes of each in terms of levels of occupational activity (C, C)	The student reality tests his broad occupational preference by systematically relating it to his achievement in different courses, part-time work, extracurricular activities (A, O)
In a flannel-board presentation, the student can label because of their tools or clothing ten different types of workers found in his community (C, K)	The student verbally differentiates his self-characteristics (e.g. interests, values, abilities, personality traits) and expresses tentative occupational choices that might provide outlets for each (C, C)	The student analyzes his present competency in skills necessary to his broad occupational preference and develops a plan by which these can be enhanced where necessary (C, An)
In an oral exercise, the student can state how different workers contribute to his well-being and the welfare of the community (C, K)	The student can appraise accurately on a written profile his measured ability, achievement level, and current interests (C, An)	Given a part-time job in school or out of school, the student is able to list the advantages and disadvantages it might offer to him in terms of his interests or values (C, C)
After viewing a movie, the student can identify most occupations in his community and describe how they support each other (C, K)	The student can place on a skilled/unskilled continuum twenty occupations about which he has read (C, K)	From a series of case studies about working conditions as they affect individuals with different characteristics, the student can identify patterns of coping behavior and discuss their implications for him under similar circumstances (C, E)
The student can check vocabulary items correctly as being names of interests, aptitudes, abilities (C, K)	From a dramatization portraying five different ways of valuing different methods of handling daily events, the student can consistently identify and describe the value set	The student executes plans to qualify for an entry-level position by choosing appropriate
From a list of fifty occupations, the student can identify those which occur primarily indoors or outdoors (C, C)		
The student can select from a list of ten alterna-		

Key: (C, K)=Cognitive—Knowledge; (C, C)=Cognitive—Comprehension; (C, Ap)=Cognitive—Application; (C, An)=Cognitive—Analysis; (C, Sy)=Cognitive—Synthesis; (C, E)=Cognitive—Evaluation; (A, Re)=Affective—Receiving; (A, Re)=Affective—Responding; (A, V)=Affective—Valuing; (A, O)=Affective—Organization; (A, CC)=Affective—Characterization by a value or a value complex.

Table 7   Sample Objectives to Facilitate Vocationalization at Different Educational
Levels   (Continued)

ELEMENTARY SCHOOL	JUNIOR HIGH SCHOOL	SENIOR HIGH SCHOOL
tives the five best reasons for planning his time (A, Re)	with which he feels most comfortable (A, V)	courses at the high school level (A, V)
The student can list correctly major breakdowns of the occupational structure: e.g. communications, manufacturing, distribution, transportation, or professional/skilled/semiskilled/unskilled (C, C)	The student can weigh alternative outcomes from different kinds of work against the public welfare and rank order his view of these outcomes (A, O)	The student produces a plan of alternative ways of accomplishing his educational (occupational) goals if his first choice is not successfully implemented (C, Sy)
The student can prepare a graph showing the different educational alternatives available: junior high school, high school, community college, area vocational technical school, college, apprenticeships, armed forces (C, Ap)	The student observes five films and then lists the major differences of the technological processes he has observed (A, Re)

Using the *Dictionary of Occupational Titles*, the student can identify ten occupations which are ranked highest in dealing with people, things, or data (C, Ap) | Given ten choices, the student decides upon a broad occupational area to study in depth. He is able in a written proposal to outline the resources he will need to develop this study, the plans necessary to gain access to these resources, and the particular outcomes he desires to obtain (C, E) |
The student can arrange in appropriate rank order the number of years of schooling normally associated with different educational alternatives (C, C)	After a field trip to a factory, the student can tell in his own words the differences in work conditions or procedures he observed in different parts of the plant (C, An)	The student can differentiate between the major occupations that make up a broad occupational area or a job cluster in terms of (1) the amount and type of education needed for entrance, (2) the content, tools, setting, products, or services of these occupations, (3) their values to society, (4) their probability of providing the type of life style he desires, (5) their relationship to his interests and values (C, E)
The student can classify the titles of courses available in his junior high school and senior high school and the types of content with which they are concerned (C, C)	The student is able to assess tentatively in rank order the value to him of each of ten occupational clusters (C, An)	
The student can choose from a list of twenty occupations those offering salaries within particular ranges (C, K)	The student can describe in essay form how knowledge and skills acquired in different subject matter areas relate to performing different work roles (C, Ap)	The student considers five different categories of post-secondary education, chooses one, and defines his reason for choosing it (C, C)
The student voluntarily discusses the importance of work and how education helps one to work effectively (A, Rs)	The student can identify and define ten forms of continuing education following high school including apprenticeships, on-the-job training, correspondence courses, armed forces service schools, evening schools, reading (C, C)	The student develops a plan of access to his next step after high school, either educational or occupational, listing possible alternatives, whom to contact, application dates, capital investment
The student can select from a table models of tools or instruments used in ten different occupations (C, An)	The student completes an	

The student can role play three occupations which he thinks most interest him (C, Sy)

The student can demonstrate how certain knowledges and skills acquired in different school subjects are applied in different work roles (C, Ap)

The student can identify the skills in which he feels most confident and role plays workers who might need these skills (C, E)

The student can role play his interpretation of the values workers might hold in four different occupations (C, E)

The student is willing to share with others the planning and presenting of a play about work and being a worker (A, V)

The student discusses the importance of team work in different work settings, cooperates with others in order to reach a common goal, and can express the importance of his contributions and that of others in reaching a common goal (A, O)

The student during his school activities expresses or demonstrates a positive attitude toward self, others, education, and different types of work roles (A, CCV)

assigned job analysis according to instructions and on time (A, Rs)

The student can compare correctly the social roles which describe a supervisor and a follower (C, Sy)

The student can tell a story in his own words about how an individual suffering a particular limitation can overcome his weakness and maximize his strength in education or in work (C, Sy)

The student can identify, locate and describe the use of five directories listing post-secondary educational opportunities at college, junior college, and technical levels (C, Ap)

The student can identify in a gaming situation future decisions he must make in order to reach different goals (C, Sy)

The student can identify, assess, and defend his analysis of possible steps he might take to minimize his limitations and maximize his assets (C, E)

The student continuously explores and synthesizes the relationships between tentative choices and demonstrated abilities (A, V)

The student is able to select two persons from history and discuss why he would like to emulate them (A, V)

The student can produce a list of resources or approaches available for learning about and assessing the world of work (C, E)

In a role-playing situation, the student can project or portray the personal and social sig-

necessary, the self-characteristics to be included on a resumé (C, Ap)

Given an identified social problem—e.g. air pollution, rehabilitation of drug users, the development of new uses for materials, creating by-products of fishery harvesting—the student can create a lattice of occupations at different levels which might contribute to resolving the problem. (The student may use as a reference the *Dictionary of Occupational Titles* or the *Occupational Outlook Handbook*) (C, E)

The student makes adjustments in planning, use of resources, and exploratory experiences necessary to maintain progress toward achievement of goals (A, O)

The student verbalizes feelings of competence and adequacy in those tasks which have relationships to his vocational preference (A, CCV)

The student is able to define the congruence between his aspirations, values, and preferred life style (C, E)

The student is able to use the ratings of him by teachers and peers to confirm his self-perceptions of competence or preference (C, Ap)

The student takes specific steps to implement a post-secondary educational plan (A, CCV)

The student takes specific steps to implement a post-secondary vocational preference (A, CCV)

The student demonstrates his ability to judge his choices in terms of situa-

Table 7   Sample Objectives to Facilitate Vocationalization at Different Educational
Levels (Continued)

ELEMENTARY SCHOOL	JUNIOR HIGH SCHOOL	SENIOR HIGH SCHOOL
	nificance that work might have in the lives of individuals at different levels within the occupational structure (C, E)	tions, issues, purposes, and consequences rather than in terms of rigidity or wishful thinking (A, CCV)
	The student can describe possible personal and environmental contingencies that could impinge upon his future decisions (C, E)	
	The student can differentiate between the several broad occupational areas in terms of (1) a potential satisfaction each might offer to him, (2) the nature of the work tasks performed, (3) the future impact technology could have on particular occupational areas, (4) the future demand for workers in broad occupational areas (C, E)	
	The student can demonstrate judgments about how different types of work can be better made to meet individual needs (A, O)	

Fundamentally, Table 7 and the discussion preceding it suggest that objectives must be defined in terms of student capability at different developmental levels, that the major reason for stating objectives is to identify specific accomplishments, or outcomes, in the course of student development from among the complex of elements that contribute to it, that different processes of vocational guidance can contribute to specific outcomes and that whether one uses tests, rating scales, or self-reports, it is necessary to evaluate student outcomes of the goals identified. In Table 7, the vocational guidance processes that are identified in particular objectives are only illustrative. Many others could be used in regard to particular objectives, but it is important to recognize the range of possibilities for use in a systems approach to vocational development.

A SAMPLE OF PROGRAM AND BEHAVIORAL DESCRIPTIONS COMBINED

In essence, the preceding materials suggest that objectives need to be posed at two levels—the program level and the behavioral level—the latter being examples of ways in which program objectives can be achieved in individual cases. Table 7 has shown how such behavioral descriptions might be cast. Finally, as different behavioral descriptions are subsumed under program objectives, it is necessary to consider alternative ways by which such objectives may be evaluated.

Table 8 shows how one school system has attempted to incorporate program objectives, behavioral descriptions, and evaluation methods in a longitudinal framework from elementary school through senior high school. It is presented here to illustrate how the input from this chapter can be incorporated into a systematic plan to guide the vocational guidance activities of a particular school district. Table 8 (pages 132-138) presents only three of the many possible program objectives for maximizing the interaction of vocational guidance and other facets of the educational process in the service of student vocationalization.

OBJECTIVES AND VOCATIONAL GUIDANCE AS TREATMENT

In this chapter little specific attention has been paid to objectives for vocational guidance as *treatment* for several reasons.

1. The application of objectives to whatever treatment approach is undertaken must be even more individualized than that for vocational guidance as a *stimulus* to vocationalization.

2. If objectives for vocationalization are first developed, then specific sets of these can be used to guide individual treatment. In other words, vocational guidance as treatment is really a process of moving the individual student through a particular aspect of vocationalization in a condensed time frame in which the specific focus is the individual's lack of information, inability to use information, general indecisiveness, or other behavioral deficit.

3. The availability of behavioral objectives relevant to vocationalization provides an inventory of possible emphases which in counselor-counselee exploration can help define the problems or the behavioral modification needed.

4. With objectives for vocationalization available as well as the activities to operationalize them, strategies for vocational guidance treatment can be selected from this pool of possibilities already existing within the school or community, in order to meet the needs of the particular student. Chapters 9 through 11 develop the concept of treatment more fully. Readers most concerned with this dimension may wish to turn to those chapters before continuing with those which immediately follow.

SUMMARY

This chapter has reviewed current approaches to designing program and behavioral objectives. It has presented current theoretical and research data which

Table 8 A Sample Longitudinal Program Showing Program Objectives K-12 and Their Respective Behavioral Objectives, Activities, and Evaluation Methods at Different Educational Levels

PROGRAM OBJECTIVES K-12*

1. Students should acquire vocabulary, knowledge, and facts for distinguishing among occupations, educational alternatives, and self-characteristics such as interests and aptitudes

2. Students should develop knowledge of their personal strengths and weaknesses and be able to understand the relationship of these characteristics to educational and vocational choices

3. Students should develop effective decision-making strategies and the skills for carrying them out

* Each of these program objectives is represented by pertinent behavioral objectives, activities to aid accomplishment of behavioral objectives, and evaluation methods of the elementary school, junior high school, and senior high school levels. Examples follow in that order.

ELEMENTARY SCHOOL

BEHAVIORAL OBJECTIVES

1. In a flannel board presentation, the student can label on the basis of their tools or clothing ten different types of workers found in his community

2. In an oral exercise, the student can identify at least six of the types of workers who contributed to building his school

3. The student can identify vocabulary words correctly as names of interests, aptitudes, or abilities

4. In an oral exercise, the student can state how different workers contribute to his well-being and the welfare of the community at large

5. From a list of fifty occupations, the student can identify those which are performed primarily indoors or outdoors

ACTIVITIES TO AID ACCOMPLISHMENT OF BEHAVIORAL OBJECTIVES

1. Class visits to police and fire stations, etc.

2. Class projects—bulletin-board displays of various occupations, exhibits of locally made products, etc.

3. Reading books on different occupations within the local community—grocer, minister, policeman, etc.

4. Films, filmstrips, and recordings illustrating various occupations of the community

5. Class plays depicting various work roles

6. Vocabulary exercises based on the world of work

7. Group guidance sessions with a trained counselor

8. Assembly programs dealing with the world of work

9. Use of occupational models

EVALUATION METHODS

1. Anecdotal records

2. Observed behavior

3. Role playing—various work roles or job situations

4. Teacher-built tests

5. Counseling contacts—individual or group

6. Vocational Knowledge Inventories—Vocational Maturity Inventories

7. Control and experimental group comparison

8. Frequency of use of occupational information resources

1. The student can role-play three occupations which most interest him

2. The student can identify the skills in which he feels most confident and role-play workers who might need these skills

3. The student can rank in order different educational alternatives according to the number of years of schooling required for each

4. The student can demonstrate how certain knowledge and skills acquired in different school subjects are applied in different work roles

5. The student can identify a particular skill which he enjoys performing and can list several types of work in which this skill might be needed

1. Daily feedback to the student on his progress in various school subjects through teacher comments, reactions, quizzes, tests, etc.

2. Feedback from standardized group testing —achievement, aptitude, interest

3. Peer reinforcement of individual strengths and weaknesses

4. Structured opportunities for students to try out a number of different roles, i.e. class leader, group member, secretary, treasurer, supervisor, etc.

5. Films, filmstrips, and readings on the performance of particular occupations, followed by discussion of such questions as:
   What particular competencies did this person demonstrate?
   How did they help him in performing his job?
   Could I do what this person is doing? Why or why not?

1. Anecdotal records

2. Case conferences with various staff members who come into contact with the student

3. Counseling contacts—individual or group

4. Observed behavior

5. Written responses such as essays or themes— "Things I'm Good At," "The Job I Would Like and Why," etc.

6. Self-ratings

1. From a list of ten reasons, the student can select the five which are the best ones for planning his time

2. From a list of occupations, the student can select one which he thinks he would like and give his reasons for making that particular selection

1. Role playing involving people in a problem situation

2. Having students plan a particular project and then analyzing the results

3. Working through illustrative case materials or games designed to identify decision factors and the alternative outcomes which result when different patterns of factors are combined

1. Observed behavior

2. Case conferences

3. Counseling contacts—individual and group

4. Gaming techniques

3. In a class project illustrating the importance of teamwork in different work settings, the student can decide on a contribution he can make to the project and discuss his reasons for his selection

4. The student can identify the advantages and disadvantages of five occupations

5. The student can identify the interdependence of five jobs within a particular field

4. Using films, filmstrips, and readings that view workers as problem solvers and asking the following questions:
What is the nature of the problem of living that this person routinely solves?
What special tools does this person use to solve problems?
What special facilities does this person need?

5. Studying community problems in class

JUNIOR HIGH SCHOOL

BEHAVIORAL OBJECTIVES

1. The student can place on a skilled-unskilled continuum twenty occupations about which he has read

2. Using the *Dictionary of Occupational Titles*, the student can identify ten occupations which are ranked highest in dealing with people, things, or data

3. After a field trip, the student can tell in his own words the differences in work conditions or procedures he can be observed in different parts of the plant

4. The student can differentiate between several broad occupational areas in terms of (1) a potential satisfaction each might offer him, (2) the nature of the work tasks performed, (3) the future impact technology could have on these particular areas, (4) the future demand for workers in these occupational areas

ACTIVITIES TO AID ACCOMPLISHMENT OF BEHAVIORAL OBJECTIVES

1. Student-planned field trips to observe workers in action

2. Reading books on various occupational fields (social, scientific, managerial, clerical, etc.—fiction and nonfiction)

3. Films, filmstrips, and recordings illustrating occupational fields

4. Use of subject matter in various classes to aid vocationalization—class discussions concerning the relationship of subject matter and selected careers, cluster concept or interdisciplinary integration based on a topic related to vocationalization such as the study of measurement

5. Exploratory work experiences

6. Counseling contacts—individual and group

7. Career Days—use of resource people in various occupations

EVALUATION METHODS

1. Individual interviews with a counselor

2. Book reports or themes in English class based on occupational readings

3. Group counseling

4. Custom-built tests

5. Inventories—questionnaires
Lee-Thorpe Occupational Interest Inventory
Brainard Occupational Preferences Inventory

6. Observed behavior

7. Frequency of use of occupational resources

1. The student can appraise accurately on a written profile his measured ability, achievement level, and current interests

2. The student can describe in essay form how knowledge and skills acquired in different subject-matter areas relate to performing different work roles

3. The student can identify, assess, and defend his analysis of possible steps he might take to minimize his limitations and maximize his assets

4. The student continuously explores and synthesizes the relationships between tentative choices and demonstrated abilities

5. The student verbally differentiates his self-characteristics (e.g. interests, values, abilities, personality traits) and expresses tentative occupational outlets for each

1. The student can describe possible personal and environmental contingencies that could impinge upon his future decisions

8. Assembly programs dealing with the world of work
9. Use of career-information kits

1. Daily feedback to the student on his progress in various school subjects through teacher comments, reactions, quizzes, tests, etc.

2. Individual interviews with a counselor (course selection, discussion of progress in various subjects, career planning, personal counseling)

3. Feedback from standardized group testing (achievement, aptitude, interest)

4. Use of films and filmstrips dealing with aptitudes, skills, interests, and their relationship to the world of work, i.e., "Who Are You?" "What Do You Like to Do?" (Filmstrips available from SRA)

5. Use of films and filmstrips pertaining to various occupational roles, followed by discussion of questions such as:
   What does it take to do that job?
   Would I like it?
   Do I have what it takes?

6. Model reinforcement group counseling
7. Exploratory work experiences

1. Counseling—group and individual with a focus on problem solving in areas with which students can identify: choosing curricula, choosing a college, how to study, etc.

1. Case conferences
2. Individual counseling contacts
   a. How the student sees himself
   b. How he uses information about himself to plan for his high school program—selection of courses
3. Written responses such as essays, themes, etc., dealing with how the individual sees himself. This could be incorporated in the regular English program
4. Observed behavior
5. Self-ratings

1. Observed behavior
2. Counseling
   a. Given proper assistance, the student is able to select appropriate high school courses or programs

2. The student can produce a list of resources or approaches available for learning about and assessing the world of work.

3. The student can identify in a gaming situation future decisions he must make in order to reach different goals

4. The student can tentatively assess in rank order the value to him of each of ten occupational clusters.

5. The student can identify, locate, and describe five directories listing post-secondary educational opportunities at college, junior college, and technical levels.

SENIOR HIGH SCHOOL

BEHAVIORAL OBJECTIVE

1. The student can differentiate between the major occupations that make up a broad occupational area or a job cluster in terms of:
   a. The amount and type of education needed for entrance
   b. The content, tools, setting, products, or services of these occupations
   c. Their value to society
   d. The probability that they will provide the type of life style he desires, their relationship to his interests and values

2. From a series of case studies about working conditions as they affect individuals with dif-

2. Study of societal problems within the framework of the regular classes—overpopulation, poverty, etc.

3. Discussion of films and filmstrips centering around the decision-making process—"What Do You Like to Do?" "Who Are You?"(SRA)

4. Role playing, sociodrama, or plays focusing upon particular content or problem areas

5. Self-directed learning programs which teach the individual the steps to be taken in effective problem solving (Magoon, 1969)

6. Gaming techniques—life career game (Boocock, 1967)

ACTIVITIES TO AID ACCOMPLISHMENT OF BEHAVIORAL OBJECTIVES

1. Reading current material on various occupations—occupational briefs, occupational monographs, specific job abstracts, Occupational Outlook Handbook

2. Films, filmstrips, and recordings on specific occupations or on how interests and abilities relate to specific occupations, etc.

3. Work experiences both in and out of school

4. Clubs or extracurricular activities such as Future Teachers, Future Nurses, etc.

5. Use of subject matter in various classes to facilitate vocationalization

b. Student identification of future decisions he must make in order to reach different goals. Assessment of possible steps he might take to minimize negative factors and maximize positive factors. Consideration of possible consequences.

3. Follow-up studies dealing with success in various high school courses which the student selected

4. Gaming situations

EVALUATION METHODS

1. Individual interviews with a counselor
2. Group counseling
3. Custom-built tests
4. Inventories—questionnaires
   a. Kuder Preference Record
   b. Strong Occupational Interest Blank
   c. Ohio Vocational Interest Survey
5. Observed behavior
6. Follow-up studies to determine frequency of use of occupational resources

ferent characteristics, the student can identify patterns of coping behavior and discuss their implications for him under similar circumstances.

3. The student is able to define the congruence between his aspirations, values, and preferred life style.

1. The student reality-tests his broad occupational preference by systematically relating it to his achievement in different courses, part-time work, extracurricular activities.

2. The student is able to use the ratings of him by teachers and peers to confirm his self-perceptions of competence or preference.

3. The student verbalizes feelings of competence and adequacy in those tasks which have relationship to his vocational preference.

6. Visits to a career resource center
7. Use of a computer-assisted occupational guidance program
8. Group guidance sessions with a trained counselor
9. Use of resource people in various occupations
10. Assembly programs pertaining to the world of work
11. Microfilm data systems—VIEW

1. Daily feedback to the student on his progress in various school subjects through teacher comments, reactions, quizzes, tests, etc.
2. Individual interviews with a counselor
   a. Course planning
   b. Progress in various subjects
   c. Career planning
   d. Personal counseling
3. Feedback from standardized group testing
   a. Achievement
   b. Aptitude
   c. Interest
4. Work experiences both outside and inside school
5. Simulated work sample techniques
6. Model reinforcement group counseling
7. Role playing of a job interview
8. Preparation of a resumé or job application

1. Case conferences
2. Individual counseling contacts
   a. How the student uses information about himself in his educational and vocation planning
   b. His view of himself compared to how others see him, his actual performance of specific tasks, etc.
3. Follow-up studies to determine student success in selected occupation or post-high school educational program
4. Resumé preparation as part of the English program
5. Self-ratings

1. The student produces an alternative plan for accomplishing his educational (occupational) goals if his first choice is not successfully implemented

2. The student considers five different categories of post-secondary education, chooses one, and defines his reasons for choosing it

3. The student develops a plan of access to his next step after high school, either educational or occupational, listing possible alternatives, whom to contact, application dates, capital investment necessary, the self-characteristics to be included in a resumé

4. The student takes specific steps to implement a post-secondary educational plan or post-secondary vocational preference

5. The student demonstrates his ability to judge his choices in terms of situations, issues, purposes, and consequences rather than in terms of rigidity or wishful thinking

6. The student executes plans to qualify for an entry-level position by choosing appropriate courses in high school

1. Counseling—group and individual with a focus on problem solving

2. Discussion of films and filmstrips centering around decision making—"Should You Go to College?" "High School Course Selection and Your Career," "Choosing Your Career" (Guidance Associates)

3. Use of a computer-assisted occupational guidance program (Impelliteri, 1968) or a manual system like Chronicle Guidance College View Deck

4. Gaming techniques—life career game

5. Role playing, sociodrama, or plays focusing on the decision-making process

6. Work experience

7. Many of the new science programs—ESCP (Earth Science Curriculum Project), Harvard Project, Physics, CHEM Study, BSCS (Biological Science Curriculum Study)—are formulated from a problem-solving approach

1. Follow-up studies to determine student success in selected occupation or post-high school educational program

2. Observed behavior

3. Counseling contacts

4. Gaming situations

The authors appreciate the assistance of Dr. Richard Warner, Director of Guidance and Counseling Services, and Mr. Richard Swails, Director, Career Resources Center, State College Area School District, Pennsylvania, in developing this information.

might serve as the content for such objectives. It has examined a rationale for a systems approach to the accomplishment of objectives at different educational levels that would move students toward increasingly complex forms of vocational maturity. And it has provided examples of different forms of objectives and illustrations of their use in local programs.

REFERENCES

Blocher, D. H.   Wanted: A science of human effectiveness.   *Personnel and Guidance Journal,* 1966, 44, 729–733.

Blocher, D. H., and Schutz, R. A.   Relationships among self-descriptions, occupational stereotypes, and vocational preferences.   *Journal of Counseling Psychology,* 1961, 8, 314–317.

*Bloom, B. S.; Engelhart, M. D.; Furst, E. J.; Hill, W. H.; and Krathwohl, D. R.   *Taxonomy of educational goals, Handbook I: Cognitive domain.*   New York: Longmans, Green, 1956.

Buehler, Charlotte. *Der menschliche Lebenslauf als psychologisches Problem.* Leipzig: Hizel, 1933.

Carter, H. D.   The development of vocational attitudes.   *Journal of Consulting Psychology,* 1940, 4, 185–191.

Clarke, R. Gelatt, H. B., and Levine, L.   A decision-making paradigm for local guidance research.   *Personnel and Guidance Journal,* 1965, 44, 40–51.

Cohen, A.   Sociological studies of occupations as a way of life.   *Personnel and Guidance Journal,* 1964, 43, 267–272.

*Cramer, S. H.; Herr, E. L.; Morris, C. N.; and Frantz, T. T.   *Research and the school counselor.*   Boston: Houghton Mifflin, 1970.

Crites, J. O.   A model for the measurement of vocational maturity.   *Journal of Counseling Psychology,* 1961, 8, 255–259.

*Crites, J. O.   Measurement of vocational maturity in adolescence: 1. Attitude test of the vocational development inventory.   *Psychological Monographs,* 1965, 79 (Whole No. 595).

Erikson, E. H.   *Childhood and society.*   2nd ed.   New York: W. W. Norton, 1963.

Flanagan, J. C.   Functional education for the seventies.   *Phi Delta Kappan,* 1967, 48, 27–32.

Galinsky, M. D., and Fast, Irene.   Vocational choice as a focus of the identity search.   *Journal of Counseling Psychology,* 1966, 13, 89–92.

Gesell, A.; Ilg, Frances L.; and Ames, Louise.   *Youth: The years from ten to sixteen.*   New York: Harper, 1956.

* Recommended for additional reading.

Ginzberg, E.; Ginsburg, S. W.; Axelrad, S.; and Herma, J. L. *Occupational choice.* New York: Columbia University Press, 1951.

Gonya, G. C. Dimensions of job perceptions. *Journal of Counseling Psychology,* 1961, 8, 305–312.

Gribbons, W. D., and Lohnes, P. R. *Emerging careers.* New York: Teachers College Press, 1968.

*Gronlund, N. E. *Stating behavioral objectives for classroom instruction.* New York: MacMillan, 1970.

Gross, E. A sociological approach to the analysis of preparation for work life. *Personnel and Guidance Journal,* 1967, 45, 416–423.

Grunes, Eilla. Looking at occupations. *Journal of Abnormal and Social Psychology,* 1957, 54, 86–92.

Havighurst, R. J. *Human development and education.* New York: Longmans, Green, 1953.

Havighurst, R. J. Youth in exploration and man emergent. In H. Borow (ed.) *Man in a world at work.* Boston: Houghton Mifflin, 1964.

Healy, C. C. Relation of occupational choice to the similarity between self-ratings and occupational ratings. *Journal of Counseling Psychology,* 1968, 15, 317–323.

Herr, E. L. Basic issues in research and evaluation of guidance services. *Counselor Education and Supervision,* 1964, 4, 9–16.

Herr, E. L. Unifying an entire system of education around a career development theme. Paper presented at the National Conference of Exemplary Programs and Projects Section of the 1968 Amendments to the Vocational Education Act, Atlanta, Ga., March, 1969.

Hershenson, D. B. Life-stage vocational development system. *Journal of Counseling Psychology,* 1968, 15, 23–30.

Hull, W. L. Evaluating pupil attainment of vocational tasks. *American Vocational Journal,* 1967, 42, 15–16.

Jordaan, J. P. Exploratory behavior: The formation of self and occupational concepts. In D. Super, R. Starishevsky, R. Matlin, and J. P. Jordaan (eds.) *Career development: Self-concept theory.* New York: College Entrance Examination Board, 1963, 42–78.

*Krathwohl, D. R. Stating objectives appropriately for program for curriculum and for instructional materials development. *The Journal of Teacher Education,* 1965, 16, 83–92.

*Krathwohl, D. R.; Bloom, B. S.; and Masia, B. B. *Taxonomy of educational objectives, Handbook II: The affective domain.* New York: David McKay, 1964.

*Mager, R. F. *Preparing instructional objectives.* Palo Alto, Calif.: Fearson, 1962.

*Metfessel, N. S.; Michael, W. B.; and Kirsner, D. A. Instrumentation of Bloom's and Krathwohl's taxonomies for the writing of educational objectives. *Psychology in the Schools*, 1969, 6, 227–231.

Mitzel, H. E. The impending instruction revolution. *Phi Delta Kappan*, 1970, 51, 434–439.

Nelson, A. G. Vocational maturity and client satisfaction. *Journal of Counseling Psychology*, 1956, 3, 254–256.

Norton, J. L. Current status of the measurement of vocational maturity. *Vocational Guidance Quarterly*, 1970, 18, 165–170.

O'Dea, J. D., and Zeran, F. R. Evaluating effects of counseling. *Personnel and Guidance Journal*, 1953, 31, 241–244.

O'Hara, R. P. Vocational self-concepts and high school achievement. *Vocational Guidance Quarterly*, 1966, 15, 106–112.

Oppenheimer, E. A. The relation between certain self constructs and occupational preferences. *Journal of Counseling Psychology*, 1966, 13, 191–197.

Pallone, N. J., and Hosinski, Marion. Reality-testing a vocational choice: Congruence between self-ideal and occupational percepts among student nurses. *Personnel and Guidance Journal*, 1967, 45, 666–670.

Patterson, C. H. Methodological problems in evaluation. *Personnel and Guidance Journal*, 1960, 39, 270–274.

Rothney, J. M., and Farwell, G. Research in guidance. *Review of Educational Research*, 1960, 30, 168–175.

Shane, H. G. A curriculum continuum: Possible trends in the 70's. *Phi Delta Kappan*, 1970, 51, 389–392.

*Shaw, M. C. *The function of theory in guidance programs.* Guidance Monograph Series I: Organization and administration. Boston: Houghton Mifflin, 1968.

Stratemeyer, Florence B.; Forkner, H. L.; McKim, Margaret; and Passow, A. W. *Developing a curriculum for modern living.* New York: Teachers College, Columbia University, 1957.

Strong, E. K., Jr. *Vocational interests eighteen years after college.* Minneapolis: University of Minnesota Press, 1955.

Strong, E. K., Jr. *Vocational interests of men and women.* Palo Alto, Calif.: Stanford University Press, 1943.

*Super, D. E. A theory of vocational development. *American Psychologist*, 1953, 8, 185–190.

Super, D. E. The dimension and measurement of vocational maturity. *Teachers College Record*, 1955, 57, 151–163.

Super, D. E. The natural history of a study of lives and vocations. *Perspectives on Education*, 1969, 2, 13–22 (b).

Super, D. E. *The psychology of careers.* New York: Harper & Row, 1957.

*Super, D. E. Vocational development in adolescence and early adulthood: Tasks and behaviors. In D. Super, R. Starishevsky, R. Matlin, and J. P. Jordaan (eds.) *Career development: Self-concept theory.* New York: College Entrance Examination Board, 1963, 79–95.

Super, D. E. Vocational development theory: Persons, positions, and processes. *The Counseling Psychologist,* 1969, 1, 2–9 (a).

Super, D. E.; Crites, J. O.; Hummel, R. C.; Moser, H. P.; Overstreet, Phoebe, L.; and Wormath, C. F. *Vocational development: A framework for research.* New York: Teachers College, Columbia University, 1957.

Super, D. E. Vocational adjustment: Implementing a self-concept. *Occupations,* 1951, 30, 88–92.

Super, D. E., and Overstreet, Phoebe L. *The vocational maturity of ninth-grade boys.* New York: Teachers College, Columbia University, 1960.

*Super, D. E.; Starishevsky, R.; Matlin, N.; and Jordaan, J. P. *Career development: Self-concept theory.* New York: College Entrance Examination Board, 1963.

*Tennyson, W. The psychology of developing competent personnel. *American Vocational Journal,* 1967, 42, 27–29.

*Tiedeman, D. V. Decision and vocational development: A paradigm and its implications. *Personnel and Guidance Journal,* 1961, 40, 15–20.

Tiedeman, D. V., and O'Hara, R. P. *Career development: Choice and adjustment.* New York: College Entrance Examination Board, 1963.

Tyler, R. W. *Basic principles of curriculum and instruction.* Chicago: University of Chicago Press, 1950.

Vriend, J. *The vocational maturity of inner-city boys.* Paper presented at the American Psychological Association Convention, San Francisco, 1968.

Weeks, C. *Career development for Philadelphia Public Schools.* Philadelphia: University City Science Center, 1967.

Westbrook, B. W., and Cunningham, J. W. The development and application of vocational maturity measures. *Vocational Guidance Quarterly,* 1970, 18, 171–175.

Wheeler, C. F., and Carnes, E. F. Relationships among self-concepts, ideal self-concepts, and stereotypes of probable and ideal vocational choices. *Journal of Counseling Psychology,* 1968, 15, 530–535.

Williams, R. L., and Cole, S. Self-concept and school adjustment. *Personnel and Guidance Journal,* 1968, 46, 478–481.

Zaccaria, J. S. Developmental tasks: Implications for the goals of guidance. *Personnel and Guidance Journal,* 1965, 44, 372–375.

SIX

VOCATIONAL GUIDANCE, VOCATIONALIZATION, AND THE ELEMENTARY SCHOOL

Children of elementary school age are fundamentally generalists in the sense that they typically are open to and interact with a broad range of stimuli and modes of behavior. In their unbridled enthusiasm and curiosity they have not yet been constrained by many of the social realities and stereotypes which plague and distort the perceptions of their older brothers and sisters and many of the adults with whom they identify. Yet they are vulnerable in the sense that attitudes and perceptions about life and their place in it are in a formative stage and are readily influenced by the environmental circumstances surrounding them.

Levels of aspiration, achievement motivation, and perceptions of self as worthy or inferior have their genesis in the early years of the family and of schooling. Here are the roots of the behavior which will manifest itself many years later under the labels of vocational identity and vocational commitment or, conversely, juvenile delinquency, early school leaving, and underemployability. If Luchin's primacy effect (1960) is a valid premise—that the information which is obtained first carries the most weight in ultimate decisions—then in the case of elementary-age children, education and vocational guidance must focus considerable attention on attitude development, decision processing, and self-awareness, as well as on knowledge of the broad characteristics and expectations of work. These are the ingredients of vocationalization, the foundations of vocationally mature behavior.

As elementary school children move through the elements of fantasy so characteristic of growth and learning at this life period, work is an important concern to them. By the time they have completed the first six grades of school, many of them have made tentative commitments to fields of work and to self-perceptions. The point here is not that the choices are irreversible or that this phenomenon is good or bad but rather that it occurs. Parker (1962), for example, found that fewer than 10 percent of 29,000 students in the seventh grade in Oklahoma described themselves as not having vocational goals. Simmons (1962) discovered that the elementary school children in his study exhibited a high degree of awareness of occupational prestige. Creason and Schilson (1970) found that of a sample of 121 sixth-graders who were asked about their vocational plans, none indicated that they had no vocational preferences, and only eight indicated that they did not know why they chose their particular preference.

In a related study, Davis, Hagan, and Strouf (1962) found that out of a sample of 116 twelve-year-olds, 60 percent had already made tentative choices. Nelson (1963) has demonstrated that as early as the third grade children have well-developed attitudes regarding occupations and levels of education and that as early as ages eight and nine children tend to reject some occupations as of no interest to them. In other words, whether or not education and vocational guidance respond to this fact, elementary school students have already begun to assimilate perceptions and preferences which may be wholesome and meaningful or distorted and ultimately harmful to aspirations and achievement.

One can speculate that not all the information and influences from which these preferences and perceptions are derived are appropriate or accurate. Frequently, unrealistic vocational plans are made at this level because of the emphasis in parental and community attitudes, as well as in textbooks, upon prestige fields, frequently defined as those requiring college preparation. Such an emphasis obscures consideration of the existence and significance of other occupations that employ large proportions of workers, offer equally potent gratifications, and are growing in demand (Lifton, 1959-60; Kowitz and Kowitz, 1959). Tennyson and Monnens (1965) found that only a small fraction of the many existing types of work are presented to children in elementary school texts; Clyse (1959) found a similarly biased picture of the world of work in basal readers.

This phenomenon is but one evidence of the fact that increasingly rigid walls have been erected between the preadolescent (and even the adolescent) and the vocational niches and educational options to which they must relate. In far too many instances, large segments of the student population—those from the culture of poverty and those from homes in which the children are economically favored but psychologically disadvantaged—have no systematic models of effective behavior or of vocational enthusiasm to which to relate and no environmental support for developing behavior which is personally and socially fulfilling. While it is probable that all children have some types of adult models with whom to identify, it is less probable that all children have models who display a range of adequate behavior and also a consistent vocational identity that provides a stable base for the child's self and vocational explorations. For many elementary school children, stultifying conditions and lack of vocational stimulation occur at a time when formation of attitudes and acquisition of the tools of the culture are in their seed stages.

The effects of a stagnated or unresponsive home or school life can be inferred from Hunt (1961, pp. 258-259). He points out that, according to Piaget,

> the rate of development is in substantial part, but certainly not wholly, a function of environmental circumstances. . . . the greater the variety of situations to which the child must accommodate his behavioral structures, the more differentiated and mobile they become. Thus, the more new things a child has seen and the more he has heard, the more things he is

interested in seeing and hearing. Moreover, the more variation in reality with which he has coped, the greater is his capacity for coping.

There is, then, the danger that when the educational process does not create flexibility of behavior and awareness of ways to obtain goals, the seeds of an anomic situation are inadvertently planted. If we hold up to children a carrot, a culturally valued goal, whether a prestige occupation or a certain level of educational attainment, without expanding equal energy in developing command of the means whereby children can obtain these goals, we have negated our concepts of individual difference and education as a process of development. Further, we are working from a narrow view of ability and propagating a restrictive definition of individual talent.

If education and vocational guidance are to form a partnership eventuating in a systematic approach to vocationalization, if they are to create the climate and the strategies basic to effective vocational behavior, they must be guided by the nature of the learner. As early as Comenius, through Dewey, and up to the more recent work of Piaget and Bruner among others, there has been support for the premise that children can grasp the success experiences and realities of the adult society and use these as bases for action if these concepts are translated into a language system and an experiential framework attuned to their levels of readiness.

Almy (1955, p. 200) states that the six-year-old lives more in a world of reality than in a world of fantasy. "He can understand a number of relationships in the physical world. . . . He knows his actions have consequences for other people and is more alert to their responses and feelings." Jersild (1951) too, has indicated that children at an early age have greater capacities for learning to meet, understand, and deal effectively with realities than has been assumed in psychological theories or in educational practice. This is not to suggest that elementary school children be robbed of their rich fantasy life or that childhood be so structured that it is a microcosm of the adult society but rather that fantasies operate from a base of knowledge, from stirring the imagination about the possible, instead of from overromanticism and stereotype.

PRINCIPLES OF VOCATIONAL GUIDANCE

Halverson (1970) has proposed several principles of vocational development in the elementary school based on characteristics of elementary school children. In paraphrased form they are:

1. The need for goals and objectives which are defined in terms of the educational needs and interests of students at this stage of development.

2. The consideration of vocational development within the larger concept of all the goals of the elementary school. It should not be a new, fragmented, or sepa-

rate piece of the curriculum but instead an integral part of goals already validated for elementary education.

3. Curriculum planning as it is influenced by vocational development should not be dominated by college-preparatory emphases.

4. Readiness for learning in terms of vocational development must take into account what has already been learned or experienced by the student, the projected goals that relate to the student's expressed or identified needs, and the general level of his intellectual, social, and emotional maturity.

5. Concrete experiences and learning must precede learning of the abstract. Younger children function more successfully in the concrete realm than in the abstract, with the readiness for abstractions increasing with age.

7. If goals for vocational development are adopted, experiences and activities must be sequenced in a manner to maximize the likelihood that students will achieve these goals.

8. There are many subject areas and activities in the elementary school which can be vocationalized. Thus vocational development can be integrated with other instructional goals.

Chapter 5 has identified some of the behavioral goals toward which vocationalization might be directed. Put simply, they are oriented toward developing preference or anticipation. At the elementary level, the concern is to orient the child to exploration and to provide him with the tools, models, and experiences through which exploration as an increasingly self-relevant process can lead to meaningful action.

Gysbers (1969) has labeled the learning phases which relate to vocational development and which span the elementary and early junior high school years thus: perceptualization, conceptualization, and generalization. The *perceptualization* phase focuses on the processes necessary for an individual to become aware of himself and his environment and to differentiate between them. In the *conceptualization* phase, essentially grades 4 to 6, concept formation is mediated by past experiences and is given direction by value systems, which are shaped by stereotypes, community and family input, and the breadth or narrowness of the student's knowledge base about work. The *generalization* phase is a period during which the student uses the already formed concepts about differences among people and occupations to generalize to wider radii in these domains.

As the individual moves through increasingly complex phases of awareness about himself and the world around him, he also moves from being a nonspecialized consumer of input to a more action-oriented investigator of selective types of input, and finally in the junior high school—senior high school years he becomes a candidate for further educational experiences or for a particularized work role. This general overview of vocational development roughly parallels the paradigms of Ginzberg, Super, Tiedeman and O'Hara, and Holland as reported in Chapter 2. The reader may wish to review these descriptions to solidify his thinking about them.

MANDATES OF VOCATIONAL GUIDANCE

On balance, the mandates of vocational guidance in the elementary grades are to provide experiences by which students can do the following (Smith, 1968, pp. 7-8; Thompson, 1969):

1. Expand their knowledge concerning the magnitude of the occupational world and the characteristics which differentiate the major foci of it.

2. Systematically diminish any distortion about the range of talents for which the occupational world provides outlets.

3. Understand the effects of change in relation to their own evolving characteristics as well as those of education and occupations.

4. Identify, understand, and interpret the significance of interests, capacities, and values as dominant factors in choice making and in the ways by which different life options can be described.

5. Acquire awareness of the influence of continuing education upon work and one's life style.

6. Establish relationships between educational opportunities and occupational outcomes.

7. Acquire decision-making skills as these find their genesis in an attitude of planfulness.

8. See themselves as value-determining agents capable of affecting their future rather than being victimized by it.

9. Develop the concept of flexibility in the work role.

10. Develop a wide base of experience regarding occupations rather than place emphasis upon early decision making.

11. Understand the importance of effective use of leisure time.

Dinkmeyer (1968, p. 309) would order and define these objectives somewhat differently.

   1. To increase the child's understanding of his abilities.

   2. To provide opportunity for the child's exploration of the aptitude, interest, and personality factors necessary on certain jobs.

   3. To make the child aware that his self-image will determine his choice of work and way of life.

4. To help children develop realistic attitudes and methods in dealing with school achievement as an aspect of vocation.

5. To help pupils understand that rapid changes taking place in the world of work will necessitate advanced training.

6. To help the child understand that all legitimate occupations are worthwhile.

These mandates are in line with the following four emphases arrived at by Hill (1969, pp. 8-9) through vocational-development research which have special significance for the educational experiences of elementary-age children:

1. The processes of growing up and meeting the developmental tasks of childhood entail many understandings and attitudes that have occupational significance and meaning.

2. The process of identification with adult models who have a strong effect upon the development of their sense of occupational identity begins early in life and persists throughout the elementary school period.

3. The child develops conceptions of himself, and these self-concepts have a profound effect upon his vocational development.

4. The understandings and attitudes, the conceptions of self, the adaptability and creativity needed in the processes of educational and vocational planning all are strongly influenced by the child's parents and by his home relationships.

Hill's observations and those which precede them make one point very clear. If vocational guidance in the elementary schools is to make a difference, simply periodically providing occupational units in which students are told about work will not do the job. A broad and varying range of activities will have to be mounted to meet the diverse needs of students at the time of their initial forays into vocational development. Parents need to be involved; and when this is not possible, some children will need to have provided for them adult occupational models with whom they can identify. Rather than be passive onlookers, counselors will have to be activists, initiating and coordinating experiences for different children both within the educational process and outside it. Educational materials and the attitudes of teachers will need to be influenced to contribute to vocationalization.

The involvement of parents in this process is not limited to their role as the prime source of influence on their child's occupational perceptions at the time he begins school. This is obviously true. Stopping with this fact assumes that because the parents have already influenced positively or negatively the child's perceptions of occupations or provided him with a meaningful or less meaningful role model, they have no further part in the process. Rather, at the elementary school level particularly, counselors should develop strategies to help parents ask the following questions and find answers to them: Why career guidance? When does career development begin? Is home environment related to career development? When should my child begin to explore occupations? What are schools and employment agencies doing in this field? How much education will my child need to succeed in a vocation? Should a parent ever choose an occupation for his child? Should a parent encourage his child to work part time while in high school? Do young people give sufficient thought to the choice of an occupation (Knapp and Bedford, 1967)? By using such a strategy, counselors are extending their influence and their expertise in ways which make parents collaborators rather than isolates in the guidance process and in the education of their children.

STRATEGIES OF VOCATIONAL GUIDANCE

As indicated in Chapter 5, objectives should precede functions and should be cast in the form of behavioral descriptions so that the counselor or teacher can evaluate whether the student has met the objectives specified for him. Assuming for the moment that one has selected from Chapter 5—or has developed on his own—objectives pertinent to his school setting and the characteristics of the students, what functional options are available to accomplish the objectives? Several suggestions have already been made in this chapter. The strategies should be concrete rather than abstract, at least in grades 1 through 3; they should involve action rather than simply verbalization; they should use multimedia approaches to the degree possible.

O'Hara (1968) adds several other observations which can be used to guide the development of functions for fostering vocationalization. First, the characteristics of vocational development discussed in this book are largely "acquired needs" pertinent to students in the United States and other developed nations of the world but are not necessarily part of the developmental needs of children in other cultures. Therefore, one must establish a readiness for vocational development. One way to do this is to reinforce—by social approval from teachers, counselors, and parents—those behaviors of children which are oriented to consideration of choices, information seeking, and participation in exploratory activities. If some teachers provide these experiences and encourage children to participate in or exhibit vocational development while other teachers convey by attitude or behavior that these things are unimportant, many students are likely not to persist in the behavior. For example, if an elementary school child is trying in his own way to raise questions about work or choice making but is constantly patted on the head and told not to worry about those things now, he is not likely to continue to consider them important. If they were, this teacher whom he admires would deal with them.

Second, since many of the vocational problems to which early efforts at vocationalization are directed are remote, we must provide direct or simulated experiences in which children can make decisions and experience their consequences. This may be done by permitting children to plan a particular project and then analyzing the results, or by working through illustrative case materials or games designed to identify decision factors and the alternative outcomes of different patterns of factors. From such immediate experiences, bridges are built from the academic world to the world of work. Further, ways must be found to convert daily intellectual problems into vocational problems and thus give children opportunity to learn a variety of responses to problem-solving circumstances. Several suggestions in this regard are presented in the chapter on information on vocational guidance.

Third, the child must be helped to develop cues by which he can distinguish those concepts and ideas that are important to him from those that are not. He also needs to have translated into notions he can understand such concepts as relative importance, compromise, irreversibility, synthesis, and developmental process.

Fourth, in order to differentiate or integrate self-characteristics or characteristics of the vocational world, he must be assisted to develop a broad repertoire of pertinent words—the language of vocations. Without them the student lacks the tools for manipulating and symbolizing the world as it pertains to him.

Hunt (1970) also has stressed the importance of symbolization but in concert with the student's ability to deal with the physical world, the social world, and the inner world as it relates to vocational development. She sees each of these three abilities as competencies which children must acquire as foundations for vocational development. In extending this line of reasoning, she recommends that children study workers primarily as problem-solvers. Regardless of whether the medium used to help students develop an understanding of different occupations is a field trip, demonstration, film, or reading, the questions students should be encouraged to ask are:

1. What is the nature of the problem of living that this person routinely solves?
2. What is the nature of this person's competencies?
3. What special tools does this person use for solving problems?
4. What special facilities does this person need?
5. Could I do what this person is doing?

What is implicit in the positions of O'Hara and Hunt is made explicit in Arbuckle's position (1963-64) that people and work are irrevocably related. Thus occupational information is valuable to the degree that it can diminish an outside-the-person focus and stimulate the child's learning and exploration as a part of seeing himself in process, as having and exhibiting freedom of choice. This emphasis upon people as workers and as problem-solvers also reinforces for the elementary school child the importance of "me" and my "characteristics" as primary influences upon "my future."

SEQUENCING VOCATIONAL GUIDANCE EXPERIENCES

Halverson's observations, previously cited, indicate the importance of sequencing vocationalization experiences from the concrete to the increasingly abstract. The activities that children in first grade are exposed to should differ from those that children in the sixth grade are exposed to, even though the themes or the attitudes to be developed remain constant. In considering sequencing, one must also consider sexual differences as these affect knowledge about or realistic attitudes toward vocational development. O'Hara (1962) has demonstrated that girls in grades 4 to 6 have a more realistic understanding of work than do boys, that they exhibit fewer fantasy choices, and are more influenced by values and interests; and that boys in grade 6 are more realistic than boys in grade 4 and are influenced by values as well as interests.

Norris (1963, p. 56) has suggested sequencing vocational guidance in the elementary schools, particularly occupational information, as follows:

Kindergarten. The child learns about the work activities of his mother, his father, and other members of his household.

Grade 1. The child learns about work in his immediate environment—his home, school, and neighborhood.

Grade 2. The child learns about community helpers who serve him as well as about familiar stores and businesses in the neighborhood.

Grade 3. The child studies the expanding community. Emphasis is placed upon transportation, communication, and other major industries.

Grade 4. The child learns about the world of work at the state level including main industries of the state.

Grade 5. The child's studies broaden to cover the industrial life of the nation. Major industries of the various sections of the United States are selected.

Grade 6. The child's program is expanded to include the entire western hemisphere. Life in Canada and in South and Central America is contrasted with life in the United States.

Bank (1969, p. 285) has provided a derivation of this grade-level theme of Norris by focusing on vocational role models exemplifying particular emphases. Examples of his approach include the following:

Kindergarten   *School role—Models*   *Principal*
                                                              Teacher
                                                              School secretary
                                                              University professor

First Grade	*Community role—Models who help feed us*	Grocer Milkman Waitress
Second Grade	*Community role—Models who protect our health*	Dentist Nurse's aide Doctor
	Models who protect our health —personal hygiene	Barber Beauty operator
Third Grade	*Models who provide shelter*	Plumber Building cleaner
	Models who protect us	Lawyer Fireman Policeman
Fourth Grade	*Models who provide transportation*	Gas station manager Bus driver Airline stewardess
Fifth Grade	*Models who provide communication*	Postman Printer Photo-journalist
Sixth Grade	*Models who provide for business*	Banker Office secretary Salesclerk

Both these conceptions show an implicit affinity for the developing radius of the interests of elementary school students and their increasing capacity for abstractions. They do not, however, suggest what kind of content to include or what emphases would help impart a knowledge of industrial characteristics or of the factors which distinguish industries. Kaback (1960) has reported on some strategies to accomplish the latter. In a first-grade project, a teacher used a broken toy chair to stimulate consideration of work and tools. After some discussion, the children decided that a broken chair leg required a carpenter. Then they decided on the tools, processes, and materials needed to repair the chair leg: "(1) Remove the broken piece of wood, (2) cut a new piece of wood, (3) nail the new piece of wood onto the chair" (p. 56). The children then went to the woodworking shop and accomplished this task. Following the repair job, they discussed the qualities needed to perform a good job. They then discussed other work activities of a carpenter. From this point they moved into discussions of the work done by their parents. Finally, they analyzed the work activities of these different occupations in terms of knowledge of the alphabet (filing), physical capacities (bending, sweeping), mental expectations (he needs to know what to do next). Such activities, with a little ingenuity, can be expanded in many different ways to provide impetus to vocationalization.

In a second-grade project, the theme was "What I Would Like to Do When I Grow Up." The teacher's objectives were to help students gain a respect for all types of work and to understand how various workers served the children themselves. Again, the children started with the occupations of their parents. Parents were interviewed. The children wrote stories about the occupations. Finally, the children role-played various occupational activities. All these student behaviors were performed under the aegis of the language arts curriculum. In the mathematics classes, students examined selected incomes and created sample budgets apportioning monies for training or educational costs, dues, work materials, etc.

In conjunction with the activities described, students also developed a newspaper that ran descriptions of occupations, their characteristics, and their requirements. Students also discussed their preferences for different occupations and the reasons for these choices. As the year progressed, students abstracted from the community newspaper, items relating to the occupations described in the class newspaper, starting an occupational file. At the same time they were learning about concepts like pride in workmanship, the interdependence of occupations, and respect for a wide range of work tasks.

In a fourth-grade project, the students moved beyond the work of their parents to other occupations in the community. They interviewed bus drivers, elevator operators, salesclerks. As they were considering the work of the bricklayer, carpenter, plumber, electrician, painter, they visited a construction site to see how these occupations interrelated and how different occupations required different tools or skills.

Hunt (1970) has argued that from kindergarten through the third grade, the emphasis should be more on manipulative direct experience than on vicarious experience. In line with Gysbers' conception of the perceptualization phase, the emphasis at these grade levels is on, Who am I? What can I do? rather than, What do others do for me or tell me about? This also means that the tools or the media that are made available in these experiences must be physically manageable. Besides helping children gain an understanding about work, it is equally important that they gain perceptions of themselves as successful with these tools or media. At the fourth- to sixth-grade levels, Hunt suggests that although concrete, direct experiences are still vital, the array of tools and media needs to be expanded in such a way as to provide more and more problem-solving challenges requiring exploration of information and acquisition of basic skills.

Hackett (1966, p. 58) has proposed bringing into the elementary school many of the elements traditionally offered in industrial arts in grades 7 through 9 in order to develop concepts such as:

1. *Man is a tool-making and tool-using animal.*

2. *Man has civilized himself through technology.*

3. *We live in an industrial-technological culture.*

4. *Technology improves man's standard of living.*

5. *Technology produces change.*

6. *Man works to be happy, useful, and successful.*

7. *All work has dignity.*

It is Hackett's contention that neither industrial arts nor any other elementary school subject can independently provide for the incorporation of these concepts into the perceptions of elementary school children. Rather, he contends that the three R's should be seen as tools for solving problems faced by workers in a variety of occupational activities. Manufactured products and the processes by which they are made would be used to illustrate the application of facts and principles now typically conceived to be within compartmentalized subject areas. Pupils might plan and prepare demonstrations and artistic displays of objects and information from different industries. They might construct models of different industrial devices to illustrate principles of communication or transportation, thus expanding the medium through which learning transpires, from paper and pencils to tools and materials.

Finally, Hackett maintains that unless the school program at the elementary level "accurately reflects work as part of our culture, it cannot purport to transmit our culture." In his view, "The specific occupations that boys and girls choose each day while in their early years are relatively unimportant; the significant thing is that they do choose occupations . . . something tangible that gives meaning to and reason for their activity" (p. 58). Broad areas of activity indigenous to industrial arts which could be used as organizing themes include: manufacturing, power, construction, transportation, services, communication, research, and management.

What Hackett does not include in this conception is the importance of the arts and humanities as occupations or cultural tools. Without reflecting an understanding of these opportunities, one is placing too much emphasis on machine technology and "hard science" as ends in themselves. Certainly, balancing what Hackett recommends with an emphasis on opportunities in the fine arts, the theater, and the literary world would also serve to bridge thought to a consideration of the evolving trends on use of leisure time. For additional emphasis on this point note the work of Lockwood, Smith, and Trezise (1968) and Gilbert (1966) in the chapter on the junior high school.

Other types of input to topics appropriate to the elementary school level stem from sociological views of work life. For example, as earlier noted, Gross (1967) has suggested that preparation for work life involves four dimensions: (1) preparation for life in an organization, involving authority, security quests, impersonality, routine, conflict, mobility, and demotion; (2) preparation for a set of role relationships; (3) preparation for a level of consumption, involving a certain style of life; and (4) preparation for an occupational career, involving changes in the nature of jobs, and different types of jobs depending on the position in the life cycle. Such topical areas lend themselves to language arts, social studies, science, geography, and, in fact, virtually any elementary school endeavor. Such themes are not confined to the elementary school population but could create organizing concepts which spiral in increasing complexity throughout the educational continuum, being elaborated upon in junior and senior high school.

Blocher (1966), too, has discussed the importance of social roles in developing human effectiveness. Students could examine social roles and the characteristics important to them such as leadership, creative or original contributions, supervision, helping relationships, and unusual levels of accomplishment. The study of social roles could be extended to occupational fields and levels of responsibility as well as to such areas as coping behaviors and their implications for growth and development.

One systematic approach to vocational development in the elementary schools which focuses on helping children in inner-city schools gain a comprehensive orientation to the world of work and of education is the Developmental Career Guidance Project located in Detroit. This project is a team effort conducted in individual pilot schools. Each school has a guidance consultant, a career community aide, and student assistants. Together with the school principal, the project staff directors, and special consultants, this team directs its efforts to the following project goals (Leonard, p. 3, undated):

1. To broaden the perceptual field of inner-city youth regarding occupations and opportunities.

2. To help overcome their lack of planning for the future. To help them make realistic plans for their future. Since so many youngsters desire immediate gratification of their needs, this is a difficult task. Furthermore, inner-city youth must be told the truth about objectives so they can plan realistically.

3. To provide better role models with whom inner-city youth can readily identify.

The school personnel who become involved in the project participate in a preliminary workshop, the objectives of which are (p. 4):

1. To stimulate participants to develop a total guidance program in their own school.

2. To prepare them to serve as an advisory committee to the guidance consultants placed in each school.

3. To broaden participants' knowledge of the community by visiting a variety of community agencies, employers, and post–high school educational institutions.

4. To help participants better understand and communicate with inner-city youth.

5. To acquaint participants with the present employment outlook.

Although only preliminary data are available for the period from January, 1965, through January, 1968, the results of contrasting students in experimental schools with those in control schools indicate the following (Leonard, p. 15, undated):

1. The level of aspiration of students in experimental schools increased significantly more than did that of students in control schools.

2. Students in experimental schools did seem to show more growth in regard to occupational knowledge and planning than students in control schools.

3. The students in experimental schools did seem to re-examine their value structure significantly more than students in control schools.

4. Students in experimental schools did show a more acceptable attitude toward counselors at the end of the project's first year of operation than did students in control schools. Interestingly, there did not seem to be a change in perception of school.

5. Students in experimental schools did perceive a greater need for professional help at the end of the project's first year than previously.

The activities which were utilized in this concentrated effort to aid vocational development include individual counseling, group counseling, dissemination of information in individual classes, field trips, speakers, direct work with parent groups as well as liaison and coordination with community agencies and neighborhood organizations.

Thus the results of the Detroit project indicate that a planned, systematic effort, using multimedia approaches and diverse personnel and nonpersonnel resources, does influence the vocational development of students in the elementary and junior high schools in positive ways.

The same results have also been demonstrated in another, less concentrated effort. In two socioeconomically different elementary schools, Goff (1967) showed that measurable increments in vocational knowledge, in level of occupational aspiration, and in realism of occupational choice can be attained through a planned vocational guidance program. Stress was placed upon developing a respect for all levels of human endeavor, gaining an understanding of personal strengths and limitations, and acquiring satisfaction in learning tasks themselves. Children were asked to work through the making of occupational choices for the purposes of testing and discussion as well as for reinforcement of the idea that early and specific choices were not expected at the elementary school levels.

In an attempt to determine whether primary-grade children could gain occupational awareness important to vocational attitude and value formation, Wellington and Olechowski (1966) found that eight-year-old youngsters could: develop a respect for other people, the work they do, and the contributions they make in providing production and services for everyone; understand that occupations have advantages and disadvantages for the worker; understand some of the interdependent relationships of workers. The group of students with whom Wellington and Olechowski worked was first exposed to a unit of study entitled "Shelter." The building industry and the variety of workers in it were explored. Initial indications were that at the conclusion of this unit youngsters did not yet understand the workers' roles and functions. Follow-up discussions then focused on methods of increasing the children's understanding. The students were assigned to interview a variety of workers. With the assistance of the teacher and the counselor, they developed questions to ask in the interviews. The interviews and the class discussions which followed were taped. After the children listened to the tapes and completed their discussions concerning the building industry and its workers, there was a significant increase in their understanding and awareness of working people and their work. The important point is that the initial lack of increased student awareness was a result of faulty techniques, not a lack of student ability to grasp the concept.

Another creative project designed to spur vocational development in grades 5, 6, and 7 was developed by personnel of the Abington School District (1967-68) in Pennsylvania. The objectives of this project were:

1. To develop learning experiences which would actively involve the students in grades 5, 6, and 7 in processes which are useful in making career choices.

2. To utilize the techniques of simulation, gaming, role-playing, decision-making, and dramatics in designing the learning experiences.

3. To develop materials and techniques which could be effectively used by teachers or counselors in conjunction with the language arts and social studies programs and in guidance activities.

4. To develop materials which would enable the counselor to participate with the students and teachers in joint activities.

5. To determine the students' interests in studying the area of careers and the processes of career selection.

In designing this project and the activities by which to accomplish the objectives, every effort was made to reveal the processes through which one can arrive at a career decision. Committees of teachers, administrators, and counselors were formed to examine the characteristics of the students to be served, ways of developing appropriate activities, and simplified procedures to administer the activities. The activities generated drew upon the resources of the school, home, and community. For each of the grade levels themes were developed which paralleled the expected interests, concept of change, and values. For example, at grade 5, the theme was "How Our Interests Develop and Their Importance in Our Lives." Sessions were held to develop sequentially the concept of interests and to help students relate this concept to their personal characteristics. The sessions were also developed in ways which would lead to their integration in the language arts curriculum and contribute to student development in spoken and written communications. The activities that were devised to develop the concept of interests were:

1. A card game which demonstrated how interests develop.

2. Short stories based upon characters with whom students could readily identify.

3. An interest inventory designed to obtain a profile of the interests of students through media relevant to their age level.

4. An open-ended play illustrating the influence of interests on personal relationships, which provided students the opportunity to write the second act showing the outcome of the situation.

5. A taped series of role-played interviews with various workers in which the students were to determine the occupation from the interests described by the person interviewed.

In grades 6 and 7, other activities were created to foster awareness of change, values, educational and occupational relationships, and similar concepts as these interacted with student development. In grade 6, all the activities developed were geared to the theme "Changes Which Are Taking Place, Decisions Which Are Made, and How They Affect Our Lives." The theme of grade 7 was "Our Values—How They Influence Our Decisions and Our Lives." In the latter two instances, slides, fimstrips, actual examples of the evaluation of tools, role playing, occupational checklists, occupational representatives, skits, field trips, values checklists, and case studies were employed to meet particular project purposes.

Like the results obtained in the other projects described, students reported overwhelmingly that they liked the activities and wished to have more of them. Teachers and principals also reported enthusiasm for the project. Parents provided considerable feedback about their interest in and support of the project even though this input was not formally solicited. The preliminary data on changes in the students evidenced considerable growth in knowledge about themselves and in interests, educational and occupational alternatives, and change. It was found that the concept of values was more difficult than the other themes for many of the sixth-grade students. It was also found that students' responses to or growth from the project was unrelated to their socioeconomic strata—low, middle, upper.

All the projects reviewed here, although derived from somewhat different sets of objectives since these were tailored to the characteristics of the children in the particular settings, give evidence of being responsive to the guidelines pervading this chapter. Their activities are also congruent with Kaback's (1966, p. 167) observation, "The younger the child the greater the interest in the actual job performance itself. Most children are natural born actors; they want to act out in order to understand what it feels like to be a carpenter or a ballplayer."

There are several important implications in Kaback's statement. First—in terms of the media of vocational development—dramatizations, role playing, and simulation each has potential for allowing children figuratively to project themselves into the characteristics of roles important to differences in occupations. An example of this is Cook's (1968) twenty-five-minute operetta, *When I Grow Up*. It is used from kindergarten to third grade to help children establish an awareness of different work roles and to help in self-concept development. Second, it is possible to help students identify with attainable vocations represented in their immediate neighborhoods or community. Finally, if children base their occupational preferences on job performance itself, this is a prime time to introduce them to the relationships between interests and occupational areas.

There are other strategies of vocational guidance in the elementary school which have not yet been identified in this chapter but also deserve mention. For example, Laramore and Thompson (1970) have suggested encouraging students to dream about what they would like to do as an adult and then pantomime the job, letting other students guess who they are and what they are doing. Other suggestions they provide include (pp. 263-264):

1. Have students discuss their hobbies and attempt to relate them to occupations.

2. Have upper-grade, elementary school children discuss any part-time jobs which they hold around the home or in the community with regard to what they like, the satisfactions they get, or how they spend the money obtained.

3. Have students write a resumé of their own skills (weeding, cutting grass, baby-sitting, ironing) and have them discuss how they might sell these skills to prospective employers in their neighborhood.

BEHAVIORAL DESCRIPTIONS

It is important to note, if only briefly, that none of the activities or projects discussed in this chapter used behaviorally defined objectives as described in Chapter 5. Without them, it is very difficult to evaluate how individual children are coping with specific objectives. The only alternative the counselor or teacher has under these conditions is to evaluate in a rather global way the progress of groups of students in meeting the objectives. While such group evaluative efforts are important, they provide little opportunity to detect individual differences in readiness for particular vocationalization experiences or individual progress in mastering these experiences. Further, it is unlikely that a viable systems approach with feedback that develops and affirms each child's movement through the vocationalization tasks important to him will result.

SUMMARY

This chapter has described an array of themes and practices which can be used in the elementary school as a base for vocationalization. Attention has been given to the characteristics of development manifested by elementary age children, and these characteristics have been set forth as the criteria to which vocational guidance efforts must be attuned. The major themes discussed were the importance of the elementary school as a shaper of attitudes toward the self and toward different aspects of the environment, as well as the need individual students have to develop a vocabulary by which they can distinguish environmental characteristics and important aspects of their evolving self.

REFERENCES

Abington School District.   *Career development activities, Grades V, VI, VII.*   Abington, Pa.: District, 1967–68.

Almy, Millie.   *Child development.*   New York: Henry Holt, 1955.

Bank, I. M.   Children explore careerland through vocational role models.   *Vocational Guidance Quarterly,* 1969, 17, 284–289.

Blocher, D. R.   Wanted: A science of human effectiveness.   *Personnel and Guidance Journal,* 1966, 44, 729–733.

Clyse, Juanita.   What do readers teach about jobs?   *Elementary School Journal,* 1959, 59, 456–460.

*Cook, H. E.   Vocational guidance materials: A survey for teachers.   *American Vocational Journal,* 1968, 13, 25–28.

*Creason, F., and Schilson, D. L.   Occupational concerns of sixth-grade children.   *Vocational Guidance Quarterly,* 1970, 18, 219–224.

Davis, P. A.; Hagen, Nellie; and Strouf, Judie.   Occupational choice of twelve-year-olds.   *Personnel and Guidance Journal,* 1962, 40, 628–629.

Dinkmeyer, D. C.   *Guidance and counseling in the elementary school: Readings in theory and practice.*   New York: Holt, Rinehart and Winston, 1968.

*Gilbert, H. G.   *Children study American industry.*   Dubuque, Iowa: Wm. C. Brown, 1966.

* Recommended for additional reading.

Goff, W. H.   Vocational guidance in elementary schools: A report of Project P.A.C.E.   Paper presented at the American Vocational Association Convention, Cleveland, Ohio, Dec., 1967. Mimeographed.

Gross, E.   A sociological approach to the analysis of preparation for work life. *Personnel and Guidance Journal,* 1967, 45, 416–423.

Gysbers, N.   Elements of a model for promoting career development in elementary and junior high school.   Paper presented at National Conference on Exemplary Programs and Projects Section of the Vocational Education Act, Amendments of 1968, Atlanta, Ga., March, 1969.

Hackett, D. F.   Industrial element for the elementary school.   *School Shop,* 1966, 25, 58–62.

Halverson, P. M.   A rationale for a career development program in the elementary school.   Paper presented to the Program Development Committee of the Cobb County, Ga., Schools, Jan., 1970.   Mimeographed.

*Hansen, Lorraine Sundal.   *Career guidance practices in school and community.* Washington, D. C.: National Vocational Guidance Association, 1970.   (This book is equally appropriate for the next two chapters.)

Hill, G. E.   Perspectives on the guidance of young children: Can we afford to delay vocational guidance?   Paper presented at the Ninth Annual All-Ohio Elementary Guidance Conference, Columbus, Nov., 1969.

Hunt, Elizabeth E.   Career development K-6; A background paper of initial suggestions.   Paper presented to the Program Development Committee of the Cobb County, Ga., Schools, Jan., 1970.   Mimeographed.

Hunt, J. McV.   *Intelligence and experience.*   New York: Ronald Press, 1961.

Jersild, A. T.   Self-understanding in childhood and adolescence.   *American Psychologist,* 1951, 6, 122–126.

Kaback, Goldie R.   Occupational information for groups of elementary school children.   *Vocational Guidance Quarterly,* 1966, 14, 163–168.

Kaback, Goldie R.   Occupational information in elementary education.   *Vocational Guidance Quarterly,* 1960, 9, 55–59.

*Knapp, D. L.; and Bedford, J. H.   *The parent's role in career development.* Washington, D. C.: National Vocational Guidance Association, 1967.

Kowitz, G. T., and Kowitz, N.   *Guidance in the elementary classroom.*   New York: McGraw-Hill, 1959.

*Laramore, D., and Thompson, J.   Career experiences appropriate to elementary school grades.   *The School Counselor,* 1970, 17, 262–263.

Leonard, G. E.   Career guidance for inner-city youth in action: The developmental guidance project.   Detroit: Wayne State University (undated). Mimeographed.

Lifton, W. M.   Vocational guidance in the elementary school.   *Vocational Guidance Quarterly,* 1959–1960, 8, 79–81.

Luchins, A. S.   Influences of experiences with conflicting information and reactions to subsequent conflicting information.   *Journal of Social Psychology,* 1960, 5, 367–385.

Nelson, R.   Knowledge and interest concerning sixteen occupations among elementary and secondary students.   *Educational and Psychological Measurement,* 1963, 23, 741–754.

*Norris, Willa.   *Occupational information in the elementary school.*   Chicago: Science Research Associates, 1963.

*O'Hara, R. P.   A theoretical foundation for the use of occupational information in guidance.   *Personnel and Guidance Journal,* 1968, 46, 636-640.

O'Hara, R. P.   The roots of careers.   *Elementary School Journal,* 1962, 62, 277–280.

*Parker, H. J.   29,000 seventh-graders have made occupational choices.   *Vocational Guidance Quarterly,* 1970, 18, 219–224.

Simmons, D.   Children's ranking of occupational prestige.   *Personnel and Guidance Journal,* 1962, 41, 332–336.

Smith, E. D.   The vocational aspects of guidance in the elementary school.   Harrisburg: Pennsylvania Department of Education, 1968. Mimeographed.

Tennyson, W., and Monnens, L.   The world of work through elementary readers.   *Vocational Guidance Quarterly,* 1963–1964, 12, 85–88.

Thompson, J. M.   Career development in the elementary school: Rationale and implications for elementary school counselors.   *The School Counselor,* 1969, 16, 208–209.

Wellington, J. A., and Olechowski, Nan.   Attitudes toward the world of work in elementary school.   *Vocational Guidance Quarterly,* 1966, 14, 160–162.

SEVEN

VOCATIONAL GUIDANCE, VOCATIONALIZATION, AND THE JUNIOR HIGH SCHOOL

When one examines the guidance needs and characteristics of students at separate educational levels—elementary, junior high school, and senior high school —it is tempting to declare that one of these is more critical than another. Yet the essence of vocational development, broadly conceived, is that each of these life stages demands that students cope with a different set of emphases within an evolving consciousness of self-characteristics and of the life options to which they must relate these characteristics. In other words, vocationalization as mediated through the educational process must be responsive to the developmental tasks which surface as children mature, as well as to the characteristics of the institutions which influence their mastery of these developmental tasks.

Johnson, Busacker, and Bowman (1961, p. ix) contend:

Neither academically inclined students nor any others can excel in their studies or realize their full potentials later unless, at the junior high school level, they—

1. attain a fairly realistic understanding of themselves;

2. make decisions about their high school programs on bases other than misinformation, personal whim, or the choices of friends;

3. are spared the experience of floundering aimlessly for lack of thought regarding even tentative vocational goals;

4. are minimally distracted by problems of growth and development or handicapped by physical or emotional difficulties;

5. negotiate effectually the change to secondary school procedures, particularly in regard to independent study;

6. have ample opportunity to discover and nourish worthwhile interests.

Likewise, the Proceedings of the National Conference on Guidance, Counseling, and Placement in Career Development and Educational Occupational Decision Making (Gysbers and Pritchard, 1970, pp. 73–74) indicate that the objectives for junior high school youth should include:

a. The student further differentiates his self-characteristics (interests, values, abilities, and personality characteristics) from those of others, and can identify broad occupational areas and levels which may be more appropriate for him.

b. The student differentiates between the several broad occupational areas in terms of (1) a potential satisfaction each might offer him, (2) the nature of work tasks performed, (3) the future impact technology might have on particular occupational areas, (4) the contribution and importance of particular occupational areas to our society, and (5) the future demand for workers in broad occupational areas.

c. The student identifies different educational areas that are available both in the immediate and more distant future, the nature and purpose of each, the avenues toward which each can lead, and tentatively assesses what each offers him in terms of his possible vocational choices. He demonstrates how knowledge and skills acquired in different subject matter areas relate to performing different work roles. He recognizes the personal and social significance that work has in the lives of individuals at varying levels within the occupational structure.

d. The student identifies future decisions he must make in order to reach different goals. He identifies those personal and environmental efforts that impinge upon his future decisions. He assesses possible steps he might take in minimizing negative factors and maximizing positive ones and considers the possible consequences each has for him.

e. The student makes a choice of a broad occupational area to study in greater depth.

f. The student can differentiate between the major occupations that make up a broad occupational area and can make some differentiation of these occupations in terms of (1) the amount and type of education needed for entrance; (2) the content, tools, setting, products or services of these occupations; (3) their value to society; (4) their ability to provide him with the type of life style he desires; (5) to what extent they can satisfy his interests and values; (6) in what ways they do and do not seem appropriate for him.

g. The student selects education or training in the light of his tentative broad career purposes.

CHARACTERISTICS OF YOUTH IN TRANSITION

The introductory points just described reflect the awareness that students of junior high school age are not the same creatures that inhabited the elementary schools a year or two earlier. As a result of experience and growth, their horizons have widened. With pubertal changes near, either in themselves or their peers, their perceptions of life change. Junior high students are more able than elementary age children to comprehend relationships and to use abstract terms and symbols. They are preoccupied with belonging and conformity, being highly influenced by their like-sexed peers and less so by their opposites, while they are also attempting to take tentative steps toward independence from their families. They are making more definitive strides in sorting themselves from the mass of students with whom they interact as they try on the multiple social roles which accompany school and community experience.

Junior high school students are immersed in the continued development, refinement, and strengthening of basic skills begun in the elementary school, and they are beginning to converge on the more specialized experience of the senior high school. Their time focus is shifting, however subtly, from the immediate present to the future. Because choices of curricula and of the specific high school or residential vocational school they will attend a year or two hence are rapidly approaching, their sensitivity to work and its relevance to them as persons in the process of becoming is accentuated.

This latter matter of choosing courses in high school and selecting a high school to attend is a matter of significant proportions in the junior high school. This is true frequently because the junior high school student or his parents are unaware that when one chooses an educational course of action, he reduces or at best alters the alternatives available to him in the future. Katz (1963, p. 26), for example, has asserted, "There is some relationship between the high school course elected and a student's future educational and occupational level." This is particularly true in the election of those courses which permit the student maximum freedom to qualify for educational opportunities beyond the secondary school while he is reality-testing whether or not such further education is necessary for his goals. Since, at the junior high school level in particular, school is work, the opportunity to use his encounters with the different content and context of courses in order to explore present and future alternatives is important. It is also manageable.

While the alternatives from which a junior high school student can choose are limited, they represent, nevertheless, the opportunity to practice collecting and analyzing information about alternatives, to anticipate outcomes, and to develop decision plans. Since such dimensions are critical to successful vocationalization, curricular decisions made in the junior high school provide the opportunity to help students consider how to maximize freedom of choice and assume responsibility for choices made while there is still time for reversing a choice and charting new educational routes if necessary.

The years of junior high school are by design transition years. They represent a period when intensive, almost frenetic, exploration can be expected whether the school aids it or simply allows it to proceed unencumbered by information, models, and experiences. It is a period when such vocational development concepts as compromise and the congruence or incongruence between aspirations and expectations become operational as realities; and when idealistic fervor or naiveté get their initial temperings in the reality-testing of curricular, athletic, and part-time work experiences. Thus unless the educational experiences provided students at this level are timely and immediate to the questions which students are asking themselves, it is unlikely that they will have a significant influence on student behavior or choice making. This is a time, then, when change in the self and the world can be used as a focal point for planning and when student responsibilities through participation in planning can be related to the consequences of decisions made.

SEX DIFFERENCES

Junior high school years are also a time when sex differences exert important influences in curriculum choice, and when choice considerations become different in kind for males and females (Cass and Tiedeman, 1960). Brough (1969) has reported that sexual differences are related to the voluntary seeking of counseling in the junior high school, with girls exceeding boys in mean number of interviews as well as in the degree to which they are interested in educational-vocational planning and personal-social development. He interprets these findings thus (p. 70):

> First, the sex-role values of the middle-class culture permit females a great degree of dependency on adults and a longer period of child-teacher closeness. By the junior high age, boys are already expected to reflect independence and "manliness" (authors' note—and this apparently precludes, in comparison with girls, their seeking help with problems).

> Secondly, while almost all students reach the age of puberty during grades seven through nine, the average age of puberty for boys is two years later than that of girls, or ages 15 and 13 respectively. Since this developmental stage involves considerable emotional crisis in our culture, it is not unusual for junior high school girls to feel the adolescent press with a greater frequency and intensity than boys.

While in the previous chapter little emphasis was placed on differences in vocationalization strategies based on sex, the intention was not to gainsay the influence of sex-typing on occupational stereotypes or on appropriate choices to be considered. Rather the assumption was that boys and girls both need a language of vocations, an orientation to preference, the rudiments of how to differentiate interests and aptitudes and relate them to future educational options and the occupational clusters available. In the junior high school, sex effects become far more pronounced and perhaps make necessary different guidance emphases. As indicated in the summary of Chapter 2, current vocational development theories give only cursory attention to differences in vocational development between males and females, but it is obvious—if for no other reason than the biological—that differences will occur in the ways young men and young women approach vocational choices.

Fortner (1970) reported that in one sample of 400 junior and senior high school girls who were compared with a similar sample of 170 boys, girls tended to show preference for professional, managerial, and skilled positions more than did boys and for semiprofessional, small business, semiskilled, and unskilled less than did boys. It was found that measured intelligence or scholastic aptitude was significantly correlated with these levels of preference. Giving initial recognition to these sex differences, Zytowski (1969) has recently presented a theory of career development for women.

The work patterns and the proportions of women in the labor force have changed significantly during the past several decades. It is expected that at least through 1975, women will enter the labor force in greater percentages than men. Thus as cultural constraints about what is acceptable work or schooling for women continue to fall away, it is expected that women will continue to seek more schooling, earlier marriages, and more employment than ever before (Surette, 1967). Yet while this process is accelerating, it remains true that the pathways and the continuity with which these pathways can be pursued are different for boys than for girls. Being a homemaker is still the model vocational expression for women (Zytowski, 1969), and bearing at least one child is now more pervasive among married women than it has been for many years (Wolfbein, 1968). These two factors alone cause either temporary or long-term discontinuities in the vocational development of women even though they less rarely negate the important presence of women in the labor force for much of their lives.

The other reality factor remains. Even though social reinforcement for working women is increasing, girls have a smaller number of job choices available to them than do boys. Similar to the discrimination which prohibits access to some occupations because of racial criteria, sex-typing can be expected to restrict women's access to some occupations in the foreseeable future even though women jockeys, baseball umpires, commercial airline pilots, and long-haul truckers are no longer without precedent.

Girls tend to get "set" in a career earlier than boys, by about age fifteen, even though they enter a career pattern with less thought than boys. For these reasons, Havighurst (1965) has advocated that counseling for girls should be different from that for boys. Whether counseling should be different in fact or should emphasize different things earlier is debatable, but it is not debatable that since the male's identity is more typically cloaked in a vocational fabric than is the female's, girls have a problem of identity achievement which differs from that of boys. Cultural influences assign to boys a primary role as the breadwinner and thus reinforce in many ways that the vocational development of males is the more critical—not necessarily because of the benefits to the male himself but because of the importance of the choices he makes to the well-being of his future family.

In studies which examine the relationships between the vocational choices of girls and various criteria, e.g. parents' occupational levels (Lee and King, 1964;

Hanson, 1965), the vocational preferences of females are found to be as high as or higher than those of males but their expectancy of accomplishing the preferences is not congruent. In other words, what they prefer to do is not what they expect to be able to do. Thus if vocational guidance strategies are to respond to the needs of females and to help them come to terms with vocationalization and vocational identity, these strategies must be mounted during the junior high school period. To wait diminishes the likelihood that vocationalization can be influenced for females in optimum ways. A more detailed discussion of the unique aspects of females as consumers of vocational guidance was given in Chapter 4.

DIFFERENCES IN MATURITY

Of the entire educational span, the junior high school years have the widest range of maturity levels in the student population. The effects of pubertal changes, differences in the rates of male and female growth, and the general unevenness of physical, emotional, and intellectual development within and between the populations of girls and boys contribute to this spectrum of maturational differences. Differences in readiness, questions of general academic progress, preoccupations with bodily change, peer conflicts, boy-girl relationships, rebellion against family restrictions—each of these coexists with and often confounds the continuing process of vocationalization. Sherman (1967, p. 5) states:

> The timing for prevocational orientation may be crucial. Once students get involved in the junior high school milieu their own social and physical maturation and the existing organizational structures (both formal and informal) and the rewards offered from these environments in which they live all influence them. They turn their attention to diverse pursuits, such as popularity, prestige, athletic and academic achievement, and appear to develop different life styles, each with a different set of values. If students are helped to focus on career development prior to becoming a part of this milieu, it could help them to build a kind of core attitude toward their personal futures which might provide a slightly different perspective on the many other concerns of this age which are so much a part of growing up.

A TIME FOR EARLY SCHOOL LEAVING

Finally, perhaps most importantly, the junior high school years are a period when many students will absent themselves from formal education permanently. Some of these students will have begun to drop out of school psychologically in the elementary grades. Others will do so in grades 7, 8, or 9. Still others who have found no meaning in school will not only terminate their psychological interaction with the educational process, they will remove themselves physically.

In several other places in this book, what the future holds for those without a high school diploma or marketable skills has been discussed. Suffice it to say here that vocational guidance and the broader educational process must respond to potential dropouts not merely by encouraging these students to remain in school or admonishing them about the monetary value of a high school diploma but by altering the educational structure to make it more meaningful to these students.

The realities are that many students who drop out are not getting anything in school that helps them get a better job, and they know it! In many instances ways have not been found to move concrete, task-oriented instruction into the junior high school, where these students can get their hands on concrete objects and tasks which relate to real work as they see it. Neither is there opportunity to combine general education and work-study opportunities at the junior high school level, which could serve to hold students in school. As Lathrop (1968, p. 3) has observed:

> Apparently society has taken the position that the youth who chooses not to (or is unable to) profit from an academic high school program forfeits his rights to any publicly supported education and must shift thereafter for himself. . . . We have, in this society, built up the myth that we are only responsible for providing one type of education, general education, which should be appropriate for all youth and that anyone who fails to profit from this social bequest is henceforth outcast economically and socially. Although many of us would deny this point of view, if confronted with it directly, the fact remains that we have moved exceedingly slowly in providing alternatives whereby youth who, for one reason or another, do not find it possible to continue in the traditional academic mold can obtain further instructional training through alternative educational arrangements.

The point is that for some youngsters at this level purely academic content holds no appeal at all unless it has immediate relevance to salable skills and this relevance is made obvious. These students need access to a skill-centered curriculum, to vocational education at what is organizationally the seventh through ninth grades. If they do not receive this opportunity, the chances are that they will leave the school as unemployable. Some of these young people do not have the tolerance or the ego-strength to wade through a morass of personally meaningless experiences until the ninth, tenth, or eleventh grades, when they can get their hands on the concrete. This does not mean that these students should not be provided experiences other than task skills to foster vocationalization. Indeed, within the context of skill development, not only can they be helped to see where they might go but prescriptions of the specific ways of implementing their goals can be developed. For those persons for whom skill-centered training is most relevant and the prime source of success experiences, training in decision making and in planning which transcends job layouts can facilitate self-understanding and recognition of alternative ways of using their evolving skills. Within this context, the concept of continuing education as a way of refining one's skills and becoming a more effective problem solver at work can be wedded to a knowledge of available apprenticeships, on-the-job training, postsecondary vocational technical schools, military service schools, and other pertinent experiences. It is clear that such task-centered, skill-oriented, and concrete experiences would be helpful to all students if used to relate self-characteristics to the alternatives available, but it is even clearer that such experiences are critical to the prevention of dropouts.

The remainder of this chapter will be devoted to the range of vocational guidance strategies for meeting specific behavioral objectives in junior high school as selected from Chapter 5 or as locally devised.

VOCATIONAL GUIDANCE STRATEGIES

Congruent with the characteristics of junior high school youth just described, Hoyt (1969, pp. 35–37) contends that the role elements of guiding vocational development in the junior high school must include the following:

1. To help each student see himself as the worthy and worthwhile person he is.

2. To help each student experience success in his own eyes.

3. To help each student find ways that school can make sense to him.

4. To help each student consider and make decisions regarding the values of a work-oriented society.

5. To help each student develop an understanding and appreciation of his own talents and interests.

6. To help each student make choices from the widest possible range of alternatives which can be made available to him.

7. To help each student formulate plans for implementing the choices and decisions he has made.

8. To help each student accept some personal responsibility for his own destiny—of making meaningful to every student that what happens to him is, at least in part, a function of what he does or fails to do.

As indicated in the preceding chapter, Gysbers (1969) has theorized that the vocationalization emphasis pertinent to the junior high school is generalization. The assumption is that if the elementary school has provided the child with perceptualization and conceptualization experiences, he is now at the point where he can use his vocabulary of self, educational, and occupational referents to expand his generalizations about the relationships of self-characteristics to work and educational options. He is also physically capable of participating in tryout, simulation, part-time work, and gaming activities. Implicit throughout this book has been an emphasis on integrating these experiences directly into curricular or other existing school goals so that they can be sequenced, thereby maintaining a constant presence in the lives of children, rather than provided as one-shot, infrequent experiences like Career Days.

A technique for synthesizing many of these suggestions is that used by Lockwood, Smith, and Trezise (1968). They took the position that if students are to begin making meaningful vocational investigations, they must first become aware of the almost infinite possibilities open to them—their world must be enlarged. A sample of students was, therefore, introduced to four worlds: the natural, the technological, the aesthetic, and the human. In the natural world, the students not only studied what nature has to offer men both materially and spiritually, but they also looked into man's preoccupation with the destruction of nature.

In the technological world, topics dealing with machines, mass production, automation, cybernetics, and computers were used to stimulate students to discuss not only how developing technology will affect the jobs of the future, but, more broadly, what it will do for man and society as a whole. In the aesthetic world, students discussed the role of the arts in modern society and the place of the artist, contemporary trends in art, the culture boom, and why the arts have a vital place in a mature culture. In the human world, students studied overpopulation, poverty, war and peace, social injustices, and the individual in mass society. Throughout these explorations students were not only exposed to each career area separately but studied the interrelations among them.

The work just reported, as well as much of that which follows, indicates that many of the concepts and methods introduced in the elementary school are—with some reshaping and extension—also viable at the junior high school level. Leonard (1969) reported on one method at the junior high school level which integrates curricula and resource persons with other media. In the seventh grade, two considerations guided the development of the program: (1) Work models should be people in the community. (2) Job discussions should be in sociological terms (see Gross, Edward, 1967, in Chapter 5). The project was placed in geography classes with the cooperation of the teachers and school counselors. Film strips like "Who Are You?" and "What Do You Like to Do?", available from Science Research Associates, were used to stimulate student interest. Student volunteers in each geography class evaluated student interest in particular work topics, selected community resource people as speakers, selected data, researched relevant job materials and presented them to the class before the speaker arrived, and developed specific questions to guide the resource person's presentation.

In the eighth grade, the theme for the project centered around community agencies and job families. History classes were used, and film strips describing families of jobs were shown to stimulate awareness. By student vote, seven job families were selected for consideration. Student volunteers in each class were organized into committees; these took seven field trips to sites representing the seven job families to obtain information for class presentation. A speaker was recruited from each of the job families to spend one entire day interacting with small groups of students. At the conclusion of the program, the students evaluated it on such factors as technical interest, variation of routine, presentation, and knowledge gained. They then analyzed this compilation of data, computing percentages of response in each category, and discussed the results.

In the ninth grade, the program was divided into four parts: vocational opportunities in the Armed Forces for men and women, college occupational areas, large company training programs, and trade schools. Like the earlier grade-level activities, speakers and small group discussions were included, and students were encouraged to pursue specific information as their interests clarified.

In addition to the themes in the approaches just cited there are other concepts which can be used to unify a program. The concept of change—change in characteristics of the self and in environmental options—has been mentioned as a possible unifying thread in vocational development and decision making. At the junior high school such a theme can be related to the accelerating application of new technological discoveries to the occupational structure. Such a theme can reinforce the validity of preparing oneself to be versatile and yet firmly grounded in the fundamental processes which undergird all occupations. The concept can be related to work habits, mechanical principles, electrical principles, structural design and architectural evolution, chemical and biological principles, numerical operations and measurements, or verbal communication as this relates to different role relationships. In this context, students can be increasingly encouraged to ask of occupational and educational areas, not only, Do I like it? but also, What does it take? Do I have what it takes? These kinds of questions can be tested in various courses, as well as in the stimulated and work experiences discussed in later sections of this chapter. Students can be encouraged to ask, Why am I taking chemistry or algebra or English? How can I use it? Teachers must be encouraged to respond to such questions as meaningful ones for which there are fairly specific answers. This is the sort of climate which supports vocationalization and connects what students are being exposed to educationally with the occupational world. It has the potential of expanding students' awareness of possibilities.

When teachers are asked to consider how the subject they teach is related to occupations or careers at different levels of education or in different interest categories, a basic difficulty often is that their formal backgrounds have not prepared them to make these kinds of translations. One important resource to offset this condition has been prepared by the Minnesota Department of Education. The Bureau of Pupil Personnel Services of this agency has developed a series of charts describing the relationship between subject-matter courses and selected careers. An example of these is Table 1, which presents information on careers related to social studies.

Obviously, this table does not exhaust all the possibilities which might be placed in the different cells, but it represents a method of connecting what one studies with how it might be used. At any point in the chart, discussions, role

Table 1 Selected Careers Related to Social Studies

LEVEL	SERVICE	BUSINESS, CLERICAL, AND SALES	SCIENCE AND TECHNOLOGY	GENERAL CULTURAL	ARTS AND ENTERTAINMENT
B.A. or above	Social worker Psychologist F.B.I. agent Counselor YMCA secretary Clergyman	Government official Industrial executive Market analyst Economist Buyer Arbitrator	Archaeologist Paleontologist Anthropologist	Judges Lawyers Philologist Editor Sociologist News commentator Reporter Librarian	Museum curators Historian (Dramatic arts)
H.S. plus technical	Police sergeant Detective Sheriff Employment interviewer	Union official Bank teller Salesman Wholesaler Retailer		Justice of the peace Law clerks Radio announcer	Tour conductor Travel bureau director Cartoonist
H.S. graduate	Policemen Religious workers Bus drivers	Floor walkers Interviewers (poll) House canvassers and agents		Library assistant	Museum guide
Less than H.S. graduate	Train porters Taxi drivers Bellhops Elevator operators Ushers	Peddlers Newspaper boys		Library page Copy boy	

Source: Minnesota Department of Education, Bureau of Pupil Personnel Services pamphlet.

playing, field trips, or other activities could be conducted to point up how social studies might be used in that particular occupation. One could relate social studies to a people-data-things conception of the occupational structure or to other emphases, always trying to extend student perceptions or possibilities and the ways of access to them.

VOCATIONAL GUIDANCE STRATEGIES FOR DECISION MAKING AND PROBLEM SOLVING

The examples just cited respond to elements of vocational development at a rather gross level and are basically similar to those activities recommended for the elementary school. To meet more specific goals, some differences in strategy or context would be useful. For example, a particular activity might be selected in order to increase student ability in problem solving and decision making. Kinnick (1968) has compared the use of group discussions and group counseling to accomplish such a purpose.

Kinnick has described group discussion "as the cooperative and constructive deliberation on a common problem by a group attempting to reach agreement on a solution to that problem" (p. 350). Typically, group discussion involves face-to-face groups of eight to fifteen members, informally interchanging information, knowledge, and ideas for the following purposes: (1) to provide a means of helping students learn problem-solving skills, (2) to help particular students improve their ability to solve their particular problems, and (3) to help students learn to work with others toward a common goal. Group discussion could be stimulated by the use of case materials presenting different types of problems with which junior high school students can identify (e.g. choosing curricula, decision making, choosing a college, how to study, job analyses); or by the use of film strips or films dealing with similar content, field trips, or resource persons. Variations on the discussion method could be initiated through the use of role playing, sociodrama, or plays focusing upon particular content or problem areas.

Group counseling that focuses on problem solving, according to Kinnick, does not depart markedly from group discussion. However, the emphasis of the latter is on problems, whereas the stress in group counseling is on the person's *approach* to problems, thus involving more personal reference, identity issues, and emotionality. One may assume, then, that more problems of a personal nature would be examined in group counseling than in most group discussions. In either of these groups, however, problem solving as a creative process of evaluation, information collection and analysis, synthesis and planning, can be aided by means of (1) these lifelike, group settings for making decisions and choices, (2) the influence of peers through group interaction and group norms, (3) the opportunity for free expression of opinions and emotions with less personal reference, and (4) the opportunity to give and receive support as a group member (Wright, 1969, p. 554).

Dilley (1968, p. 247) maintains that there are five counselor actions that foster decision making:

1. *Encourage the development of personal responsibility beliefs—this means reinforcing student statements about self-responsibility, anticipating the future, or thinking before doing.*

2. *Encourage the use of a decision strategy—this may involve reinforcement of a decision strategy in clients or the actual presentation of such a strategy.*

3. *Encourage expansion and specificity of decision deliberations—this means helping the student consider as many alternatives to reaching his goals or, indeed, to the goals themselves as is possible.*

4. *Assist in the processing of decision-relevant information—this means not just helping the student determine that alternatives are available but also helping him to sort out, through whatever strategies seem necessary, those which are most personally relevant.*

5. *Let the client make his own decision—while this action is self-evident to most counselors, the point is that you are, through each of the actions Dilley cites, helping the individual develop his decision-making skills, you are not passing judgment on what he decides.*

Dilley further suggests that the way in which a particular counselor implements the first three actions—the encouraging actions—is primarily a matter of philosophy but that ways which hold promise include: (1) discussing or presenting decision material in printed form, (2) supplying a model, (3) reinforcing appropriate client responses.

Evans and Cody (1969) reported on teaching eighth-grade students a specific decision-making process in a counselinglike setting. Students were provided a series of problems requiring decisions. Their responses were then evaluated in terms of whether they were based on the following (p. 428):

1. *A consideration of alternative courses of action*

2. *A consideration of the consequences of each of the alternative courses of action*

3. *A consideration of past experiences appropriate to the problem*

4. *A consideration of the desirability of the consequences occurring from alternate decisions*

5. *The selection of a decision based on the considerations listed previously*

The conclusions of this study were: that a process for decision making can be taught in a counselinglike situation in which counseling is seen as in reality a learning situation employing the counselor as a model to help students become competent decision-makers; that directed learning of decision making is more effective than nondirected practice (no specific attention to the particular considerations inherent in decision making); and that directed learning appears to aid transfer of decision-making skills to real-life circumstances outside the counseling setting.

Even more directly focused on the fostering of decision-making skills is the work of Krumboltz and his students. For example, Ryan and Krumboltz (1964) found that systematically reinforcing decision and deliberation statements of students in counseling did increase the rate of deliberation and decision statements significantly and that this reinforced behavior generalized to noncounseling settings.

Yabroff (1969) has demonstrated the importance of specific information if the counselor wishes to increase the realism of choices of ninth-grade students. He used experience tables (probability tables based on what has happened to students having different levels of achievement, etc., when such students entered colleges, employment, or high school courses) to reinforce the importance of obtaining (1) specific facts about the choice, (2) a knowledge of alternatives, and (3) some estimate of the possible consequences. Yabroff found that his sample of ninth-grade students selected high school courses and made post-high school plans more commensurate with their abilities than did students who do not receive such information.

Magoon (1969) has developed a self-directed learning program which teaches the student the steps to take in effective problem solving. The student considers and evaluates the relevant data about a problem, integrates the data, and develops several alternative plans of action based on how this information fits his own educational-vocational concerns. Bergland and Krumboltz (1969) have also reported on the use of occupational problem-solving kits to stimulate exploratory behavior. They used a problem-solving booklet about law enforcement to accomplish the following: (1) to teach the student some of the basic aims of police work and some of the fundamental facts necessary to solve law-enforcement problems, (2) to enable the student to solve a short, simple problem like those solved by policemen, and (3) to virtually guarantee that the student would succeed in solving the problem. The results were that eleventh-grade students were stimulated more than tenth- or ninth-grade students to seek information through this technique. This was, of course, a group finding rather than an individual finding, suggesting that some ninth-graders were stimulated by this technique to engage in more intensive exploratory behavior.

A final and very specific type of simulation is provided by the job-experience kits developed at Stanford and discussed by Johnson (1970). These kits attempt to engage students in tasks normally performed by different workers, i.e. appliance servicemen, x-ray technicians, policemen, salesmen, laboratory technicians. Each job kit derives from an extensive job analysis of a particular occupation, and the conversion of this analysis into simulated tasks has been evaluated and authenticated by a representative of the particular occupation. In Johnson's words (p. 31):

> Each kit briefly introduces the occupation, asks the student to imagine that he is employed in that occupation, presents problems to be solved, provides information and materials necessary for solution, and finally lets the student know whether or not his solutions are correct. Instructions, where necessary, are programed. Illustrations are liberally used and printed text kept to a minimum.

Most of the work in social modeling and imitative learning as stimuli to information seeking or decision making has used senior high school students; these techniques are reported in the following chapter. The reader may wish to turn there now to consider the use of some of these techniques with junior high school youth or to wed these techniques with others reported in this chapter.

SIMULATION AS A VOCATIONAL GUIDANCE STRATEGY

In discussing simulation, This (1970, p. 20) has stated:

> Desirable as it may be, it is not always possible to bring reality into the classroom or into the training situation. When this is not possible, we try to replicate in the learning experience the nearest thing we can to the phenomenon of the real world. It does not matter whether we are talking about a piece of equipment or an emotional experience. We call this simulation.

This goes on to say that in order for simulation to result in changes in behavior, the following elements are generally considered to be necessary:

1. A supportive climate
2. Exposure of the individual's normal behavior
3. Feedback
4. Experimentation
5. A cognitive map
6. Practice
7. Planning application

In a sense, most of the work reported in the previous section has used some form of simulation of reality to stimulate exploratory behavior in students. In each instance some form of technology—films, modeling, audiotapes—has been used. Until recently, educational technology has been more concerned with how to communicate than what to communicate. It has, however, clear and powerful potential for simulating real-life experiences as an aid to vocational development, decision-making processes, contingencies, and outcomes. It can also serve as a medium for information retrieval accessed on the basis of student characteristics. A number of relevant projects already exist and will be discussed next.

One of the most intriguing techniques to stimulate decision making is the Life Career Game (Boocock, 1967). In this game, students plan the life of a fictitious student or older person within simulated environments—education, occupation, marriage and family life, and leisure. Unplanned event cards give players a sense of the possible effect of intervening variables. As decisions are made, feedback is obtained about the possible consequences of the decisions, and various alternative actions are examined in terms of their consequences.

The Life Career Game can be used to build an entire curriculum devoted to decision making or occupational-educational exploration; to enrich group discussions and group counseling (as a short-term technique); to promote specific kinds of information seeking or planning behavior; and to provide treatment for certain individuals who lack information on how to sequence decision-making steps. The game can be used from the sixth grade through the twelfth and also with out-of-school youth when appropriate. Varenhorst (1969) has reported that the Life Career Game encompasses: learning through social means, discrimination learning through selective reinforcement, and skill building. She contends that this approach is an influential counseling technique having important potential for use in the junior high school.

In recent years, there have emerged several projects which have attempted to tie together exploration, simulation, and information retrieval with computer technology. One is the work of Loughary, Friesen, and Hurst (1966) in developing Autocon, a computer-based, automatic counseling simulation system. This approach attempts to identify which counselor activities might be accomplished by computers, thus freeing counselors to collaborate with students on a more specific, individualized basis. A somewhat more comprehensive approach to the use of computers was reported as a Man-Machine Counseling System by Cogswell, Donahue, Estavan, and Rosenquist (1966). Through computer application this system provides a way to track students through their school progress, identifying at the earliest possible time those in need of counselor assistance because of difficulty in studies or in educational-vocational planning. Automated interviews were also used to develop computer-student dialogues about course programming, post-high school educational planning, and vocational exploration.

Three computer application systems which are among those most relevant to junior high school age students are the following:

1. *The Computer-Assisted Occupational Guidance Program* (Impelliteri, 1968) has three objectives: to provide an easily updated, occupational-information retrieval system; to develop a process whereby youth could build up their own individualized frameworks of the occupational structure; and to help youth acquire ways of relating their abilities and interests to occupational opportunities by means of simulation practice. This system uses student terminals, which are typewriterlike devices tied to a computer by telephone lines. Information

on the abilities, preferences, and educational plans of those students who will use the terminals are stored in the computer. Students are oriented to the system before interacting with it. At that time, each student is given a list of forty occupations with corresponding codes. The computer's first request is to ask the student to select one of the forty occupations about which he would like to know more. After the student responds by typing an occupational code number, the computer then types out a short paragraph describing the occupation. The student is then asked if he wishes to find out more about the occupation. If he responds positively, four sequential activities follow: (1) discrepancies which may exist between the student's ability-preference profile and requirements for the particular occupation are typed out; (2) a two-minute taped interview with a worker in the occupation is played; (3) an image is projected on the slide-projector screen depicting the worker undertaking four typical tasks in the occupation; (4) a 150- to 200-word description of the occupation is typed out for the student to read and to keep for later use. Perhaps the major differences between this system and the two to be described subsequently are, first, that the emphasis in this one is on using GATB cut-off scores as part of the discrepancy or accessing procedure and, second, that the occupations presented are those clearly tied to particular vocational-technical curricula available to the students participating.

2. *The Computerized Vocational Information System* (Harris, 1968) was developed by the guidance staff of the Willowbrook High School, Illinois. It evolved to meet two persistent needs: getting students interested in reading vocational material and in learning how to relate it to their own abilities and interests. It uses Roe's two-dimensional system to divide occupations into eight interest categories and six levels (levels are based on amount of training required and degree of responsibility assumed by the worker). Localized information is then placed into the system describing the following: companies in DuPage County (where the school is located) which hire high school graduates or school leavers in the field specified by the student; how to choose a first job; local apprenticeship opportunities; trade and technical schools within a 100-mile radius including technical programs in the local college of DuPage; sources of scholarship aid; information about specific colleges based on decisions students have made regarding cost, distance, major fields of study, as well as the characteristics of each student's achievement record and testing information. This system also computerizes the permanent records of students as base data for developing computer dialogue and for identifying discrepancies between a student's choices and his achievement or interest patterns.

Like the previous system described, the student accesses the computer through a terminal. He types his student identification number so that the computer can recall his permanent record. Conversations between the student and the computer script are then initiated, with the computer typing messages and presenting questions on a cathode-ray tube, from which the student selects appropriate answers from multiple possibilities. Once the student has selected an interest category and training level, the computer types out appropriate lists of occupations, definitions of them, descriptive information, references to further sources of information, and other pertinent data. The student can change interest categories and levels of training in order to work through as many possibilities as he wishes. Counselors also have access to any of the information stored in the computer, including the paths followed by each of their counselees. In addition, they receive major and minor discrepancy statements indicating students who need counselor collaboration at any particular point.

The major point about this system is that it was designed and developed by the guidance staff of one high school. It is not a system purchased from some other school but one which meets local needs and responds to local information.

3. *The Educational and Career Exploration System* (Thompson, Lindeman, Clack, and Bohn, 1970) is an experimental system developed jointly by IBM and personnel of Teachers College, Columbia University, under the project direction of Donald Super. It is now undergoing field testing in grades 8 to 12 in Montclair, New Jersey, schools. The objectives relative to the student are: (1) to increase his knowledge about himself in relation to the world of work; (2) to permit him to explore some of the implications of his educational preference; (3) to aid the process of selecting an institution of higher education. The objectives relative to the counselor are: (1) with many of the information preliminaries accomplished by the computer, the counselor can begin working with students at a higher level of problem solving; (2) he can have available a comprehensive, up-to-date library, easily accessible to the student.

The student terminal, tied to a time-shared IBM computer at another site by telephone lines, includes a film-image display unit, a numeric keyboard, and a typewriter printer. There is also a student reference guide, which provides system orientation as well as a complete listing of the occupations, schools, and major fields covered by the system.

Student profiles and self-estimates on a variety of factors are placed in the data bank and used as points of reference as the student explores tentative career preferences, clarifies specific occupations, and proceeds through specific problem-solving situations relevant to occupations, educational orientation, and a post-high school educational search.

This system has the most comprehensive data base and exploratory potential of the three described. One of its exciting components is the opportunity provided for students to actually work through problems or sample work tasks found in the occupations under consideration.

While there are other systems under or through development which also have important implications for aiding the exploratory activities of junior high students, notably the Information System for Vocational Decisions at Harvard under the leadership of Tiedeman et al. (1968), which is now operational under the aegis of Interactive Learning Systems (Boston), the three just described represent a range of objectives from the specific to the highly complex. There is little doubt that the availability and application of these systems will expand in the next decade. Perhaps the most significant fact is that these systems are not intended to supplant either teachers or counselors. Instead, they provide these professionals with new tools for expanding their energies in ways which will make their collaboration with students more relevant and more personally oriented. Further discussion of man-machine interaction can be found in Chapter 11.

INFORMATION RETRIEVAL

Although Chapter 11 will discuss the use of information in vocational guidance and information retrieval in some depth, the importance of this topic is acknowledged here by the description of two particular approaches to it.

One system is entitled Vocational Information for Education and Work (VIEW) (Smith, 1968). The VIEW system was conceived for use in the San Diego County, California, schools. It consists of decks of IBM cards with apertures into which are inserted microfilm presentations of occupational and educational information on opportunities in the San Diego area. These decks, which are easily updated, are prepared in a central county school office and disseminated to all the schools in the county. Counselors and students can access appropriate cards on the basis of codes, using such criteria as aptitudes, measured interests, and related school subjects. The student inserts these cards in a microfilm reader (available in the counseling office) to determine whether the particular opportunity described is of interest to him. If he wishes to have printed copies of the information to discuss with his parents or to explore the opportunity further, he can insert the card in the adjacent microfilm printer. Such an approach, which is now being used in several states, insures that the information on which student planning is based is as current and accurate as it is possible to make it. It also permits the counselor and the counselee to spend their time in considering the relevance of the information to the student rather than in locating what is available.

A similar, but less comprehensive, attempt to make available local occupational information has been made by counselors, vocational educators, and representatives of industry in Santa Cruz County, California (Elder, 1969). As part of a funded county-wide workshop, counselors gathered the following data from firms in the area during the academic year.

1. Job titles within the firm
2. Entry-level requirements for each job
3. Training and educational requirements for each job
4. Wage rates
5. Employment potential and possible growth
6. Desirable related high school courses
7. Contact persons within the firm

Occupational data were obtained on 907 different jobs. The information was coded, cross-referenced, and published in a directory, which was made available for counselor and student use.

It is important to recognize that the development of information and of systems of retrieval can be accomplished in many ways other than the two just described. In a larger sense, the examples cited throughout the chapters on the elementary school, the junior high school, and the senior high school are ways of delivering information, of responding to the characteristics of the consumers, of providing students the context in which they can project themselves into the information being considered and reality-test the personal meaning of it.

Many studies confirm the importance of access to information for students in the junior high school. Only two will be cited here. Kraskow (1968) studied a group of ninth-grade boys, using among other techniques an occupational test divided into two parts: (1) a multiple-choice test on general occupational information, and (2) an essay test of specific questions about a preferred occupation. His conclusions and the implications of them are (p. 278):

1. This study confirmed the poor background exhibited by most ninth-grade boys at the time of choosing high school curriculum.

2. The study shows that those boys who selected a vocational curriculum actually had less vocational information than those who chose an academic course. Students knowing the least number of alternatives were making the most crucial decisions.

3. Students' responses on the essay part of the test indicated a lack of occupational realism and of self-information.

4. This study indicated that information about a preferred occupation was greater than that about occupations in general.

Some of his recommendations are (p. 279):

1. That a developmental occupational information service be started in the elementary school, and that at the junior high school level occupational integration with subject courses be part of the program.

2. Practice in decision making should be coordinated with the occupational information service.

3. The use of an occupational information test early in junior high school might identify students exhibiting retarded vocational development.

4. In-service training of teachers could promote a better understanding of vocational development and provide a vehicle for the implementation of an effective classroom-centered information service.

Betz, Engle, and Mallinson (1969) took a random sample of 350 non-college-bound high school graduates from four north-central states and studied their perceptions of the education and guidance they had experienced. Among the conclusions was that, in general, the youth interviewed could not articulate a meaningful concept of self. These youth, contrary to some other data, did not perceive parents as being especially helpful in resolving personal, educational, or vocational problems and concerns, and there were no other significant adults to help them because counselors were perceived as not available, too busy, too involved with college-bound students, or simply unknown to this group. Finally, these ex-students were in agreement that a dichotomy in information available, encouragement, and help with vocational-identity questions favoring the college-bound over the non-college-bound exists in the schools from which they came.

These findings again affirm that the ingredients of vocationalization discussed throughout this book are important to all students, not just to some strata of them. They also reemphasize that although information availability and help with sorting out one's self-implications are not the whole of vocationalization, they are an important component of it. Finally, by implication, it is clear that the provision of information cannot be delayed until students are at the point of leaving school but data must be continuously accessible throughout the course of education.

VOCATIONAL GUIDANCE STRATEGIES AND WORK

As indicated earlier in this chapter, work itself is integral to access to skill-centered vocations for some students and a powerful stimulus to exploration for many students seeking other vocations. For many students work is the best of all try-out experiences. For some, organized work and study programs are ways of shortening the period of economic and psychological dependence under which so many youth chafe. If such work experience is also to facilitate voca-tionalization, it should be more than casual, unsystematic ventures into whatever chance opportunity presents itself. The behavioral goals cited in Chapter 5 are pertinent here also. They represent motivational as well as diagnostic possibilities to which work can be related. If such goals are to be realized, however, education and industry must come together in mutually creative exchanges in order to provide such opportunities systematically. One requirement would be that schools accept responsibility for helping youngsters find part-time or summer jobs in which they can make use of what they have learned. Equally important, guidance and counseling activities must be directed to helping students examine the work that they are doing as they are doing it if it is to help the vocationaliza-tion of these students.

Thomas Gambino, Director of the Introduction to Vocations Program spon-sored by the New Jersey Department of Education, relates a story that illustrates this point (1970). He speaks of a nonverbal student whose counselor was having a great deal of difficulty in getting him to consider alternatives, make decisions, and examine vocational education opportunities. The student was, however, in-volved in some industrial arts experiences which moved him among work tasks of different types. To try to improve communication, the counselor took pictures of the boy doing various kinds of work. He then used these as points of reference for the boy to discuss, expressing how he felt about these work tasks, which he liked best, why, what really pleased him. The transformation in the boy's attitude was remarkable. He was no longer talking about abstractions—he was talking about himself in action. The pictures represented concreteness which he felt comfortable and adequate in talking about.

One attempt in the junior high school to use work as a way of accomplishing some of the goals cited here is the Forsyth Program conducted in Forsyth County, Georgia. This is an effort to reconstruct at grades 7, 8, and 9 the total educational environment to make it meaningful to socioeconomically disadvantaged students who are indifferent to abstract curricula or to work. The concrete elements of a particular vocational program such as industrial arts, home economics, or agriculture is used as the core of the basic academic curriculum (math, science, and communication skills). Students are placed in work stations within the school or outside the school, and their experiences are used as the basis for group counseling sessions. The group counseling sessions are conducted by an educational and work-experience coordinator (a person with both counseling and vocational education background). This person also places and supervises students in their work stations and coordinates the activities of those teachers assigned to work with students in the project (Bottoms and Matheny, 1969; Royston, 1970).

Another example of a work-experience program for ninth-grade students, as well as for tenth-, eleventh-, and twelfth-grades—particularly potential dropouts —has been mounted in Oshkosh, Wisconsin. The adaptations to the regular school program required by such an approach are reported by Bunda and Mezzano (1968, p. 272) as including:

1. *Placement of the potential dropout on a job for half of the school day*

2. *Reduction of the potential dropout's academic load*

3. *Intensive counseling with the potential dropout*

4. *Continuous communication with the employer and the home by the coordinator of the program*

As a result of this program, it was found that the average number of half-day absences dropped from 28.36 to 8.56 per student and the academic average moved from 3.57 (D) to a 4.57 (C). Teacher comments on attitudes and behavior also reflected the general improvement of student participants.

It is obvious that paid work has limited possibilities for fostering behavioral modification or vocationalization in many parts of the nation because of federal, state, or local restrictions on age, the amount of time a student can commit to work, and the type of work he can do. There are, however, junior high school students to whom none of these restrictions apply. There are others for whom opportunities could be made available if the job needs which exist were communicated to educators or counselors by such community agents as the chamber of commerce, industrial personnel people, representatives of the National Alliance of Businessmen, or the United States Employment Service.

VOCATIONAL EDUCATION

Another approach to fostering the vocationalization of students, particularly those likely to be early school leavers, is called the cluster concept. The cluster concept can be viewed as providing a ladder of vocational education opportunities which become increasingly specific the longer one remains in the program. At the junior high school level, in particular, the intent is to provide individual students with the skills, knowledge, and attitudes required for entry level in a family (a cluster) of occupations. Vocational education has traditionally attempted to provide intensive preparation for a narrowly focused occupation, e.g. carpentry, auto mechanics. The cluster concept would prepare the individual student for several of the occupations within a cluster such as construction, metal forming and fabrication, electromechanical installation and repair, graphic reproduction, graphic presentation, transportation, health services, and food services. The jobs or tasks within each of the constellations start at a very basic level and become more complex and specific the further up the hierarchy one proceeds. Thus in metal forming and fabrication, the skills required by an assembler also relate to those of a sheet-metal worker, a welder, a machinist, a job setup man, and a tool and dye maker. However, the latter tasks require incremental skills forming a continuum from very basic skills to those of a skilled craftsman at the highest level of sophistication short of professional engineering.

Implicit in the cluster-concept form of vocational education in junior high is the integration of academic areas. Thus mathematics, science, communications, and social studies each helps prepare the student to acquire the skills important to the cluster tasks rather than functioning as separate entities. Short of restructuring the total curriculum of the junior high school around a cluster concept, this means that instructional teams must be mounted to integrate learning through such techniques as flexible or modular scheduling, team teaching, independent study, and individualized instruction.

While an instructional team is providing the integrated skill or academic components of the program, the work of the school counselor should be to assist the students to gain self-knowledge, decision-making prerequisites, and knowledge of the job and of continuing educational opportunities for use of cluster skills.

Seventeen school systems participating in the ES '70 Project are now serving as test/demonstration sites to examine the feasibility of new curricula which use occupational interests to develop general and vocational skills through the interweaving of concepts which cross subject-content lines (Bushnell and Rubel, 1968).

In addition, Carr and Young (1967, p. 304) have reported a project in which a new program relates each subject to the other subjects in the curriculum as well as the whole course to the outside job market.

> To study measurement, students learn decimals and fractions, geometry and
> trigonometry. . . . In shop class, they use these skills to construct cardboard

models of heating ducts, make blueprint drawings, and convert them into aluminum ducts. They discuss history of measurement and its impact on Western Civilization in social studies and air flow and the measurement of air pressure in science. They then write up the whole project for English class. Throughout the program, the key idea is cooperation. One boy's draw-ings are used by another for fashioning into a duct, which must fit exactly the sector being made by a third. This is the method of the course; such is the method of industry.

Other schools, too, are training students in families of skills rather than in a single skill. Some are creating flexible curricula by which students leaving school at any point can do so with a marketable skill or with jointly marketable skills and prerequisites for different post-secondary educational opportunities including college. Other approaches to this goal will be discussed in the next chapter.

STAFFING FOR VOCATIONAL GUIDANCE

Chapter 12 will discuss some of the major links between counselors, teachers, and personnel in the larger community that can contribute to the broad goals of vo-cational guidance. While this book contends that the school counselor has a central role in vocational guidance and vocationalization, it also acknowledges that he cannot do the job alone. Indeed, some persons ask whether the school counselor really has a significant part to play at all. We think he does, if certain facets of his role are emphasized more than is presently typical even though a comprehensive program of guidance services continues to prevail. These points have been raised throughout this book so they will not be restated here. Rather, this section will identify some staffing models for serving the vocational guid-ance needs of students.

Carey (1970) has questioned whether differentiated staffing is the answer to vocational guidance for all. He has suggested a guidance organization which would systematically use the services of individuals with different training, skill levels, and interests. In particular, he has identified four categories of guidance personnel: (1) paraprofessional, (2) guidance teacher, (3) school counselor, and (4) specialist/coordinator.

The use of paraprofessionals in guidance or in education is not a new theme. Carlson, Cavins, and Dinkmeyer (1969), as well as Salim and Vogan (1968) among others, have discussed the usefulness of selecting, training, and assigning guid-ance functions to such persons. Under paraprofessionals Carey has classified the secretary-clerk, the paid or volunteer aide, and the technician. He has suggested that these persons could help students use vocational information and assist in test administration and scoring, placement, follow-up studies or community sur-veys, and the operation of data-processing and computer procedures.

The guidance teacher, in Carey's terms, would be a person trained to teach in curricula typically labeled career orientation or prevocation orientation. The mode guidance teachers would use is identified as group guidance. The assumption is further made that these proposed guidance teachers would find "new and creative ways to combine school and community resources, such as computerized information systems, simulation and gaming techniques, multimedia systems, field trips, and work experience" (p. 69) to accomplish the group objectives for orientation of students.

The school counselor in such an organization would be freed of many current, time-consuming tasks in order to work with other staff members in developing curricular and career activities; to conduct research; and to provide more effective counseling and placement services.

The specialist/coordinator would provide for guidance workers, teachers, and others, system-wide, in-service programs on different aspects of vocational guidance, and he would coordinate all clearly vocational facets of the overall guidance program: i.e. placement, interrelations between education and work.

Carey (1970, p. 69) contends that the advantages of differentiated staffing include the following:

1. *It should result in more guidance services, provided to more people more effectively, than can be expected of a traditional approach.*

2. *It should result in more efficient utilization of personnel and consequently reduce the per-student cost of services.*

3. *It would provide a career ladder for guidance which would permit persons with a variety of backgrounds to enter at different points.*

4. *It should offer better opportunities for guidance personnel, vocational educators, and community resource personnel to team up to create more relevant educational and career-development programs.*

5. *It would lend itself to the kind of planning, evaluation, and accountability that are increasingly required in education.*

Such a plan also has disadvantages. It would probably not be feasible for small schools. More important, however, state certification and financing, as well as preparation requirements for counselors, teachers, and paraprofessionals, would each need to be substantially revised from their current forms to insure that such a pattern of staffing is developed meaningfully rather than allowed to grow haphazardly.

Bottoms and Cleere (1969) have also reported on several models for deploying resources in the junior high school most effectively in order to aid vocational development. Among these are full-year exploratory courses conducted and coordinated by a school counselor, school counselor–industrial arts teacher teams to maximize the use of industrial arts in career development; and work-experience programs to develop employability skills, led by a work-experience coordinator serving with a school counselor. The point seems to be that regardless of who assists the school counselor to implement vocational guidance programs in the junior high school, objectives need to be stated to give substance to what is done; multimedia approaches which combine the concrete and the abstract and which respond to the differential readiness or learning patterns of students need to be mounted; and continuous coordination of the program should be developed so that it is purposeful, not random, in its influence upon the lives of students.

SUMMARY

This chapter examines the implications for vocational guidance of youth in exploratory transition at the junior high school level. Themes and practices previously recommended for the elementary school level are longitudinally extended and reshaped to make them appropriate for the junior high school. The needs for increased access to concrete tasks and for reconceptualized forms of vocational education are considered.

REFERENCES

Bergland, B. W., and Krumboltz, J. D.   An optimal grade level for career exploration. *Vocational Guidance Quarterly,* 1969, 18, 29–33.

Betz, R. L.; Engle, K. B., and Mallinson, G. G.   Perceptions of non-college-bound, vocationally oriented high school graduates. *Personnel and Guidance Journal,* 1969, 47, 988–994.

Boocock, Sarane S.   The Life Career Game. *Personnel and Guidance Journal,* 1967, 45, 328–334.

Bottoms, J. R., and Cleere, W. R.   *A one-week institute to develop objectives and models for a continuous exploratory program related to the world of work from junior high through senior high school. Final report.*   Carrolton, Ga.: West Georgia College, Sept. 1969.

Bottoms, J. R., and Matheny, K.   Occupational guidance, counseling, and job placement for junior high and secondary school youth.   Paper presented at the National Conference of Exemplary Programs and Projects Section of the Vocational Education Act, Amendment of 1968, Atlanta, Ga., March, 1969.

*Brough, J. R.   A profile of junior high school counseling. *The School Counselor,* 1969, 17, 67–72.

*Bunda, R., and Mezzano, J.   A study of the effects of a work-experience program on performance of potential dropouts. *The School Counselor,* 1968, 15, 272–274.

* Recommended for additional reading.

Bushnell, D. S., and Rubel, R. G.   A skill and a choice. *American Vocational Journal,* 1968, 43, 31–33.

Carlson, J., Cavins, D. A., and Dinkmeyer, D.   Guidance support for all through support personnel. *The School Counselor,* 1969, 16, 360–366.

Carey, E. Neil.   Vocational guidance for all: Is differential staffing the answer? *American Vocational Journal,* 1970, 45, 68–69.

Carr, H. C., and Young, M. A.   Industry-education cooperation. *Vocational Guidance Quarterly,* 1967, 15, 302–304.

*Cass, J. C., and Tiedeman, D. V.   Vocational development and the election of a high school curriculum. *Personnel and Guidance Journal,* 1960, 38, 538–545.

Cogswell, J. B.; Donahue, C. P.; Estavan, D. P.; and Rosenquist, B. A.   The design of a man-machine counseling system.   Paper presented at the American Psychological Association Convention, New York, Sept., 1966. Mimeographed.

*Dilley, J. S.   Counselor actions that facilitate decision-making. *The School Counselor,* 1968, 15, 247–252.

Elder, L. A.   An in-service community occupational survey. *Vocational Guidance Quarterly,* 1969, 17, 185–188.

Evans, J. R., and Cody, J. J.   Transfer of decision-making skills learned in a counselinglike setting to similar and dissimilar situations. *Journal of Counseling Psychology,* 1969, 16, 427–432.

Fortner, Mildred L.   Vocational choices of high school girls: Can they be predicted? *Vocational Guidance Quarterly,* 1970, 18, 203–206.

Gambino, T.   Letter, April 23, 1970.

Gysbers, N. C.   Elements of a model for promoting career development in elementary and junior high school.   Paper presented at the National Conference on Exemplary Programs and Projects Section of the Vocational Education Act, Amendment of 1968, Atlanta, Ga., March, 1969.

Gysbers, N. C., and Pritchard, D. H.   *Proceedings, National Conference on Guidance, Counseling, and Placement in Career Development and Education-Occupational Decision-Making.*   Columbia: University of Missouri, Oct., 1970.

Hanson, J. T.   Ninth-grade girls' vocational choices and their parents, occupational level. *Vocational Guidance Quarterly,* 1965, 13, 361–364.

*Harris, JoAnn.   The computerization of vocational information. *Vocational Guidance Quarterly,* 1968, 17, 12–20.

*Havighurst, R. J.   Counseling adolescent girls in the 1960's. *Vocational Guidance Quarterly,* 1965, 13, 153–160.

Hoyt, K. B.   Role, function, and approach for guidance in career development of youth from junior high through senior high. In J. R. Bottoms and W. R. Cleere (eds.). *A one-week institute to develop objectives and models for a continuous exploratory program related to the world of work from junior high through senior high school. Final report.*   Carrolton, Ga.: West Georgia College, Sept., 1969.

Impelliteri, J. T.   *The development and evaluation of a pilot computer assisted occupational guidance program. Final report.*   Harrisburg: Pennsylvania Department of Public Instruction, July, 1968.

*Johnson, M., Jr.; Busacker, W. E., and Bowman, F. Q., Jr.   *Junior high school guidance.*   New York: Harper & Brothers, 1961.

Johnson, R. G.   Simulation techniques in career development.   *American Vocational Journal,* 1970, 45, 30–32.

*Katz, M.   *Decisions and values: A rationale for secondary school guidance.*   New York: College Entrance Examination Board, 1963.

Kinnick, B. C.   Group discussion and group counseling applied to student problem solving.   *The School Counselor,* 1968, 15, 350–356.

Kraskow, B. S.   Occupational information as a factor in the high school curriculum chosen by ninth-grade boys.   *The School Counselor,* 1968, 15, 275–280.

Lathrop, R. L.   A point of view about the place of vocational education in contemporary education.   University Park: Pennsylvania State University, 1968. Mimeographed.

Lee, Billie Louise, and King, P. R.   Vocational choices of ninth-grade girls and their parents occupational levels.   *Vocational Guidance Quarterly,* 1964, 12, 163–167.

Leonard, Rachel.   Vocational guidance in junior high: One school's answer.   *Vocational Guidance Quarterly,* 1969, 17, 221–222.

Lockwood, Ozelma, Smith, D. B., and Trezise, R.   Four worlds: An approach to vocational guidance.   *Personnel and Guidance Journal,* 1966, 45, 641–643.

Loughary, J. W., Friesen, D., and Hurst, R.   Autocon: A computer-based automatic simulation system.   *Personnel and Guidance Journal,* 1966, 45, 6–15.

Magoon, T. M.   Developing skills for educational and vocational problems. In J. D. Krumboltz and C. E. Thoresen (eds.) *Behavioral counseling: Cases and techniques.*   New York: Holt, Rinehart, and Winston, 1969, 343–396.

Royston, W., Jr.   Forsyth County Vocational High: An investment in youth.   *American Vocational Journal,* 1970, 45, 58–61.

Ryan, T. Antoinette, and Krumboltz, J. D.   Effect of planned reinforcement counseling on client decision-making behavior.   *Journal of Counseling Psychology,* 1964, 11, 315–323.

Salim, M., and Vogan, H. J.   Selection, training, and functions of support personnel in guidance: The counselor assistants project.   *Counselor Education and Supervision,* 1968, 7, 227–236.

Sherman, Vivian S. *Guidance curriculum for increased self-understanding and motivation for career planning.* American Institute for Research in Behavioral Sciences. ERIC Document, EDOIO 626.

*Smith, E. D. Innovative ideas in vocational guidance. *American Vocational Journal,* 1968, 43, 19–21.

Surette, R. F. Career versus homemaking: Perspective and proposals. *Vocational Guidance Quarterly,* 1967, 16, 82–86.

This, L. E. What is simulation? *American Vocational Journal,* 1970, 45, 20–22.

Thompson, A. S.; Lindeman, R. H.; Clack, Sylvia; and Bohn, M. J., Jr. *The educational and career-exploration system: Final trial and evaluation in Montclair High School.* New York: Teachers College, Columbia University.

Tiedeman, D. V.; Landy, E.; Fletcher, W. J.; Ellis, A. B.; Davis, R. G.; and Boyer, E. G. *An information system for vocational decisions. Annual report, 1967-68.* Cambridge, Mass.: Harvard Graduate School of Education, 1968.

Varenhorst, Barbara B. Learning the consequences of life's decisions. In J. D. Krumboltz and C. E. Thoresen (eds.) *Behavioral counseling: Cases and techniques.* New York: Holt, Rinehart and Winston, 1969, pp. 306–319.

Wolfbein, S. L. *Occupational information.* New York: Random House, 1968.

Wright, E. W. Multiple counseling: Why? When? How? *Personnel and Guidance Journal,* 1959, 37, 551–557.

*Yabroff, W. Learning decision-making. In J. D. Krumboltz and C. E. Thoresen (eds.) *Behavioral counseling: Cases and techniques.* New York: Holt, Rinehart and Winston, 1969, pp. 329–342.

*Zytowski, D. G. Toward a theory of career development for women. *Personnel and Guidance Journal,* 1969, 47, 660–664.

EIGHT

VOCATIONAL GUIDANCE, VOCATIONALIZATION, AND THE SENIOR HIGH SCHOOL

The transcendent factor with which senior high school students must deal is the imminence of reality. Like other factors in decision making and intermediate choices, reality—defined as the way the individual approaches alternatives in his post-secondary school life—will have different implications for each individual.

Post-secondary school reality for different students might be cast in any of the following forms:

1. Choosing a post-secondary vocational or technical school to pursue some skilled specialty

2. Gaining access to a college and selecting a major field of study with its myriad implications for later vocational endeavors

3. Converting part-time work experience while in school into a full-time position in the labor market

4. Entering the labor market for the first time

5. Deliberating about military service, marriage, combining work and continuing education

6. Acquiring an apprenticeship opportunity

However, there will also be a sizeable number of students for whom none of these possibilities seems viable or appealing; for them the future and its reality represent threat or trauma. For some of these students, the future beyond high school represents a confrontation with the ramifications of a general state of indecisiveness regarding life and their place in it. Others will find the burden of decision making untenable and will use various avoidance behaviors to escape or postpone facing directly such an awareness.

Since students in the senior high school will have arrived at these differing degrees of vocational maturity by differing routes of continuity or discontinuity vocational guidance activities for them must be threefold: stimulating vocationalization, providing treatment, and aiding placement. (The latter refers to student movement to the next educational level or to the immediate life of worker, consumer, and citizen.) Conceptually, it is important to recognize that in terms of vocational development, some senior high school students will be no more mature than are elementary school students. Thus whichever of the above three vocational guidance emphases is mounted in the individual case must depend upon where the student is in his vocational development and what he needs most at a given time: reassurance, information, reality-testing, emotional release, attitude clarification, or work exposure. Obviously, vocational guidance activities at the senior high school level, as at other educational levels, must be predicated upon individual needs, readiness, and motivations.

In one sense, the principal emphases must be upon the intensity of planning, readiness to participate in life as an independent person, and the level of goal-directedness which characterize the individuals to be served. In support of such premises, the National Conference on Guidance, Counseling, and Placement in Career Development and Education-Occupational Decision making (Gysbers and Pritchard, 1969, p. 74) recommended the following objectives for vocational activities in the secondary school:

1. *The student develops awareness of his need for more specific implementation of his career purposes.*

2. *The student develops more specific plans for implementing his career purposes.*

3. *The student executes plans to qualify for entry-level jobs by taking appropriate courses at the high school level, by on-the-job training, or by pursuing further training in college or post-secondary vocational education leading toward qualifications for some specific occupation.*

These objectives must be elaborated and cast in behavioral terms as recommended in the preceding chapters, particularly Chapter 5. But the significant point here is that vocational guidance activities in the senior high school must take each student from where he is in coping with developmental tasks integral to vocationalization, and lead him to the creation and the achievement of a set of specific preferences and plans to implement them. For many students the senior high school years are the crucible in which they test their vague aspirations through developing specific strategies for converting these aspirations into reality. Vocational guidance, in its repertoire of possible emphases, represents the last opportunity for students to rehearse in a protected context different coping behaviors, alternative actions and plans, and to assess these against a back-drop of self-characteristics and value sets before their induction into the adult society.

Hence, perhaps more than at any other point in the educational continuum, vocational guidance activities in the senior high school must help the individual prescribe with logic and with system how he can realize his motivations and prepare himself psychologically to cope with their implications. Given such a reality, it is not sufficient that vocational guidance strategies be designed only to help students gain awareness that opportunities exist or how these can be related to self-characteristics; it is equally necessary that they be helped to plan specifically how to gain access to these opportunities.

As vocational guidance activities are implemented, students in the senior high school are likely to be found more rigid in their educational and occupational values and preferences than are their younger contemporaries. Thompson (1966) has reported that ninth- and tenth-graders' view of their vocational choice may be well established when they enter high school and may not change readily. Astin (1967), too, has shown that on the basis of Project Talent data derived from a sample of 650 male high school seniors, the students' measured interests and expressed career choice at the ninth-grade level were the best predictors of career outcomes at the twelfth-grade level. Perrone (1964) has demonstrated that senior boys with similar scores on cognitive measures tend to indicate a preference for similar occupational groups. Hollender and Parker (1969) have shown, consistent with Holland's theory (see Chapter 2), that the occupational stereotypes held by high school sophomores are related to their needs as measured by the Adjective Check List and that these stereotypes represent a foundation for vocational choices. Other studies, however, indicate that many high school seniors appear to be unrealistic or unaware of their characteristics as related to the occupation selected (Milliken, 1962), even if they approach such choices rigidly and with determination.

The fact that some senior high school students base their choice making upon occupational stereotypes or upon a lack of awareness of self-characteristics and the fact that some evidence less malleability in values and preferences would seem to be expected where systematic efforts to foster vocationalization have not occurred in the elementary and junior high schools. It is apparent that the vocational guidance activities in the secondary schools are not yet at a sufficiently developed level to influence some of these student behaviors even though the limitations inherent in waiting until this period are known. Campbell (1968) reported the results of a national survey of vocational guidance in secondary education among 353 schools representing urban comprehensive, rural comprehensive, urban general academic, rural general academic, urban vocational, and area vocational-technical. From these six types of secondary schools, usable questionnaire returns were obtained from 308 counselors, 324 principals, 1,405 teachers, 3,038 students, and 1,409 parents. Among the selected findings of this survey were:

1. Learning about the world of work and study habits counseling were least frequently checked as available and most frequently checked as needed by students.

2. Although 81 percent of the students indicated that they had had an opportunity to read publications about occupations, 35 percent of them checked that the kind of job information they wanted and needed was not readily available in their school. Sixty-three percent of the rural comprehensive and 59 percent of the rural general academic students indicated that they had not had the opportunity to read occupational information, compared to 19 percent for the four other types of schools.

3. In terms of time available for individual counseling conferences, counselors reported that the median percentage of students having two or more 15-minute conferences over the past year was 31; 15 percent of the counselors reported that no students in their schools had had two or more 15-minute conferences.

4. Students were also asked about the frequency and length of individual conferences. Only the responses of senior students who had been in the same school for three or four years were analyzed. The median number of individual conferences for all years was four, 13 percent reported that they had had none, and 25 percent indicated that they had had nine or more over the years. The median length of individual conferences was 16 minutes per conference.

5. For seventeen guidance services enumerated, teachers reported that they "could assist" more with guidance services than they were currently doing. The majority of the teachers saw themselves as being able to "assist with aid in course selection" and "aid in choosing an occupation."

These admittedly selective findings suggest that although students desire vocational guidance, they are not getting it; at least they are not getting it in the systematic and comprehensive ways which this book contends are necessary. One reason, which is implied throughout Campbell's findings, is the lack of counselor time for individual conferences. That reality, however, in no way negates the importance of vocationalization to students' overall development and the necessity of finding alternate ways of aiding that development through vocational guidance and the larger educational process.

Such a necessity exists not simply because students need help in selecting an occupation but because existing research suggests that the degree to which high school students are acquiring the ingredients of vocationalization, as defined in this book, corresponds with their personality development, academic achievement, and generalized style of life. In another context, after an extensive summary of the interaction between college inputs and outputs, Herr and Cramer (1968, p. 116) were led to conclude:

> The importance of desiring what one has chosen rather than being at the whim of others without any personal investment in the choice is a factor in academic success. Vocational ambitions and/or appropriate goals are very important. Men and women students with identifiable educational goals— reasons which are related to why they are doing what they are doing—seem consistently to be better prepared for college than students who have no such reasons for being in college.

Apparently, similar relationships exist between the elements of vocationalization and high school achievement. For example, Oakland (1969) reports relationships between levels of high school achievement and personal traits such as the following: being motivated to succeed; assuming responsibility; being competitive, persistent, self-confident; exhibiting interest in leadership; planning work efficiently; planning and organizing things; being a dependable worker. Each of these traits represents components found in assessments of vocational maturity and, in a sense, are among the personal characteristics which vocationalization strategies are designed to foster. For individual students who lack these traits, vocational guidance can respond either longitudinally through one of the many vocationalization approaches described throughout this book or by condensed vocational guidance approaches designed to treat a particular behavioral deficit.

The importance of this matter is emphasized in other research (O'Hara, 1966), which suggests that the concept a person has of himself influences his achievement to a significant degree. In particular it was found "that self ratings of vocational attributes are significantly related to the vocational developmental task of achievement in a college preparatory course in high school" (p. 111). Pine (1964-65), in a sample of 683 pupils in grades 9 and 12, reported significant relationships between educational and occupational aspirations and the degree of individual involvement in delinquent behavior. Related to such findings are those of vocational rehabilitation personnel working with emotionally disturbed and delinquent boys (Research Utilization Branch, 1968). In the latter case, it has been found that a requisite of effective treatment of youth in trouble is to help them develop desirable work habits, favorable attitudes toward work, and the stability necessary to hold a job.

On balance, this brief introduction outlining some of the characteristics of senior high students, their heterogeneity, their needs for vocational guidance, as well as a brief excursion into the current status of vocational guidance, provide a framework for the remainder of this chapter, which presents vocationalization, treatment, and placement strategies for the senior high school population.

VOCATIONALIZATION, VOCATIONAL GUIDANCE, AND VOCATIONAL EDUCATION

A persistent theme in the chapters on vocational guidance in the elementary and junior high schools has been the need for many of the objectives of vocationalization to be met within the goals of particular curricula. Implied has been the need for students continuously to connect what they are doing educationally with the future consequences in terms of occupational and educational alternatives, the styles of life they represent, and their general requirements. Mention has also been made of the importance of teacher attitudes in encouraging planfulness among students; an appreciation of the spectrum of occupational alternatives in which knowledge of English, social studies, mathematics, languages, business education, or other disciplines are used; and other elements of vocational maturity.

In the chapter on the junior high school, the cluster concept of vocational education was introduced as one method of providing early school leavers with entry-level, saleable skills; as a way of providing other students with exploratory opportunities without negating the possibility of their pursuing a range of other educational interests; and as a way of integrating academic disciplines around occupational interests and of using concrete vocational education to spur student development in other academic areas. These discussions also acknowledged that the educational process must create a greater diversity of opportunities to find meaning in the school program for both those students who are comfortable with verbal abstractions and those who are not.

The school counselor has a role in directly encouraging the development of such experiences as well in collaborating with teachers to assist them in the vocationalization of students. The school counselor needs to exert leadership in helping administrative and curriculum groups respond to the architect's dictum that form should follow function as plans are made to incorporate more flexibility, interdisciplinary integration, variable time blocks, individualized programming, multimedia approaches, and self-teaching devices than now exist in many educational systems.

Perhaps one of the most fruitful efforts of the school counselor will be his work in direct collaboration with vocational educators to reshape both the image and the substance of their disciplines. Vocational education has been called "the bridge between man and his work" in a report so titled (Advisory Council on Vocational Education, 1968). This book contends that such an appellation must come to describe to a greater degree the total educational process, not just a segment of it. If any part of education (or all of it) is to deserve this label by bringing into the lives of individual students the complex of experiences necessary to bridge education and work, more than narrowly defined job training is involved. This very specificity of trade or job training is what has led to cries of obsolescence in vocational education and of unresponsiveness to the dynamics of the occupational structure.

One evidence that these charges have some validity is the first nation-wide study of the employment experience of male graduates of trade and industrial occupational courses. This study shows that the majority of these graduates for their first job do not enter the trade for which they trained in high school, nor do many tend to enter the trade in later years (Eninger, 1965, p. 25). Perhaps the criterion used in this study is unrealistic or too simplistic, but it leads to speculation about whether the traditional, narrowly focused training is sufficiently viable given the needs of young workers entering the labor force.

The important point about vocational education is that it has been seen for too long as useful only to a highly restricted sample of the total student population rather than to all or most students. Its image has been that of a second-class alternative for those with low verbal skills or for those with interests in working with their hands rather than their minds. In the process, many students in such programs and many vocational educators have become defensive about their alleged inferior status, have moved further into an isolationist stance divorcing themselves from so-called academic education, and have tied themselves to training experiences rigidly defined by time and content. This latter condition has occurred not necessarily because vocational educators want it that way but because factors such as legislative funding and union or apprenticeship regulations have in some instances forced such restrictions.

Regardless of the reasons for the situation, the fact remains that many students who desperately need what vocational education and vocational experiences can offer have been blocked from this access. Such a condition has added further fuel to the arbitrary separation of students into supposedly homogeneous categories of college-bound and non-college-bound, with the educational experiences offered each group seen as essentially mutually exclusive.

The means of releasing more of the potential contribution of vocational education to vocationalization and, indeed, to vocational guidance lies not in assigning to or recruiting more students for a vocational education track but in making vocational education an equal partner with all other aspects of the educational process. All the relationships between "general education" and vocationalization which have been suggested apply to vocational education with equal force. They must be incorporated into a reshaping of the many thrusts of vocational education in such a way that the lines, or at least the image, which presently separates vocational education and general education are made to blur or vanish.

These comments about vocational education are not intended to preclude the continuation of specific job training for some students but rather to convey the urgent need to broaden the present interrelationships and pathways within vocational education and between it and other educational experiences. Indeed, it is important that there be developed even more specific vocational education programs which truly respond to both the low and the high ends of the intellectual continuum—whether the preparation is for becoming a helper, a waiter, a lawnmower repairman, an industrial landscape gardener, a heavy construction equipment operator, or a computer programmer. The need is to create more tactics not only for fitting youth to programs but also for fitting programs to youth. The existing lockstep of certain training durations and specified training experiences as the only route to vocational education must be broken to exploit the enlarging opportunities in the occupational structure for individuals with a wide range of capability.

If vocational guidance is to be fully effective, vocational education courses must not only teach skills for specific occupations or skills across families of jobs; they must also develop within students the elements of vocationalization which will free them to discern the alternative ways in which these skills can be used and to attain the personal competence to capitalize upon these skills. Further, more avenues must be created for all students to move freely between general and vocational education, with the criteria for such movement being individual need, readiness, interest, motivation, and the blend of academic and vocational experiences which can meet these criteria. As Moss (1968, p. 21) has indicated, it is "the relative pre-vocational value of various patterns of preparation that is of prime educational significance."

To aid students in patterning and mixing general and vocational educational experiences, counselors and teachers will need to collaborate in developing probability data, as well as multiple discriminant data, for comparing the characteristics of students contemplating a particular blend of experiences with the characteristics of individuals who have completed similar and different sequences of experiences and the outcomes of these. Chapter 10 will discuss some of the possible ways of doing these things. Such procedures will need to be continuing and complementary reinforcements of decision making, value refinement, and personal planning as these occur not only in the selection of educational experiences but within the experiences themselves. While such strategies may seem to be too future-oriented, the reader is referred to the time-shared computer capabilities in vocational guidance reported in Chapter 11, with which these objectives could be meshed.

The zero-reject concept of curriculum planning used in the San Mateo Unified School District, San Mateo, California, is one example of the comprehensive planning required by the objectives implicit in the preceding paragraphs. The zero-reject concept assumes (Champion, 1969, p. 4):

1. That the state of the art in education today makes it possible for every student to earn a high school diploma with significant standards and a broad liberal and vocational education.

2. That more individualization of education is possible through a wider range of known learning strategies, even though much more research is needed in this field.

3. That vocational education and general education are mutually supportive and equally necessary; one does not take precedence over the other.

4. That work in and of itself can be a rewarding element of the full life beyond economic independence, and it is a common denominator of concern for all Americans.

5. That practically speaking there are no unskilled jobs, only unskilled people.

6. That the schools have the responsibility for seeing that students are employable whenever they choose to leave school.

7. That educational goals can be expressed in terms of cognitive, affective, and psychomotor skills, and that each occupation requires a differing mix.

8. That occupations can be grouped by clusters and by levels, and that they form ladders of progression through the various educational levels.

9. That education is a lifelong process and that the school provides the direction and climate for continued learning.

Obviously, neither traditional conceptions of vocational education nor the newer forms of it, such as the cluster concept, nor a greater freedom of movement between general and vocational education is the only way to provide vocational guidance and vocationalization. At the senior high school level, the integration of work experience with schooling can be a reality. The age and sex of the student are no longer the contingencies they are at the junior high school level. Blocks of time can be developed when students will actually report to jobs instead of school for two or three weeks or perhaps a term at a time. While the economic appeal is obvious, the training and exploratory value of such experience must be fitted to individual needs. Hence if a particular student is interested in electronics, a program could be made available by which he can complete his high school work and simultaneously secure the on-the-job training available through part-time employment. With creative industry-education cooperation, programs could be mounted providing training at work stations in the community in the late afternoon or morning hours with the remainder of the day devoted to general education in the school. For some students, this could be pretechnical training, for others, a permanent job, and still others, exploration prior to baccalaureate study.

Probably the more common name for such programs of work-study is cooperative vocational education. A specific definition of such programs is provided by the National Conference on Cooperative Vocational Education (University of Minnesota, 1969):

> A cooperative work-study program of vocational education for persons, who, through a cooperative arrangement between the school and employers, receive instruction, including required academic courses and related vocational instruction, by the alternation of study in school with a job in any occupational field, but these two experiences must be planned and supervised by the school and employers so that each contributes to the student's education and to his employability. Work periods and school attendance may be on alternate half-days, full days, weeks, or other periods of time in fulfilling the cooperative vocational education work-study program.

The National Conference tended to view cooperative vocational education as an "application learning laboratory" for students in conjunction with vocational education and as a vehicle for the "self-exploration function of supervised work experiences" which would foster long-range career development. More particularly, the National Conference recommended that the essential elements of a quality program of cooperative vocational education should include:

1. A well-qualified, highly dedicated teacher-coordinator

2. Related instruction focusing on technical competencies, career development, and occupational adjustment taught by the teacher-coordinator.

3. Adequate time for the teacher-coordinator to supervise instruction and on-the-job training

4. *Adequate facilities, equipment, and materials to provide instruction related to the student's job and career goal*

5. *Placement and instruction matched to the student's career interests, abilities, and aspirations*

6. *Pre-vocational education and guidance services which prepare students for selecting the most appropriate training opportunity*

7. *A student-directed youth organization like FFA, DECA, etc.*

8. *A selection of cooperative vocational education programs to serve the needs of students of different abilities, career interests and aspirations— including the disadvantaged, the nonprofit private school students, and the dropouts*

9. *Full wages and credit toward graduation while receiving on-the-job instruction*

10. *Written training agreements and individual training plans developed and agreed upon by the employer, training sponsor, students, and coordinator*

11. *Community involvement in planning, organizing, and supporting cooperative programs*

12. *An advisory committee composed of representatives from business, industry, labor, the school, and the students enrolled*

13. *Compliance with all state and federal laws regarding employment practices*

14. *Continuous evaluation and revisions based on followup of student trainees and achievement of program objectives*

15. *Ancillary services to provide in-service teacher education, supervision, development of curriculum materials, evaluation and research for the improvement of cooperative education*

16. *Adequate funds to support a quality cooperative vocational education program*

Many prototype programs designed to exploit school-community work relationships for students with differing needs are already under way. Among them are projects in Santa Barbara, California, Champaign, Illinois, Cranston, Rhode Island, and Kansas City, Missouri (Burchill, 1969).

The Santa Barbara Program as described by Burchill (p. 8) is a part of the regular curriculum and has three distinct parts:

1. *The exploratory work-experience education phase permits students to explore their vocational interests and aptitudes through a variety of part-time jobs in industry, business, or the professions. Students are super-*

vised by school personnel, receive school credits toward graduation, but receive no pay.

2. The general work-experience education phase *is intended to give students experience in work settings where they meet regular work standards. They work for pay and school credits, during or after school hours, on part-time jobs supervised by school authorities.*

3. The vocational work-experience education phase *is set up to provide students paid jobs in the field directly related to the occupation they want to enter after they leave school. It is a laboratory experience for them while they are still enrolled in school.*

In the project, a full-time school coordinator for each high school, together with members of the counseling staff and selected teachers, oversees the placement of students, supervises students on their stations, coordinates their activities with parents and employers, and reports on the progress of each student.

The other three programs described by Burchill have a more specific focus than the one in Santa Barbara. The program in Cranston, Rhode Island, is designed to prepare girls for post–high school employment as nurse's aides, ward secretaries, and medical secretaries. The program's typical yearly enrollment includes senior girls exploring and learning nonprofessional-level vocations in hospital settings. Some are good students with definite vocational goals. Others use these experiences to explore medical vocations. Still others are potential dropouts who see the worth of continued education in a practical work-study curriculum. In this one-year program, students alternate two-week periods of class attendance with two-week periods of work in local hospitals. The class is divided into two sections and rotated from one setting to the other every two weeks. The students receive a weekly stipend for work performed in the hospital.

The program in Kansas City, Missouri, is a work-study experience designed to prevent juvenile delinquency. This is a three-stage program designed specifically for children fitting the definition of alienated youth. The first stage is a general orientation period consisting of half-day classes and half-day group work assignments. The students perform socially useful work in and around the school for half of each day and spend the other half studying an academic program geared to their level and interests. The second stage is for boys from fifteen to seventeen years of age who have completed the first stage. They are placed on community jobs for half of each school day and continue academic classwork during the other half of the day. Cooperating employers and the school employment coordinator supervise them on their jobs. To be eligible for the third stage boys must be between the ages of sixteen and eighteen and must have completed stage two successfully. In this third stage the employment coordinator-supervisor helps them find full-time employment and oversees their adjustment from school to work.

VOCATIONAL EDUCATION AND HANDICAPPED STUDENTS

The program in Champaign, Illinois, also described in Burchill (1969), is designed to provide pre-vocational services for physically or mentally handicapped youth. The first phase of the project involves rehabilitation through a complete special-education program in small, sheltered class environments. This phase is concerned with the social adjustment of the students as well as with pre-vocational education—the provision of those experiences which foster the attitudes, habits, skills, and knowledge necessary for effective vocational adjustment. Students successful in this phase, particularly with social adjustment, are placed on part-time work assignments in school, where they are supervised by school personnel and where their work assignments and classwork can be coordinated.

The students progress from this stage to half-day job assignments in the community, where their adjustment is helped by the cooperative efforts of employers, program supervisors, state rehabilitation counselors, school social workers, and special teachers. Finally, when they complete school students are helped to find regular employment and continue to receive follow-up assistance from school personnel until their transition from school to work is complete. Throughout the program, the handicapped pupil's interests and aspirations, and the counselor's understanding of the child, are the bases for selecting individual programs.

The inclusion of handicapped children in vocational education requires an assessment of their work potential. Like any other group, handicapped students are not homogeneous. They differ in interests, skills, and aspirations, and such individual characteristics must be identified. Merachnik (1970), in outlining such an approach in the public schools, recommends the following considerations, which the authors have paraphrased:

1. The assessment of work potential should focus upon the strengths of the handicapped child rather than upon his weaknesses.

2. Handicapped students should not be compared directly with nonhandicapped students since the former have probably suffered restrictions on exploratory experiences leading to the development of interests and skills. Even in the case of handicapped students who appear to possess little interest, skill, or aptitude in anything of a work nature, the search must be made for a possible work motif. Even the simplest activities must be considered in terms of potential for work since these may furnish the clues which lead eventually to realistic work activity.

3. Handicapped conditions differ in the degree and kind of restriction. Within this population, any one or a combination of the following conditions may be present: physical (as in the case of a below the knee amputee), mental (as in the case of an educable mental retardate), social (as in the case of a badly burned adolescent isolate), emotional (as in the case of a withdrawn schizophrenic youngster), educational (as in the case of a slow learner). Regardless of

the handicap or its secondary effects, it will be necessary to determine what special needs—whether prosthetic, mechanical, or therapeutic—are required to maximize the student's work potential.

4. Because of lack of experience, unfamiliarity with test-taking, or an emotional overlay, which calls for interest or aptitude testing of the handicapped child, it is probably necessary to do such testing on an individual rather than group basis.

5. Parents must be consulted and counseled when work plans are made for their handicapped offspring. Acceptance of a realistic plan for work may well depend upon how they have accepted the fact of their youngster's limitations.

6. Because of the lessened mobility of many handicapped students and their resulting propensity to remain within the geographic area in which they have lived, local labor market data related to work opportunities unimpaired by their handicapping condition are essential.

7. Placement of handicapped students may involve helping prospective employers determine how through improvisation or the use of mechanical aids a particular job routine can be altered in such a way that the handicapped youth can adequately function in it.

8. Community agencies will need to be used in terms of their special expertise on specific handicapping conditions for purposes of assessment, support, and/or placement.

Pruitt and Longfellow (1970, p. 8) have indicated that work evaluation concerns itself with two basic types of clients: "those who are aware of their need to work and those who, because of a number of psychological factors, deny this need." They further suggest that the common problems which work evaluation must take into account include: developmental problems, attitudinal problems, readiness problems, and role problems. In terms of the vocabulary used in this book, some handicapped students will have suffered a lack of vocationalization and will need to have this matter attended to before or at least at the same time that specific behavioral or attitudinal deficits are dealt with. Sankovsky (1970) has indicated that vocational evaluation is the following process:

1. Establishing criteria and vocational goals
2. Collecting information regarding vocational potential
3. Analyzing information regarding vocational potential
4. Decision making on potential vocational goals and predicting outcome
5. Determining the effectiveness of the evaluation process by feedback obtained through follow-up

Obviously, these processes involve concern for the physical and the psycho-social condition of the youngster as these interact to determine where vocational evaluation must start and the degree to which common measurement techniques, manual dexterity tests, work sample assessments, job analysis, pre-vocational education (vocationalization), or other vocational guidance strategies need to be employed either prior to or with vocation education, general education, and placement.

Probably it is fair to predict that school counselors as they more fully implement the vocational aspects of guidance will need to gain understanding of the implications of work sample theory for vocationalization or vocational guidance as treatment. This is true both for handicapped students and for nonhandicapped students. There is a need for knowledge of work sample theory whether school counselors involve themselves directly in work sample activities or provide the cooperative links with employment service counselors and rehabilitation counselors described in Chapter 12.

In brief, work samples are of three types: *the simulated work sample,* which is a mock-up or a close simulation of an actual work activity, not essentially different from the kind of work required in a specific kind of job; *the actual work sample,* which is a small sample from an actual job involving the use of the same materials, equipment, and/or tools, e.g. typing letters or operating a machine, and differs only from the actual job in terms of the work setting; *the isolated-trait work sample,* which assesses a specific trait, such as finger dexterity or sorting ability, common to a number of different jobs (Pruitt, 1970).

The importance of work sample techniques lies not only in their direct application to vocational evaluation and in their more direct relationship to a particular criterion of job performance but also in the fact that they represent a substitute for the more typical psychological tests which are highly dependent upon the manipulation of verbal symbols and frequently reading ability as well as academic achievement. This is not to suggest that work sample techniques should or can be used in isolation from assessments of broader abilities, dispositions, beliefs, attitudes, response-styles, and the like (Neff, 1970); rather, it is to say that for many students, e.g. the handicapped and the nonverbal, work sample techniques provide more concrete and direct ways to get measures of actual job potential from which other self-characteristics can be evaluated. As Barton (1970) has indicated, vocational evaluation and work sampling can be considered a requisite to work adjustment, and vocational evaluation can also be considered a vocational development experience. The important point here is that the strategies inherent in vocational evaluation and work sampling represent powerful tools not only for relating the handicapped student to vocational education and subsequent work placement but for enhancing the vocationalization of all students as these techniques are tied to simulations, gaming, or diverse exploratory activities.

In summary, Johnson (1969, pp. 10-11) has outlined the fundamental principles to follow in organizing vocational education for the handicapped:

1. A single approach to the solution of how to provide an appropriate vocational education for the handicapped does not lie in the organization of segregated classes nor in integrated classes per se. The answer to the correct educational placement of a child lies only within him. . . .

2. Segregated and integrated programs, as usually defined, are mechanistic approaches; structures that in and of themselves solve no problems. Once programs are conceived to provide for the vocational education of all potential recipients, the appropriate structures can be developed. . . .

3. No single characteristic can be used to determine the appropriate class placement of a child. Thus, his placement is not determined by his handicap.

4. Separate, segregated instruction should be recommended and provided only when no existing class can be used to give the students the kind and level of instruction necessary. . . .

5. When a handicapped child is placed in a regular or existing class, he should have the necessary skills and abilities to participate on an equal basis with the rest of the children in the group. . . .

6. Supportive, ancillary services should be provided. . . .

7. In the placement of a child his strengths and positive characteristics are the fundamental considerations. . . .

VOCATIONAL EDUCATION FOR MINORITY-GROUP OR DISADVANTAGED YOUTH

The development of vocational education programs (and, indeed, other vocationalization activities) for minority-group youth—like those for handicapped youth—require special considerations. In particular, Dennard (1969) has suggested that planning for vocational education programs must take into account socioeconomic constraints such as socioeconomic needs, industry-needs surveys, and special socioeconomic problems that focus on the following (p. 6):

1. Hiring practices of minority members
2. Entry-level requirements
3. Apprentice union practices
4. Percent of minorities in the local population
5. Percent of minorities in the local work force
6. Percent of minorities in the in-school population
7. Percent of minorities in the out-of-school population
8. Types of educational/occupational opportunities existing

In addition, Dennard suggests that the occupational fields and courses provided in vocational and technical education should be those which will improve the local socioeconomic *employment* situation for disadvantaged students rather than the school situation. This requires attention to local manpower projection studies and their implications for curricula, as well as to surveys of the supply of students and their occupational preferences.

Feldman (1969), speaking from the focus of programs funded by Ford Foundation, contends (p. 1), "Vocational education has a serious and important message to deliver in the education of the poor for reasons that are even more important than the fact that it does provide economic mobility." In the case of the poor child, he states (p. 6):

> *We now believe we must create the experiences which build learning. The experiences will come from those programs now defined as industrial or vocational education. We often lose sight, however, of the fact that doing is only the beginning—thinking–follows–feeling–follows–doing is the specific form which later generalizations will follow. We in vocational education can provide a high proportion of doing if it were used properly for comprehensive education purposes. . . . The processes of vocational education require the student's active participation and greatly enhance his motivation to learn. They help relate his educational experience to any number of adult roles as well, which are particularly applicable to the poor. . . . In an effective comprehensive program, youngsters would be introduced to the concept of choice between achievement through verbal or abstract performance and achievement through manipulation and demonstration of real objects.*

Mangum (1969, p. 11), speaking on vocational education for the disadvantaged from the perspective of experience in government-funded programs, emphasizes that meeting the needs of these youth through vocational education in the senior high school must be part of a longitudinal program that takes into account the following needs and facts:

1. Early childhood education

2. Elementary school orientation to the world of work

3. The need to view vocational education as a teaching method and an educational objective rather than a separate educational system with especial value for its contributions to relevance and motivation

4. The critical need for and the methods of remedial basic education, communications and job hunting skills, work adjustment, and prevocational training

5. The value of vocational education to previously neglected clients such as prisoners, reservation Indians, the disadvantaged in general, and the employed needing upgrading

6. The possibilities and the motivating and training value of direct links between the school and the job

7. The irrelevance and often the perverseness of many of the credentialing requirements for vocational education personnel and the critical need for sympathetic and relevantly trained staffs

8. The arbitrariness and inflexibility of many curriculum and scheduling practices, the perverseness of entrance requirements and testing methods, and reminder [sic] that adaptation of the school to the individual needs rather than vice versa is the only defensible stance

9. The variety of institutional, social, and personal handicaps confronting the disadvantaged individual, his critical need for supportive services, and the number of cooperating institutions emerging to meet his needs

10. The fact that the disadvantaged are not appreciably different in their yearnings and ambitions from anyone else, once the possibilities of upward mobility are clear and realistic

The observations made in the last two sections on the handicapped and the disadvantaged and minority youth reaffirm the thrusts of this book. To deal with the vocationalization needs of youth, one has to consider what levels of knowledge, personal experience, self-understanding, interests, and motivational dispositions characterize the individual case. Determination must then be made of the particular sets of exposures or experiences which will foster the individual's further vocational development. If the problems for any individual or any group of individuals can be seen whole, then the response must be a systems emphasis either over the longer range—kindergarten through twelfth grade—or the shorter range, which incorporates those resources—remedial, attitudinal, knowledge, skills, general education, vocational education, simulations, work-study—that appear to be able to improve the life perspective of the individual.

VOCATIONALIZATION AND GENERAL EDUCATION

The amount of emphasis in this chapter on vocational education, cooperative vocational education, and the interrelationships necessary between vocational education and general education is not intended to indicate that vocational guidance and vocational education are synonyms nor to denigrate the potential of general education to influence vocationalization. Rather, the intent of this emphasis is to heighten the school counselor's and the vocational educator's awareness of the more comprehensive role which can be played by vocational education if it is reshaped to provide greater numbers of students with access to it.

To increase the vocationalization potential of general education in the senior high school requires incorporating and adopting many of the themes and activities emphasized in the chapter on the junior high school and supplementing them with simulation, group processes, or work-study opportunities. For example, a continuing vocational development theme in courses designed to prepare students for college will diminish the persistent assumption that college is an end in itself. It, too, is an intermediate vocational choice for the vast majority of students who enter college. With such an emphasis, students can be helped to see college less as a way of deferring career thinking and more as one of the alternative ways to achieve particular vocational goals. As indicated previously, many of the students for whom college is the immediate step following high school can also profit from direct work experience or from access to vocational education experiences in the school itself in order to heighten the purpose with which they approach college.

Not all the students to whom vocationalization strategies in general education and vocational guidance have relevance will have college as their major intent or work after high school as their immediate goal. Hoyt has mounted a major research project concerned with those whom he has described as "the specialty oriented" (Hoyt, 1965). He contrasts the specialty–oriented and the liberal arts–oriented student, with the former also having post-secondary educational aspirations but inclined to trade, technical, or business school training rather than college. He speaks of the specialty oriented as those whose prime educational motivation is to acquire an occupational skill or set of skills which could be used to enter the labor market.

Hoyt indicates that for the specialty–oriented student, guidance practices should include increased use of information in the counseling process and counseling for specific decision making. He asserts (p. 235), "I think far too many students leave the secondary school today with, at best, some general notions of what they may do but without the slightest idea of when or how they will be able to convert these general notions into realistic actions."

Throughout this book the authors have echoed similar concerns about the need to provide meaningful and relevant information to expand student freedom of choice and the range of possibilities from which students may choose. It has been our contention that information can be delivered in many ways— through curriculum, role playing, modeling, simulation, work, work-study, and others. We have also contended in this chapter that counseling and other vocational guidance activities must foster specific decision making. In the preceding chapter, some of the strategies for fostering decision making among junior high school youth were introduced. The next section will extend that discussion to the senior high school population.

VOCATIONAL GUIDANCE STRATEGIES TO FOSTER DECISION MAKING

Many different guidance strategies independent of or combined with various media have been used to promote the different aspects of decision-making behavior among senior high school students. Jones and Krumboltz (1970) in one study examined the matter of stimulating vocational exploration through film-mediated problems. The experiment was replicated in two high schools; one a predominantly white middle-class school and the other a school in which 46 percent of the students were Mexican American and Puerto Rican, 7 percent were black, 1 percent were oriental, and the remainder were white. In both these high schools, three versions of an experimental film were shown; the film presented five jobs that represented a cross section of employment opportunities available for men and women in banking. A representative problem situation in each job was enacted on film for five or six minutes to the point where a decision had to be made.

The three versions of the film differed in the type of response each requested from the students in the experimental group: active-overt participation (students recorded their solutions in workbooks), active-covert participation (students were asked to think about their solutions but did not write them down), passive participation (no questions were asked of the students). One control group of students viewed regular banking career films; another read printed banking career information, and questions for them to consider were suggested; a third control group read printed general career information. The conclusions were (1) that the experimental film versions were more effective than were materials selected for comparison purposes and (2) that the active participation versions of the experimental film were more effective than the passive participation version.

In another study, Krumboltz and Schroeder (1965) randomly assigned 54 eleventh-grade volunteers for educational and vocational counseling to three treatments: (1) reinforcement counseling (information-seeking responses reinforced), (2) model-reinforcement counseling (tape recording of a male counselee played to each student prior to reinforcement counseling), and (3) a control group. The findings were (a) that the experimental groups engaged in more information seeking outside the interview than did control group members; (b) that reinforcement counseling produced significantly more information-seeking behavior outside the interview (e.g. reading resources, talking about opportunities) for females but not males as compared to control group behaviors; (c) that model-reinforcement counseling produced significantly more information-seeking behavior outside the interview for males than for females as compared to controls; and (d) that the ratio of information-seeking responses to other responses in the interview was positively correlated with external information-seeking behavior.

In a related study, Krumboltz and Thoresen (1964) randomly assigned 192 eleventh-grade pupils to individual and group counseling settings in which the following four procedures were used by counselors: (1) reinforcement of verbal information-seeking behavior, (2) presentations of a tape-recorded model interview followed by reinforcement counseling, (3) presentation of film or filmstrip plus discussion as a control procedure, and (4) inactive control. The findings were (a) that model-reinforcement and reinforcement counseling produced more external information-seeking behavior than control procedures; (b) that with a male model, model-reinforcement counseling surpassed reinforcement counseling for males but not females; (c) that group and individual settings were about equally effective on the average, but interactions were found to be affected by counselor variables, schools, set of subjects, and treatments.

Meyer, Strowig, and Hosford (1970) in a similar study assigned 144 female and male eleventh-grade students in three rural high schools to four behavioral-reinforcement counseling treatments and controls in individual and small-group settings. Base line data on the information-seeking behaviors of the students were collected prior to initiating the treatments. Local high school counselors were trained and used as the experimental counselors. The treatments used were: (1) reinforcement of verbal information-seeking behavior, (2) tape-recorded model interview plus reinforcement, (3) sound film plus reinforcement, and (4) no-treatment control. The findings were (a) that all behavioral-reinforcement treatments produced significantly more information-seeking behaviors than no-treatment control procedures; (b) that on the average, reinforcement counseling was as effective as model reinforcement and film reinforcement for promoting the criterion behaviors; (c) that insignificant differences occurred between small-group and individual counseling settings; and (d) that for most treatments, females showed a greater amount and variety of information-seeking behavior than males.

Hosford (1970) has discussed the unpublished work of Thoresen and Hamilton, who in 1969 tested the effect of structured stimulus materials, peer social modeling with structured materials, and insight group counseling to promote knowledge and use of career information on the part of eleventh-grade male students at three schools. Four group sessions were employed for each treatment group. Hosford (p. 16) reports:

> The structured stimulus materials treatment involved the subjects in specific listening, talking, writing, and enacting activities. The sessions included (1) setting up expectations for a career and learning how to ask relevant questions, (2) practice in asking relevant questions, (3) determining credibility of career information, and (4) formulating a tentative plan of action. The peer social modeling treatment consisted of four 15-minute video tapes in which the models discussed behaviors highly similar to those in the stimulus materials treatment. . . . Peer social modeling with structured materials utilized the content and sequence of the first two treatments. The fourth treatment, insight group counseling, involved verbalization of feelings and ideas about future plans and career possibilities.

The results obtained from this study were mixed in the sense that in some schools the structured-materials approach was more effective than modeling, while at another school this condition was reversed.

Krumboltz, Varenhorst, and Thoresen (1967), in a study examining the relationships of sex, model counselor attentiveness, and prestige to later information-seeking behavior, found among a sample of 168 female eleventh-grade students that the use of relevant female social models did increase the information-seeking behavior of female students. Thus, when these results are wedded with those of other studies reported in this section, it appears that an appropriate social model increases the information seeking of both males and females. Additional data received in the study led the authors to further suggest (p. 417), "It appears quite plausible that the prestige and the attentiveness of a counselor are major variables in his effectiveness."

In another related study, Thoresen, Krumboltz, and Varenhorst (1967) reported that when four types of social model audiotapes (male counselor and male student, male counselor and female student, female counselor and male student, and female counselor and female student) were used to foster imitative behavior, a male counselor–male student model was most effective for males when presented by a male counselor. For females, the significant variable was the sex of the counselor, not the sex of the model student.

Thoresen and Krumboltz (1968), in studies of the effect of peer group models on imitative learning, found that different athletic-model success levels caused significant differences in the frequency of information-seeking behaviors by students. This finding, however, was not confirmed for students whose self-perceptions athletically, socially, or academically were low. These low self-concept students, who were aspiring to high success, engaged in more information-seeking behavior after exposure to low- or medium-success models.

Collectively, the studies reported here, although not exhaustive, provide insight into the potential of reinforcement-behavioral counseling, modeling, imitative learning, and filmed and audiotaped presentations of specific stimulus materials, to influence different components of decision-making and information-seeking exploratory behavior among high school students. Perhaps more important, they demonstrate that sex and other individual characteristics are related to the effects of these different approaches. In other words, they emphasize the necessity of matching technique with individual characteristics and needs.

Finally, it is apparent that while these approaches have validity for vocationalization objectives, they also hold promise for the treatment of specific behavioral deficits. In terms of the latter, Woody (1968) has discussed the use of behavioral techniques in vocational counseling. In particular, he has described the following as behavioral techniques having validity in vocational guidance and counseling: social recognition and object rewards; social modeling; verbal reinforcement; systematic desensitization; assertive practice; and clinical suggestion.

VOCATIONAL RESOURCE CENTERS AND CONFERENCES

In addition to aiding vocationalization through the many strategies discussed thus far, there is also the possibility of physically concentrating these efforts in one center within the school, typically near the office of the school counselor. One example is the Career Guidance Resources Center in the Public Schools of Newton, Massachusetts (Smith, 1968). This center integrates the career information library, the placement program, and follow-up services. In addition, it administers a vocational testing service and various group guidance activities designed to foster vocational development, and disseminates relevant information to those who guide the career exploration and decision making of students. Finally, the center is the liaison with the local business-industrial community, coordinating community resources to support vocational development needs of students.

Another way of focusing attention upon the vocational guidance needs of students and enlisting the support of community resources to meet them is through what Unger and Karlin (1969) have described as a Vocational Resources Conference. Initially, representatives of the multiple agencies serving youth in New York City were brought together with school personnel to discuss cooperative efforts. One outcome was a Youth Vocational Resources Conference, which convened in a local high school. This conference provided small-group, informal discussion among school counselors and representatives of the various youth service agencies. The format did not consist of speeches but of opportunities for each person to visit with agency representatives to discuss the services available, to learn who the contact person was, and to obtain other similar data. Students were not involved. This was primarily conceived as a meeting of professionals from different settings who had similar concerns but a range of strategies for meeting them. Another outcome of this approach was the identification and compilation of data about existing community resources, ways of access to them, hours available, and ways in which services could be combined across agencies.

Johnson (1969) has reported on an Occupational Information Center for Education-Industry. This agency, serving seven school systems in and around Atlanta, Georgia, represents the combined efforts of faculty members of Georgia State College, representatives of about one hundred local businesses and industries, as well as the Georgia State Department of Education. Specifically the goals identified for the center include (p. 41):

1. To provide for high school counselors and other educators in metropolitan Atlanta, a specific, detailed source of up-to-date information about employment opportunities, and to recommend ways in which students may prepare themselves to take advantage of these opportunities

2. To establish and maintain lines of communication between local business firms and school personnel

3. To develop projects which will build upon and improve this communication

4. To update the training of counselors who work with high school students and to keep them current on employment needs and trends in the metropolitan area

5. *To assist principals and counselors in the development of career-information programs for school assemblies, career days, faculty meetings, and parent meetings*

6. *To develop new ways to present career information to students, including such media as films, filmstrips, videotapes, recordings, and other audio-visual aids*

Among the many concentrated activities of the center in developing information useful for counselors and students was the use of a standardized interview schedule with employers. In addition to providing information about the work of the firm, what it does and how it is done, availability of public transportation, number of new employees hired, minimum age and education requirements, the project classified the jobs available in four ways:

1. Jobs for the young person who has not finished high school
2. Jobs for the high school graduate
3. Jobs for the young man or woman who entered college but did not stay
4. Jobs for the college-degree holder

These three approaches are, of course, only representative of the many approaches and organizations across the nation which attempt to accomplish similar objectives and to muster resources both in and out of schools to meet the manifold vocational guidance needs of youth. Implicit in each is an awareness that educational processes and vocational guidance cannot operate in isolation from the community in which they are located, nor can they be effective without aiding the movement of youth from schools to participation in the occupational activities of the community.

Finally, then, vocational guidance must concern itself with placement as a culmination of all the preceding efforts in vocationalization. The next section will deal with this area.

PLACEMENT

Historically, vocational guidance, counseling, and placement have been considered mutually exclusive events. The contention of this book is that while vocational guidance, counseling, and placement are not synonymous, neither are they mutually exclusive—nor are they events. From the viewpoint of a systems approach, vocational guidance as a stimulus to vocationalization is a process which contributes to placement. In a very real sense, effective placement of students in the labor market is the end product of readiness for vocational planning (Gribbons and Lohnes, 1968) or of crystalizing a vocational preference (Super, Starishevsky, Matlin, and Jordaan, 1963). Each of these is in itself a level of vocational maturity at which is developmentally synthesized attitudes, knowledge of alternatives, planfulness, self-awareness, and other characteristics discussed in Chapters 2 and 5.

Such observations do not preclude the fact that individuals will come to placement in different conditions of readiness for decision making based upon considered alternatives. The assumption is that these conditions will depend upon the degree to which such persons have been exposed to the elements of vocationalization in concert with general educational experiences from elementary school through senior high school. If such development has not occurred in the personal history of the student to be placed, the school counselor or whoever else is responsible for placement will find it necessary to provide the student with the conditions and the resources, within an abbreviated time frame, which will foster the prerequisites to placement the individual lacks. In these instances, the school counselor must counsel or provide information in such a way that the student can test for himself the possible consequences of different placement alternatives. In other instances, particularly those in which placement responsibility is assumed by someone other than the school counselor, the student might need to be referred to another specialist who can assist him acquire the attitudinal, emotional, or informational placement prerequisites necessary.

If placement is viewed as a transition process for the student as well as a point in time, the school counselor can help him prepare himself psychologically for placement. This may require role-playing interview situations, assistance in completing or recognizing the importance of employment applications, or provision of information about jobs available in the local setting. It will also involve support and follow-up while the individual is moving through the placement process. In some cases, the school counselor must lend strength to individual students who encounter initial rebuffs until their confidence and self-esteem are reinforced through being accepted by a firm.

To be effective in the placement process, it is obvious that the school counselor will need to communicate with persons outside the school active in placement—personnel or training people in business and industry, employment service counselors, rehabilitation counselors, and others. Such communication will require that the school counselor be able to talk knowledgeably about the competence level, goals, and characteristics of persons to be placed, as well as to secure information about openings which is relevant, accurate, and localized.

Since not all students to be placed will be high school graduates, school counselors concerned with placement will need to know of jobs available for the school dropout as well. The Atlanta Occupational-Educational Center, discussed in the previous section, exemplified ways of obtaining such information. At the point of placement of school dropouts, the counselor needs to reject the temptation to admonish about how much monetary difference exists between them and high school graduates or why this choice condemns them to a life-long position of unskilled or semiskilled work. The appropriate course is to provide the dropout with help in obtaining employment, information about ways he can continue his education, and the reassurance that if and when he is interested in resuming his high school program he will be welcome to do so.

The fact is that placement for students entering the labor market has seldom been seen as a major responsibility of the school. It is true that vocational educators in different curricula, business teachers, and some school counselors have engaged in placing students. But it is less true that these activities have been performed with purpose under the rubric of vocational guidance or have been seen as a natural extension of this process. This situation is a continuing paradox in the face of the intensity with which schools and school counselors pursue the placement of students in college.

Bottoms and Matheny (1969, p. 15) have suggested that three sequential steps are necessary to a high school job-placement program:

1. Preparation for entrance into the world of work which includes assessments of one's own desires, abilities, etc., and the acquisition of knowledge about occupations and what is expected of a person in a work setting

2. Locating and accepting a job, which includes making plans for moving from school to work and in implementing plans as well as contracting in potential employers

3. Follow-through personal contact and counseling for students once they are placed on a job to assist them in retaining the job and in establishing plans for moving up the job ladder

These three steps reemphasize the importance of viewing placement as more than an isolated event. They also affirm the importance of placement as a service that brings students and employers together. If the school already participates in the types of work-study or cooperative vocational education programs previously described in this section, part of this task has already been accomplished. If it does not, strategies to enlist school-industry cooperation must be devised. Cooperative linkage with employment service counselors is one step in this direction; vocational resources conferences, community advisory groups, utilization of Chambers of Commerce, and the National Alliance of Businessmen are others.

In a different and more comprehensive context, Bottoms and Thalleen (1969) have described Georgia's state-wide job-placement program for area vocational technical schools. While of greater scope than would be developed in a specific school system, the approach offers suggestions worth considering. Included in the Georgia program are guidance units presented to students prior to the Techdays—the days when employers come to the schools. These units deal with such topics as How to Prepare a Resumé, How to Complete a Job-Application Form, Your Job Interview, etc. Each of these units is intended to create in students an attitudinal set, understandings, and skills which will permit them to approach placement interviews with maximum personal effectiveness. Among other coordinating and supporting responsibilities, the State Department of Education conducts a state-wide mailing to industry, provides publicity for the program through news releases, television, radio spots, and posters, and originally consulted with local area school guidance personnel as they formulated their programs.

The Techdays program provides opportunities for students to meet in group sessions to hear company representatives describe the opportunities provided by their firms. Interested students are then offered an opportunity to be interviewed personally by these representatives or to make appointments to visit particular firms subsequent to the program. In 1968, 643 companies participated in twenty-three area vocational technical schools in Georgia, and 1,978 job offers were made to students. Not all the students were interested in the jobs offered them, but the results seemed to evidence that these students, like those who accepted employment, felt that they had benefited from the experience and were better equipped for later interviews. Programs such as this serve the employment and public relations needs of industry; they develop community and industrial awareness of the areas in which students receive training and foster favorable attitudes concerning the quality of this training. More important, however, they give evidence to students that the school is interested in them and that placement does ensue by system rather than by chance.

SUMMARY

This chapter has discussed vocational development in the senior high school as it is conditioned by the imminence of various forms of reality with which students must cope. Continuing themes regarding a systems approach to vocationalization which were begun in elementary school finally converge at the senior high school level. Implications for intensity of planning and the fostering of goal-directedness in different individuals are considered as correlates of different forms of behavior following high school. The mutual contributions of vocational education and general education to vocationalization are examined as recommendations are developed for greater meshing of these two elements of the educational process.

REFERENCES

*Advisory Council on Vocational Education.   Vocational education: The bridge between man and his work.   *Highlights and recommendations from the General Report.*   Washington, D. C.: U. S. Office of Education, 1968.

*Astin, Helen S.   Career development during the high school years.   *Journal of Counseling Psychology,* 1967, 14, 94–98.

Barton, E. H., Jr.   Vocational evaluation and adjustment: Vocational development companions.   *Journal of Rehabilitation,* 1970, 36, 35–37.

* Recommended for additional reading.

Bottoms, J. R., and Matheny, K.   Occupational guidance counseling and job placement for junior high and secondary school youth.   Paper presented at the National Conference on Exemplary Programs and Projects Section of the Vocational Education Act, Amendments of 1968, Atlanta, Ga., March, 1969.

Bottoms, J. R., and Thalleen, W.   Techdays: Georgia's state-wide job-placement program for area vocational-technical schools.   *Vocational Guidance Quarterly,* 1969, 18, 10–14.

Burchill, G. W.   Work-experience educational programs for secondary youth.   Paper presented at the National Conference on Exemplary Programs and Projects Section of the Vocational Education Act, Amendments of 1968, Atlanta, Ga., March, 1969.

Campbell, R. E.   Vocational guidance in secondary education: Selected findings on a national survey which have implications for state program development.   Paper presented at the National Conference on Vocational Guidance, Development of State Programs, U. S. Office of Education, Washington, D. C., Jan., 1968.

Champion, G.   New and improved career-centered curriculum models to serve college and non-college-bound students and young workers.   Paper presented at the National Conference on Exemplary Programs and Projects Section of the Vocational Education Act, Amendments of 1968, Atlanta, Ga., March, 1969.

Dennard, C. L.   Vocational education for the disadvantaged: Planning, organizing, and operating through a systems approach.   Paper presented at the National Workshop on Vocational Education for the Disadvantaged, Atlantic City, N. J., March, 1969.

Eninger, M. W.   The process and product of T. & I. high school level vocational education in the United States.   Unpublished paper, American Institute of Research, Institute for Performance Technology, Pittsburgh, Pa., Sept., 1965.

Feldman, M. J.   Vocational education for the disadvantaged: Lessons from Ford Foundation–funded programs.   Paper presented at the National Workshop on Vocational Education for the Disadvantaged, Atlantic City, N. J., March, 1969.

Gribbons, W. D., and Lohnes, P. R.   *Emerging careers.*   New York: Teachers College Press, Columbia University, 1968.

Gysbers, N. C., and Pritchard, D. H.   *Proceedings,* National Conference on Guidance, Counseling, and Placement in Career Development and Educational-Occupational Decision-making.   Columbia: University of Missouri, Oct., 1969.

Herr, E. L., and Cramer, S. H.   *Guidance of the college-bound: Problems, practices, perspectives.*   New York: Appleton-Century-Crofts, 1968.

Hollender, M. A., and Parker, H. J.   Occupational stereotypes and needs: Their relationship to vocational choice.   *Vocational Guidance Quarterly,* 1969, 18, 91–98.

Hosford, R. E.   Behavioral counseling: A contemporary overview.   *The Counseling Psychologist,* 1969, 1, 1–32.

*Hoyt, K. B.   High school guidance and the specialty-oriented student research program.   *Vocational Guidance Quarterly,* 1965, 13, 229–236.

*Johnson, Beverly B.   An occupational information center for education-industry.   *Vocational Guidance Quarterly,* 1969, 18, 41–44.

Johnson, G. O.   Integrated and segregated vocational education programs for the handicapped.   Paper presented at the National Conference on Vocational Education, Pittsburgh, Pa., Feb., 1969.

Jones B., and Krumboltz, J. D.   Stimulating vocational exploration through film-mediated problems.   *Journal of Counseling Psychology,* 1970, 17, 107–114.

Krumboltz, J. D., and Schroeder, W. W.   Promoting career planning through reinforcement and models.   *Personnel and Guidance Journal,* 1965, 44, 19–26.

Krumboltz, J. D., and Thoresen, C. E.   The effect of behavioral counseling in groups and individual settings on information-seeking behavior.   *Journal of Counseling Psychology,* 1964, 11, 324–333.

Krumboltz, J. D.; Varenhorst, Barbara; and Thoresen, C. E.   Nonverbal factors in effectiveness of models in counseling.   *Journal of Counseling Psychology,* 1967, 14, 412–418.

Mangum, G. L.   Vocational education for the disadvantaged: Lessons from government-funded programs.   Paper presented at the National Workshop on Vocational Education for the Disadvantaged.   Atlantic City, N. J., March, 1969.

*Merachnik, D.   Assessing work potential of the handicapped in public school.   *Vocational Guidance Quarterly,* 1970, 18, 225–229.

Meyer, J. B.; Strowig, W.; and Hosford, R. E.   Behavioral-reinforcement counseling with rural high school youth.   *Journal of Counseling Psychology,* 1970, 17, 127–132.

Milliken, R. L.   Realistic occupational appraisal by high school seniors.   *Personnel and Guidance Journal,* 1962, 40, 541–544.

Minnesota, University of.   *A guide for cooperative vocational education.*   Minneapolis: College of Education, Division of Vocational and Technical Education, University, Sept., 1969.

Moss, J.   The prevocational effectiveness of industrial arts.   *Vocational Guidance Quarterly,* 1968, 17, 21–26.

*Neff, W. S.   Vocational assessment: Theory and models.   *Journal of Rehabilitation,* 1970, 36, 27–29.

Oakland, J. A.   Measurement of personality correlates of academic achievement in high school students.   *Journal of Counseling Psychology,* 1969, 16, 452–457.

*O'Hara, R. P.   Vocational self-concepts and high school achievement.   *Vocational Guidance Quarterly,* 1966, 15, 106–112.

Perrone, P. A.   Factors influencing high school seniors' occupational preference.   *Personnel and Guidance Journal,* 1964, 42, 976–979.

Pine, G. J.   Occupational and educational aspirations and delinquent behavior.   *Vocational Guidance Quarterly,* 1964-65, 13, 107–111.

*Pruitt, W. A.   Basic assumptions underlying work sample theory.   *Journal of Rehabilitation,* 1970, 36, 24–26.

*Pruitt, W. A., and Longfellow, R. E.   Work evaluation: The medium and the message—guest editorial.   *Journal of Rehabilitation,* 1970, 36, 8–9.

Research Utilization Branch.   Youth in trouble: A vocational approach.   *Research Brief,* Division of Research Demonstration Grants, Social and Rehabilitation Service, Department of Health, Education, and Welfare, Washington, D. C., Sept., 1968.

Sankovsky, R.   Toward a common understanding of vocational evaluation.   *Journal of Rehabilitation,* 1970, 36, 10–11.

Smith, E. D.   Innovative ideas in vocational guidance.   *American Vocational Journal,* 1968, 43, 19–22.

*Super, D. E.; Starishevsky, R.; Matlin, N.; and Jordaan, J. P.   *Career development: Self-concept theory.*   New York: College Entrance Examination Board, 1963.

Thompson, O. E.   Occupational values of high school students.   *Personnel and Guidance Journal,* 1966, 44, 850–853.

Thoresen, C. E., and Krumboltz, J. D.   Similarity of social models and clients in behavioral counseling: Two experimental studies.   *Journal of Counseling Psychology,* 1968, 15, 393–401.

Thoresen, C. E.; Krumboltz, J. D.; and Varenhorst, Barbara.   Sex of counselors and models: Effect on client career exploration.   *Journal of Counseling Psychology,* 1967, 14, 503–508.

Unger, M. B., and Karlin, Muriel.   A vocational resources conference.   *Vocational Guidance Quarterly,* 1969, 17, 300–301.

*Woody, R. H.   Vocational counseling with behavioral techniques.   *Vocational Guidance Quarterly,* 1968, 17, 97–103.

NINE

HELPING STRATEGIES IN VOCATIONAL GUIDANCE

One can read almost any book dealing with the role of vocational guidance in the schools and construct a summary list of goals which, while not necessarily all-inclusive, would look very much like the following:

1. Vocational guidance is an integral part of pupils' all-round education and preparation for life.

2. Practical work experience in socially useful labor helps pupils gain interests, skills, and proper attitudes toward labor.

3. Pupils should have freedom of choice in making their vocational decisions.

4. The needs of the economy and opportunities for job placement must be taken into account.

5. Pupils' interests, aptitudes, abilities, and personalities must be considered when helping them choose a vocation.

6. Health information about each pupil, as well as information about the physical and mental requirements of occupations, must be considered.

7. Vocational guidance must begin in the lower grades.

8. A wide variety of means, media, and people must be incorporated into vocational guidance work.

9. Pupils must learn to see the necessity for general educational preparation as well as for scientific, theoretical, and practical preparation for a given vocation.

10. Vocational guidance work must be connected with both in-class and out-of-class activities.

11. Pupils must learn the beauty and strength of labor expressed in all occupations.

12. Ties between school and enterprises must be established beginning in the lower grades.

13. While their orientation to labor should begin with a consideration of the economic region in which they live, pupils should not be restricted in their choice of occupation by their immediate geographical area.[1]

[1] Copyright © 1968 by the American Personnel and Guidance Association. Reprinted by permission.

Incongruous as it may seem, the above precepts describe vocational guidance in the schools of the Soviet Union (Smith, 1968). Theoretically, it would appear that the task of the Soviet schools is to prepare the pupil, by means of various activities, to select a vocation that corresponds both to his personal attributes and proclivities and to the needs of Soviet society. Emphasis is evidently placed on the student's responsibility to his government and to the Soviet people. It is this latter characteristic that distinguishes Soviet society from American society. While it would be desirable for individual personal leanings and American societal requirements to dovetail, the American system of guidance places paramount emphasis on the individual and on the personal nature of his choice. To be sure, his choice is affected by factors of need in the national economy (see Chapters 1 and 2), but that choice is not appreciably dictated by such factors as it appears to be in Soviet society.

This freedom of choice makes the decisions of American youth infinitely more complex than those of their Soviet counterparts. Guidance in the United States removes vocational imperatives; there are no "musts," "shoulds," or "oughts." The choice is that of the individual (or his parents, in some cases). The school does not impose a choice upon the individual.

Because the choice is unique for each individual—as opposed to the situation in some other societies—he must be given assistance in the process of decision making. He must be helped to discover those personal characteristics in himself that make a vocational difference; he must be aided to be aware of the array of alternatives open to him; and he must be assisted to process the dimensions of these two worlds on both an affective and a cognitive level. This task is usually accomplished directly by means of individual counseling and group methods in their various forms and indirectly by environmental treatment. The utilization of the one-to-one counseling strategy, of group methods, or of environmental treatment to enhance vocational decision making is appropriate in both vocational guidance viewed as vocationalization and vocational guidance considered as treatment. However, the individual counseling approach is more frequently used in treatment aspects, and the group methods and environmental treatment are more prevalent in vocationalization activities.

Each of these helping strategies—individual, group, and environmental treatment—will be discussed in terms of their relevancy for vocational guidance in the schools.

INDIVIDUAL COUNSELING

DEFINITION

There are hundreds of definitions of counseling. Some focus on process; others are primarily concerned with relationship variables; others tend to highlight content; many are technique oriented; and still others stress the importance of the characteristics of the counselor. In an earlier work (Herr and Cramer, 1968), the present authors indicated that the best definition of counseling—in terms of their own biases—was that offered by Gilbert Wrenn (1951, p. 59). That definition we still find appropriate with two small additions. Wrenn proposed, "Counseling is a dynamic and purposeful relationship between two [or more] people in which procedures vary with the nature of the student's needs, but in which there is always mutual participation by the counselor and the student with the focus on self-clarification and self-determination [and action] by the student." The words in brackets have been added to indicate that effective counseling may take place within a group setting and that evaluation of the success of counseling must be based on behavior change in the counselee.

Counseling, then, is regarded as both *dynamic* and *purposeful*. This suggests that the counselee is constantly changing, that the counselor is ever changing in terms of the inferences he draws regarding the counselee, and that the dynamics of the relationship between the two—although certain basic elements are relatively constant—are also in a state of flux. There is movement in the counseling experience. Hopefully, that movement is in the direction of the resolution of factors that may be hindering the decision-making process.

This brings us to the concept embodied in Wrenn's definition that *procedures vary* according to student needs. Each school or theory of counseling proposes its unique and sometimes not-so-unique set of procedures and techniques for dealing with counselee problems. The authors of this volume are convinced that there are very few "truths" in counseling. Each counseling approach can lay claim to its share of successes—at least insofar as one can gauge successes from reports of clinical activities and can accept varied definitions of the term.

However, clients vary; each comes with need systems, backgrounds, and psychological sets that militate against undifferentiated treatment. Some counselees want information; some want help in "thinking through" a problem; some wish assistance in exploring feelings; some desire aid in ridding themselves of unwanted anxieties. And so it goes. Each counselee stimulus presents the counselor with an opportunity to make a differentiated, tailored response. Psychologists frequently speak of inappropriate responses made by a client; however, the obverse is equally true. The counselee who seeks information and finds himself confronted by a counselor who clarifies, explores, diagnoses, reinforces, extinguishes, or engages in all sorts of behaviors *except* giving information has reason to wonder about the appropriateness of the counselor's response. All these behaviors are appropriate to various stimuli; their indiscriminant use, however, is unproductive. Thus counseling procedures or behaviors will vary according to the needs presented by the client.

The words in Wrenn's definition "procedures vary according to the student's needs" mean that the counselor will remain "cognitively flexible" (Sprinthall, Whiteley, and Mosher, 1966). Cognitive flexibility refers to the counselor's remaining open-minded, adaptable, and resisting premature closure in his perception and cognition. The opposite of flexibility is rigidity; a rigid counselor has no tolerance of ambiguity, has an excessive need for structure, and has great difficulty in adapting to the needs of the student. Flexibility thus implies an avoidance of either excessive structuring or complete ambiguity.

Certain types of counselor behaviors are appropriate in certain situations and are inappropriate in others. For example, if the goal of vocational counseling is to promote information-seeking behavior on the part of the counselee, evidence suggests that the techniques of reinforcement are effective (Krumboltz and Schroeder, 1965). On the other hand, there are specific vocational counseling problems and concerns that might be better approached by other procedures. It may help at specific times to clarify or reflect feelings in order to make clear to the counselee. It may be of value at other times to summarize, restate, or interpret. There are occasions when a counselee is ready for confrontation, and that technique will be effective. On a more cognitive level, the counselor may want to point out alternatives or to give information. At still other points in a relationship, the counselor may allow the counselee to have catharsis and thus help to desensitize him. In the manner of some behavioral counselors or rational-emotive counselors, he may elect to give homework assignments—that is, assign the counselee tasks outside the counseling setting which are related to his problem. At times, the counselor may even attempt to persuade the counselee. These examples of counselor behaviors are by no means exhaustive. However, they do exemplify the diversity of approaches in a helping relationship, and their very diversity argues for their discriminate use.

The next phase of the definition of counseling stresses relationship and the notion of *mutual participation* by the counselor and the counselee. If the counselor assumes all responsibility for participation, then the interview is nothing more than advice giving—a kind of Sermon on the Mount. If the counselee is given all responsibility for participation, the interview becomes a soliloquy, and while some catharsis may result, little else emerges. These extreme examples of the structure—nonstructure or the directedness—nondirectedness continuum suggest that the counseling relationship is not a superordinate-subordinate one; the counselor and the counselee are equally responsible for participation. Because of individual differences in personality, type and level of training, and experience, some counselors will tend to be more active than others. Likewise, some counselees will tend to be more verbally active in the relationship than others. But each—counselor and counselee—must interact in dynamic fashion if counseling is to have an impact on the counselee's decision making.

In terms of the counseling relationship, much has been written recently regarding the concept of facilitative conditions (Carkhuff and Berenson, 1967; Berenson and Carkhuff, 1967; Carkhuff and Truax, 1966). Briefly, this concept argues that the counselor's effectiveness transcends any theory of counseling. The crucial variables in his success are assumed to be attitudes and sensitivity that create a "therapeutic" atmosphere. Among the dimensions which operate here are the accuracy of the counselor's empathic understanding of the counselee, the respect he shows for the counselee, his genuineness within the counseling session, and the degree of concreteness or specificity with which problems are confronted. Presumably, if these conditions exist, the counselee will explore himself and deal with his problems more constructively than he otherwise would. Greater self-understanding and self-experiencing, then, it is hypothesized, lead eventually to behavior change.

Adequate research has not yet been conducted in sufficiently objective fashion to permit the authors of this volume to completely endorse the concept. Certainly, we agree that the conditions of the counseling relationship should be therapeutic but are not convinced that the conditions outlined above are all-inclusive nor persuaded that even these conditions can be measured with sufficient objectivity. We note also the high intercorrelations of these variables with each other, suggesting a unidimensional factor (Hansen, Moore, and Carkhuff, 1968). Finally, we are not yet convinced that the absence or presence of these conditions bears a linear or nonlinear relationship to counseling outcome.

It does appear that the various counseling theories have more similarities in terms of relationship than differences (Fiedler, 1950), but precisely what relationship variables are crucial is still moot. For example, Geis (1970) has postulated that in addition to the conditions advocated by Truax, Carkhuff, and Berenson, others which one might reasonably expect to be facilitative are: communicated competence, authoritativeness, confidence and wisdom; noncondemnation of the counselee as a person; objectivity; flexibility; high intelligence; absence of serious emotional disturbance; absence of communicated disruptive personal values; and personal style.

The final aspect of the definition of counseling relates to outcomes—*self-clarification, self-determination,* and *action.* The first of these outcomes involves assisting an individual to acquire a realistic and accurate picture of himself in terms of a host of variables and to learn to relate these variables to external criteria—in this case, decisions of a vocational nature and the development of vocational identity. The second outcome variable suggests that decision making is an individual responsibility and that this function cannot be usurped by the counselor (although it is frequently usurped by parents). Finally, the third outcome, action, connotes that some sort of appropriate behavior will result as a consequence of counseling.

London (1964) indicates that counseling approaches can be divided into two categories: the *action* counselors on the one hand, and the *insight* counselors on the other hand. In broad terms, action-oriented counselors are concerned with behavioral change and are not particularly interested in etiology, self-insights, or self-understanding. Primarily, they will attack the external symptoms of the counselee and seek to change these. The insight counselors, on the other hand, argue that treatment of a symptom is at best palliative, that the counselee must understand his own behavior—although such understanding does not necessarily mean that he will change it. In terms of outcome, the action counselor takes behavior change as the criterion of the "goodness" of counseling; the insight counselor is likely to employ criteria other than or in addition to behavior change, e.g. expressed satisfaction, paper-and-pencil inventories, etc.

We agree with the action counselors that behavior change is the *ultimate* measure of the effectiveness of counseling. It is necessary, therefore, as with other aspects of treatment in a systems approach, to devise immediate and in-termediate behavioral goals for counseling, since the ultimate goal of counsel-ing in vocational guidance—adequate performance and satisfaction in an occu-pation and life style—is a goal that cannot be measured for years.

Thus the concept of counseling as used in this book refers to (1) a largely verbal process in which (2) a counselor and counselee(s) are in dynamic inter-action and in which (3) the counselor employs a repertoire of diverse behaviors (4) to help bring about self-understanding and behavior change in the form of "good" decision making in the counselee, who has responsibility for his own actions.

COUNSELING FOR DECISION MAKING

We have indicated that a major criterion of the effectiveness of counseling should be the ability of the counselee to make "good" decisions. This view of voca-tional counseling as training in decision making is not new, but it is a concept to which we eagerly subscribe. For example, Tyler (1961) has suggested that counseling concentrates on the willingness to make choice and commitment in accord with a clear sense of ego identity. Moore (1961) argues that counseling, especially at the secondary school level, is concerned primarily with the making of choices by the counselee. And Samler (1968) advocates that vocational counseling should be a learning experience in decision making. The problem he sees is basically one of identifying and weighing alternatives and the personal factors pertinent to each alternative. The factors to which Samler alludes are presented later in this chapter.

If good decisions are the outcome of vocational counseling, it is necessary to define a good decision. There are two ways to view the adequacy of de-cision making, either of which is appropriate for vocational counseling. Dilley (1967) proposes that decision making be differentiated in terms of outcome and process. In the outcome view, a good decision is one which has favorable results. In the process view, a decision is good in terms of looking at the indi-vidual who made it at the time it was made. It is thus conceivable that a de-cision considered good in terms of process may be considered bad years later when an outcome criterion is used.

Dilley (1968) also describes five counselor behaviors that he feels help stu-dents to the decision-making goal. He suggests that counselors encourage the development of personal-responsibility belief, encourage the use of a de-cision strategy, encourage expansion and specificity of decision deliberations, assist in the process of decision-relevant information, and let the client make his own decision.

One decision strategy is that of Clarke, Gelatt, and Levine (1965), who advo-cate that the decision to be made must first be clarified and made explicit. Various possible alternatives are then investigated and each considered in terms of probable outcomes. These probable outcomes are then evaluated in terms of desirability. That outcome which most closely combines the probable and the desirable is then selected. The reader will recall that Chapter 2 provides a framework for viewing decision theory.

Counseling for decision making does not mean that students should be forced into making irrevocable choices. Indeed, students should be encouraged continually to scrutinize the tentative decisions they do make. As Stewart (1968, p. 106) states, "The counselor must rid himself of the middle-class feeling that a person's character is strengthened by his capacity to make a decision and, irrespective of what changes occur in his life and regardless of how ill-conceived the decision was, to stick to it." What *is* being said here is that movement toward decision making, action taken toward many mini-decisions, and the process of actually making good decisions are the purpose of vocational counseling.

Hershenson (1969) proposes that various stages of vocational development require diverse skills or procedures that the client must master. He argues that different assistance techniques are necessary for each stage and that the techniques may vary according to whether one is dealing with vocational guidance as vocationalization or as treatment. A summary table of his analysis is reproduced on page 228.

The social amniotic stage concerns the development of a self-concept based on acceptance or rejection of environmental stimuli—the production of a functioning awareness of one's unique life style. This, in turn, determines a set, or program, through which future stimuli are processed. Attainment of this stage leads to the second stage, self-differentiation, wherein the various inputs are actually processed and decisions are made regarding what is appropriate to one and what is inappropriate. In the third stage, competence, only appropriate inputs (or go's) are processed and assessed, decision-making skills are gained, and choices are formulated. The fourth stage, independence, relates to the application of choices; and ultimately the investment of energy in those choices produces the final stage, commitment. In other words, one goes through the following sequence in vocational decision making: achieving awareness of self, determining appropriate aspects of self, differentiating aspects of self, testing aspects of self vocationally, investing the self vocationally.

THE DANGER OF THERAPY MODELS

It should be kept in mind that counseling is taking place within a school setting and that the imposition of therapy models of counseling in this sort of situation may be unwise. The school counselor is working with a predominantly normal population. As Aubrey (1969, p. 277) states the case:

> What the schools need are theoretical models congruent with educational purposes, and/or realistic designs which will enable guidance personnel to modify or change existing educational structures and practices. Those

Table 1   Techniques for Assisting Vocational Life-Stage Transitions

STAGES	TRANSITIONAL PROCEDURE	TRANSITIONAL CONCEPT	ASSISTANCE TECHNIQUES		PROTOTYPE THEORIST OR SCHOOL
			FACILITATION	REMEDIATION	
Social amniotic					
	Determining program (set)	"me"	Life style analysis	Environmental manipulation; psychotherapy	Adler
Self-differentiation					
	Information input	"go-versus-no-go"	Guidance		Trait-and-factor
Competence					
	Information processing	"go-versus-go"	Content: Client-centered Process: Training in decision making		Rogers Tiedeman Krumboltz
Independence					
	Information utilization	"application"	Intrapsychic: Existential Situational: Job matching		Frankl Beck Herzberg
Commitment					

From: D. B. Hershenson, Techniques for assisting life-stage vocational development, Personnel and Guidance Journal, 1969, 47, 778. Copyright © 1969 by the American Personnel and Guidance Association. Reprinted by permission.

psychotherapeutic models and techniques which fail to take into account the counselor's training and background, the conditions under which he works, the involuntary nature of many counselees in a school setting, the limitations of time and scheduling, the institutional expectations, and the structure of the school setting should be approached with extreme caution.

A school counselor is not a therapist. Much of his work will be of a therapeutic nature in the sense that he will foster conditions of mental health in both individual and the school setting. However, his work will not be therapy insofar as that term denotes the correction of pathology, disease, or generally severe dysfunctional behaviors.

The counselor assists the general population of students to accomplish normal developmental tasks and to make the decisions necessary and appropriate at each departmental stage. In vocational guidance as treatment, the counselor may find it necessary to revert to a previous developmental stage of a student in order to correct faulty or missed vocationalization, but he is not concerned with the remediation of faulty basic personality structure or of deeply ingrained psychotic behaviors. His focus is on students with basically normal personality structure, the capacity for normal reality orientation, and the ability to make decisions and to bear responsibility for them.

A BROAD VIEW OF VOCATIONAL COUNSELING

Vocational counseling cannot be viewed in a narrowly defined sense. It cannot be neatly compartmentalized and separated from Gestalt, developmental, and therapeutic counseling in general, which take into account an individual's total personality and his culture. Brammer and Shostrom (1960) point out that vocational counseling can be construed in several ways. First, they speak of vocational counseling simply as a process of confirming a choice already made by a counselee. Second, they see vocational counseling largely as a process of clarifying vocational objectives. Finally, they view vocational counseling as allowing counselees to discover facts about themselves and the working world. In this latter view, vocational counseling is a process whereby occupational-choice limits are broadened and effective vocational planning really becomes a part of life-planning.

Historically, the genesis of school counseling is "pure" vocational counseling. In the 1930's, many counselors began to realize that pure vocational counseling was a goal as illusory as the Loch Ness monster, and consequently they began to assimilate into vocational counseling those variables usually subsumed under the rubrics of educational counseling and personal-social counseling. This development did not strike a responsive chord in some diehard vocationalists, one of whom wrote an article advocating that the schools rid themselves of a piece of "educational rubbish"—that rubbish being all counseling in the schools *except* vocational counseling (Kitson, 1934). In some respects, this argument has continued to the present. We find ourselves in substantial agreement with Boy and Pine (1963, p. 225), who argue in the following manner:

> *The proponents of "vocational guidance" state quite emphatically that the school counselor's first job is vocational counseling and that therapeutic counseling is purely secondary. Yet in the light of the Super, Roe, and Ginsberg theories of vocational development, with their stress on the significant role of the self-concept in the process of vocational development, how can vocational counseling be divorced from therapeutic counelisng? If, as Super indicates, the process of vocational development is essentially that of developing and implementing a self-concept, can effective vocational counseling take place just through dispensing and discussing occupational information without considering the psychodynamics of the self-concept? If vocational counseling is a primary task, should not school counselors provide the student with the opportunity to reach new insights, to explore and see his self-concept, to deveolp and to implement it?*

In a previous chapter we have alluded to the thoughts of Drucker regarding work in the future. His ruminations are not dissimilar to those of Wrenn (1964), who suggests that vocational *and* nonvocational aspects of an individual's life should be a "committed or responsible whole in which one works for both self-fulfillment and for the fulfillment of others." This concept, too, argues for a broad rather than a narrow approach to vocational counseling; it looks to the total life goals of an individual and to his subsequent life style.

Thus we are addressing ourselves to integrative vocational counseling. In order to illustrate aspects of this approach and to provide the counselor with one possible methodology of attacking the process, we offer a diagnostic system.

A DIAGNOSTIC SYSTEM

The variables which influence the decision-making process in vocational guidance have been outlined in a previous chapter. In gross terms, these factors can be classified into those relating to individual development, to individual environment, and to educational and vocational opportunities. These are not mutually exclusive categories because in large measure individual development is a product of individual environment, and, obviously, the scope and thrust of available educational programs and occupational opportunities represent significant dimensions of one's environment, and are critical to the fostering of individual development.

For the school counselor concerned with facilitating student choice making, such gross categories are valuable to the degree that they help him become cognizant of the complexity within which choices are made. In the last analysis, however, the school counselor must possess some framework by which he can organize the influences affecting a given student.

One such model which is useful for classifying the factors influencing choice and for examining the relative importance of such factors in influencing different individuals is that proposed by Flum (1966). In this model, influences upon choice making are grouped in the following manner:

1. Inner-limiting factors
2. Inner-directing factors
3. Outer-limiting factors
4. Outer-directing factors

The factors which may be inner-directing for a given student include his desire for status, for security, for "being someone"—in a sense, the things which he values and has an interest in obtaining. The factors which might be inner-limiting could include the degree to which he possesses aptitudes, achievements, skills, motivation, persistence, and responsibility whereby to learn and progress in a multitude of educational and occupational tasks. He might also be inner-limited because he is unaware that he has certain potentials or characteristics or unaware that outlets exist by which he can find a satisfactory route toward those things to which his inner-directed urges prompt movement. He may be unaware of the variety of levels and contexts which might satisfy his inner-directed urges; or he might be suffering considerable conflict or distortion between what his inner-directed images prompt him to do and what he is equipped to do.

As important as these two intrinsic elements of the self are, they do not operate in a vacuum. One must also come to terms with the outer-directing and the outer-limiting factors. Consequently, what an individual's inner urges prompt him to do and what his parents, peers, community, or social class direct, expect, or reward his doing may be quite different. And, finally, what one would like to do—assuming one can do it and be valued for doing it—is dependent upon whether or not it is available to do or if ways exist by which one can be prepared to do it.

Conceptually, the classification might be conceived as a simple problem in arithmetic for a given individual, i.e. by adding and subtracting all a person's limiting and directing factors, the counselor might define the field of possibilities (e.g. curricular choice, occupational choice) for that individual. Further, such a framework permits consideration of the personal-conflict influences which may exist between the inner-limiting and the inner-directing factors, or between the inner-directing and the outer-limiting factors, or even within the inner-directing group. Regardless of the infinite number of combinations possible in a given population, these influences are uniquely organized within the individual in such a way as to shape his self-concept system and to define the range of choices he is free to make and implement.

Table 2 illustrates some of the factors which might be subsumed under the separate categories of inner and outer forces impinging upon the choices of a given individual. These are not pure or independent factors either within or across groups.

Table 2   Examples of Self and Environmental Factors Influencing Choice

INNER-LIMITING	INNER-DIRECTING	OUTER-LIMITING	OUTER-DIRECTING
Intellectual ability	Values	Rural-urban	Social-class
Aptitudes	Interests	Accessibility of	expectancies
Skills	Life goals	occupational	Family aspirations
Achievements	Perceived prestige of	opportunities	and expectancies
Experiential	various occupa-	Accessibility of	Peer influences
history	tions (curricula)	educational	Community attitudes
Motivation	Perceived stereo-	opportunities	and orientation
Responsibility	typed attitudes	Scope of occupa-	toward education
Perseverance	toward occupa-	tional opportuni-	or work
Punctuality	tions (curricula)	ties	Teacher or counselor
Warmth	Psychological cen-	Scope of educational	influences
Openness	trality of occupa-	opportunities	Image of vocational
Rigidity	tion or curriculum	Lines of communica-	education or other
Ego strength	in values	tion to the self	options
Sex differences	Getting ahead as	Requirements of	High school climate
Self-esteem	satisfaction of	occupations	and reward system
Decision-making	intellectual	Requirements of	
ability	curiosity	curricula	
Vocational			
maturity			

This organizing frame of reference brings us to the point where the counselor must order his system of strategies for working with counselees. Obviously, the techniques and the attitudes which guide his professional behavior must take into account the inner-limiting, inner-directing, outer-limiting, and outer-directing factors.

These factors also describe the counselor's perception of the counselee's freedom of choice. Guidance practitioners have continued to emphasize as part of their credo the creation in their counselees of free and informed choice. However, free and informed choice is a function not only of personal attributes and understandings but also of the environmental conditions which affect the counselee. Consequently, the counselor's role is not confined to working in a one-to-one relationship with the counselee but requires interaction with several of the components that make up the outer-limiting and outer-directing elements of the student's total environment. The functions in which the counselor engage are expressions of each of these roles.

The Counselor and the Student's Internal Frame of Reference. The objectives of counseling include, at the outset, assisting the counselee to cast in bold relief those factors which are for him inner-limiting and inner-directing. Some two decades ago, Super (1951, p. 92) proposed a definition of vocational guidance which emphasized not solely the provision of occupational information at a particular point in time or a simple matching of man and job but rather a "process of helping a person to develop and accept an integrated picture of himself and his role in the world of work, to test this concept against reality, and to convert it into a reality, with satisfaction to himself and to society." This definition blends those dimensions of guidance sometimes arbitrarily separated into the personal and the vocational, into a totality with interlocking relationships. Further, this process is seen as oriented to the self-concept, primarily focusing on self-understanding and self-acceptance. To these can be related the self-relevance of the outer-directing and outer-limiting factors, which define the environmental options available to the individual.

This approach also stresses the importance of counseling's resting upon a base of self-attitudes and value sets, which the individual understands and accepts and uses to maximize his own freedom to choose the opportunities which seem to meet his needs, desires, and inner urgings. A counseling relationship so defined means, in addition, that the counselee and the counselor come to understand which of the inner limits of the individual are unchangeable and which are modifiable. The counselee can then proceed with self-understanding to the matter of engaging in appropriate vocational behaviors.

In order to deal effectively with the latter dimension of the counseling process, the counselor will need to be an appraiser as well as an interpreter of data about the counselee. Essentially, three broad classes of information are important (Goldman, 1964). The order in which they are dealt with is in large measure a result of the counseling orientation the individual counselor espouses.

The first set of appraisal information is concerned with the inner-limiting data—predictor variables. A given counselor may determine that he should begin counseling a given individual by presenting what he has learned about him through information from tests of aptitude, achievement, interest, personality; school grades; hobbies; work history; family background; expressed attitudes. Frequently, counselors who start from this base treat each of these pieces of information as fixed and unmodifiable, as having a high relationship to certain future outcomes which the individual should consider. Because of the overwhelming amount of such information which can be collected about a given individual, much of it may be irrelevant to the set of questions which a student has, or he may accept the interpretation of the predictor variables as having a sophistication or expertness which permits him little room in which to maneuver. More important, the counselee may play a passive and dependent role awaiting, with little personal investment or acceptance, the expert's judgment on what he can and cannot do or what he should and should not do. Recall that counseling is an activity of *mutual* participation.

A second set of appraisal data relates to certain pathways the counselee might follow. Should he take vocational education? Should he take a specific vocational education sequence? Should he attend a post-secondary business or trade school? Should he go into the Armed Forces? Should he enter college? Some counselors may choose immediately to compare the requirements for each of these avenues with the information available about those predictor variables (inner-limiting data) which describe the particular student. This, like starting immediately with predictor variables, is a trait-and-factor approach, which if treated superficially or mechanically can be irrelevant to the real issues. For example, the student who asks where he should go to college may really be asking whether he should go to college at all. Why are my parents so insistent upon my attending college? Are there some other things I might do which can get me to where I want to be? A counselor sensing the underlying questions may choose, instead of immediately turning to college catalogs and the predictor variables which describe the student, to help the student sort out what he would expect to gain as a result of pursuing one pathway rather than another. What are the outcomes which he considers personally important (inner-directing factors)?

A third piece of appraisal information with which the counselor might begin are the outcomes that are of consequence to the student at his present level of development. What kind of person are you? What do you see as your major strengths or limitations? As you think about the future, are you primarily interested in obtaining satisfaction from the work activity in which you are engaged or the work situation? Do you feel the need for regularity and security, or do you desire variety and change? Do you like to work alone or with others? Are you principally concerned about income levels or prestige? What possible choices have you already considered and why? What are your values? What influences are most important to you as you have shaped personal answers to these questions—parents, peers, generalized attitudes in your community?

From the beginning of the counseling relationship this approach encourages the counselee to tune into himself and organize those parts of his self and self-concept which he thinks are of most significance. Super (1957, p. 308) addresses this point in the following manner:

> *Since vocational development consists of implementing a self-concept, and self-concepts often need modification before they can be implemented, it is important that the student, client, or patient put his self-concept into words early in the counseling process. He needs to do this for himself, to clarify his actual role and his role aspirations; he needs to do it for the counselor, so that the counselor may understand the nature of the vocational counseling problem confronting him.*
>
> *This calls for the cyclical use of nondirective and directive methods. Schematically, vocational counseling can be described as involving the following cycle:*
>
> *1. Nondirective problem exploration and self-concept portrayal*
>
> *2. Directive topic setting, for further exploration*

3. Nondirective reflection and clarification of feeling for self-acceptance and insight

4. Directive exploration of factual data from tests, occupational pamphlets, extracurricular experiences, grades, etc., for reality-testing

5. Nondirective exploration and working through of attitudes and feelings aroused by reality testing

6. Nondirective consideration of possible lines of action, for help in decision-making

Such a frame of reference then provides the counselor and the student an opportunity to identify those predictor variables and those avenues which appear to be most self-relevant to the student. Further, having such a frame of reference from which to operate provides the counselor an opportunity to help the counselee identify and clarify possible distortions between how he sees himself and how all the information about him suggests he operates most effectively or typically.

For example, a student who overestimates his mechanical skills may not perform very effectively as a machinist. In other words, the individual ascribes to himself characteristics which he actually does not possess. Following our previous line of thought, this student's inner-limiting factors and inner-directing factors do not seem to be congruent. Such a situation raises several questions for the counselor and the student. Is the degree to which one possesses mechanical skills modifiable? Are the elements of mechanical skill which this student thinks he has but appears not to have a matter of manual dexterity or a matter of experience? If it is the former, his chances of becoming an effective machinist are minimal. If it is the latter, are there possible pathways in the school or community by which he can acquire experience in mechanical activities to heighten his skill proficiency? Another question is, of course, what prompts him to want to be a machinist? Is it the work activity or the work situation? Is it because he knows people who are machinists and is influenced by them or because he has been told that machinists are in great demand and thus gain good income and security? Is it because he wants to remain in his present community and the machining industry is a prominent one? If he is concerned about something besides the work activity as a machinist, does he possess other skills or strengths upon which he can capitalize to gain the same outcomes he perceives as resulting from becoming a machinist?

The second part of this concern is that choosing an occupation also includes choosing a life style. In Western culture, one is largely labeled by the occupational title he carries. From an existential frame of reference, Simons (1966) has contended that occupational choice is ultimately a result of an array of decisions leading to self-objectification. It is these sequential decisions which give the individual the option of standing out as fully responsible before his fellowman, of being objectified, or of conforming to certain stereotypes which permit him to escape the painful process of having others see him as he really is. Hence it is the ego strength which he builds and commits to these decisions that ultimately determines whether or not he is going to spend his life in dynamically realizing his potential, or spend it in the frustration of fighting his own innate drive toward fulfillment. But it must be realized that this, too, is an important ingredient of choice—deciding how much of one's self one desires to express in his occupational commitment. How ego-involved is the student in work, in a curriculum choice, or in school? How committed does or can this individual become (Herr, 1969)?

A counselor and a counselee need to understand that a measured interest, whether it be from the Kuder Preference Record or the Strong Vocational Interest Blank, may indicate what one will direct his efforts to but does not say how much effort he will apply to get there. To cite an extreme analogy, a person may have an interest in going to Tahiti, and this interest may remain constant throughout his life. But interest alone does not indicate that the individual will take the steps or raise the finances which will get him to Tahiti. So it is with tentative occupational aspirations. The individual will have to be helped to examine whether he has the "capacity for deep involvement, devotion to task, commitment, absorption, giving of self to the task" (Samler, 1964), which is required by specific choice options. This, too, is a matter of inner limits and characteristics of the self which may or may not be present or possible to acquire.

But the capacity for deep involvement relates also to the meaning one attaches to a particular occupational life style. How important is it to a particular student to be tagged as a machinist? Important enough to delay certain personal gratifications through a lengthy apprenticeship? Important enough to labor over applied mathematics or physics? Important enough to permit himself to be placed on the midnight shift rather than working from 8 A.M. to 5 P.M.? Important enough to gamble that he will attain seniority privileges before being laid off because of reduction in force or an economic recession? Important enough to practice being punctual, reliable, dependable? Important enough to try to be a machinist even if the odds are high that he will not make it? These are not necessarily the right questions, but they are the types of questions which counselors and counselees must work through as the inner-limiting and inner-directing factors, as the self and the self-concept, are described and clarified.

GROUP PROCESSES

The second major strategy for implementing vocational guidance programs in the schools is the use of groups of one type or another. In the chapter dealing with information, we have alluded to several possibilities for the use of group processes in disseminating and utilizing educational, occupational, and personal information and in developing attitudes toward vocational planning and work. This section presents an overview of the group strategy in vocational guidance.

RATIONALE

It becomes clear that in a systems approach to vocational guidance in the schools, a great many objectives of vocational guidance can be achieved through group methods. Traditionally, it has been argued that group processes provide *efficiency* and *effectiveness*. If, for example, the dissemination of information is a goal of vocational guidance at a specific point along the K-12 continuum, it is clearly more efficient to present the information once to a group than to present it individually to each member of the group. Also, if the goals of vocational guidance entail problem solving or if the immediate objective of vocational guidance is to treat dysfunctional behaviors affecting vocational development, then group methods are appropriate, for groups have been found consistently to perform better in certain types of problem-solving tasks and under certain conditions than do individuals attacking the same problems (Olmsted, 1959). In terms of correcting dysfunctional behaviors, it is argued that these behaviors are learned in group settings and are therefore best unlearned in the same milieux and substitute behaviors learned.

Currently, approximately 70 percent of all employed persons work within the framework of corporate structures wherein the primary modus operandi is the group as a procedural vehicle (Hansen and Cramer, 1971). It would seem beneficial for youngsters to become used to functioning in this manner as a part of their pre-vocational experience. Suggested themes by which such learning might be facilitated in groups are presented in Chapters 6, 7, and 8.

CHARACTERISTICS OF THE GROUP

Much of what we have come to call group guidance is really misnamed. In fact, counselors have frequently worked with collections of individuals or aggregates rather than with true groups. In a social psychology sense, a group is characterized by at least six criteria (Hansen and Cramer, 1971, p. 81):

1. Members of the group are in interaction with one another; that is, there must be at least two-way communication.

2. Members of the group share a common goal. This goal may be set by the group itself, or it may be imposed by external forces.

3. The group members set norms which give direction and limits to their activity. Certain behaviors come to be rewarded; others are punished in some way.

4. The members develop a set of roles. Certain functions are performed by group members.

5. *The group members develop a network of* interpersonal attraction *(likes and dislikes for each other).*

6. *The group works toward the* satisfaction of the individual needs of group members.

Clearly, these characteristics will be present or absent in varying degrees. The more in evidence they are, the more the likelihood that a group exists; the more these characteristics are lacking, the greater the chances that an aggregate exists. Large assembly programs, for example, deal with aggregates. Successful discussion, problem solving, and counseling work via groups. A collection of individuals can still provide utility for counselors. The point is simply that a distinction should be made between groups, which offer great potential inner resources for guidance, and aggregates, which are a convenience.

Pearson (1968) has termed work with aggregates mass procedures. As opposed to group procedures, mass procedures are characterized by lack of interaction among individuals and do not satisfy individual needs. Other members of the mass in no way affect any given individual. While mass procedures have some initial value in and of themselves for the acquisition of intellective or cognitive material, there must be feedback and follow-up if the individual is to internalize the information in some meaningful fashion.

If the counselor works with true groups, then he must understand at least basic elements of group dynamics. As a group interacts, it becomes dynamic; members are constantly adjusting and changing in relation to each other. As a group restructures and adjusts, tensions are reduced, conflicts eliminated, and problems solved. The study of the variables underlying group movement is called group dynamics. Understanding group dynamics leads to evolving the techniques for effective group actions and decisions by using the forces that facilitate or inhibit group functioning. Such forces include the manner of interaction among the members, the amount of participation, the degree of group cohesiveness, the group values, the kind and quality of group leadership, and the internal structure of the group (e.g. degrees of permissiveness, competition, and communication).

The preceding brief section is not a primer in group methods. We wish only to point out here that the counselor skills necessary for effective functioning with groups are unique. Given sensitivity and communication ability as a base, however, the counselor can learn these skills.

THE USES OF GROUPS

The uses to which groups can be put in vocational guidance are limited only by the imagination and energy of the counselor. The following section presents some suggestions which are not all-inclusive but which should provide an idea of the array of possibilities. Purposes for groups are first offered; these are followed by several specific examples.

Purposes.   1. *Information dissemination.* Information about the world of work is a prerequisite for good decision making. Certain elements of that information are pertinent only for given individuals; other elements are needed by all individuals. Information regarding the occupational structure, post–high school educational opportunities, and courses of study at various educational levels, to cite but a few examples, are needed by every student and can be transmitted by means of mass procedures, which will, of course, require follow-up. Techniques for information dissemination in large groups can be found in Cramer and Cramer (1971).

2. *Persuasion.* The term "persuasion" connotes propaganda, which, in turn, has a negative connotation. However, persuasion here relates to motivation, to the concept of convincing students of the value of some aspect of vocational guidance, whether that aspect involves the need for vocational planning in a broad sense or the need to take aptitude tests, for instance, in a much narrower sense.

3. *Teaching.* The most obvious application of group techniques occurs in the teaching process. There is a place for teaching in vocational guidance. At least one theoretician (Goldman, 1962) has argued that group guidance has typically failed because counselors have dealt with guidance concerns by means of teacher behaviors. In other words, the process of teaching is seen as inappropriate for the content of guidance. This charge certainly is true in terms of the more affective elements of guidance content, but, as has been repeatedly stressed throughout this book, much of vocational guidance begins with a cognitive base. The goals of developing a vocabulary of work in youngsters or of imparting decision-making skills are effectively accomplished via a teaching strategy (Varenhorst and Gelatt, 1971).

4. *Practice.* Role playing, dramatization, gaming, and other simulation techniques allow students to rehearse or to practice vocational guidance behaviors in groups. Whether the practice is as specific as role-playing a job interview or as complex as playing the Life Career Game, group situations permit the rehearsal of necessary vocational behaviors in a protected context.

5. *Attitude Development.* Attitudes are learned predispositions to respond in characteristic ways to certain stimuli. Since they are learned, they can be unlearned. Since they are learned within the family and other groups, they are logically unlearned and relearned within a group structure. Hence the clarification of vocational attitudes and values (e.g. the worth and dignity of all work) and the crystallization and development of attitudes toward oneself (e.g. self-concept) can be fostered within groups.

6. *Counseling.* Related to attitude development but more specific in nature is group counseling. Mahler (1969, p. 11) defines group counseling as follows:

The process of using group interaction to facilitate deeper self-understanding and self-acceptance. There is a need for a climate of mutual respect and acceptance so that individuals can loosen their defenses

*sufficiently to explore both the meaning of behavior and new ways of be-
having. The concerns and problems encountered are centered on the
developmental growth tasks of members rather than on pathological blocks
and distortions of reality.*

This definition emphasizes group counseling with a developmental focus
which can benefit all youngsters within a school setting. It is a means of helping
students to recognize and use their more affective aspects.

7. *Exploration.* Since school-aged youngsters are in the exploratory stage of
vocational development, various group activities designed to stimulate and to
enhance that exploration are beneficial. Such exploration may take the form of
vocational development lessons (McCourt, 1971), described elsewhere in this
volume, or field trips and career conferences, to cite just a few examples.

Methods.   The chapter on information on vocational guidance presents several
methods of implementing vocational guidance through groups. Assemblies,
field trips, career days and career conferences, classroom activities, vocational
group-guidance courses, the vocational development lesson, simulation and
gaming activities of various types, case studies, and homerooms are all discussed in some detail.

Fundamentally, group guidance should provide an opportunity to test or
discover one's own characteristics as related to particular environmental options. The following questions reflect such an intent: Knowing what I know
about myself, how would I probably behave or perform in a situation that has
the characteristics identified? Knowing what I know about a given occupation,
what characteristics of mine can I compare and contrast with those required by
the occupation?

Through role playing, case studies, selected audiovisual devices, discussion,
speakers, etc., an atmosphere can be created which will encourage students
to project themselves figuratively into a given choice situation and to analyze
how they, personally, would feel in that situation. Of course, it is not possible
to create all the situations from which one might be able to choose or to have
complete information. Also, it is possible to present irrelevant information to
a group or to fail to encourage students to consider the characteristics of their
behavior and performance which are related to choice making.

Whether one deals with individual counseling or with group processes, the
same questions are relevant. Both should support those experiences which reinforce for students the validity of the questions: Who am *I*? What do *I* want to
be? Why do I want to be *this*? Am I able to be what I wish to be? What is my
life likely to be if I succeed in becoming what I choose to be?

Throughout the guidance process, individually and in groups, the counselor
not only must insure that the student has access to accurate, relevant information about his personal characteristics and create conditions which will help
him to understand the implications of this information, but the counselor also

must insure that the student has accurate, relevant information about the options open to him. In the final analysis, one's self-perceptions or the self-labels which direct his behavior relate to persons, objects, and possibilities which lie outside the self. In other words, one's self-descriptions, whether they be such adjectives as dull-bright, capable-incapable, leader-follower, have meaning only in comparing oneself with others and with the requirements of specific situations. Appropriate information, much of which can be gleaned through groups, is vital to making good decisions about oneself as well as about what opportunities exist and what they require as one tests his personal fit with these opportunities.

Too often a group strategy is employed simply because someone feels that it is time to launch a group guidance venture. Nothing comes before; very little comes after. The group guidance experience becomes a moment in time for its own sake. Unlike the poem which declares that "beauty is its own excuse for being," group guidance is not its own raison d'être. In a systems approach to vocational guidance in the schools, one first determines his goals and states them in behavioral terms; he then decides what treatments are appropriate for achieving those goals; finally, he evaluates to discover if those goals have been attained. One or more of the possible treatments may entail the use of one or more groups. This approach is quite a different matter from deciding to use a group strategy and then finding a focus for it. Intent determines strategy, not vice versa.

As has been stated earlier, the possibilities for utilizing groups in vocational guidance in the schools is almost limitless. To illustrate, the following examples of group activities are presented. They are only a few of the many that have taken place or that could take place, but they should provide a flavor of the diversity.

At the elementary school level, in addition to those group activities presented in the chapters on the elementary school and information, the following group activity is noteworthy. Thompson (1969, p. 209) suggests that four objectives can be accomplished in the elementary school by means of group guidance (again, however, the objectives are not stated in sufficiently specific behavioral terms):

1. *To help the child appreciate all kinds of work in our society*

2. *To develop the concept of flexibility in the work role*

3. *To provide a wide base of experience regarding occupations rather than to place emphasis upon early decision making*

4. *To stress the importance of the effective use of leisure time*

Each of these objectives can be implemented within the classroom as a part of the on-going educational process. The marriage of education and vocational guidance can thus be consummated by a systematic approach.

One simulation technique that has not been previously discussed to any appreciable degree is dramatization. Drama can stimulate meaningful group discussion just as do case studies, role playing, and other techniques. Perry (1970), for example, has developed a skit for imparting career information at the junior high school level and above. On a more affective level, psychodrama and sociodrama can prove effective tools for gaining self-knowledge.

Another simulation technique was utilized in social studies classes in a Minnesota junior high school (Braland and Sweeney, 1970). It consisted of having students plan a typical work week in a student's life during each of his high school years, including class time, study, leisure, part-time work, and family interaction. Involved, too, was post–high school planning. As is the case at present with most gaming and simulation techniques, this approach was not carefully evaluated, but it does seem promising.

In another junior high school, counselors adopted a four-world approach to vocational group guidance (Lockwood, Smith, and Trezise, 1968). Rather than focusing on specific career areas, counselors attempted to broaden the students' overall understanding and awareness of the world. The four worlds introduced to the students were: the natural (ecology); the technological (automation, cybernetics); the aesthetic (arts and the culture boom); and the human (overpopulation, peace, the individual in a mass society). This project was accomplished in a one-semester, required, occupational-guidance class, and students discussed career areas related to each world.

The preceding are but a few examples of the variety of foci that can be employed in group work for vocational guidance. Again, group methods must be part of a unified systems approach and must be directed toward the achievement of specific goals.

ENVIRONMENTAL TREATMENT

The third major helping strategy, in addition to individual counseling and group work, is what is here termed environmental treatment. This concept relates to the counselor's need to concern himself about the school's total atmosphere for learning and personal development. By doing so the counselor can be a vital agent in bringing about change in the school. Such a counselor is as much concerned with adapting the school to the individual as he is with adapting the individual to the school. This idea is frequently expressed by labeling the counselor an "expert in human relations," an "environmental manipulator," a "human development engineer," a "change agent," or a "social engineer." We prefer to use the term "environmental treatment."

The goal of environmental treatment is two-fold: (1) to change individual behavior, and (2) to provide optimal conditions for educational and personal experiences for all students. The first goal—changing individual behavior—simply refers to altering a given student's reality situation. If, for example, a student and a teacher are in conflict and that discord cannot be resolved in a mutually satisfactory fashion, the counselor may place the student in another class. This sort of assistance is frequently valuable in and of itself. If, however, there are underlying problems which are transferred to the new situation, then the change of environment has only temporary value. If, on the other hand, the change of environment leads to a learning of permanent new behaviors, the environmental engineering is effective.

The second goal—creating positive school conditions for learning and for personal development—relates to the counselor's assuring that negative psychonomic factors are either eliminated or prevented from occurring. He searches out variables in the school, home, and neighborhood environments that may be mentally unhealthy or that may impede adequate vocational development. To illustrate this helping strategy, we return to the diagnostic paradigm employed earlier in this chapter.

In the discussion of the inner-limiting and inner-directing aspects which affect an individual's decision making, emphasis was placed upon counselor-guided self-appraisal, self-understanding, and self-acceptance. The reason for this emphasis was, of course, that unless the student knows what personal resources he has to commit to a specific choice and where he is heading, he has no particular guidelines for deciding whether a particular option is of value to him. But there is more to free and informed choice than coming to terms with one's inner-limiting and inner-directing characteristics. Stopping at the point of personal freedom which these represent would naively assume that the social system assigns equal value to all possible choices and provides for all of them diverse pathways to their achievement. That is obviously not true. Consequently, the counselor must recognize that dealing with the factors previously described as inner-limiting or inner-directing is only part of the total effort.

Free choice of curriculum or of vocational options can exist only when the social structure, i.e. teachers, parents, the community at large, ascribes equal value to the differential options available to the student. In addressing himself to the democratic antecedents of the Vocational Educational Act of 1963, Senator Wayne Morse (1963) of Oregon made the following observations:

> It is in keeping with the American tradition that the many tasks of the world of work are equally important—that the man who works with his hands should be just as well-trained, have just as many opportunities, be just as respected as the man who works at a desk. It is also in keeping with the democratic ideal that every man and woman should have access to the education and training needed, to develop to his highest potential.

The values implicit in this statement find expression in the outer-limiting and outer-directing factors with which students must cope as they are in the process of choice making. The degree to which there exist curricular pathways to prepare students for wide-ranging occupational opportunities is a measure of the outer-limiting factors. The support or lack of support of student choices ranging across the occupational spectrum is a measure of the outer-directing factors.

The first concerns accessibility. Are there curricula available that are responsive to the needs of students and relevant to where any student is in his search for a larger context of purpose? Or are students forced into existing curricula without regard for personal needs, abilities, desires? It is distressing to help students see themselves in adequate and accurate ways, to help them mobilize their personal resources, to help them adopt goals for defining intermediate choices, but not to provide them with effective educational experiences to achieve these goals.

The second—the outer-directing factors—concern attitude. Does the community of the school in which the counselor finds himself foist upon students a negative image of certain curricula or occupations? Are the students in vocational education regarded less highly than those in college-preparatory programs? Are there stereotyped attitudes toward occupations which correspond to whether or not college education is required for entry? Does the counselor or do teachers have personal preferences or biases about the dignity of certain preparation programs and occupations by which they consciously or unconsciously influence student choice? What is the effect of the high school climate on student aspirations? On what bases are parental aspirations for their children developed? Does this community recognize that the right of access to higher education is not the requirement that all students go on to higher education?

What, then, are the responsibilities of guidance programs and of school counselors regarding these outer-limiting (accessibility) and outer-directing (attitudes) factors? The principal professional source for such decisions (ASCA, 1965) recommends thirty-seven or more functions which the school counselor should perform or cause to be performed. At least half of these can be broadly described as change-agent or environmental-engineering functions, in which the counselor is expected to be in contact with the significant others of the students' environment: teachers, administrators, other personnel services specialists, parents, community referral agencies.

In support of these functions a recent paper synthesizing the reports of seven conferences sponsored by the United States Office of Education drew the following inferences (Herr, 1968, p. 2):

Schools need to be geared for change. Consequently, counselors and guidance workers must be prepared to serve as educational leaders, reformers, agents of change. This change requires that counselors be more than test technicians and interviewing specialists; and, thus, in counselor education programs, they must be provided courses not only in changes in the meaning of work, but also courses about change as a process. The counselor of the future will likely serve as a facilitator of the environmental and human conditions which are known to promote the counselee's total psychological development, including his vocational development, as well as a strong sense of self-identity with which he can cope with change. Thus, the conference participants expect the counselor to be active, to assume a positive offense, to be more committed and willing to fight for what he considers correct.

In more pragmatic terms, counselors must be oriented to get out of their offices and to the places where the action is. If counselors have a mandate to help youngsters sort out and cope with the demands upon them, then counselors also have a mandate to get to the points where such unrealistic demands are generated and to work with others—teachers, parents, employers—to look at these demands, expectations, and attitudes and modify those which can be modified.

School counselors must bring their insights about the needs of children to bear upon the matter of developing new or improved educational programs. The lockstep of certain training durations and training experiences must be broken and more attention given to the needs of particular groups of students. Educational programs must be created to match the needs and characteristics of children in a continuous effort to counteract the pervasive tendency to fit students into existing programs. This assumes that school counselors can help those responsible for curricula development to identify and understand the heterogeneous student values and benefits that reside in one cluster of educational options compared to those that reside in another. Such a task cannot depend exclusively upon professional opinion but must rest also upon a firm body of information about the characteristics and aspirations of the students to be served. Campbell (1968) has recently reported data which suggest that how counselors and others perceive the needs of students and the services they require is not necessarily congruent with how students view the same issues.

These observations further suggest that school counselors must be aware that they cannot do the job alone. A guidance counselor and a guidance program are not necessarily synonymous. By definition the latter must be an integral part of a set of objectives which weave throughout the educational process. Other educators and school counselors must work in harmony to determine what students seek for themselves and what kind of vocational preparation is appropriate for different groups of students at different levels. Such information must be made available to and considered by all concerned.

As the counselor works with others, he needs a special set of skills if he is to be effective in environmental treatment. Jenkins (1949), for example, has postulated four general steps in environmental treatment to bring about educational change: (1) analyzing the present situation, (2) determining the changes which are required, (3) making the changes, and (4) stabilizing the new situation so that it will be maintained. The latter two steps are discussed in detail in the last chapter of this volume.

The first two steps relate to discovering those outer-limiting variables of accessibility and those outer-directing variables of attitudes that hinder vocational development. In discovering these variables, the counselor will want to observe both the "driving forces" in the environment (those factors which push for change) and the "restraining forces" (those factors which hold back change). Inasmuch as each type of force has a valence and an intensity, change will occur only when the driving force exceeds the restraining force. To modify forces, one can either reduce or remove restraining forces, strengthen or add to driving forces, and/or change the direction of the forces.

To do any of these, first the counselor must determine what forces have to be dealt with. What are the prevalent attitudes toward work in the community? What are the forces causing these attitudes? Can these forces be reversed or opposing forces strengthened? Is there a reasonable likelihood that these forces can be changed? Which opposing forces can be reduced with the least effort? Which driving forces can be increased? In short, the counselor must try to do what can be done.

SUMMARY

This chapter has considered three major helping strategies for systematically providing vocational guidance in the schools: individual counseling, group work, and environmental treatment. While all three strategies are appropriate to both vocational guidance as treatment and vocational guidance as vocationalization, counseling and environmental treatment will be emphasized more often in treatment, while group work will be applied most frequently to vocationalization. The counselor employs that strategy which seems most likely to satisfy his objectives. Finally, it should be noted that the primary consideration in vocational guidance is the building of attitudes, values, general vocational knowledge, and decision-making skills rather than the imparting of highly specific information or the forcing of a decision.

REFERENCES

American School Counselors Association.   The guidelines for implementation of the ASCA Statement of Policy for secondary-school counselors.   In J. W. Loughary, R. O. Stripling, and P. W. Fitzgerald (eds.), *Counseling: A growing profession.*   Washington, D. C.: American Personnel and Guidance Association, 1965.

Aubrey, R. F.   Misapplication of therapy models to school counseling.   *Personnel and Guidance Journal,* 1969, 48, 273–278.

Berenson, B. G., and Carkhuff, R. R.   *Sources of gain in counseling and psychotherapy.*   New York: Holt, Rinehart and Winston, 1967.

Boy, A. V., and Pine, G. J.   *Client-centered counseling in the secondary school.*   Boston: Houghton Mifflin, 1963.

Braland, R. G., and Sweeney, W. L.   A different approach to vocational counseling in junior high.   *The School Counselor,* 1970, 17, 260–261.

Brammer, L. M., and Shostrom, E. L. *Therapeutic psychology.* Englewood Cliffs, N. J.: Prentice-Hall, 1960.

Campbell, R. E. Vocational guidance in secondary education: Selected findings of a national survey which have implications for state program development. Paper presented at the National Conference on Vocational Guidance, Development of State Programs, U. S. Office of Education, Washington, D. C., Jan., 1968.

Carkhuff, R. R., and Berenson, B. G. *Beyond counseling and therapy.* New York: Holt, Rinehart and Winston, 1967.

Carkhuff, R. R., and Truax, C. B. Toward explaining success and failure in interpersonal learning experiences. *Personnel and Guidance Journal,* 1966, 46, 723–728.

*Clarke, R.; Gelatt, H. B.; and Levine, L. A. A decision-making paradigm for local guidance research. *Personnel and Guidance Journal,* 1965, 44, 40–51.

Cramer, S. H., and Cramer, Rosalind. Information dissemination in large groups. In J. C. Hansen and S. H. Cramer (eds.), *Group guidance and counseling in the schools.* New York: Appleton-Century-Crofts, 1971, 89–95.

Dilley, J. S. Counselor actions that facilitate decision-making. *The School Counselor,* 1968, 15, 247–252.

Dilley, J. S. Decision-making: A dilemma and a purpose for counseling. *Personnel and Guidance Journal,* 1967, 45, 547–551.

Fiedler, F. E. The concept of an ideal therapeutic relationship. *Journal of Consulting Psychology,* 1950, 14, 239–245.

*Flum, Y. Hatsaa lesivug hegoremim hakoveim et behirat hamiktsoa (Proposal to Classify Factors in Determining Occupational Choice). Megamot, 1966, 14 (1-3), 225–228.

Geis, H. J. Toward a comprehensive framework unifying all systems of counseling. *Educational Technology,* 1969, 9, 19–28.

Goldman, L. Group guidance: Content and process. *Personnel and Guidance Journal,* 1962, 40, 518–522.

Goldman, L. The process of vocational assessment. In H. Borow (ed.), *Man in a world at work.* Boston: Houghton Mifflin, 1964, 389–410.

*Hansen, J. C., and Cramer, S. H. *Group guidance and counseling in the schools.* New York: Appleton-Century-Crofts, 1971.

Hansen, J. C.; Moore, G. D., and Carkhuff, R. R. The differential relationships of objective and client perceptions of counseling. *Journal of Clinical Psychology,* 1968, 24, 244–246.

* Recommended for additional reading.

Herr, E. L.   Implications for state vocational guidance program development from selected Office of Education—supported conferences.   Paper presented at the National Conferences on Vocational Guidance, Development of State Programs, U. S. Office of Education, Washington, D. C., Jan., 1968.

Herr, E. L.   Guidance and the vocational aspects of education: Some considerations.   *Vocational Guidance Quarterly,* 1969, 17, 178–184.

Herr, E. L., and Cramer, S. H.   *Guidance of the college-bound: Problems, practices, and perspectives.*   New York: Appleton-Century-Crofts, 1968.

Hershenson, D. B.   Techniques for assisting life-stage vocational development.   *Personnel and Guidance Journal,* 1969, 47, 776–780.

Jenkins, D. H.   Social engineering in educational change: An outline of method.   *Progressive Education,* 1959, 26, 193–197.

Kitson, H. D.   Getting rid of a piece of educational rubbish.   *Teachers College Record,* 1934, 36, 30–34.

Krumboltz, J. D., and Schroeder, W. W.   Promoting career planning through reinforcement.   *Personnel and Guidance Journal,* 1965, 44, 19–26.

Lockwood, O.; Smith, D. B.; and Trezise, R.   Four worlds: An approach to occupational guidance.   *Personnel and Guidance Journal,* 1968, 46, 641–643.

London, P.   *The modes and morals of psychotherapy.*   New York: Holt, Rinehart and Winston, 1964.

*Mahler, C. A.   *Group counseling in the schools.*   Boston: Houghton Mifflin 1969.

McCourt, H.   The vocational development lesson. In J. C. Hansen and S. H. Cramer (eds.), *Group guidance and counseling in the schools.*   New York: Appleton-Century-Crofts, 1971, 172–183.

Moore, G. D.   A negative view toward therapeutic counseling in the schools.   *Counselor Education and Supervision,* 1, Winter, 1961, 60–68.

Morse, W.   Foreword to the Vocational Education Act of 1963.   PL 88210. Washington, D. C., 1963.

*Olmsted, M. S.   *The small group.*   New York: Random House, 1959.

Pearson, R.   Working with the disadvantaged through groups. In W. E. Amos and J. D. Grambo (eds.), *Counseling the disadvantaged youth.*   Englewood Cliffs, N. J.: Prentice-Hall, 1968, 61.

Perry, Pauline E.   Tommy's career choice.   *The School Counselor,* 1970, 17, 182–187.

*Samler, J.   Occupational exploration in counseling: A proposed reorientation. In H. Borow (ed.) *Man in a world at work.*   Boston: Houghton Mifflin, 1964, 411–432.

*Samler, J.   Vocational counseling: A pattern and a projection.   *Vocational Guidance Quarterly,* 1968, 17, 2–11.

Simons, J. B.   An existential view of vocational development.   *Personnel and Guidance Journal,* 1966, 44, 604–610.

Smith, R. E.   Vocational guidance in Soviet schools.   *Personnel and Guidance Journal,* 1968, 46, 790–793.

*Sprinthall, N. A.; Whiteley, J. M.; and Mosher, R. L.   Cognitive flexibility: A focus for research on counselor effectiveness. *Counselor Education and Supervision,* Summer, 1966, 5, 188–197.

Stewart, J. A.   Vocational choice theories: Helps and hazards for practitioners. *The School Counselor,* 1968, 16, 103–107.

Super, D. E.   *The psychology of careers.*   New York: Harper & Brothers, 1957, 308.

Super, D. E.   Vocational adjustment: Implementing a self-concept.   *Occupations,* 1951, 30, 81–92.

Thompson, J. M.   Career development in the elementary school: Rationale and implications for elementary school counselors.   *The School Counselor,* 1969, 16, 208–212.

Tyler, Leona E.   *The work of the counselor.*   New York: Appleton-Century-Crofts, 1961.

Varenhorst, Barbara, and Gelatt, H. B.   Group-guidance decision making. In J. C. Hansen and S. H. Cramer (eds.), *Group guidance and counseling in the schools.*   New York: Appleton-Century-Crofts, 1971, 107–123.

*Wrenn, C. G.   Human values and work in American life. In H. Borow (ed.) *Man in a world at work.*   Boston: Houghton Mifflin, 1964.

Wrenn, C. G.   *Student personnel work in college.*   New York: Ronald Press, 1951.

TEN

ASSESSMENT AND EVALUATION
IN VOCATIONAL GUIDANCE

We have been told so often that we live in an age of extraordinary complexity, technology, specialization, and growth we frequently fail to realize the implications of this situation. We take for granted the vast proliferation of knowledge, the social mobility and flux of social roles, and the substantial changes in occupational structure and opportunity that characterize our time. Yet this "progress" presents us with problems unparalleled in history.

Two problems directly relevant to vocational guidance are the training and allocation of manpower in order to ensure maximum utilization of this most valuable of all resources. We need talent of diverse specializations; we require a means of identifying that talent. The chief one that has evolved is the standardized test.

In addition, we have come to accept the premise that assessment procedures help individuals to understand themselves not only in terms of their talents but also in terms of their interests, values, and personality characteristics. The greater the degree of accurate self-understanding an individual has, the more likely he is to make realistic, satisfying educational and vocational choices, it is assumed. While accurate self-understanding does not guarantee good decision making, good decisions probably cannot be made without a realistic picture of one's abilities and interests. Again, assessment devices provide a vehicle that contributes to student self-understanding and accurate appraisal.

In the United States we have not yet resolved the argument regarding the relative contributions to human potential of nature and nurture (Anastasi, 1958; Burt, 1955; Goslin, 1963; and Jensen, 1969). Other countries, for better or for worse, seem to have made this decision. England, for example, takes the view that human abilities are largely innate. Because of this belief, testing is regarded as highly important because it is the vehicle for talent *discovery*. On the other hand, Russia has adopted the notion that human abilities are largely acquired. Tests, therefore, are of little importance because the emphasis is on talent *development* rather than on talent discovery. The idea prevalent in the United States appears to be that both inherited and acquired factors contribute to human potential but in degrees not yet specified and in ways not yet discerned.

Regardless of *what* we are measuring, there is no doubt that schools are indeed measuring *something* in startling numbers. Almost all schools in this country administer standardized tests. The median annual expenditure for pupil-appraisal programs (including materials and scoring services but not salaries of personnel) is about forty cents per student. The numbers of tests administered vary from state to state and from community to community. In 1961 the state legislature in California passed a bill mandating every public school to administer standardized tests of intelligence, reading, arithmetic, and language usage to all pupils in the fifth, eighth, and eleventh grades each year. Obviously, per-pupil appraisal expenditures in California are considerably above the median. This is also the case in New York State, where state regulations assign each local school responsibility for "identifying children who fail or underachieve, discovering the causes of failure or underachievement, and effecting aid to bring about change" (Bureau of Guidance, 1967). The primary tool used to "identify" and "discover" in the implementation of this ingenuous statute is testing. At the same time, however, several large-city school districts have exorcized tests of scholastic aptitude on the grounds that they are unfair to the cuturally different students who often constitute a majority of the large-city school population.

This chapter considers four major uses of tests, or assessment procedures. Dealt with first are the *predictive* uses of tests with standardized appraisal data serving to forecast success in educational and vocational behaviors. Second, this chapter discusses the use of tests and inventories for *discrimination*—that is, for permitting an individual to discover what occupational and/or educational groups he most resembles or is most like. Third, the *monitoring* function of tests is discussed. In a systematic approach to vocational guidance in the schools, it is important that those responsible for such guidance be able to identify the vocationalization stage of any individual or group and to identify their attitudes toward work. Finally, this chapter deals with the use of tests to *evaluate* how well goals are being achieved with the treatments or guidance processes provided. Thus the fourfold purpose of assessment is: prediction, discrimination, monitoring, and evaluation.

PREDICTION

Quite apart from other uses to which testing is put (e.g. curriculum planning, assessment of teaching effectiveness, selection and placement, etc.), the identification of talent remains the primary raison d'être of testing in vocational guidance. However, identification is merely a first step. A relationship must be established between performance on a test and the behaviors of some type of job or educational achievement in order that predictions can be made.

When events are not random but are seen to be natural consequences of previous events, they are said to be ordered and therefore lawful. When one can group these lawful events, these facts, into a body of knowledge, it is possible to make predictions—that is, to forecast in a reasonably accurate manner what will occur in a future event. The prediction is usually made in a way that expresses some degree of uncertainty.

The uncertainty is expressed in terms of probability. One can present odds describing the likelihood of an event's occurring under given conditions. The method of describing all this is largely through measurement and the calculus of probability. In guidance, the prevailing beliefs about measurement have been neatly summarized by Beck (1963, p. 130):

> It is possible and desirable to collect data sampling types of behavior from which actuarial predictions can be made. The actuarial prediction derived from testing can often prove of value in estimating or predicting behavior of humans who share traits in varying degrees.

Hence it is possible to predict performance on some future measure on the basis of some previously measured variable. This prediction can be made if there is a clear relationship between the two variables being measured. For example, if there is a known relationship between height and weight, it is possible to predict, within a prescribed error range, what an individual's height is if we know only his weight. The correlation coefficient (r) is usually the measurement used to express the degree and direction of the relationship. The actual means of prediction is usually a regression equation.

Once it has been determined that a relationship exists between two variables, the next question is the degree or significance of the relationship. In this regard, various categorical descriptions have been proposed. There is some agreement among those who work with educational and psychological tests that the following descriptions are useful (Garrett, 1958, p. 285):

r from   .00 to ± .20   denotes indifferent or negligible relationship

r from ±.20 to ± .40   denotes low to moderate correlation—present but slight

r from ±.40 to ± .70   denotes substantial or marked relationship

r from ±.70 to ±1.00   denotes high to very high relationship

These categories are broad and are dependent upon several other factors. First, it is necessary to consider the characteristics of the variables being correlated. Reliability coefficients, for example, are typically considerably higher than validity coefficients. More apropos to vocational guidance, as we shall see later in this chapter, correlations between tests and criterion measures rarely are higher than .50. Yet prediction of practical significance can be gained even with this relatively moderate relationship. Finally, there is no such thing as the correlation between an aptitude measure and a criterion. Rather there is a correlation between certain measures of an aptitude (e.g. perceptual speed and accuracy) and certain criteria (e.g. success in secretarial training, success in a clerical job, etc.).

In vocational guidance what all this means is that if there is a relationship between scores on a battery of tests, for example, and performance on a given job, it is possible to predict via a regression equation the likelihood of an individual's job performance if we know his test performance. Decisions regarding probable success made in this manner are invariably better than decisions made on the basis of subjective judgment.

However, several qualifying conditions must be considered when discussing the accuracy of predictions made from regression equations. The first of these is the *standard error of estimate,* a statistical measure which indicates the range in an individual forecast (i.e. comparing the predicted measure to the actual measure). Only when a correlation coefficient is ±1.00 is there no error of estimate and each score is predicted exactly. The standard error of estimate depends upon the standard deviation of the measure being predicted. Thus adequate prediction is possible only when there is a relatively high correlation coefficient and the variability of the predicted score distribution is small. When one or both of these conditions fail to exist, prediction is relatively worthless.

A second consideration in forecasting involves the relative accuracy of group versus individual predictions. Correlation is much more accurate in forecasting the performance of groups than of a given individual. Actuarially, it is possible to achieve normative predictions more precisely than it is to forecast individual performance. Knowing the correlation between a battery of tests and a criterion of importance (e.g. success in training), one can tell with some assurance how many in a given group whose test scores are available will succeed. However, for any specific individual in that group, prediction can be made with less assurance.

A third factor influencing forecasting efficiency is the interpretation of the correlation coefficient. The correlation coefficient will vary according to the heterogeneity of the group. The more homogeneous the group, the lower the correlation will be. This principle explains, for instance, why correlations between scholastic aptitude and grades in school become progressively lower as one moves through the educational system. By the time one gets to college, the student population is much more homogeneous in scholastic aptitude than it was at the elementary school level. Another factor in interpreting correlation coefficients is the so-called regression effect. There is a tendency for all scores predicted from a regression equation to converge toward the mean. Thus if a group is retested, the high scores tend to move downward toward the mean and the low scores to move upward toward the mean. Lastly, it should be remembered that a correlation coefficient is a measure of relationship and not an indicator of causation.

In summary, when the effectiveness of tests is evaluated in vocational guidance, the concern is how well test performance predicts some future performance (e.g. success in training, success on the job, etc.). The test is called a predictor; the variable being predicted, a criterion. The entire procedure is one of establishing the predictive validity of a test. The higher the predictive validity of a test (as summarized in a correlation coefficient), the more adequately we can forecast group achievement and to a lesser extent individual achievement.

CLINICAL VERSUS STATISTICAL PREDICTION

The actual process of making a prediction on the basis of test data can take one of two forms or can combine elements of both. The first of these methods is the clinical or case-study method. Here the counselor operates as a clinician, and on the basis of test data and other observations made of an individual, he formulates some hypotheses regarding the dynamics of the counselee. On the basis of these hypotheses, the counselor predicts subsequent counselee behavior. This approach is largely intuitive and is probably the prevalent modus operandi for most counselors.

The second method of prediction is the actuarial or statistical method. Here the counselee's test data are classified into a category which represents his performance. The counselor then uses an actuarial table which provides statistical frequencies of behavior of other persons classified in the same way. The data are thus mechanically combined (e.g. by means of a regression equation or an expectancy table), and a probability figure results.

A continuing argument in vocational guidance centers on the relative effectiveness of these two methods of making predictions from test data. Meehl's (1954) early work in this regard is instructive. He investigated nineteen studies having unambiguous results which predicted success in some kind of training or schooling, recidivism, and/or recovery from a major psychosis. Ten of these studies failed to find a difference between the two methods; nine found differences in favor of the statistical method of prediction; none produced a difference in favor of the clinical approach.

Meehl's pioneering work has been supported by later studies by Watley (1964). He used three groups of counselors (high school, university counseling center, and university advisor's office) and one group of freshman college students as predictors to forecast grade-point average, persistence in major, and extracurricular achievements for a group of college freshmen. In general, his results were as follows: Given basic data about individuals, increasing increments of information had no effect on predictive accuracy. There was very little difference between the predictive performance of groups of counselors, and their performance was not extraordinarily higher than that of the student predictors. The number of correct predictions made by statistical methods was higher than the same predictions made by different groups of clinical judges. There was great variability in the ability of individual counselors to make accurate predictions; generally, more accurate predictors tended to be more capable in abstract verbal reasoning ability, more compulsive, least confident about their predictions, and they used no consistent model of prediction from case to case. There was some evidence to suggest that those counselors who predicted most accurately also did the best job of counseling.

The message that emerges from these studies is clear. In vocational guidance, the making of clinical predictions should be approached with extreme tentativeness. Further, whenever it is possible to collect the necessary data to make statistical predictions, this method is preferred. Therefore, it is mandatory that we know with what our tests correlate and precisely what we are predicting.

THE VALIDITY OF APTITUDE TESTS FOR VOCATIONAL GUIDANCE

It is safe to say that aptitude tests predict school performance better than success in training for an occupation and performance in an occupation. The use of typical tests of scholastic aptitude produce correlation coefficients between test performance and grade-point average at the graduate school level ranging from .20 to .60 with a mean of .40 and at the baccalaureate level from .30 to .70 with a mean of .50. At the high school level, ability and grades are correlated at about .60 (Lavin, 1965). Personality factors add very little to predictive accuracy when they are combined with intellective factors.

The prediction of vocational training and success in an occupation shows much more modest results. One of the monumental and frequently criticized studies in this regard was carried out by Thorndike and Hagen (1959). Their results represent a devastating condemnation of the validity of tests in predicting job performance. Approximately ten thousand men who had taken a one and one-half day battery of tests during World War II as applicants for air-crew training were followed up twelve years later in civilian life. The tests yielded twenty separate scores in the areas of verbal, numerical, spatial, perceptual, and motor abilities. The sample was sorted into one hundred and twenty occupational groups, with each subject rated in terms of "success in the occupation." Within each occupational grouping, success indicators were correlated with each of the twenty test scores.

There were group differences in mean scores in sensible directions (e.g. accountants scored better on numbers tests than on any other tests and also scored better than writers, for instance, on the measure of numerical ability). However, there was wide variability within occupational groups which was almost as great as the variability in the total group of ten thousand (e.g. some accountants had numerical scores as low as the lowest truckdriver's score). In general, the twelve thousand correlations clustered around zero with as many in the negative direction as in the positive direction. The conclusion reached was that tests given at about age twenty cannot predict occupational success twelve years later.

Thorndike and Hagen offer some possible explanations for their findings. The most valid of these is probably the proposition that beyond survival in an occupation, "success" is a meaningless concept. Because of the institutionalization of rewards in many occupations (Civil Service, teaching, unions, etc.), in which pay scales, hours and output are set by schedules or agreements, it is virtually impossible to secure a differential measure of success in an occupation. Yet even granting this fact, the results of the research are most discouraging and point, at best, to the need for short-range rather than long-range vocational counseling.

A brighter picture of the validity of occupational aptitude tests is offered by Ghiselli (1966). He reviewed all the studies made prior to 1965 on the accuracy of tests in predicting training success and proficiency in occupations. For all occupations the average of the validity coefficients is .30 for training criteria and .19 for proficiency criteria. This difference on the order of .10 in favor of training criteria holds for just about all occupational groups. Thus predicting success in training for a job is more accurate than predicting success in the job itself.

Table 1   Comparison of Validity Coefficients for Training
and Proficiency Criteria by Type of Test

TYPE OF TEST	MEAN VALIDITY COEFFICIENT		NO. PAIRS OF COEFFICIENTS
	TRAIN.	PROF.	
Intellectual abilities	.35	.19	38
Intelligence	.34	.21	16
Immediate memory	.23	.18	5
Substitution	.27	.23	4
Arithmetic	.42	.15	13
Spatial and mechanical abilities	.36	.20	28
Spatial relations	.38	.19	13
Location	.24	.17	6
Mechanical principles	.41	.24	9
Perceptual accuracy	.26	.23	15
Number comparison	.25	.24	4
Name comparison	.24	.29	3
Cancellation	.58	.19	1
Pursuit	.18	.17	4
Perceptual speed	.30	.27	3
Motor abilities	.18	.17	24
Tracing	.18	.15	4
Tapping	.15	.13	6
Dotting	.15	.14	4
Finger dexterity	.16	.20	7
Hand dexterity	.24	.22	2
Arm dexterity	.54	.24	1
Personality traits	.05	.08	2
Interest	.05	.08	2
All tests	.30	.19	107

Table 1 also presents data on the comparison of validity coefficients by type of test. It is clear that while certain types of tests have significantly higher predictive power for training than for proficiency criteria, others do not. It seems that tests of intellectual, spatial, and mechanical abilities are more effective in predicting trainability than in predicting job proficiency. On the other hand, tests of perceptual accuracy and motor abilities predict trainability and job proficiency equally well.

Thus the accuracy of aptitude tests in forecasting occupational success and trainability is moderate. For any given job, tests of one kind give better predictions than others. The predictive power of a test must be determined for a specific job. When this is done, the maximal power of tests to predict success in training jumps to .47 and success on the job itself to approximately .35.

Finally, we have been speaking only of the predictive power of single tests. Combinations of two or more different types of tests yield even greater validity. The evident conclusion is that tests hold a sufficiently high degree of predictive power to be of substantial practical value in the selection of personnel and to be of some value in counseling.

USES OF TESTS: COUNSELING VERSUS PERSONNEL SELECTION

As we have just noted, tests may be used both for personnel selection and for counseling. In terms of personnel selection, the obvious aim is to use those tests that will ensure a maximal hit rate and, conversely, a minimum miss rate. In terms of guidance and counseling, the object is to select tests that will help an individual to achieve a more accurate picture of his potentialities. When tests are employed for personnel selection purposes, their use is *institutional* since the results lead to organizational decisions. When tests are used for counseling purposes, their use is *individual* since the results lead to individual decision making.

There are several recognized methods of choosing personnel selection tests. If only a single test is to be used, then one selects the test which has the highest correlation with the criterion measure. If one wishes to use two or more tests, he selects those tests which have the highest correlation with the criterion measure and at the same time the lowest intercorrelation with each other. For example, suppose we are interested in using tests to help select applicants for some sort of job training, and we have the following four variables:

Test 1 $r_{14} = .50$ $r_{12} = .50$

Test 2 $r_{24} = .60$ $r_{13} = .60$

Test 3 $r_{34} = .50$ $r_{23} = .80$

Success in
  training 4

In this case, we would choose tests 1 and 2 because both correlate reasonably well with the criterion measure of success in training and at the same time have the lowest correlation with each other. A low correlation between tests indicates that they are measuring different things. This is a quick and simple rule-of-thumb method.

A more complicated technique, when there are many tests from which to choose, is to use the Wherry-Doolittle Test Selection Method, which provides a means of solving certain types of multiple correlation problems with minimum statistical labor. This method selects the tests of a battery analytically and adds them until a maximum multiple correlation coefficient (R) is obtained. A step-by-step process can be found in most statistics books.

To determine the effectiveness of a test used in a personnel selection procedure, we must know two things in addition to the correlation coefficient, however. We must first know the *cutting score*—that is, the point at which we make a decision of successful or unsuccessful (e.g. a "C" average, 100 words per minute in shorthand, etc.). This figure would then describe how many individuals were *false positives* (those who would not have been accepted using the specified cutting score but who would have succeeded had they been given the opportunity) and how many were *misses*[1] (those who would have been accepted but who would have failed). Whether one type of error is more serious than the other depends upon one's philosophy and the purpose of the selection. For example, the typical open-door admissions policy assumes that a miss is much preferable to a false positive; medical schools, on the other hand, because of the limited number of places available, the high cost of training, and the potential danger of incompetence to society, place a premium on false positives and attempt to minimize misses.

Second, we need to know the *base rate*—that is, the proportion of persons who succeeded before the use of the test. The proportion of correct decisions made when the test is used (the validity rate) must be determined and compared with this base rate:

Helmstadter (1964, p. 125) summarizes the procedures for evaluating a test used in a personnel selection situation:

1. Administer the test to all individuals who would be selected under the procedures as they would be followed without *the test.*

2. Allow all *persons so tested to work on the task until an adequate measure of their criterion performance has been obtained.*

3. Determine, for alternate cutting scores, the number of misses, the number of false positives, and the total proportion of errors made when so

---

[1] If one is interested only in misses, it is possible to use a Taylor-Russell table to determine base rates and correlations for given selection ratios.

using the test. By subtraction, obtain the total proportion of correct decisions.

4. Compare the proportion of correct decisions made with the test with those without the test (that is, compare the validity rate with the base rate).

The selection of tests for counseling purposes poses a problem that cannot be handled quite so mechanically. The primary consideration is that tests should possess the characteristics set forth in the American Psychological Association's *Standards for Educational and Psychological Tests and Manuals* (1966). This document presents over 150 specific statements classified as essential, very desirable, and desirable. The statements are categorized into six areas: dissemination of information, interpretation, validity, reliability, administration and scoring, and scales and norms.

Beyond this point, however, there is little agreement regarding selection of tests for counseling and guidance. Argument continues on several issues because research thus far has not provided suitable answers. The first point of disagreement is whether one should use tests at all. Opponents of the use of tests in counseling suggest that because tests are so frequently abused and misused, they should not be employed at all. It is frequently further argued that the use of tests removes responsibility for decisions from the client and transfers it to the tests themselves and that tests pose an anxiety threat that detracts from the atmosphere of the counseling relationship. Granting the misuses of tests, however, it seems silly to throw out the baby with the bath or to assume that tests are ends in and of themselves. Almost all counselors recognize the potential value of tests in the counseling process.

Yet even those who agree that tests should be used are divided on the question of how they should be employed. The polarized viewpoints that have emerged may be classified as the testing-as-needed approach versus the testing-program-for-all approach. In schools, the latter strategy has been prevalent, with all students in given grades taking the same tests each year. The antithesis of this approach is for counselors to administer tests to meet individual needs of students as these needs emerge in counseling. Goldman (1961b, p. 305) argues, largely on the basis of the concept of readiness, "Students might be served more adequately by individualized methods of selection." However, readiness in the context of psychological testing probably refers more to interpretation than to administration. Therefore, it makes sense economically and psychologically to test programmatically in the schools. External to school settings, on the other hand, one would find himself in agreement with Goldman.

A final argument centers on who should select the tests used in counseling. Here, too, opinions span a continuum. In relatively clinical situations, perhaps the ideas of Bordin (1955) make the most sense. He proposes that client participation in selecting tests is essential because it serves as a stimulus to return for further interviews, enhances understanding of abilities, and provides motivation to do well on the tests. This notion has never received conclusive support from research. Nor has the obverse point of view—namely, that the counselor, not the student, has the required technical knoweldge and competencies for test selection. It seems that "it makes little difference what process is used so long as the most appropriate tests are administered and skillfully interpreted" (Goldman, 1961b, p. 40).

Again we emphasize that this book presents a systems approach to vocational guidance in the schools. And because a systems approach demands programmed activities at various points, because goals have to be relatively specific, measureable, realistic, and attainable, and because a total program spans time beyond the here and now of a client's perception, the following concepts of testing for vocational guidance in the schools appear to pertain:

1. It is necessary to collect data regarding various criterion measures for local school districts so that the predictions made are based on similar clientele. In other words, just as school districts frequently determine local educational norms, they should also determine local vocationalization norms.

2. Tests contribute to vocational guidance only to the extent that the results are used. If tests are not to be interpreted and the interpretation is not to be worked into the total spectrum of student decision making, they may as well not be given.

3. In terms of the testing-as-needed versus testing-for-all debate, it seems that in a systems approach the two viewpoints are not mutually exclusive. It is postulated that all students need various types of tests at different developmental stages. At the same time, unique individual needs will mandate certain nonprogrammatic testing for some students.

4. Because the parameters of vocational guidance in the schools include grades K-12 and because few, if any, students can have broad perspective on such parameters, the vocational testing program is best determined by the counselors and other professional staff of a school district.

TYPES OF APTITUDE TESTS

Assessment in the cognitive domain is usually achieved by administering a standardized battery of tests or individual tests measuring common aptitudes for which adequate criterion data are available. An aptitude may be defined as "readiness for learning" (Thorndike and Hagen, 1969, p. 644). An aptitude test is, therefore, one that predicts success in some occupation or training course (Cronbach, 1970, p. 38). At present, the number of aptitudes for which psychologists have determined adequate validity data is relatively limited. At best, it includes: intelligence (verbal, numerical, and performance), perceptual speed and accuracy (clerical), manual dexterities, mechanical, spatial visualization, aesthetic judgment, artistic ability, and musical talent (Super and Crites, 1962). Of these, the latter two are highly specialized and have limited application. Thus we are left with five basic aptitudes.

Various individual tests are capable of assessing aptitudes in each of these areas. However, for purposes of vocational guidance testing, the selection of individual tests poses problems. The main obstacle is that they have been standardized on different populations, and therefore norms are not consistent from test to test. Also, some individual tests fail to provide specific norms—that is, occupational and educational norms—which would be useful in vocational guidance. Finally, choosing individual tests to assess multiple potentialities can typically run to large costs and present clerical problems in scoring.

Because of these deficiencies, psychologists have developed the test battery. Here a number of tests are employed together to predict various criteria. Individuals have a number of different aptitudes, or patterns of strengths and weaknesses, that contribute to their total potential. The battery yields a multiscore summary of these differential patterns. Since all the tests of a battery are standardized on the same group, norms take on added meaning.

The two instruments of this sort most widely used in schools are the Differential Aptitude Tests (DAT) and the General Aptitude Test Battery (GATB). Each of these will be discussed briefly.

The Differential Aptitude Tests (Psychological Corporation).   The DAT requires approximately four hours for administration and consists of six aptitude tests (verbal reasoning, numerical ability, abstract reasoning, spatial relations, mechanical reasoning, and clerical speed and accuracy) and two achievement tests (spelling and grammar). The intercorrelations of these tests are moderate, indicating the presence of a general factor but also unique factors for each. The most recent revision and restandardization of the DAT occurred in 1963. The most recent manual was published in 1966. It is designed for use in grades 8 to 12.

Following the principle that a test is probably most valid for the middle portion of the range for which it is intended, the DAT is probably best administered at the end of grade 9 or the beginning of grade 10. In practice, it is frequently administered earlier because critical choice points in some school systems come at the end of grade 8.

The validity data on the DAT are voluminous but largely predict educational achievement in high school and college. Some occupational norms exist, largely as a result of two follow-up studies (four years and seven years), but the predictive validity of the DAT regarding occupational criteria is relatively meager. Because the verbal and numerical subtests together correlate on the order of .70-.80 with tests of scholastic aptitude, these two subtests are frequently used as a general intelligence measure. As is usually true of the relationship between interests and aptitudes, the DAT correlates only moderately with the results of such interest inventories as the Strong Vocational Interest Blank and the Kuder Preference Record-Vocational.

Finally, individual profile reports are ingeniously devised so that when scores are plotted, a difference of one inch is required before one can say that performance on one subtest differs from performance on another to the extent that the standard error of measurement is exceeded. Scores may be reported in both percentiles and stanines.

In summary, the advantages of the DAT are in the extensive educational norms and the highly competent technical development of the tests. The disadvantages are the amount of time required for administration and the relative lack of occupational norms.

The General Aptitude Test Battery (United States Employment Service).   Probably the most scientifically developed battery is the GATB. Devised on the basis of factor analysis, the battery contains twelve tests which measure nine factors: G (intelligence), V (verbal aptitude), N (numerical aptitude), S (spatial aptitude), P (form perception), Q (clerical perception), K (motor coordination, F (finger dexterity), and M (manual dexterity). Approximately two and one-half hours of time are required for testing. Scores are reported on a standard-score basis with a mean of 100 and a standard deviation of 20. Cut-off scores on several tests rather than regression equations have been established for various occupational groups and for job families. These scores relate to the *Dictionary of Occupational Titles* (see Chapter 3). Few educational norms are available.

Although the primary use of the GATB has been in state employment service offices, the battery can be used by schools, colleges, Veterans' hospitals, prisons, agencies, etc. Recently, selected schools have been permitted to administer and interpret the GATB on their own.

In summary, the GATB has two advantages not inherent in the DAT: strong occupational norms and a relatively short testing time. Its primary disadvantages are in the lack of educational norms and the use of cut-off scores rather than regression equations.

The Dailey Vocational Tests (Houghton Mifflin Company).   The Dailey Vocational Tests are designed for use with non-college-bound youngsters in grades 8 to 12 and with adults. The battery consists of three tests: the technical and scholastic test, the spatial visualization test, and the business English test. These three yield a total of twelve subscores.

As validation of this battery has proceeded over a number of years, initially disappointing and incomplete data on reliability, validity, and norms have improved to the point that this instrument can be used with a reasonable degree of psychometric confidence.

This battery may be used in comprehensive high schools with non-college-bound youth in lieu of more academic batteries. Its advantages include its "face" validity for specialty oriented students. A primary disadvantage is that it takes approximately 140 minutes of testing time.

Other Batteries.   Other test batteries are, of course, available. None, however, offers the comprehensive norms, years of validation, or technical proficiency of either the DAT or the GATB. Among the more promising but still not fully developed batteries are the Flanagan Aptitude Classification Tests (FACT), published by Science Research Associates; and for younger children the Academic Promise Tests (APT), published by the Psychological Corporation; and the Tests of Primary Mental Abilities (PMA), published by Science Research Associates.

TWO SPECIAL POPULATIONS IN VOCATIONAL TESTING

Testing two populations—the disadvantaged and the handicapped—presents special problems in vocational guidance. Each of these populations will be discussed briefly.

The Disadvantaged.   Designated by whatever euphemism is currently in fashion —the disadvantaged, culturally different, culturally deprived, etc.—this group, which includes all races, represents those who have experienced educational, cultural, and/or economic lacks of some magnitude. Although the range of test scores of such populations is typically as wide as that of the general population, the average scores of these groups are depressed in comparison with the average scores of middle-class subjects. Therefore, it is frequently contended that tests which may be appropriate for the middle-class majority are totally inappropriate for the disadvantaged. Acting on this assumption, several large-city school districts have eliminated I.Q. testing.

The specific charges made against the use of tests with the disadvantaged range from low motivation and anxiety on the part of the examinees, to unfair cultural content of the questions, to score interpretation that fails to take into account the background of the examinees, to lack of relevance of the test in relation to the requirements of various work situations. To compensate for these alleged drawbacks, several strategies have been proposed, including: retests to alleviate anxiety; "culture-fair," "cross-cultural," "culture-common," or "culture-laden" test items; use of bonuses or separate norms for the disadvantaged; and more restrictive testing and criterion refinement in order to assess only those behaviors mandatory in specific work situations.

All the above criticisms of testing with the disadvantaged and the proposed solutions seem reasonable. In actual fact, however, *tests are still as good predictors (or as poor) for the disadvantaged as they are for the advantaged* (Boney, 1966; Hewer, 1965; Munday, 1965; Stanley and Porter, 1967; Thomas and Stanley, 1969). This is true largely because the same factors measured in the test —the predictor—are also measured in the criterion (e.g. success in training, success on the job, etc.). The most promising way of breaking this self-fulfilling prophecy appears to be to change the educational treatments of various sorts between the predictors and the criteria. This rationale would explain, for example, the existence of various preschool programs such as Head Start and the many special collegiate programs such as SEEK and Upward Bound.

The Handicapped.   Testing the handicapped presents two unique problems: administration and interpretation. Some types of handicaps preclude use of the usual testing procedures. A blind student cannot read a test unless it is set in Braille; a victim of cerebral palsy would have a difficult time with a speeded test; a deaf student cannot hear oral directions given over a loudspeaker. Goldman (1961a) suggests that when speeded tests are administered to the handicapped, the examiner should note the point where the examinee is at the end of the standard time allotment but should allow the examinee to complete the test. Hence two measures will emerge: a direct comparison with published norms (timed) and a score that can be clinically interpreted (untimed). A second approach is to develop separate norms for different types of handicapped individuals after determining how individuals with given scores actually perform in various work situations.

Some evidence suggests that differential predictability for the handicapped is necessary (Banas and Nash, 1966; Hallenbeck and Hallenbeck, 1963) because aptitude measures are usually less predictive of the handicapped client's performance than they are of the nonhandicapped. Hence, adaptation of existing tests or standardization of tests with given exceptional populations may make some sense. At present, however, the evidence is too sparse to make a definitive statement in this regard. The best that can be said is that test scores of handicapped students must be held suspect and investigated thoroughly.

TEST INTERPRETATION

The effective use of tests in a counseling relationship depends upon the extent to which the client understands and accepts the results of his test performance. Since we are considering the use of test results in a school program, where everyone takes the same tests, our major concern is with group interpretation. Some research findings comparing various methods of group interpretation are summarized below:

1. Whatever the method used, student attitudes toward the counselor or toward the value of the test are much the same. However, recall of test results appears to be highest when the student has been dominant in the interpretation interview after a learning set for test interpretation has been created (Holmes, 1964).

2. Scholastic aptitude may be a significant variable in interpretation. Students with lower scholastic aptitude seem to recall scores more accurately with the use of audiovisual aids. There is also some evidence to suggest that acceptance of test results is facilitated in individual sessions more than in group sessions (Walker, 1965).

3. Those who have the most accurate pictures of themselves before testing tend

to learn most about themselves as a result of test interpretation, regardless of the interpretive technique utilized (Gustad and Tuma, 1957).

What these illustrative studies and many others suggest is that no one method of test interpretation can be considered superior for all students. Given this finding, the following recommendations for test interpretation offered by Lister and McKenzie (1966, pp. 62–63) are extremely helpful:

1. The student must experience a need for the test information. Therefore, the counselor's role in motivation is most important. He must assist students to see that a knowledge of test performance will be beneficial to them.

2. The student's questions must be translated into operational terms that are acceptable to him. This means that the interpretation must be made in terms of some criterion of importance to the student.

3. The information must be clearly communicated to the student. Lister and McKenzie argue that the evaluation of the effectiveness of test interpretation must be based on more than simple accurate recall of test information, that recall must be accompanied by significant behavior change. Some type of action must be taken. A student who understands and accepts test results given in the form of a probability statement would play the odds. His behavior would be consistent with the test results and with other data.

DISCRIMINATION

It is generally conceded that at least two types of measurement are required for vocational guidance: assessment of various capacities or aptitudes and assessment of interests. Each of these two should be surveyed at various stages of an individual's development. The results should be communicated to the client in two ways: first, in terms of the groups that he most resembles and, second, in terms of the groups he may succeed in. The "most like" type of description is achieved by means of a statistical technique called discriminant analysis. The latter "goodness" type of probability statement emerges as a result of the regression analysis procedures discussed earlier in this chapter. Hence it is necessary to assess personal traits from both the cognitive and the noncognitive domains and to report results both in terms of the groups an individual is most like (discriminant analysis) and in terms of his probability of success in given groups (regression analysis) (Sprinthall, 1967). Interest measurement is the most common application of discriminant analysis in vocational guidance.

INTERESTS

Super and Crites (1962) have observed that we may assess an individual's interests in four ways. We may look to *expressed interests*—what an individual says he is interested in. Second, we may observe *manifest interests*—what an individual actually does as an indication of what his interests are. Third, we may assess interests by *testing*—using an instrument like the Michigan Vocabulary Test on the grounds that if an individual is really interested in something, he will know the vocabulary involved in that area. Finally, we may look to *inventoried interests*—determining the pattern of an individual's interests from his responses to lists of occupations and activities.

This last technique is by far the most common means of assessing interests. Basically, two types of inventories have emerged. One is the so-called empirically keyed inventory, which results in interest scores related to specific occupations. The Strong Vocational Interest Blank (SVIB), the Clark Minnesota Vocational Interest Inventory, and the Kuder Preference Record (DD) are examples of inventories of this sort. Non–empirically keyed inventories yield score profiles in areas, rather than in specific occupations. Examples of this type of inventory are the Kuder Preference Record—Vocational (CH), the Ohio Vocational Interest Survey (OVIS), and the Brainard Occupational Preference Inventory. The most commonly used inventories are the Strong and the Kuder. Each of these will be briefly described, also the OVIS.

The Strong Vocational Interest Blank (Stanford University Press). The Strong Vocational Interest Blank (SVIB) has separate forms for men and women, although the men's form is occasionally used for both sexes. This inventory was developed for use with and standardized on college students, but research indicates that it can also be used with high school students (Stefflre, 1947). Because of the complexity of scoring, the SVIB is usually farmed out to a scoring service. The great majority of the fifty-four men's and fifty-eight women's occupational scales are professional in nature.

Scores are reported in terms of letter ratings from C to A. In addition to individual occupational ratings, it is possible to lump scores into primary, secondary, and tertiary patterns. The 1969 versions also provide content-oriented scales called basic interest scales (twenty-two for men; nineteen for women).

In addition to occupational scales and basic interest scales, the SVIB includes two other scales. One deals with the following eight nonoccupational, empirical scales which compare two contrasting groups: AACH (academic achievement), AR (age-related interests), DIV (diversity of interests), MFII or FMII (masculinity-femininity or femininity-masculinity), MD (managerial orientation), OIE (occupational introversion-extroversion), OL (occupational level), and SL (specialization level). The final scale presents administrative indices which help detect problems in administering and scoring SVIB responses.

All in all, the 1966 revision of the Men's Blank and the 1969 revision of the Women's Blank offer contemporary measures of interests, both occupational and general. The disadvantages of the SVIB are the almost mandatory need for a scoring service and the fact that the letter-grade system of reporting entails interpretation problems. The nonoccupational scales are largely related to research and are not as yet sufficiently developed for general counseling uses.

The Kuder Preference Record—Vocational (Science Research Associates). The Kuder Preference Record—Vocational (Form C) is perhaps the interest inventory most widely employed in secondary schools. It measures interest preferences in ten broad categories rather than in specific occupations: outdoor, mechanical, computational, scientific, persuasive, artistic, literary, musical, social service, and clerical. Activities are listed in triads, and the responder is required to make a choice in each triad in terms of the activity he likes most and the activity he likes least. The answer booklet is self-scoring and involves pin-pricking appropriate answers. Occupational keying of Form C is relatively meager. Scores are plotted on a chart in terms of percentiles based on a large normative group. A verification score enables the examiner to check for misunderstandings or for socially desirable responses. There is some evidence that the Kuder can also double as a personality measure, although considerably more research is required to substantiate this idea. The Kuder is designed for grades 6 to 12 and requires only a sixth-grade reading level.

In summary, the Kuder Preference Record—Vocational (Form C) is an easily administered, self-scoring measure of broad occupational interests. Score reporting is easily understandable in terms of percentiles. Its primary disadvantage is that it cannot be employed as a predictive instrument at all because of a lack of occupational keying.

A newer form of the Kuder—the Occupational Interest Survey (Form DD) (OIS) seeks to make up for this lack of occupational keying. This criterion-keyed instrument presents eighty occupations and twenty college major fields for men and thirty-six occupations and twenty-five college major fields for women. Results are offered in terms of a correlation coefficient indicating the degree to which an individual's interest pattern matches the interest pattern of a given occupational group. A verification scale and eight experimental scales also emerge from the instrument.

The obvious advantage of the OIS is its possibilities for predictive as well as discriminant use and the fact that it utilizes specific occupational groups for criterion groups rather than a general group (like the Strong). At this point, the primary disadvantage is the newness of the instrument and the fact that adequate validity data have not yet been established.

The Ohio Vocational Interest Survey (Harcourt Brace Jovanovich). Another relative newcomer to the interest measurement scene is the Ohio Vocational Interest Survey (OVIS). Using the data-people-things cubistic model of the *Dictionary of Occupational Titles* (see Chapter 3), the OVIS yields scores on twenty-four homogeneous interest scales, ranging from manual work through customer services to medical (D'Costa and Winefordner, 1969).

The reading level of the OVIS is approximately grade 8, and it usually requires from one hour to ninety minutes for administration. In addition to the interest inventory, the OVIS solicits information on a student questionnaire, which includes data on job preferences, school subject likes, high school program, plans for future education or training, and availability of and preference for vocational or business programs. The inventory itself consists of 280 job activities, to which students respond on a five-point continuum from "dislike very much" to "like very much."

The OVIS is presumably helpful in assisting students with educational planning, aiding dropouts to determine vocational plans, guiding counselors in planning group guidance occupational units, providing a framework for an occupational information file, and identifying groups of students interested in specific educational and vocational programs. Since the General Aptitude Test Battery is also tied into the *Dictionary of Occupational Titles* system, the OVIS provides an interest measure compatible with the aptitude measurement of the GATB. Initial validity and reliability data on the OVIS are adequate, but a great deal of further development is necessary.

Other Interest Inventories.   The Kuder and the Strong, in all their various forms, are by far the most widely used and standardized interest inventories. The OVIS holds considerable promise. Several other inventories are available. For specialized interests in the trades only, the Minnesota Vocational Interest Inventory (Psychological Corporation) is a well-validated instrument. The California Occupational Preference Survey (California Test Bureau) is a promising instrument which currently lacks adequate validity and reliability data. Much research has been conducted of late on the Holland Vocational Preference Inventory (Consulting Psychologists Press). This instrument is still undergoing validation, and initial results are somewhat disappointing. It is discussed in detail in Chapter 11.

MONITORING

This book has repeatedly stressed the idea of vocationalization. This concept, an analogue of the concept of socialization, refers to the interplay of psychological, sociological, cultural, and economic inputs in producing such outcomes as effective vocational behavior, decision-making ability, and vocational maturity. It has to do with the total Gestalt of experiences in an individual's life that play upon the process whereby he acquires work values, occupational knowledge, and vocational skills, eventually leading to effective vocational behavior. It is useful, therefore, to have some assessment of the stage of vocational development or vocational maturity of an individual or of groups of individuals. In a sense, monitoring can be thought of as evaluation of the vocational progress of an individual. It tells where an individual is vocationally and where he is to go. The needs of students determine the goals of a systems approach and the subsequent treatments that they will receive; monitoring permits a continual check on these needs. Two types of assessments of this sort are vocational maturity measures and work values measures.

VOCATIONAL MATURITY MEASURES AND WORK VALUES MEASURES

A relatively recent development in measurement for vocational guidance has been the standardization of scales to assess an individual's vocational maturity. Super (1955) postulated five dimensions which might indicate mature and immature vocational behavior during adolescence:

1. Orientation to vocational choice
2. Information and planning about the preferred occupation
3. Consistency of vocational preference
4. Crystallization of traits
5. Wisdom of vocational preferences

Two years later, Super (1957, p. 132) defined the construct of vocational maturity thus:

Vocational Maturity I *focuses on life stages and is indicated by the actual life stage of an individual in relation to his expected life stage (based on his chronological age).*

Vocational Maturity II *focuses on developmental tasks and is represented by the behavior of the individual in handling the developmental tasks with which he is coping.*

Vocational Development Inventory.   To measure vocational maturity as the construct was defined by Super, Crites (1965) developed the Attitude Test (AT) of the Vocational Development Inventory, which seeks to determine choice of and attitude toward an occupation in terms of empirical behaviors. This instrument consists of sixty questions cast in true-false form which yield both a vocational maturity scale and a deviate scale. Reading level is about grade 5. The rationale of the instrument is that if a counselor knows the rate and level of a counselee's development in regard to career matters, he can work more effectively with him. The Vocational Development Inventory was standardized on approximately five thousand students in Iowa. It is still largely experimental, but all indications are that it can be employed by counselors in a practical manner. In addition, it has obvious research value.

Readiness for Vocational Planning.   A second instrument designed to measure vocational maturity has been developed by Gribbons and Lohnes (1964a and 1964b). This instrument takes the form of an interview scale and is called Readiness for Vocational Planning. Eight dimensions are assessed: factors in curriculum choice, factors in occupational choice, verbalized strengths and weaknesses, accuracy of self-appraisal, evidence for self-rating, interests, values and independence of choice. The instrument requires some short-term training for counselors so that it will be administered with maximum validity and reliability. This assessment device, too, is largely experimental and research-oriented. However, early use of it indicates that it has considerable practical value, especially in terms of its use in a systems approach.

As a result of research utilizing both the Crites and the Gribbons and Lohnes instruments, several findings have already emerged. Two of special note are increase in vocational maturity with chronological age and the fact that lower-class students typically lag as much as two years behind in vocational maturity compared to their middle-class peers (Ansell, 1970; Maynard, 1970). Thus far, however, such measures have not demonstrated predictive ability, with the exception of the curriculum section of the Readiness for Vocational Planning (Gribbons and Lohnes, 1967).

Work Values Inventory (Houghton Mifflin Company).   The final instrument to be discussed is Super's Work Values Inventory. Rather than a vocational maturity measure, this instrument assesses fifteen values relating to success and satisfaction in work. The fifteen values are: intellectual stimulation, job achievement, way of life, economic returns, altruism, creativity, relationships with associates, job security, prestige, management of others, variety, aesthetics, independence, supervisory relations, and physical surroundings. These fifteen values can be further distilled into four factors: material, goodness of life, self-expression, and behavior control.

Designed for grade 7 through adult, the WVI requires only fifteen minutes for administration. Stability coefficients appear minimally adequate; construct, content, and concurrent validation are promising. Thus far, however, no predictive validity has been established. All in all, the Work Values Inventory appears to be an instrument of high potential which measures a greater variety of values than other instruments.

EVALUATION

Built into any systems approach is the process of evaluation. Evaluation is simply an activity or a series of activities designed to determine how closely goals have been achieved. As such, evaluation implies valuing—saying what is desirable or good. Wellman (1970) proposes, "The ultimate goal of evaluation is to provide the kinds of information needed to predict the probability that a specified outcome will result when a defined guidance process is used in a particular situation with a given type of student."

Zaccaria (1969, p. 241), drawing on Froelich (1949), has identified seven common approaches to the evaluation of guidance services:

1. External criteria. *The program is evaluated in terms of the general practices of the program. It is assumed that if a program has adequate practices, it is a good program.*

2. Follow-up. *Students are evaluated in terms of various criteria after they have left the school. It is assumed that a good guidance program will have beneficial results in students in terms of success, satisfaction, adjustment, etc.*

3. Client opinion. *Students are asked to evaluate the services provided by the guidance program. It is assumed that effective guidance will be reflected in client satisfaction with the help received.*

4. Expert opinion. *Experts evaluate the guidance program in terms of a survey of the facilities of the program. It is assumed that a good program must have good facilities.*

5. Specific techniques. *The guidance program is evaluated in terms of the effectiveness of specific techniques. It is assumed that the program can best be evaluated by focusing upon practices and results.*

6. Within-the-group changes. *Clients are evaluated before and after having received guidance. It is assumed that changes in clients result from the guidance they receive.*

7. Between-the-group changes. *This is the traditional experimental approach in which one of two matched groups of students receives guidance, and the other serves as a control. It is assumed that if the experimental group improves more than the control group, the improvement is due to the guidance received.*

Each of these seven approaches contains inherent methodological weaknesses. The assumption has usually been made, however, that evaluation conducted by one or more of these approaches is better than no evaluation at all. This assumption seems reasonable. A systems approach to evaluation offers the means of softening these weaknesses and of providing both a comprehensive and an intensive evaluation of goals.

In a systems approach, one looks for a relationship between vocational guidance processes (input) and student behavioral outcomes (output). In order to determine the strength of such a relationship, one must consider certain elements in the systems model. These have been dealt with in an earlier chapter; by way of review, selected aspects of the components of a systems approach are presented as they have been categorized by Wellman (1970).

1. *Needs.* The various developmental stages through which students pass determine their needs at various developmental levels and, in turn, determine the goals of vocational guidance.

2. *Objectives.* Objectives or goals, which arise from student needs, are stated in both global and behaviorally specific terms. More about this crucial variable in evaluation is given after this list.

3. *Process.* Process or treatment refers to specific activities carried out to achieve

objectives. Treatments are dependent upon and arise from the base built prior to their implementation and subsequently determine future process.

4. *Student variables.* Since certain vocational guidance processes are dependent upon selected characteristics of the students who are exposed to those processes, it is frequently necessary in evaluation to conduct crossbreaks—that is, to determine differential effects of process on students because of differences in sex, socio-economic level, culture, ability, etc.

5. *Situational variables.* It is equally likely that vocational guidance processes may have differential effects in different situations. What works in a vocational school may not work in a comprehensive high school; what is effective in a rural area may not be effective in an urban area, etc.

6. *Outcome variables.* Outcome variables are defined by objectives which are behaviorally specific and which must, in some cases, present immediate, intermediate, and long-range goals.

7. *Feedback.* This concept refers to the need for continuous evaluation. Just as one continually uses monitoring procedures to keep aware of students' vocational needs, he employs continual evaluation to determine how closely goals are being achieved. If goals are not being achieved, then processes must be changed for future groups.

Perhaps the most crucial aspect of evaluation in a systems approach relates back to objectives, for "the key characteristic of evaluation is that it must state what behavior, performance, or activity the learner will be doing when he has achieved the goal of that particular objective" (McAshan, 1969). In order to perform this aspect of evaluation, one must first define level of success. Mager (1962) suggests that it can be defined (1) by specifying by name the kind of behavior that will be accepted as evidence the student has achieved the objective; (2) by describing the important conditions under which the behavior must occur; and (3) by stipulating how well the student must perform.

To expand this idea, McAshan (1969, p. 13) suggests three levels in the development of behavioral objectives:

> Goal Statement (Nonbehavioral). *This consists of the basic goal statement and check for communication. It is a general objective. . . .*
>
> Minimum Level (behavioral-program level). *This level consists of the goal statement general objective plus the basic evaluation statement, but does not include the check for quality standards.*
>
> Desired Level (behavioral-instructional level). *This level consists of the goal statement level plus the basic statement for evaluation and the check for quality standards.*

The following statements illustrate each of the three levels, proceeding from the basic goal statement, through the basic evaluation statement, to the quality standards statement.

1. *Goal Statement:* To improve the student's understanding of the occupational structure

2. *Minimum Level:* To improve the student's understanding of the occupational structure as determined by:
   a. A locally devised test which measures understanding of the DOT
   b. Ability to order the categories of the NORC prestige scale
   c. Ability to describe which categories of occupations will show increased demands for workers in the future and which will require fewer workers

3. *Desired Level:* To improve the student's understanding of the occupational structure as determined by:
   a. Each student's achieving a score of at least 80 percent on a locally devised test which measures understanding of the DOT
   b. Each student's ordering categories of the NORC prestige scale with not more than two rank order differences
   c. Each student's identifying at least three occupational categories that will have increased demands for workers in the future and at least one that will have a decreased demand

It is obvious that within a systems approach, the common categories of evaluation described earlier will still be utilized. The major difference is that they will be used within the structure of behaviorally stated goals and that their use will be continual and systematic. For a detailed description of evaluation techniques which even the counselor who is unsophisticated in research procedures can accomplish, see Cramer, Herr, Morris, and Frantz (1970).

In summary, the procedures for evaluation within a systems approach are as follows:

1. Formulate the broad goals of the vocational guidance program.

2. Classify these goals so that an economy of thought and action can be achieved. Decide what developmental stages require which guidance processes for implementation.

3. Define objectives in behavioral terms.

4. Suggest situations in which the desired objectives and behaviors might be observed.

5. Develop or select appraisal techniques such as standardized tests, monitoring instruments, questionnaires, etc.

6. Gather and interpret performance data and compare these data with the stated behavioral objectives.

This system of evaluation is, in a sense, an absolute system, since no comparisons are made between the vocational guidance program in the given school district and the program in any other school district. Those responsible for planning, implementing, and evaluating a systems approach to vocational guidance may wish to make such comparisons to determine relative effectiveness.

SUMMARY

This chapter has discussed the use of measurement and assessment procedures in four areas relating to vocational guidance in the schools: prediction, discrimination, monitoring, and evaluation. Selected aspects of each of these areas, with descriptions of measuring instruments, were presented. Prediction and discrimination techniques provide data for individual decision making; monitoring and evaluation procedures enable counselors to plan more effectively in providing vocational guidance in a systems approach. The use of any specific assessment instrument, whether commercially standardized or locally developed, depends upon the unique characteristics of a given school system. Therefore, there is no such thing as *the* testing program in vocational guidance or *the* evaluation instruments. School districts should be flexible and imaginative as they build their own assessment programs.

REFERENCES

Anastasi, Anne. Heredity, environment, and the question "How?" *Psychological Review,* 1958, 65, 197–208.

Ansell, Edgar M. An assessment of vocational maturity of lower-class Caucasians, lower-class Negros, and middle-class Caucasians in grades eight through twelve. Unpublished dissertation for the Doctor of Education degree, State University of New York at Buffalo, 1970.

Banas, Paul, and Nash, Allan. Differential predictability: Selection of handicapped and nonhandicapped. *Personnel and Guidance Journal,* 1966, 45, 227–230.

Beck, Carlton E. *Philosophical foundations of guidance.* Englewood Cliffs, N. J.: Prentice-Hall, 1963.

Boney, J. Don. Predicting the academic achievement of secondary school Negro students. *Personnel and Guidance Journal,* 1966, 44, 700–703.

Bordin, E. S. *Psychological counseling.* New York: Appleton-Century-Crofts, 1955.

Bureau of Guidance. *Guidance and the underachiever.* Albany: New York State Education Department, 1967.

Burt, C.   The evidence for the concept of intelligence.   *British Journal of Educational Psychology,* 1955, 25, 158–177.

*Cramer, S. H.; Herr, E. L.; Morris, C. N.; and Frantz, T. T.   *Research and the school counselor.*   Boston: Houghton Mifflin, 1970.

*Crites, John O.   Measurement of vocational maturity in adolescence: Attitude test of the vocational development inventory.   *Psychological Monographs,* No. 595, 1965.

Cronbach, Lee J.   *Essentials of psychological testing.*   (3rd ed.) New York: Harper & Row, 1970.

D'Costa, A., and Winefordner, D. W.   A cubistic model of vocational interests.   *Vocational Guidance Quarterly,* 1969, 17, 242–249.

Froelich, C. P.   *Evaluating guidance procedures.*   Washington, D. C.: U. S. Office of Education, 1949.

Garrett, Henry E.   *Statistics in psychology and education.*   New York: Longmans, Green, 1958.

*Ghiselli, Edwin.   *The validity of occupational aptitude tests.*   New York: John Wiley & Sons, 1966.

Goldman, Leo.   Testing handicapped clients.   *Rehabilitation Counseling Bulletin,* Dec., 1961a, 162–169.

Goldman, Leo.   *Using tests in counseling.*   New York: Appleton-Century-Crofts, 1961b.

Goslin, David A.   *The search for ability: Standardized testing in social perspective.*   New York: Russell Sage Foundation, 1963.

*Gribbons, W. D., and Lohnes, P. R.   Relationships among measures of readiness for vocational planning.   *Journal of Counseling Psychology,* 1964a, 11, 13–19.

*Gribbons, W. D., and Lohnes, P. R.   Validation of vocational planning interview scales.   *Journal of Counseling Psychology,* 1964b, 11, 20–26.

*Gribbons, W. D., and Lohnes, P. R.   Predicting five years of development in adolescents from readiness for vocational planning scales.   *Journal of Educational Psychology,* 1967, 56, 244–253.

Gustad, John W., and Tuma, Abdul.   The effects of different methods of test introduction and interpretation on client learning in counseling.   *Journal of Counseling Psychology,* 1957, 4, 313–317.

Hallenbeck, C. E., and Hallenbeck, R. N.   Using standard tests to predict job performance in hospital workshops.   *Rehabilitation Counseling Bulletin,* Sept., 1963, 6–11.

* Recommended for additional reading.

Helmstadter, G. C. *Principles of psychological measurement.* New York: Appleton-Century-Crofts, 1964.

Hewer, Vivian H. Are tests fair to college students from homes with low socioeconomic status? *Personnel and Guidance Journal,* 1965, 43, 764–769.

Holmes, June. The presentation of test information to college freshmen. *Journal of Counseling Psychology,* 1964, 11, 54–58.

Jensen, Arthur R. How much can we boost I.Q. and scholastic achievement? *Harvard Educational Review,* Winter, 1969, 39, 1–123.

*Lavin, David E. *The prediction of academic performance.* New York: Russell Sage Foundation, 1965.

*Lister, James L., and McKenzie, Donald H. A framework for the improvement of test interpretation in counseling. *Personnel and Guidance Journal,* 1966, 45, 61–66.

Mager, Robert F. *Preparing instructional objectives.* Palo Alto, Calif.: Fearon, 1962.

Maynard, Peter. *Assessing the vocational maturity of inner-city youths.* Unpublished dissertation for the Doctor of Philosophy degree, State University of New York at Buffalo, 1970.

*McAshan, H. H. *Writing behavioral objectives.* Gainsville: Florida Educational Research and Development Council, 1969.

Meehl, Paul E. *Clinical versus statistical prediction.* Minneapolis: University of Minnesota Press, 1954.

Munday, Leo. Predicting college grades in predominantly Negro colleges. *Journal of Educational Measurement,* 1965, 157–160.

Sprinthall, Norman A. Test interpretation: Some problems and a proposal. *Vocational Guidance Quarterly,* 1967, 248–256.

Standards for educational and psychological tests and manuals. Washington, D. C.: American Psychological Association, 1966.

Stanley, Julian C., and Porter, Andrew C. Correlation of scholastic aptitude test score with college grades for Negroes versus whites. *Journal of Educational Measurement,* 1967, 5, 199–217.

Stefflre, B. The reading difficulty of interest inventories. *Occupations, 1947,* 26, 95–96.

Super, Donald E. The dimensions and measurement of vocational maturity. *Teachers College Record,* 1955, 57, 151–163.

Super, Donald E. *The psychology of careers.* New York: Harpers, 1957.

Super, Donald E., and Crites, John O. *Appraising vocational fitness.* New York: Harper & Brothers, rev. 1962.

Thomas, Charles L., and Stanley, Julian C. Effectiveness of high school grades for predicting college grades of Black students: A review and discussion. *Journal of Educational Measurement,* 1969, 6, 203–215.

Thorndike, Robert L., and Hagen, Elizabeth. *10,000 careers.* New York: John Wiley & Sons, 1959.

Thorndike, Robert L., and Hagen, Elizabeth. *Measurement and evaluation in psychology and education.* (3rd ed.) New York: John Wiley & Sons, 1969.

Walker, Joseph L. Four methods of interpreting test scores compared. *Personnel and Guidance Journal,* 1965, 44, 402–404.

*Watley, Donivan, and F. L. Vance. *Clinical versus actuarial prediction of college achievement and leadership activity.* Final report, Project No. 2202, Cooperative Research Program. Washington, D. C.: Office of Education, U. S. Department of Health, Education, and Welfare, 1964.

Wellman, Frank E. Evaluation of vocational guidance: Local level. Paper presented at the 64th annual Vocational Convention, New Orleans, December, 1970. Mimeographed.

Zaccaria, Joseph. *Approaches to guidance in contemporary education.* Scranton, Pa.: International Textbook, 1969.

ELEVEN

INFORMATION IN VOCATIONAL GUIDANCE

The average youngster is directly exposed to very few occupations. He is aware, sometimes only vaguely, of the occupations of his immediate family and perhaps those of a small coterie of family-connected individuals. Because of the mass media, he may also be acquainted with an additional small number of occupations, frequently stereotypes. During the process of his socialization, he has learned that some types of occupations are desirable and that others are taboo, at least within his cultural sphere. In attempting to relate self-characteristics to various occupations, then, he typically has few alternatives through which to sort unless some type of direct intervention occurs. This intervention usually takes the form of exposure to occupational information.

In addition to his need for occupational information, an individual requires educational and personal information if his vocationalization is to be complete. Since educational decisions are intermediate choices within the total context of vocational decision making, students must possess and be able to use information about various curricular opportunities, post–high school educational possibilities, and the relationship between education and work. If the college decision has been made, students need to understand such factors as how collegiate environments differ, how the overt characteristics of institutions of higher education (e.g. size, selectivity, geographical location, curriculum, etc.) affect individuals, how to go about the application process, how to investigate financial-aid opportunities, how to determine what national tests are required, and how to cope with many other variables in the process of college choice. If students are specialty-oriented, they must have similarly important information about opportunities for post–high school training.

Both educational and occupational information have meaning only insofar as such data are evaluated within the framework of what an individual knows about himself. Self-information is crucial to a student's seeing the relevance of the educational and/or occupational data which he receives. A student needs an accurate picture and acceptance of his strengths and weaknesses in both the cognitive and the noncognitive domains in order to realize fully the value of the information regarding the worlds of work and education. He must be aware of his diverse aptitudes, his interests, his values, and his attitudes toward learning and work. Only then can he truly evaluate the information which he receives. In effect, he asks, Knowing what I know about myself, how can I use this information?

The process of vocationalization requires that information continually reinforce planfulness; the interaction of educational alternatives, occupational alternatives, and self-characteristics is mandatory if good vocational decision making is to occur. Suggestions for enhancing the interaction of these topics are offered in Chapter 9.

This chapter suggests guidance processes to achieve the goals for vocational guidance in the elementary, junior high, and high schools, offered earlier in this volume. It suggests a range of delivery systems by which the concepts, knowledge, and attitudes integral to vocationalization can be attuned to the needs and characteristics of various consumer publics. It seeks to identify the range of possibilities available within the many facets of the educational enterprise and within the community for reinforcing vocationalization—for helping the student develop a vocabulary of work, acquire necessary vocational knowledge, develop healthy vocational attitudes, learn adequate decision-making skills, etc. Specifically, this chapter sets forth the principles for effectively using information and discusses the evaluation of information, types of delivery systems, and illustrations of some of the more promising systems. Finally, it speaks to the special salience of information in elementary schools and for dropouts and terminal students.

PRINCIPLES FOR USING INFORMATION EFFECTIVELY

It is obvious that exposure to information is insufficient. The mere availability of information about occupations, educational opportunities, and the self-characteristics of an individual does not mean that the information will be used or, if used, that it will be employed effectively. In order to increase the probability that data will be efficiently utilized, one must consider aspects of motivation, the quality of the information, and how information is assimilated.

MOTIVATION

O'Hara (1968) highlights the importance of the concepts of need and readiness whether one views vocational guidance as vocationalization or as treatment. In emphasizing the more cognitive aspects of vocational learning, he suggests that all such learning is a function of motivation. Motivation, in turn, is based on a student's attempt to satisfy a vocational need. In other words, no need, no action; no action, no vocational learning. To satisfy these conditions, O'Hara proposes (p. 638), "Guidance personnel have an obligation to impose a formal learning situation, with formal academic sanctions, in order to create the goal-directedness necessary for increased understanding of the world of work and the numerous possible responses to it." The formal learning situation would emphasize the language of vocations in order that the world of work can be explored vicariously. Without this experience, the student is likely to be a "vocationally deprived child." O'Hara, then, points up the first principle in the use of information: motivation for use.

Cooley's (1969, p. 65) view coincides with O'Hara's.

I believe a necessary ingredient would be an extensive guidance curriculum. Through a variety of approaches—such as independent study, small group discussions, career games, and computer-assisted instruction—principles involved in goal setting, planning toward goals, self-direction, and decision-making need to be taught. . . . Such a curriculum could provide the student with a body of relevant knowledge regarding those processes (goal setting and planning) so that the counselor and student can more easily work together in those tasks. The guidance curriculum must try to prepare the student to make effective use of the counseling interview.

While we are not advocating in this chapter the development of a formal occupational curriculum, we are in agreement with both O'Hara and Cooley that a great deal of vocational guidance is composed of cognitive learnings. Almost all learning theories place a premium on motivation, readiness, and the establishment of a set in the learner. Vocational guidance processes would do well to follow this example. To become motivated, students must be assisted to see how their needs are being met by whatever information is being delivered.

EVALUATION OF INFORMATION

A second factor in the effective use of information is the caliber of the data. Whatever the vehicle by means of which the information is transmitted—print, film, slide, record, computer, simulation, etc.—there is a need to evaluate it in terms of some criteria of "good" information.

One important criterion is the source of the information. Some material is produced for recruitment, and although many such presentations are acceptable, some, because of their overzealousness, are misleading. Other materials are produced specifically for guidance purposes and thus can frequently be considered more accurate at face value.

Other important considerations are the recency, validity, and applicability of the data (Herr and Cramer, 1968). Recency refers to the up-to-date nature of the information. Newness does not guarantee accuracy, but it is unlikely that information will be accurate unless it is relatively recent. Validity refers to the accuracy of the information insofar as the data may be affected by such factors as the zealous recruitment motive discussed above. Finally, applicability may be considered from two points of view: (1) Are data presented in such a manner that they can be easily utilized? (2) Is the level at which data are presented appropriate to the consumer?

The National Vocational Guidance Association has suggested other guidelines for evaluating occupational materials in terms of the completeness of presentation (NVGA, 1964). Depending upon how closely a piece of occupational information adheres to the NVGA recommendations, it is classified as highly useful, recommended, or useful. Following are some of the recommendations:

Basic Concepts

1. A basic standard for any occupational publication should be the inclusion of a clear statement as to its purpose and the group to whom it is directed.

2. Occupational information should be related to developmental levels which will vary with age, educational attainment, social, and economic backgrounds.

3. Consideration should be given to the implications of the material for all groups in our society.

4. The description of an occupation should be an accurate and balanced appraisal of opportunities and working conditions, which should not be influenced by recruiting, advertising, and other special interests.

5. Occupational information should include the nature of personal satisfactions provided, the kinds of demands made, and the possible effects on an individual's way of life.

Guidelines for Content

The quality and specificity of detail in occupational materials will vary with the intended use of the publication. For example, a publication intended for adults considering retraining or additional training should include more specific information about earnings and fringe benefits than one designed to help students explore the job world. The following is intended not as a schedule for analyzing occupations but as a checklist to insure that a particular publication contains the necessary information.

Definition of the occupation as given in the Dictionary of Occupational Titles or as determined by the U. S. Employment Service. (The DOT title should be included if definitions are provided by state employment services, professional and trade associations, unions, licensing bodies, or job analysis.)

History and development of the occupation including its social and economic relationships.

Nature of the work such as duties performed, tools or equipment used, relationships to other occupations, possible work settings, and fields of specialization.

Requirements such as education and training, aptitudes, temperaments, interests, physical capacities, and working conditions.

Special requirements such as licensure or certification imposed by law or official organizations.

Methods of entering the occupation such as direct application, personal reference, examination, apprenticeship. (Explanation should be made of the assistance which may be offered by unions, employers, professional and other organizations, public or private employment agencies, school and college placement offices.)

Opportunities for experience and exploration through summer and part-time employment, work-study programs, programs of the Armed Forces or voluntary agencies such as the Peace Corps, youth organizations, and community services.

Description of usual lines for advancement or of possibilities for transfer to related occupations either through seniority, experience, on-the-job or in-service training, additional education, and examinations.

Employment outlook as suggested by trends likely to affect employment the next five, ten, or twenty years. (Factors affecting particular groups such as geographic area, age, sex, race, physical disabilities, and the like should be considered, as well as factors affecting outlook such as supply and demand, retraining programs, replacement needs, automation, and other technological developments.)

Earnings, both beginning and average wage or salary according to setting, locality, and other significant factors, as well as supplementary income and fringe benefits such as commissions, tips, overtime, bonuses, meals, housing, hospitalization, vacations, insurance and retirement plans. (Related to earnings are costs or deductions for tools, equipment, uniforms, supplies, and the like.)

Conditions of work and their implications for the individual's way of life, including where significant, daily and weekly time schedules, overtime, seasonality, physical conditions such as travel required, setting—indoor or outdoor, noise, confusion, temperature, health hazards, and strength demands.

Social and psychological factors such as work satisfactions, patterns of relationships with supervisors and other workers, and with unions, associations, or other organizations in which membership may be required or desirable.

Sources of additional information such as books, pamphlets, trade and professional journals, motion pictures, slides and other visual aids, pertinent literature provided by government agencies, union, associations, industry, schools, colleges and universities.

Criteria for Style and Format

The intended use of the occupational material will be a critical factor in the consideration of style and format.

Style should be clear, concise, interesting, and adapted to the readers for whom the material is intended.

Publishers are encouraged to be creative and imaginative in presenting factual information in a stimulating fashion. The typography should be inviting, the total format pleasing, and the illustrations should be of a quality to enhance the effectiveness of the material and to make it appropriate for the age level for which it is planned.

Charts, graphs, or statistical tables should be properly titled and interpreted. Sources and dates of basic data should be given.

The occupational book or pamphlet should state specifically the publisher, date of publication, the sponsoring organization, group, or individual, and the author. Information about the author's training and experience should be provided. Pages should be numbered in sequence, and the price, when applicable, should be included.

In view of the changing nature of occupations, it is important that information be kept up to date. Provision should be made for review and revision when the original publication is issued, and new editions should state whether or not contents have been revised. Dates of original publications and of the data used should be given on both first and revised editions. When information about wages or other data subject to relatively rapid change is used, date and source should be indicated.

A similar guide for the evaluation of occupational films was published by NVGA in 1966. Among the points stressed in this pamphlet is that films should possess the following content:

1. The interdependence of related occupations
2. Activities of the worker
3. The setting of the work
4. Preparation required
5. Contribution of the occupation to safety
6. Excellence of workmanship
7. Levels of occupational opportunities
8. Personal rewards of the occupation
9. Organizations related to the occupation
10. Factors affecting growth of the occupation

In addition, style and format are judged important, including: length of film, implications for motivation, implications for social and ethnic groups, basic information, and credits.

There are several other ready-made evaluation devices for assessing occupational information, for example, *The Ohio University Check List and Rating Scale for Evaluating Occupational Literature* (Hill, 1966). These types of instruments are helpful. However, it should be recalled that appropriateness is a criterion of "good" information. It is entirely possible that some information will not conform to all the standards recommended and yet be highly useful and appropriate for some individuals.

STUDENT USE OF INFORMATION

The manner in which individuals use information in decision making is, in many respects, a highly personalized matter. Several generalizations are possible, however, on the basis of research conducted by Halpern and Norris (1968, p. 240). They investigated the role of information in the curriculum decisions of tenth-grade students.

1. The students tended to select information which counselors had judged to be most relevant.

2. Their information search sampled the available information areas with the exception of values, which tended to be neglected.

3. Their information-search pattern changed as they received information, i.e. information at first considered important was often reclassified as unimportant (and vice-versa) as new information was received.

4. The information areas of abilities was considered the most important, plans and interests less important, and values least important.

When these findings are coupled with the results of research reported in other chapters, namely, the concepts of cognitive dissonance (Festinger, 1957) and the so-called primacy effect (Luchins, 1960), it is easy to understand that the manner in which information is assimilated, processed, and accepted or rejected is very complex and idiosyncratic. Just as the intake of information is individualized, so too is the output of information as it affects decision making.

Indeed, individualizing information appears to be a key requirement for its effective use. Hollis and Hollis (1969, p. vi) argue, "The more information processes can be personalized, the better the individual can understand and integrate information through both his cognitive and affective processes." What this means is that there is a variety of approaches by which information can be gathered and that the effectiveness of these approaches will vary from individual to individual. As the counselor assists a student to sort through, comprehend, assimilate, and find meaning in information, the effectiveness or lack of effectiveness of such data becomes apparent. It is, therefore, at this point appropriate for the counselor to survey the types of delivery systems currently available in order to evaluate potential effectiveness.

TYPES OF DELIVERY SYSTEMS

The problem before us is a basic and complicated one—the storage, retrieval, and dissemination of information. The information or knowledge explosion is a well-known reality. Knowledge in some fields doubles itself every few years. The generation of new knowledge, in fact, as achieved by various research and development programs, is mainly responsible for the changing occupational structure described in Chapter 3. New jobs and occupations come about because new products, services, and industries evolve from new knowledge; these new jobs, in turn, generate more new jobs and occupations. The assault of information and new knowledge forces us to grope with new methods by which to store the information in order that it can be retrieved with maximum efficiency and disseminated in the most effective manner. The various delivery systems are outlined in the following pages.

PRINTED MATTER

The most common and traditional type of vocational information is published material. These materials, of course, range from occupational briefs to the *Dictionary of Occupational Titles* and the *Occupational Outlook Handbook*, from biographies to popular magazines, from booklets, catalogues, and brochures to newspapers. A variety of methods have been devised for filing such information. There are diverse prepackaged or home-grown systems available. These are described in detail in a number of good texts (Hollis and Hollis, 1969; Isaacson, 1971). It is beyond the scope of this chapter to recapitulate filing methods for educational, occupational, and personal information.

Unfortunately, experience with occupational and educational literature indicates that all these systems present dissemination problems. The data are easily stored and readily retrieved, but they appear to be insufficiently utilized. Perhaps the motivation of the student is missing. Perhaps the effort of reading is too much. Perhaps the printed word is dry and uninspiring. Whatever the reason, it is clear that while students are aware of the types of printed information which the school has stored and know that it can be retrieved, they do not in general make use of the information (Gibson, 1962). It is apparent that methods other than or in addition to traditional printed materials are necessary or that counselors must deal more effectively with motivational concerns if students are to use printed data more extensively.

OTHER MEDIA APPROACHES

In addition to printed matter, various audio and visual means of disseminating information are used: bulletin boards and exhibits, commercial and closed-circuit television, slides, films, filmstrips, and microfilm. At the elementary school level, activities in this category might even include "show and tell" exercises.

A study by Norman (1969) suggests that the use of an audio aid often encourages students to seek additional vocational counseling. He transmitted vocational information to one group by means of a tape and presented the same information in mimeographed form to another group. More of the audio-group clients returned for further counseling than did the visual-group students.

Another noteworthy project which makes use of various media is the Career Information VIEW System. By means of microfilm, recorder devices, and computers, this system—which began in San Diego County, California, and has spread across the country—attempts to provide secondary school students who are largely non-college-bound with current information about job opportunities in a local area. In effect, this project establishes a Regional Career Information Center, breaking down the provincialism of local school districts (Pierson, Hoover, and Whitfield, 1967).

Audio and visual approaches provide an interesting and sense-appealing method of transmitting information. Clearly, they are more effective in vocationalization than in treatment because of their limited coverage, with the exception of the placement aspect of treatment.

FORMAL GROUP APPROACHES

Occupational, educational, and personal information can also be disseminated via assemblies, career days or nights, and vocational panels either in large groups or in class-sized groups. In classes, for example, the vocational implications of various subject matter—e.g. mathematics, science, etc.—are frequently discussed.

An example of an approach of this sort is presented by Osipow and Alderfer (1968), who investigated the effects of a high school speech course oriented toward assignments on career development and decisions. Their results suggest that such a course increases the frequency of student discussion concerning career plans.

An occupational unit taught through social studies classes in fifth grade is described by Thompson and Parker (1971). Comparing an experimental and a control group, they found that teaching an experimental occupational unit by means of interviews, role playing, filmstrips, audiotapes, bulletin boards, group discussion, counseling, and brainstorming led to the experimental group's gaining greater knowledge of community careers and occupation patterns than the control group.

Here, again, the methodology is primarily useful in vocationalization, in assisting young people to build a vocational vocabulary. Individualization occurs only after students have had opportunity to discuss the information and sort through it in terms of its relevancy to them personally.

INTERVIEW APPROACHES

Educational or occupational information can be gathered by means of a variety of person-to-person and group interactions with individuals who represent various careers, occupations, jobs, and educational institutions or with individuals also learning about the world of work or educational opportunities. The career conference or career day is one such approach. Here adult individuals represent their vocations, and students are free to talk with and/or listen to as many as possible within a restricted amount of time. The dangers inherent in this procedure are many: superficial or selective coverage of an occupational area, overemphasis on function to the exclusion of self-factors, proselytizing in the most negative sense, circus atmosphere, etc. Students also tend to go to hear people who represent jobs and occupations in which they are already interested and about which they already know something; thus no new possibilities are explored. An educational analogue of this activity is the college night.

In a similar but more in-depth approach, the student interviews workers in various jobs or personnel directors who are familiar with the requirements of a relatively wide range of jobs. The youngster is not limited to those occupations represented at a career conference; he is free to explore any occupation available in the community. He may be given an interview guide to ensure that important aspects of the occupation are covered in the conference. Again, however, this approach assumes that the youngster has some prior interest in an occupation and that he seeks to broaden his knowledge of it.

A still more detailed and thorough approach is the job analysis. In this case, the student supplements direct-interview data with data he gathers from other sources, such as occupational literature. While this technique offers a comprehensive and intensive view of a single occupation, it can be a tedious exercise which turns off youngsters if their motivation is not relatively strong.

A final interview-type approach to occupational information is the job clinic. Whereas the career conference has relatively long-range goals, the emphasis in the job clinic is on immediate goals, usually job placement. The job clinic brings together many individuals who have jobs to offer (and frequently many counselors). Other individuals who need jobs come to the clinic and decide whether their attributes and interests match the available jobs. This type of activity is most common in employment agencies of one type or another and, of course, emphasizes vocational guidance as treatment—for what can be more treatment-oriented than immediate placement?

It is likely that job clinics will be obsolescent in the very near future. Computer technology has made the actual physical presence of a number of employers in one setting anachronistic. Computerized job banks already are operating extensively via state employment services, especially in New York, Wisconsin, Utah, and California. They allow for daily updating and listing of jobs in a fairly wide geographical area. When people and jobs can be matched with this type of nonbiased efficiency, there is really no need for a job clinic.

SIMULATION APPROACHES

There are many simulation or gaming techniques by which students can vicariously explore careers as well as educational opportunities. Simulation must be used properly—that is, not in isolation as an end in itself but along with meaningful discussion, follow-up, and explanatory materials. If not used properly, simulation can lead to distorted understandings (Kaplon and Gordon, 1967). When employed properly, however, simulation is valuable in that it brings down to manageable proportions a very complicated aspect of life. There is some disagreement about the relative merits of simulation. Cherryholmes (1966) has concluded that students who participate in simulation activities do not learn significantly more facts and/or principles than those engaged in other methods of learning. On the other hand, Boocock and Coleman (1966) have demonstrated that gaming has produced significant differences, especially in students' attitudes.

The simplest form of simulation is role playing of various types. For example, students may role-play job interviews in order to be more relaxed and prepared when an actual employment interview comes. Students may also dramatize potential conflicts in work situations (e.g. promptness on the job) on the premise that such an exercise will serve a preventive function when they actually begin to work.

Taking role playing a step further, McCourt (1965) has developed what he calls the vocational development lesson. In this type of simulation, groups of youngsters are exposed to an occupation by means of a role model. The role model may be represented in person, in a film, or in literature. The role model tells what he does, but, more important, he relates the personal meaning of his work—his satisfactions, frustrations, etc. In short, he gives a picture of the kind of person he is and helps the group try to be for a short while a member of the occupation he represents. For example, a psychologist might present the students with a case study concerning an individual with whom he has worked and invite the group to attempt a diagnosis and prescribe treatment. After the role model has been presented, students are asked to engage in reflective thinking, to compare and contrast what they know about themselves with what they know about the role model and his work. Thus students explore vicariously the relevance to them of the particular occupation under consideration. McCourt's early evaluations of this technique suggest that it is highly promising. Certainly, it is the type of activity that integrates the primary types of information: educational, occupational, and personal.

Based on a similar premise, Krumboltz et al. (1967) have produced a series of vocational problem-solving kits which provide students with experiences in a variety of occupations. A student can, for example, achieve some notions regarding the work of an accountant by actually balancing a mini-set of books. He can then read about the personal and educational requirements for the occupation of accountant. Hamilton and Krumboltz (1969) report that the initial impact of such simulated activities appears to be considerable. They utilized an Electronics Technician Kit with tenth-grade, non-college-bound students and compared them with a group that used a less "real" type of experience. They found that the experimental group enjoyed the experience more, had a greater desire for further information, and wanted more experiences of the same sort. It is noteworthy that although Science Research Associates is publishing these kits, it has chosen to publish them in the form which Krumboltz found least effective in his research.

Another simulation technique of great potential is gaming. Perhaps the best-known occupational game is the Life Career Game, developed by Boocock (1969). The goals are to provide high school and college students some ideas about the contours of the future, information about occupational and educational alternatives or opportunities, a feeling for the total life cycle of an individual, and practice in decision making. The game is played by teams of from two to fifteen students, who compete against each other in making decisions about a fictitious individual for eight years into the future. By means of this simulation, a student presumably acquires an understanding of the labor market, educational opportunities, marriage, and leisure patterns. There is no doubt that Life Career is fun to play; the determination of whether or not it contributes to vocationalization requires empirical evidence that has not yet been obtained. A number of doctoral dissertations designed to answer this question are currently under way.

Career clubs provide still another type of simulation activity. Future Teachers of America and Junior Achievement are examples of this approach. In the former, youngsters with an interest in teaching as a career can hear speakers, go on field trips, and sometimes actually gain experience in teaching. Prelaw, premedicine, and other professions-related clubs are also in operation. In the latter, students gain real experience in setting up and running a business enterprise.

A final simulation delivery system uses the vehicle of the workbook. Two examples of this activity are Holland's (1970) Self-Directed Search for Educational and Vocational Planning and the Educational Guidance Information System of the College Entrance Examination Board (1970). The Holland materials consist of a self-administered, self-scored, and self-interpreted system. There are two booklets: an assessment booklet that yields a three-letter occupational code (see Chapter 4) and an occupational classification booklet that the student uses after he determines his occupational code. The object is to provide a simulation—in thirty to fifty minutes—of a vocational counseling experience of several interviews' duration. In short, while other simulation experiences suggest that they are an adjunct or input to counseling, Holland's system was developed as a substitute for counseling or as a parallel experience. Another workbook, the Educational Guidance Information System (EGIS) of the College Entrance Examination Board, is designed for use at high school level. This planning guide attempts to help the student integrate information about his current plans, interests, job requirements, abilities, past performance, and future plans. It elicits information about other decision-making variables also.

Both these types of simulation are on the edge of moving in the directions advocated in this volume. They are exciting possibilities. They require a great deal of further development and research, but they are a step in a healthy direction.

FIELD TRIPS

Field trips to plants, offices, educational institutions, etc., are a common method of gaining occupational and educational information. The opportunity to see work performed in an actual job setting and to interview those who perform the jobs, or the opportunity to get the feel of an educational institution can be a valuable experience. Too often, however, field trips are accomplished only en masse with little or no thought given to the interests of students. It is likely that a field-trip program which is individualized to the extent that arrangements can be made for a single student's visit will be a better program. Group trips can be useful, especially for expanding the educational and vocational worlds of the culturally deprived, but they must be preceded by careful planning and followed up with feedback. Regarding preparation for field trips, Dale (1954, p. 167) suggests the following points:

1. *Arouse student interest in the trip (by class discussion, photographs, bulletin board, and other similar materials).*
2. *Discuss with students the problems that the trip can help solve.*
3. *Make clear to students the purpose or purposes of the trip.*
4. *Develop background by consulting reference materials.*
5. *Work out with students the specific points to observe during the trip.*
6. *Set up with the students the standards for safety and behavior.*
7. *Prepare and distribute to students any materials that can be used profitably in the course of the trip.*

Follow-up or debriefing activities include discussion individually and in groups regarding the values gained from the trip. Such questions as How does the information which I gained relate to me? and How does what I observed affect my decision making? are appropriate.

FORMAL CURRICULUM APPROACH

Earlier in this chapter the views of O'Hara and Cooley regarding the need for a formal vocational guidance curriculum in the schools were presented. The authors concur with that view only to the extent that we believe certain aspects of vocationalization and even a limited number of treatment applications are perhaps best accomplished by means of structured and direct teaching-learning. But these applications can take place within the existing curriculum.

Hence occupational units within existing courses of study, vocational courses, and even an integrated occupational curriculum are possibilities. The professional literature is replete with possibilities for the content and process of such units and courses. For example, Fibkins (1969) included the following topics in a one-week unit in an American History class which used popular songs as a stimulus.

1. The significance of man in the present world

2. The changing pattern of family life due to contraceptives, working women, changing responsibility of man and woman

3. The changing pattern of family life due to increased population in an already crowded environment

4. The relation between work availability and increasing population

5. The relation between food supply, foreign policy, and available occupations

6. Adolescent military obligations and foreign policy

7. The change from a rural to an urban population and the present urban crisis

8. Negro people and occupations, housing

9. Increasing political power of people under twenty-five

10. The selection of a life style including education, occupation, marriage, and recreation

This unit is presented because it illustrates some of the pitfalls inherent in units and courses. One such danger is the attempt to do too much in too short a time. Another is the use of seemingly disjointed or unrelated topics. A third factor is the offering of an isolated unit without something relevant preceding or following. A fourth peril is the failure to provide for evaluation of the unit. And the final factor is the failure to ascertain whether the shotgun approach is relevant for all the students in the class.

The thrust of this book is that a systematic approach to vocational guidance is necessary from kindergarten through grade 12. One cannot create unrelated units or courses and expect the goals of vocational guidance to be achieved. Planfulness of a total nature is necessary. Even a one-semester course must be recognized as a second-best measure if one agrees that vocationalization is developmental and lifelong. Obviously, the incorporation and integration of vocational learnings and attitudes within an existing curriculum throughout the K-12 educational span would be most beneficial. A fortress cannot be stormed with a peashooter; a total assault is required. At best, isolated, unrelated units are palliative; they do not strike to the core of vocationalization. What is required is a sequential, developmental, and systematized integration with the existing curriculum that extends beyond the classroom.

DIRECT EXPERIENCE

The axiom that the best way to learn something is to do it probably holds true for the acquisition of information. Direct work experience clearly allows an individual to learn a great deal about a specific job. Work experience, is, therefore, a valuable strategy when vocational guidance is viewed as treatment and, in some cases, can be an aid to vocationalization. Many schools offer work-experience programs. Retailing students, for example, are freed from school for a half day to work in retail establishments. This cooperation provides on-the-job training and the benefit of experiential learning. Part-time and summer jobs also provide exploratory opportunities which make the individual more occupationally aware. Again, however, these opportunities increase in value as students have a chance for feedback to reinforce or stimulate vocational learnings.

COMPUTERS

Electronic data-processing techniques appear to be the promise for the future in guidance. Computer utilization may take two forms: (1) computer-assisted instruction (programmed instruction) whereby an individual may learn his way through a vocational workbook or (2) computer-assisted information systems that provide almost immediate retrieval and dissemination of information. Once information has been retrieved, however, it is transmitted to the user by means of the printed word.

There are currently at least nineteen projects which try to use computer technology in vocational guidance. Some are merely information vehicles; others are more ambitious, attempting something closer to a counseling approach.

1. Development of a System of Vocational Exploration Through Use of the *Dictionary of Occupational Titles* and the Ohio Vocational Interest Survey—Ohio Department of Education, Columbus, Ohio 43212

2. Vocational Guidance in Education (VOGUE, a Demonstration System of Occupational Information Dissemination for Career Guidance)—Board of Cooperative Services, Jericho, New York 11753

3. Project PLAN—American Institutes for Research, Palo Alto, California 94302

4. Computerized Vocational Information Systems (CVIS)—Willowbrook High School, Villa Park, Illinois 60181

5. A Study of Intellectual Growth and Vocational Development—Educational Testing Service, Princeton, New Jersey 08540

6. Vocational Information System Involving Occupational Needs (Project VISION)—Wisconsin State Employment Service, Madison, Wisconsin 53702

7. Computer-assisted Occupational Guidance Program—Pennsylvania State University, University Park, Pennsylvania 16802.

8. Multiple-Message Transmission of Educational Information Regarding College Major Fields of Study—Counseling Center, University of Maryland, College Park, Maryland 20740.

9. Media Interactive System for Vocational Development—Indiana State University, Terre Haute, Indiana 47809

10. Experimental Education and Career Exploration System (ECES)—IBM, Yorktown Heights, New York 10598

11. It's About Work—Dover, Delaware 19901

12. Career Information: The VIEW System—San Diego, California 92111

13. Total Guidance Information Support System—Bartlesville Public Schools, Bartlesville, Oklahoma 74003

14. Information System for Vocational Decisions (ISVD)—Harvard University, Cambridge, Massachusetts 02138

15. Rochester Career Guidance Project—Rochester City Schools, Rochester, New York 14614

16. Exploratory Study of Information-processing Procedures and Computer-based Technology in Vocational Counseling—System Development Corporation, Santa Monica, California 90404

17. Computer-based Course Selection Program—Palo Alto Unified School District, Palo Alto, California 94302

18. The Counseling Information System 9/10 (CIS)—University of Oregon, Eugene, Oregon 97403

19. Who Does What? A Guidance Career Game—State University of New York at Buffalo, Buffalo, New York 14214

The above list does not include the dozens of commercial businesses that offer the service of sorting through colleges and providing lists for prospective applicants.

The authors have chosen to devote a relatively large amount of space to technological delivery systems and less space to more traditional ones. It is clear that these traditional methods have not proved so effective as one might desire. There are many possible reasons for this relative failure. In some cases, they have been spontaneously mounted with no thought of what came before or what would come after; they have lacked adequate preparation and feedback opportunities. Whatever the reasons, we are not suggesting that schools give up traditional approaches. They represent activities that require very little expenditure of money; they need no fantastic hardware; they call for no new educational system. Simply put, the effective use of traditional methods is dependent upon teacher-counselor-administrator attitudes, and in many instances these methods can be incorporated within existing approaches by slightly readjusting program gyroscopes. It is equally clear, however, that in a systematic approach to vocational guidance, technology assumes a greater role than it otherwise would (Hosford and Ryan, 1970).

The use of technology is not accomplished without concomitant problems. A financial outlay is necessary, of course, although mini-computers and time-sharing plans are bringing costs down to manageable proportions. Beyond financial outlay, however, the use of technology opens other concerns. Walz (1970) points out that technology forces the student to come to grips with his values and goals, which might have otherwise remained unexamined. The result is frequently conflict. Invasion of privacy, or lack of safeguards for confidentiality, also can be troublesome. Fadism, intemperate usage, and "depersonalization" are further possible outcomes of technology. Yet with judicious planning and utilization, technology can provide a strong weapon among many in the arsenal of the counselor.

Loughary (1970) delineates at least three ways in which computers can be used in guidance. In the first application, computers serve as data-processing tools for counselors by storing pupil data and subsequently reporting it in various ways. Second, computers can be used as substitutes for some counselor functions that go beyond simple information processing. Here one may think in terms of reference systems which often permit the user and the computer to engage in a dialogue. Examples are the matching of students and colleges, or the matching of workers and jobs. In the third application, the machine is viewed as a substitute counselor, at least for some counseling functions which involve systematic, consistent, and selective use of a limited number of simple skills.

In terms of the first two categories, Miller (1970, pp. 215-216) has divided information systems into four classes:

1. *Educational development and planning systems are student information systems containing test scores, grades, personal characteristics, etc., and are usually state-based.*

2. *Locally oriented occupational information systems are designed to communicate general and local occupational information to students for use in vocational planning and placement.*

3. *Information systems to facilitate vocational decision making emphasize providing the student with information about self, educational opportunities, and the world of work, and also helping him develop skills in effective vocational decision making.*

4. *Information systems for staff training and program development contain information about current educational programs, practices, and research.*

In order that the reader may get a feel for the type of usage possible with computers, an excerpt from an existing computer project follows. It was developed by Lohnes (1970) and is geared to the concept of readiness for vocational planning. Assessment instruments for this project are further described in Chapter 10. A student of approximately eighth-grade reading level sits at a terminal which is plugged into a time-sharing computer. After brief instruction in how to interact with the machine, the student answers a series of questions. A sample print-out follows:

WHO DOES WHAT? A CAREER GUIDANCE GAME

IN THIS GAME YOU TYPE THE NUMBER OF THE ANSWER YOU SELECT
AND THEN HIT THE RETURN KEY.

WHAT IS A CAREER? CHOOSE FROM THESE ANSWERS
[1] HOW A PERSON FEELS ABOUT HIS LIFE AND WORK.
[2] SOMETHING PEOPLE LIKE ENTERTAINERS AND ATHLETES HAVE.
[3] A PERSON'S HISTORY OF MAKING HIS WAY IN THE WORLD.
TYPE THE NUMBER OF YOUR CHOICE AND HIT RETURN.
? 3
GOOD, PSYCHOLOGISTS LIKE ANSWER 3 BEST, TOO.
IS WHAT YOU DO IN SCHOOL PART OF YOUR CAREER? CHOOSE
[1] NO, BECAUSE ONLY ADULTS HAVE CAREERS.
[2] YES, SINCE WHAT YOU ACCOMPLISH IN SCHOOL CONTRIBUTES
TO WHAT YOU ACCOMPLISH WITH YOUR ENTIRE LIFE.
? 1
PSYCHOLOGISTS THINK THAT CAREER DEVELOPMENT STARTS IN
CHILDHOOD AND DEFINITELY INCLUDES WHAT PEOPLE ACCOMPLISH
IN SCHOOL.
IS BEING A HOUSEWIFE PART OF A CAREER? CHOOSE FROM
[1] NO, IT'S WHERE WOMEN HIDE FROM CAREERS.
[2] YES, IT'S A WAY OF MAKING ONESELF USEFUL IN SOCIETY.
? 2
MEN DON'T ALWAYS ADMIT IT, BUT BEING A HOUSEWIFE IS AN
IMPORTANT CAREER.
WHY DO PEOPLE HAVE SUCH DIFFERENT CAREERS? CHOOSE FROM
[1] IT'S ALL DETERMINED BY WHO YOUR PARENTS ARE, WHAT YOUR
BACKGROUND IS, WHAT SCIENTISTS CALL HEREDITY AND ENVIRONMENT.
[2] THE CAUSES OF CAREER DIFFERENCES ARE INDIVIDUAL DIFFER—
ENCES IN PERSONALITY, INTELLIGENCE, SPECIAL ABILITIES,
INTERESTS, ETCETERA.
[3] PEOPLE CHOOSE THEIR CAREERS. PERSONAL DECISIONS ARE
THE MAIN FACTOR.
[4] MOSTLY IT'S A MATTER OF CHANCE OR LUCK. CAREER IS A BIG
LOTTERY, ALMOST LIKE RUSSIAN ROULETTE.
[5] NONE OF THE ABOVE IS AN ADEQUATE ANSWER. THERE IS NO
REALLY GOOD ANSWER.
? 5
WE HATE TO ADMIT IT, BUT NUMBER 5 IS TRUE. THERE IS TRUTH
IN 1, 2, 3, AND 4, BUT EACH IS ONLY PARTLY TRUE. ALSO, OUR
KNOWLEDGE OF CAREERS AND WHY THEY DIFFER IS INCOMPLETE.
DON'T TAKE WHAT YOU LEARN FROM THIS GAME AS GOSPEL, BUT ONLY
AS SOME OF WHAT PSYCHOLOGY HAS TO SAY AT PRESENT ABOUT
CAREER DEVELOPMENT.
ANYWAY, CONGRATULATIONS ON A SMART CHOICE.
PSYCHOLOGICAL RESEARCH SHOWS THAT PERSONALITY IS RELATED
TO CAREER IN MANY WAYS. BUT FIRST, WHAT DO YOU SUPPOSE
PSYCHOLOGISTS MEAN BY PERSONALITY? CHOOSE FROM
[1] ALL THE WAYS A PERSON DIFFERS FROM OTHER PEOPLE.
[2] THE WAYS A PERSON IS SEEN BY OTHER PEOPLE.
? 1
GOOD CHOICE.
PSYCHOLOGISTS DEFINE PERSONALITY AS THE SYSTEMATIC WAYS ONE
PERSON DIFFERS FROM OTHER PEOPLE. IN EACH SPECIFIC PERSONAL
CHARACTERISTIC YOU ARE SIMILAR TO SOME OTHER PEOPLE, BUT IN
THE PROFILE OF ALL YOUR CHARACTERISTICS YOU ARE A UNIQUE
PERSONALITY.

WHAT SEX ARE YOU?   ANSWER 1 FOR MALE, OR 2 FOR FEMALE.
? 1
WE ASK BECAUSE SEX IS A MOST IMPORTANT PERSONALITY ATTRIBUTE.
DOES SEX INFLUENCE CAREER?   ANSWER 1 FOR YES OR 2 FOR NO.
? 1
EASY QUESTION.   OF COURSE SEX INFLUENCES CAREER.   HOW MANY
WOMEN ARE AIRLINE PILOTS OR MEN ARE HOUSEWIVES?   SOME,
BUT NOT MANY.

SEX IS A QUALIFICATION FOR SOME TRAINING AND WORK POSITIONS.
SEX ALSO INFLUENCES INTERESTS, WHICH IN TURN INFLUENCE
CAREER DEVELOPMENT.   THUS, BOTH CAREER OPPORTUNITIES AND
CAREER INTERESTS DEPEND PARTIALLY ON SEX.

PSYCHOLOGISTS LIKE TO DISTINGUISH BETWEEN PEOPLE WHO ARE
PRIMARILY INTERESTED IN THINGS AND THOSE WHO ARE PRIMARILY
INTERESTED IN PEOPLE.
IF YOU ARE MOSTLY INTERESTED IN SCIENCE, TECHNOLOGY, OR
CRAFTMANSHIP YOU ARE SAID TO BE THING-ORIENTED.
IF YOU ARE MOSTLY INTERESTED IN BUSINESS, SOCIAL
SERVICE, POLITICS, HISTORY, CULTURAL OR LITERARY MATTERS
YOU ARE SAID TO BE PEOPLE-ORIENTED.
WHICH ARE YOU?   EVEN IF YOU ARE NOT SURE, CHOOSE FROM
[1] THING-ORIENTED, OR [2] PEOPLE-ORIENTED.   TYPE 1 DIGIT.
? 2
OK, YOU SAY YOU ARE A PEOPLE-ORIENTED BOY.
IS THIS CORRECT?   ANSWER 1 FOR YES, OR 2 FOR NO.
? 1
WHAT PERCENT OF 8TH-GRADE BOYS WOULD YOU GUESS ARE PEOPLE-
ORIENTED?
TYPE 2 DIGITS [A GUESS BETWEEN 00 AND 99] AND HIT RETURN.
? 75
TOO HIGH.
PSYCHOLOGISTS ESTIMATE THAT 40 PERCENT OF 8TH GRADE BOYS ARE
PEOPLE-ORIENTED.
SO, SEX IS RELATED TO INTERESTS, BUT...
THIS RELATIONSHIP MAY CHANGE WITH AGE.   CAN YOU GUESS
WHAT PERCENT OF 25-YEAR-OLD MEN ARE THING-ORIENTED?
TYPE A 2 DIGIT GUESS.
? 50
GOOD GUESS.
ABOUT 40 PERCENT OF 25-YEAR-OLD MEN ARE THING-ORIENTED,
AND ABOUT 60 PERCENT ARE PEOPLE-ORIENTED.
CAN YOU GUESS WHAT PERCENT OF 25-YEAR-OLD WOMEN ARE
THING-ORIENTED?
TYPE 2 DIGITS AND HIT RETURN.
? 20
GOOD GUESS.
THE ANSWER IS ABOUT 20 PERCENT.
MANY MALES CHANGE FROM PRIMARY THING INTERESTS TO PRIMARY
PEOPLE INTERESTS DURING ADOLESCENCE OR EARLY ADULTHOOD.
THE PERCENTAGES REMAIN CONSTANT FOR FEMALES, BUT OF COURSE
INDIVIDUAL WOMEN MAY CHANGE THEIR INTERESTS.
WHETHER A PERSON PLANS TO GO TO COLLEGE MAKES A BIG
DIFFERENCE FOR MANY CAREERS.
DO YOU PLAN TO GET A FOUR YEAR COLLEGE DEGREE?
TYPE 1 FOR YES OR 2 FOR NO, AND HIT RETURN.
? 2

```
OK, YOU DO NOT PLAN TO GET A 4-YEAR COLLEGE DEGREE.
IF THIS IS CORRECT, TYPE A 1.  IF IT IS WRONG, TYPE A 2.
? 1
YOU HAVE DESCRIBED YOURSELF AS A BOY WHO IS PEOPLE-
ORIENTED AND WHO DOES NOT PLAN TO GET A 4-YEAR COLLEGE
DEGREE.  THIS PLACES YOU IN A NON-COLLEGE BUSINESS OR
SOCIOCULTURAL CATEGORY [EVEN THOUGH YOU MAY BE PLANNING
ON SOME COLLEGE EDUCATION].  RESEARCH SHOWS THAT ABOUT
20 PERCENT OF 25 YEAR OLD MEN BELONG IN THIS CATEGORY.

HERE IS A TABLE OF PERCENTAGES OF 25-YEAR-OLDS OF EACH SEX
IN EACH OF FOUR CAREER PLANS CATEGORIES.

                                       MALES       FEMALES

COLLEGE SCIENTIFIC                      15            5
NON-COLLEGE TECHNICAL                   25           10
NON-COLLEGE BUSINESS OR SOCIOCULT.      25           70
COLLEGE BUSINESS OR SOCIOCULTURAL       35           15

WE HOPE IT IS INTERESTING TO YOU TO SEE HOW 25-YEAR-OLD
PEOPLE ARE DISTRIBUTED AMONG THESE CATEGORIES.  THIS TABLE
IS AN EXAMPLE OF CAREER DEVELOPMENT RESEARCH.

THANK YOU FOR PLAYING THIS GAME.
YOUR GAME SCORE WAS EXCELLENT.


K = 4         V = 35


TIME:  19 SECS.


BYE

*** OFF AT 13:52.
 H@
```

It should be noted at this point that computerized informational systems are typically based on one or another of the occupational classifications described in Chapter 3. For example, the Willowbrook High School Computerized Vocational Information System (Harris, 1968) is based on Roe's two-dimensional classification of field and level. The system relates objective data about each student to the two-dimensional classification system. For example, after student data input is accomplished, the computer will print out for Levels 1 and 2 a decision-making conversation about college, a list of suggested schools to be investigated, and information regarding scholarship aid. For Levels 3 and 4, the computer provides information about local and 100-mile radius technical programs and about apprenticeships. For levels 5 and 6, output consists of first-job information. It is equally possible to take any of the classification systems (e.g. DOT, Holland, etc.) and to program appropriately for the storage, retrieval, and dissemination of information.

It is clear that computer technology can provide help in implementing a systems approach to vocational guidance in the schools. A great deal of development is still necessary to make computers even more effective. Their development is currently at the toddler stage, but they are likely to mature and grow. Their growth, however, will require considerable change in the counselor's perception of himself and of his role (Wrenn, 1970). Counselors who regard their function as primarily providing information will have to concede that a computer can do that with greater facility, dispatch, and, probably, accuracy. To use the computer effectively, the counselor will have to acquire a whole new set of learnings. As Blocher (1969) points out, ". . . counselors will need to understand thoroughly the area of data processing and learn to generate, code, store, retrieve, and communicate appropriate information to client systems."

OCCUPATIONAL INFORMATION IN THE ELEMENTARY SCHOOL

Most informational systems and materials are directed at the secondary school level. Elementary schools must often rely on the ancillary use of materials prepared for purposes other than educational or occupational information. For this reason, a brief discussion about information in the elementary school is included at this point as a supplement to the chapter on Vocational Guidance, Vocationalization, and the Elementary School.

Kaback's (1968) survey of occupational information in the elementary school suggests that what elementary counselors are doing in this regard is not necessarily what they would like to do in the future. As might be expected, the use of published materials, the emphasis on occupational material in the curriculum, assembly programs, group guidance, films and filmstrips, and teacher workshops were found to be the primary activities in disseminating information. Employed to a considerable degree were trips, bulletin boards, invited speakers, individual interviews with children, radio programs, and parent workshops. Not currently used but projected into the future were such activities as the development of positive attitudes toward work and of motivation for future educational and vocational activities, and the development of occupational information programs which begin early and continue through later grades, geared to the developmental interests of children.

Innovative and creative occupational information activities at the elementary school level included: presentation in assembly programs of photographs of local occupations taken by the counselor; collection by children of pictures of various occupations used to stimulate discussions regarding skills, potentialities, and attitudes; and collection of photographs from around the world to spark discussions of world-wide occupational similarities and differences. Also utilized were tape recordings of interviews with various workers; daily want ads, which revealed labor market trends and occupational requirements; and the preparation of bibliographies on educational and occupational information by the school librarian. Other activities involved committee work to explore occupations, the return of junior high school students to their elementary school to discuss requirements of junior high school and their feelings about the new experience, and panel discussion by the children about occupational films they viewed.

Goodson (1968) investigated the library holdings of nine selected elementary schools and identified 178 books which had value in terms of occupational information, either because they were career fiction books, because they offered business and industrial descriptive literature, or because they presented occupationally descriptive literature. She found books appropriate in reading level for kindergarten through grade 9, with the preponderance of occupational material at grade 3 reading level and tapering off at the higher grades. In rank order, the occupations most frequently described were: policemen, post-office worker, secret serviceman, engineer, fireman, and librarian. The great bulk of the books were obsolescent. In summary, the occupations represented did not reflect the occupational structure, the books were antiquated, and as the children drew nearer to the ninth-grade curriculum decision point, they had less occupational information to draw upon than they did in the lower grades.

Both the Kaback and Goodson studies are instructive in terms of how information is used at the elementary school level. It is clear that more and better occupational literature as well as occupational and educational materials in general are necessary for younger children. It is also evident that to make up for this deficiency, counselors will have to engage in creative and innovative practices in collecting and disseminating data.

Bugg (1969, p. 171-172) neatly summarizes the role of information at the elementary school level in the following manner:

> There is no indication that the elementary school should encourage children to make specific vocational choices. The job of the grade school is to focus the attention of children on the general meaning of work in our society and to assist them in gaining information about the total range of occupational opportunities. Considerable attention should be given to the individual differences of both workers and jobs and to the varying rewards (intrinsic and extrinsic), social and physical characteristics, and general training requirements of different occupational fields. The elementary school program should attempt to communicate to children why people work; why all honest work is important; the fact that some-day they, too, will work; and the impact that a job is likely to have on them personally.

The counselor's role in the area of information in the elementary school has been outlined by a committee of the National Vocational Guidance Association (NVGA, 1969). Among their recommendations are the following (p. 3):

Recommends, and upon request, selects occupational materials for the use of the teacher, the principal, parents, and pupils.

Assembles for the guidance office collection of books and pamphlets about workers and industries.

Consults with the school librarian on the selection, acquisition, and circulation of occupational materials.

Provides the principal and teachers with information about the occupational composition of the community.

Helps teachers find individuals in the commur.ity who can provide first-hand information about occupations and places of work.

All these considerations are dealt with in considerable detail in the elementary school chapter. Again, it is only because of the special problems of information at the early grade levels that the topic is supplemented in this chapter.

OPPORTUNITIES FOR DROPOUT AND TERMINAL STUDENTS

From the beginning of the educational spectrum we now jump to what is the end of formal schooling for many—the dropout stage. When the dropout leaves school, he often is ignored in terms of vocational guidance or placement. He frequently has some notion of an entry-level job that he can get or he already has such a job, and the counselor assumes that the choice is appropriate. Eight of every ten dropouts have never had any counseling by school or employment-service counselors (Arnow, 1968). In addition, a study by Krasnow (1968) demonstrates that ninth-grade students who choose vocational curricula have a lesser amount of vocational information than those who choose academic curricula, even though they make the narrower decisions. It is clear that these same students are likely to be dropouts and that they will not perceive enough alternatives or possess the decision-making skills or have adequate self-knowledge to make an effective choice.

There are obviously jobs available for the 25 percent of students who do not complete high school. But the range of these jobs is constricted. In fact, the dropout has relatively few job alternatives open to him. For example, of dropouts in 1967-1968, 29.4 percent were employed in white-collar jobs, 29.5 percent in blue-collar jobs, and 37.9 percent in service jobs. These figures may be compared with those for 1968 high school graduates—66.9, 16.4, and 15.7 percent respectively (U. S. Department of Labor, 1969).

The factors that contribute to the making of a dropout are varied. One evident factor is that the decision by males of whether or not to complete high school is directly related to the level of educational attainment of their fathers. If the father graduated from high school, the chances are almost nine out of ten that the son will graduate; if the father did not graduate, the chances are only six out of ten that the son will earn a high school diploma (Arnow, 1968).

It is also clear that lack of academic aptitude is not a primary cause for school leaving. One comprehensive study (Lichter, et al., 1962, p. 253) suggests that the emotional problems of dropouts are severe but emphasizes the heterogeneity of the dropouts in other respects.

Apart from the large issue of severe emotional disturbance, no other single factor could be isolated to account for school malfunctioning and premature leaving of school. Though the drop-outs had emotional problems, some kinds more frequently than others, there was no typical emotional disorder that characterized them; they ran the gamut of diagnostic classifications. In environmental aspects, the range of individual differences was also broad. The students not only came from homes of varying degrees of stability but the parents had a diversity of attitudes and character problems. In addition, some schools offered more understanding than others. Thus, the drop-outs were subject to a variety of stresses, and each youngster had his individual vulnerabilities, deficiencies, and capacities. It follows that there is no easy, over-all solution to the problem of school malfunctioning or early school leaving. Help must be individualized for each student in accordance with the particular circumstances that create the emotional problems and school difficulties.

The schools are often accused of creating conditions within themselves that force children to leave, thus making them push-outs rather than dropouts. While it is probably true that the educational enterprise is not doing as much as it might to provide youngsters with what they themselves can regard as meaningful education, and while it is also probably true that some schools are responsible for the etiology of student difficulties, it is equally true that youngsters who leave school early have certain predispositions in that direction which are extremely heterogeneous in nature, as we have just seen. Yet even with that heterogeneity, it is possible to identify the likely dropout as early as ninth grade and to apply appropriate preventive measures (Walters and Krangler, 1970).

Regardless of the causes of early school leaving, counselors have a special obligation in terms of vocational guidance as treatment. Much of this obligation concerns the provision of adequate educational and occupational information and assistance in relating this information to important self-characteristics. Rosen (1969) suggests that counselors of non-college-bound students and dropouts should be aware of employment opportunities in the skilled trades and should make clear to students the diverse paths open to them and the fact that some can be followed even if they fail, drop out, or are otherwise blocked. His point is that vocationally oriented youngsters need the same type of career counseling as their college-bound counterparts. One way to achieve this goal is by means of better local and national labor market information provided in a systematic way. Earlier vocational guidance and more work-study opportunities would also be helpful.

While agreeing with the findings of the Lichter study that no single cause of school leaving is identifiable, an Ohio study of school dropouts (Nachman, et al., 1964) recommended, "Provisions should be made for secondary course offerings to meet the varying needs of the student body, including work-study units in special education, occupational training, and group guidance, as well as the more widely available academic and vocational programs."

All the preceding suggestions seem to be potentially effective means of heading off those who might be school leavers. But what of those who are actually leaving? In this case, the counselor has a dual responsibility: On the one hand he must provide information regarding the availability of jobs and of additional training opportunities. On the other hand, he may see his role expanded to include the placement function.

In terms of providing information regarding job opportunities in the community, the staff of the *Occupational Outlook Quarterly* has separated all jobs described in the 1968-1969 *Handbook* according to levels of education necessary for entry and has published these in five pamphlets available for a minimum cost from the Superintendent of Documents, Washington, D. C. The five pamphlets are entitled (*Occupational Outlook Quarterly*, 1969):

Jobs for which a high school education is preferred, but not essential

Jobs for which a high school education is generally required

Jobs for which apprenticeship training is available

Jobs for which junior college, technical institute, or other specialized training is usually required

Jobs for which a college education is usually required

In the first pamphlet, for example, which applies directly to high school dropouts, some seventy-one jobs are listed in health services, clerical and related occupations, service occupations, building trades, driving occupations, machining operations, mechanics and repairmen, manual operations, foundries, government post-office occupations, hotels, and railroads. Yet, seventy-one job categories present relatively few jobs for some six million expected dropouts in this decade.

Another responsibility in helping the dropout and the terminal student is to provide them with—and help them think through the implications of—federal- and state-financed programs. It is extremely important that the counselor keep informed on such programs because each new legislative session produces changes in the opportunities available. There are many programs for helping students find jobs which are implemented through such agencies as the United States Training and Employment Services (USTES), the National Alliance of Businessmen (NAB), Youth Opportunity Centers (YOCS), Concentrated Employment Programs (CEPs), Model Cities Programs, and Neighborhood Service

Centers. Training, programs are currently offered by such projects as Manpower Development and Training (MDTA), wherein jobless or underemployed are trained for existing jobs by means of classroom instruction, on-the-job training, or both; Neighborhood Youth Corps (NYC), which is for those from 14-21, in or out of school, and which includes on-the-job experience; and a variety of Experimental and Demonstration Programs (E & D), which test new ideas for preparing hard-core unemployed for jobs.

In addition, apprenticeship programs of one type or another are in operation. More than 350 skilled trades and crafts offer such programs to youth from ages seventeen to twenty-six generally. A special program, the Department of Labor Apprenticeship Outreach, finds and prepares individuals for various apprenticeship programs provided by industry.

Finally, dropouts should be made aware of the many forms of continuing education other than the college. Home or correspondence schools, trade schools, proprietary business schools, business schools, and adult and continuing education programs are possibilities (Stevic and Hayden, 1970). A series of books by Sloan and Clark (1960, 1962, 1964, 1966) highlights the fact that educational opportunities in the armed forces, retail businesses, and industry are available in astounding number and diversity.

An excellent project aimed at the terminal student is Hoyt's (1965) Specialty-Oriented Student (SOS) project. Specifically, this project is directed at those students who seek post–high school training in trade, technical, or business school settings. This project has yielded much valuable data regarding specialty-oriented students and the institutions which they attend. On the assumption that typical information is too general for specialty-oriented students and/or is not oriented toward answering the kinds of decision-making questions posed by these students, the SOS project offers information on over forty specific training programs. This information is highly specific (How would I be likely to find a place to live? What is it likely to cost to go through this program?) and readable. Increasing numbers of states are now adopting the SOS approach.

To recapitulate, then, the role of the counselor with the dropout student may take the following forms: (1) Communicating occupational, educational, and personal information to the student while he is still in school and helping him to integrate it; providing him with information on jobs and training opportunities when he comes out. In some cases, this function will require referral to various agencies for assessment, counseling, placement, job coaching, training, and/or follow-up and support services. (2) Working for the establishment or improvement of early employment experiences, whether in the form of part-time jobs, work-study programs, cooperative education, or the like. (3) Implementing a systematic approach to vocationalization that will hopefully reduce the need for the emphasis on vocational guidance as treatment.

SUMMARY

This chapter has discussed information in terms of criteria for "good" information and for effective use of information. Various possibilities for the storage, retrieval, and dissemination of information have been explored. Special consideration has been given to the use of information in the elementary school and for the dropout. Underlying this chapter has been the view of the counselor's role as that of helping students to integrate educational, occupational, and personal information in the decision-making process. The fostering of planfulness and vocational development involves not only helping students acquire information but also helping them to apply the knowledge to their personal characteristics.

REFERENCES

Arnow, P. *Bridging the gap between school and work.* Washington, D. C.: U. S. Department of Labor, 1968.

Blocher, D. H. Counseling as a technology for facilitating and guiding change in human systems. *Educational Technology,* 9 (March, 1969), 15-18.

Boocock, S. S. *Instructor's manual for life career.* New York: Western, 1968.

*Boocock, S. S., and Coleman, J. S. Games with simulated environments in learning. *Sociology of Education,* 1966, 33, 215–236.

Bugg, C. A. Implications of some major theories of career choice for elementary school guidance programs. *Elementary School Guidance and Counseling,* 1969, 13, 164–173.

Cherryholmes, Cleo. Some current research on effectiveness of educational simulations: Some implications for alternative strategies. *American Behavioral Scientist,* 1966, 10, 4–7.

College Entrance Examination Board. *Looking ahead: Your ECIS planning guide.* New York: CEEB, 1970.

Cooley, W. W. Computer systems for guidance. In *Computer-based vocational guidance systems.* Washington, D. C.: U. S. Government Printing Office, 1969, 61–71.

Dale, E. *Audio-visual methods in teaching.* New York: Dryden Press, rev. 1954.

Festinger, L. *A theory of cognitive dissonance.* Evanston, Ill.: Row, Peterson, 1957.

Fibkins, W. A different approach to sharing occupational information. *School Counselor,* 1969, 16, 390–393.

* Recommended for additional reading.

Gibson, R. L. Pupil opinions of high school guidance programs. *Personnel and Guidance Journal*, 1962, 40, 453–457.

Goodson, A. Occupational information materials in selected elementary and middle schools. *Vocational Guidance Quarterly*, 1968, 12, 128–131.

Halpern, Gerald, and Norris, Lila. Student curriculum decisions. *Personnel and Guidance Journal*, 1968, 47, 240–243.

Hamilton, J. A., and Krumboltz, J. D. Simulated work experience: How realistic should it be? *Personnel and Guidance Journal*, 1969, 48, 39–44.

Harris, J. A. The computerization of vocational information. *Vocational Guidance Quarterly*, 1968, 17, 12–20.

Holland, J. L. A theory-ridden, computerless impersonal vocational guidance system. Presidential address, Div. 17, American Psychological Association, Sept., 1970. Mimeographed.

*Hollis, J. W., and Hollis, L. U. *Personalizing information processes.* New York: Macmillan, 1969.

Hosford, R. E., and Ryan, T. A. Systems design in the development of counseling and guidance programs. *Personnel and Guidance Journal*, 1970, 49, 221–230.

Hoyt, K. B. High school guidance and the specialty-oriented student research program. *Vocational Guidance Quarterly*, 1965, 13, 229–236.

Isaacson, L. *Career information in counseling and teaching.* Boston: Allyn and Bacon, 1971.

Kaback, Goldie R. Occupational information in elementary education. *Vocational Guidance Quarterly*, 1968, 12, 203–206.

Kaplon, Alice J., and Gordon, M. S. A critique of "War and Peace": A simulation game. *Social Education*, 1967, 31, 383–387.

Krasnow, B. S. Occupational information as a factor in the high school curriculum chosen by ninth-grade boys. *The School Counselor*, 1968, 15, 275–280.

Krumboltz, J. D.; Sheppard, L. E.; Jones, G. B.; Johnson, R. G.; and Baker, R. D. *Vocational problem-solving experiences for simulating career exploration and interest.* Final report of Project OE 5-85-059, U. S. Office of Education, 1967.

Krumboltz, J. D., and Bergland, B. W. Experiencing work almost like it is. *Educational Technology*, 9 (March, 1969), 47–49.

Lichter, S. O.; Rapien, E. B.; Siebert, F. M.; and Sklansky, M. A. *The dropouts.* Glencoe, Ill.: Free Press, 1962.

Lohnes, P. R. *Career development project.* Washington, D. C.: U. S. Office of Education, final report on Project No. 70-0001, 1970.

Loughary, J. W. The computer is in! *Personnel and Guidance Journal,* 1970, 49, 185–191.

Luchins, A. S. Influence of experience with conflicting information on reactions to subsequent conflicting information. *Journal of Social Psychology,* 1960, 5, 367–385.

McCourt, H. The vocational development lesson. Unpublished Ed.D. Thesis, Teachers College, Columbia University, 1965. Mimeographed.

Miller, J. Information-retrieval systems in guidance. *Personnel and Guidance Journal,* 1970, 49, 212–218.

Nachman, L. R.; Getson, R. F.; and Odgers, J. G. *Ohio study of high school dropouts: 1962–1963.* Columbus: State Department of Education, 1964.

Norman, R. P. The use of preliminary information in vocational counseling. *Personnel and Guidance Journal,* 1969, 47, 693–697.

Norris, W. *Occupational information in the elementary school.* Chicago: Science Research Associates, 1963.

NVGA Commission on Vocational Materials for Elementary Schools. *Assisting vocational development in theh elementary school.* Washington, D. C.: American Personnel and Guidance Association, 1969.

*O'Hara, R. P. A theoretical foundation for the use of occupational information in guidance. *Personnel and Guidance Journal,* 1968, 46, 636–640.

Perrone, P. A., and Thrush, R. S. Vocational information processing systems: A survey. *Vocational Guidance Quarterly,* 1969, 17, 255–266.

Pierson, G. N.; Hoover, R.; and Whitfield, E. A. A regional career information center: Development and process. *Vocational Guidance Quarterly,* 1967, 15, pp. 162–169.

Rosen, H. Vocational guidance: Room for improvement. *Manpower,* 1969, 1, 6–8.

Sloan, H. S., and Clark, H. F. *Classrooms in the factories.* New York: Teachers College Bureau of Publications, 1960. See also *Classrooms in the stores* (1962), *Classrooms in the military* (1964), and *Classrooms on Main Street* (1966).

Stevic, R. R., and Hayden, C. E. Noncollegiate post–high school opportunities. In S. H. Cramer (ed.) *Pre-service and in-service preparation of school counselors for educational guidance.* Washington, D. C.: American Personnel and Guidance Association, 1970, 43–51.

Thompson, C. L., and Parker, J. L. Fifth-graders' groove in the work world scene. Unpublished report of research, University of Tennessee, 1971. Mimeographed.

U. S. Department of Labor. Employment of high school graduates and dropouts. *Monthly Labor Review,* June, 1969, 40.

U. S. Department of Labor.   What's in the barrel for the dropout?   *Occupational Outlook Quarterly,* 1969, 13, 4–7.

Walters, H. E., and Kraszler, G. D.   Early identification of the school dropout. *The School Counselor,* 1970, 18, 97–104.

*Walz, R.   Technology in guidance: A conceptual overview.   *Personnel and Guidance Journal,* 1970, 49, 175–182.

Wolfbein, S. L.   *Occupational information: A career guidance view.*   New York: Random House, 1968.

Wrenn, C. G.   The dangers within.   *Personnel and Guidance Journal,* 1970 *49* 183–184.

TWELVE

COOPERATIVE EFFORTS IN VOCATIONAL GUIDANCE

This book persistently supports the fact that many persons do and should contribute to the accomplishment of the objectives of vocational guidance. In various contexts, parents, teachers, counselors, administrators, employers, workers, have each been mentioned as either influencing directly the attitudes and knowledge which make up vocationalization or as having the potential to exert such influence if they are systematically included in the process. We have also noted the growing tendency in guidance and in education to consider the potential of differentiated staffing, including the use of paraprofessionals or aides, as one means of mustering the range of expertise needed to accomplish the many different vocational guidance objectives.

The latter portion of this chapter will discuss the ways by which persons in education, in community agencies, and in business and industry can strengthen their cooperative efforts and accentuate their contributions to vocational guidance within the constraints of their primary responsibilities. Before turning to the potential contributions of these separate specialists, who operate essentially within local community or educational settings, the early sections of this chapter will be devoted to the importance of state-level leadership in guidance. If one is to consider creating a systems approach to vocational guidance in the schools, it is necessary to recognize the importance of the planning and the leadership of all governmental units, particularly those charged with state-wide responsibilities.

In this chapter there is no intent to argue for new kinds of specialists beyond the role possibilities in the existing personnel resources in education, governmental agencies, and business or industry. Nor is there an attempt here to argue that school counselors by themselves, can accomplish all the tasks subsumed within a systematic approach to vocational guidance. It is contended, however, that cooperation and coordination are the key to the attainment of a systems approach to vocational guidance.

SOME FACTORS SPURRING COOPERATIVE EFFORT

The complexity of the influences which shape vocationalization and the fact that many of these influences are direct consequences of the behavior displayed by adults to students combine to give face validity to efforts to spur systematic cooperation in vocational guidance among adults in school and out of school.

But it is not just face validity or logic which supports the need for cooperative efforts to accomplish vocational guidance objectives. Increasingly, federal legislation, program funding criteria, and an insufficient supply of counselors emphasize this need.

During the past decade, federal legislation and supporting appropriations have emphasized directly or indirectly the importance of vocational guidance in different agencies and for different populations. Examples include: anti-poverty legislation; federal aid to elementary, secondary, and higher education; the Vocational Rehabilitation Act, as amended; the Area Redevelopment Act of 1961; the diverse combinations of the G.I. Bill; the various amendments to the National Defense Education Act; the Manpower Development and Training Act of 1962; and the 1968 amendments to the Vocational Education Act of 1963. Collectively, these pieces of legislation validate the importance of counselors in the maintenance and progress of the American society in its respect for individual differences, informal free choice, and opportunities for constructive adulthood. In the legislation cited, counseling is seen as integral to manpower policy and to the increased employability of persons from all segments of the population (Pritchard, 1965).

The facts of the matter are, however, that for the foreseeable future, the need for counselors will outstrip the supply (Shertzer and Stone, 1966, p. 83). A conservative estimate (Hitchcock, 1965) is that by 1975 there will be a need for 159,391 counselors in elementary and secondary schools, junior colleges and universities, the United States Employment Service, rehabilitation agencies and various Office of Economic Opportunity programs. Comparison of the figure projected for 1975 with Hitchcock's estimated need for 45,241 counselors in 1965 and 98,880 in 1970 is one index of the accelerating need for counselors.

Since group and individual needs for jobs, for education, for improved earning power, and for personal dignity have become more visible in the years since these projected counselor needs were formulated, it is probable that these needs are understated. For example, using ratios of one full-time counselor per 750 college students, one to 300 secondary school students, and one to 600 elementary school students (which are criteria espoused by various professional counseling organizations), Shertzer and Stone (1966, p. 83) contended that in 1964-65 there was a shortage of 79,000 counselors to serve the population identified in education. This is a figure much in excess of that in Hitchcock's projections. Moreover, in view of the fact that elementary school, secondary school, and college populations have continued to burgeon, it seems likely that the extent of the shortage indicated in this figure will hold for some time to come.

If the supply of counselors available is unlikely to meet the probable future or current demand, we must examine alternative ways of meeting the vocational guidance, counseling, and placement needs of persons through the most positive strategies available to us at this point in history. If the job to be done is larger than can be accomplished by any one set of specialists in any one institutional setting, then to whom do we turn and what contributions do we seek?

At the outset, it must be clear that if persons representing different specialties and different settings are all to have a part in assisting individuals "to select, prepare for, and enter occupations" (Arnold, 1967), rigid territoria' imperatives and defensive grasping for compartmentalized, splintered approaches to the concerns at issue must go. The alternative is coordination and cooperation among all resource groups.

PLANNING FOR COORDINATION AND COOPERATION

Coordination and cooperation among persons having contributions to make to vocational guidance can occur in at least two ways. One is to sharpen persons' awareness of certain goals toward which their efforts might be directed or redirected and then help them adopt the attitudes, gain the knowledge, and develop the strategies for accomplishing such goals within their own disciplines. This requires at the outset identifying the contributions that particular people can make (teachers, school counselors, and rehabilitation or employment counselors) and then—through training, administrative arrangement, or whatever is necessary—providing the conditions by which they can realize their contributions. The second way to achieve coordination or cooperation is to create a master set of goals and a set of strategies to meet these goals. Specific resource contributions can then be related to these goals and strategies.

To formulate a master plan for vocational guidance at either local or governmental levels, it is necessary to establish the following (Herr, 1969, p. 32):

1. *The outcomes which vocational guidance or vocationalization are to facilitate*

2. *The processes by which persons attain such outcomes and the factors which thwart or negate such development*

3. *The preparation, the competencies, the skills which must be possessed by those who will facilitate the outcomes subsumed under (1) as these are mediated by (2)*

4. *The potential impact of different persons as defined by the characteristics of the populations they have contact with it—e.g., the age, the period of exposure—as well as by the characteristics and constraints of the setting in which these personnel operate—e.g., Are they permitted by legislation to work with only certain persons? Must they have only one- or two-session contacts?*

5. *The technology or media which can strengthen the potential impact of the persons identified in (4), given the characteristics of the populations to be served*

Such a "systems analysis" would eliminate the sporadic, arbitrary, and tenuous attachment of different specialists to pieces of the system. It would also eliminate the practice of pushing specialists into work they have no preparation for. It would more clearly indicate what duties and functions should be performed by a counselor (whether he be in the school, the Employment Service, or the Bureau of Vocational Rehabilitation) as compared with what duties should be performed by a teacher or by personnel in business or industry. Also, such a master plan would make clear that no particular specialist can operate in a vacuum but that his efforts to accomplish the goals of vocational guidance must be meshed with and reinforced by those of other persons having contributions to make to the system.

The kind of master plan for vocational guidance just identified as necessary has yet to be charted. Nevertheless, for a vocational development system to function effectively through the educational institutions in this nation, planning of outcomes and resources to accomplish them should be given high priority.

STATE-LEVEL LEADERSHIP IN VOCATIONAL GUIDANCE

In looking at the array of needs and the various recommendations for improving the vocational aspects of guidance, the focus of much of this book has been upon the efforts of practitioners in schools, in community agencies, and in business or industry. However, for a systems approach to have validity, it is also necessary to consider all these matters in the context of leadership at the state level. For example, what is the role of a state guidance staff in facilitating, throughout a given state, educational climates, procedural strategies, and goals which emphasize the links between general education and vocational education; between vocational guidance in the schools and counseling services in the community; between school and community guidance approaches and business or industrial resources?

Hoyt (1966) has provided a perceptive analysis of the forces impinging upon the role of state supervisors of guidance over the last several decades. In essence, he contends that state guidance supervisors need to be restored to the *degree* of influence held in the early period of missionary work for guidance but not necessarily to the *same* influence. In fact, neither counselors, schools, nor counselor educators require services from the state guidance supervisor for the same reasons they needed him in the past. When once the overriding goal of the state guidance supervisor was to influence both the nature and conduct of guidance programs within his state, today many would question whether the state supervisor any longer has such a right. As a variety of basic changes in the acceptance, the integration, and the manifestations of guidance have taken place, some wonder what state guidance supervisors should be doing and others question whether or not they have anything to offer.

Regardless of the role confusion which faces state supervisors of guidance, and, indeed, school counselors, counselor educators, and vocational educators, all these persons need each other more intimately than ever before. The question really is: As the functions of all these positions change, how can each complement the other? How can each—the supervisor, the preparer, the practitioner—proceed from a set of objectives which are appropriate to his responsibilities but which, when combined with those of other specialists, move effectively toward all that the changing social order requires to be accomplished? In McCully's words (1964), how can each of these persons create a troika rather than three horses stampeding off in opposite directions?

In a very real sense, the changes apparent in both federal and state legislation present both a challenge and a set of tools for the state supervisor of guidance that must change his main focus from quantity to quality, from global or platitudinous concerns to in-depth, integrated ones. The provision of quality guidance services in local settings in any state depends, to a large extent, on the vision, enthusiasm, and leadership of the state staff. There must be provided at this level the framework in which guidance programs at the local level can find their impetus, raison d'être, and models. Since the state supervisor commands the best perspective on current status and on existing and future needs within his state, all the activities for developing quality guidance services should be geared to a set of objectives or a systems analysis that represents the posture of the state agency for education.

Like the guidance program's relationships to the educational philosophy of a particular school, the state guidance program must be related to the broader educational program of the state department of education:

1. It must have clearly stated and well-defined objectives which cover all phases of the guidance program as these relate to certain behavioral outcomes of the state's student population.

2. After each objective, attainable goals must be identified and strategies for achieving them enumerated. Systems analyses techniques must be used by state staff to identify such interrelationships as those between guidance and curriculum, pre-service and in-service counselor education, interdisciplinary approaches to all dimensions of guidance programs, and necessary research.

3. Ways of evaluating the accomplishments under each goal must be identified and continuously evaluated.

Each of these requirements supports the need for state guidance staff members to assume an aggressive stance in identifying and providing the conditions by which all those who can make a contribution to effective, purposeful guidance programs will be able to do so. The contributions to school vocational guidance programs which agencies outside the school and industrial personnel can make, as described briefly later in this chapter, should be viewed from the perspective of the total guidance program of the state and integrated where and how appropriate. Although perhaps this point has been obscured in the focus of this book, the vocational aspects of guidance cannot and should not operate separately from the other guidance services. Thus the state staff must assume responsibility for a total program of guidance services from kindergarten to twelfth grade or into the community college as appropriate, a program which is related to the characteristics of the various subpopulations of students inhabiting that state.

If state leadership is to be a vital force in improving local guidance programs, the state staff cannot afford to provide a service and then wait for counselors to come and take advantage of it—any more than a school counselor can afford to help only those students who come seeking his aid. Through constant and positive reaching out to school counselors, state leadership must provide opportunities for them to review, refresh, and reorient their perspectives, strategies, and goals, paying continuous attention to the changing needs of the publics to be served and the emerging alternative ways of strengthening the guidance services.

Finally, before turning to some specific dimensions of state leadership in vocational guidance, the factor of diversity among state departments must be recognized just as the diversity among local school and community settings is recognized. As the need for improvements in the vocational aspects of guidance, the change strategies, and the specific implications here are considered, the differences in opportunity to deal with these areas that different state supervisors have must be seen. This is true because of differences in legal authority, state agency role expectations for supervisors of guidance, resources available, staff available, state department and state guidance structure, size of state, and other factors which affect individual state operations.

The areas of state guidance-staff leadership which follow do not exhaust all possibilities, but they do represent significant parts of a systems approach to improving vocational guidance in the schools (Herr, 1967, p. 14):

1. Legislation

In light of current societal demands, an expanding economy, advancing technology and the necessity for a continuum of guidance services which cross institutional lines, state supervisors of guidance should be more concerned with the broad and specific mandates for guidance services in existing as well as in projected future legislation, both at the federal and state levels. This concern should include both counselor preparation and guidance practices as these affect various segments of the general population—the vocationally ignorant youth, the advantaged as well as the disadvantaged, and the unemployed, underemployed, displaced, or discouraged older workers.

This concern should be manifested by sensitivity to the implications of existing legislation and reaction to projected legislation so that the maximum impact of legislation can be realized by the ultimate recipient, the counselee. Further, state supervisors of guidance should seek full cooperation with those in vocational education to include cooperative funding, information sharing, and a general but purposeful expansion of guidance services at both the state and local level. In the administration of any funds for guidance from the state level, provision should be made to insure that vocational aspects of guidance are given adequate emphasis at the local level.

2. In-Service or Staff Development

It is apparent that theory and research in the area of vocational development are more advanced than that which validates current guidance practices. Since much of the research is too current to have been included in the counselor education programs through which many practicing counselors have passed, it is necessary to provide continuing opportunities by which counselors can translate theory and research into practice. There is a tripartite need for university personnel, local district supervisors and state supervisors to create a meaningful network of in-service programs tailored to focus on strengthening specific counselor competencies. Since counselor educators, local guidance supervisors, and state supervisors of guidance each have different response sets, concerted efforts at in-service program development should blend the emphases of each in ways more appropriate than any of the three can accomplish alone. With the apparent necessity for field experience to equip counselors more adequately, the following are some of the programs which give promise of effectiveness: seminars with industry; internships for counselors in industry and in other state agencies; institutes for counselors; workshops combining counselors and vocational educators on national, state, and local levels as well as workshops combining counselors, vocational educators, and representatives of industry and labor.

Finally, in addition to more structured in-service activities, the state staff must continue to improve and/or increase the number of contacts with local schools. There is really no substitute for the person-to-person contacts between state supervisors and school counselors which such opportunities provide. State supervisors must begin where the local school guidance program is in a consultative, as opposed to a regulatory, effort to build into the existing local program alternative strategies which give promise of more effectively meeting the objective of the local program.

3. Resources and Technology

The volume of materials, techniques, procedures and research data with which school counselors are expected to be familiar and which they are expected to integrate into programs is rapidly increasing. The current answer to this matter resides in the use of systems designed to cope with the magnitude of information. State guidance supervisors should become more active in taking steps to wed information to technology, to develop methods of instantaneous retrieval, to design controls which can be included in such systems where questions of confidentiality interact with the use of data about students, to create networks of demonstration projects which have a resource/demonstration/in-service as well as an evaluative capability.

In addition to the potential which some state departments have for centralizing such data repositories and upgrading them, leadership and funds must be expended in efforts to develop materials for counselors and students in the area of vocational education opportunities. Such materials should convey realistic information on vocational education and the employment opportunities which can result. Examples of such information include: directories of vocational education opportunities; descriptions of secondary and post-secondary educational opportunities; the characteristics of those students who find success in various vocational education programs; follow-up data on vocational education graduates.

4. Leadership Skills

In order for counselors to effectively facilitate change, educational leadership, and coordinated attacks on such things as the establishment of compensatory programs of career development and the development of materials designed to help students explore vocational and educational opportunities, state supervisors should take the lead in insuring that counselors are taught the parameters of leadership and the strategies of change much as these are taught to management in the business-industry community.

5. Certification

A priority area for the attention of state guidance personnel is the development of certification patterns that include provisions for insuring that counselors possess competencies in the vocational aspects of guidance services. This objective necessitates collaboration between school administrators, counselors, counselor educators and state guidance and vocational education personnel as certification patterns are designed which stimulate progress and effectiveness in providing staff for comprehensive guidance programs from K-12. Certification should serve to stimulate counselor competency and creativeness in preparation patterns rather than serve as a block to positive change in such areas.

6. Counselor Education

State supervisors must work cooperatively with counselor educators in providing an opportunity for counselor-trainees to acquire knowledge, skills, and attitudes needed to acquaint students with vocational education opportunities at all levels as well as providing opportunities for counselor educators, local counselors, vocational educators, business leaders, labor representatives, and others to meet for the purpose of reviewing and discussing the vocational aspects of guidance and means of strengthening counselor competencies in this area. State supervisors should also exert leadership influence on counselor education programs to provide and require supervised practice aimed at developing counselor awareness, understandings, experiences, and strategies necessary to serve all students. The latter should be linked to the appropriate provision of field experiences for counselor-trainees as possible. It also seems necessary to promote improved counselor education in the use of effective group processes designed to disseminate vocational and educational information, to enhance student internalization and testing of such information, and to attend to procedures by which group processes can be integrated into the larger educational enterprise. State personnel in concert with counselor educators should also insure that counselor-trainees are able to translate the concepts of vocational development into understanding of counselee needs and behaviors on an interdisciplinary basis.

7. Curriculum

Increased attention to the importance of curriculum concerns must be given by the school counselor. The curriculum is a valuable means of fostering the broader concept of vocational maturity instead of the more restrictive concept of occupational choice. Curricular provisions have to be made to explore leisure activities, vocational interests, attitude development, and acquisition of knowledge and skills. It is also true that increased attention must be given to the instrumental relationship between vocational opportunities and academic content. While work is not losing its value, the value is apparently changing. Therefore, the total curriculum must support the individual's need to sort out the concepts of job, vocation, and leisure. The preparing of youth, both psychologically and mentally, to be receptive to retraining and continuous education throughout adulthood is yet another problem that can be partially, if not totally, attacked via the curriculum.

The implications for the state guidance supervisor in the area of curriculum are several. He can make recommendations to his colleagues in other segments of the state education agency to insure that state curriculum regulations and minimums for program approval or subsidy reflect the need for inclusion of the concepts described above, that the vocational guidance function is only part of a broader process of vocational development. Certainly, the state plan for guidance must have reciprocal support from the state plan for education at all levels from the elementary forward as emerging vocational motives are acquired and refined through a developmental prism.

8. Research

Since there is considerable concern among many educational groups with the "dissemination lag" and the adoption in local programs of effective innovations, i.e., expediting research results into action, state supervisors should not only work to modify arbitrary policies which retard such efforts but continuously communicate with and encourage consideration among their many publics about the implications of research. In addition, the state staff in cooperation with counselor educators, vocational educators, school administrators and others should identify questions of significance for which answers must be found, create avenues by which approaches to these questions can be effectively undertaken, and provide continuous feedback through multi-media to those who have the potential to implement the results of research and innovative endeavors. While it is probably not feasible for most state supervisors of guidance to undertake basic research themselves, they must maintain a research consciousness as the objectives and projected activities of their program unfold, identify priority questions, and collaborate with those complementary agencies in the state education agency, regional laboratories, universities or local schools which can execute appropriate research.

9. Coordination

Coordination is another central responsibility of the state guidance staff. As has been suggested earlier, guidance programs per se cannot and should not shoulder the responsibility for all aspects of the vocational development of students. This means that the state guidance staff must foster a widening dialogue among educational and noneducational specialists, research and development centers, the state employment service, the business-industrial community, organized labor and other relevant service organizations in efforts to focus all the coordinated and concentrated efforts on the vocational aspects of guidance services and the vocational development of youth wherever they are found.

Although the focus for leadership in the areas identified has been the state staff in guidance, many parallels could be drawn for the activities of guidance personnel in the United States Office of Education. Similar to state responsibilities but with a national cast, they must create a posture for guidance within national educational policy, contribute to and monitor the shaping of federal legislation as it affects guidance, and establish lines of communication with their counterparts at state and local levels to facilitate quality program development. These are only examples of some of the many tasks confronting United States Office of Education personnel. However, the current trend in federal legislation is to place greater emphasis on program development or on the translation of legislative intent into the hands of the individual state agencies responsible for education, labor, and guidance rather than the federal agencies. This tendency will change the role of guidance personnel at both the state and federal levels.

It is also worth noting that in the nine areas identified there are many impli-cations for the leadership of guidance directors in local school systems, particu-larly in large or urban situations. Some directors of guidance in city systems have as great a responsibility in terms of professional personnel supervised or the heterogeneity and numbers of students for whom they have responsibility as do state supervisors in some smaller states. Thus city guidance directors have as much potential influence on and as much concern about certification, legis-lation, research, and the other areas identified as they plan systems of vocational guidance, as do their counterparts in state agencies.

The point remains, however, that whether one is creating a plan for a systems approach to vocational guidance at the federal, state, or local level, the possible contributions which separate specialists can make must be identified. The fol-lowing sections will discuss briefly some of the influences which teachers, school counselors, rehabilitation counselors, employment service counselors, business and industrial personnel, and paraprofessionals can exert on vocational guidance in local settings (Herr, 1969).

TEACHERS

Teachers, whether at the elementary school or secondary school level or in rehabilitation or industrial settings, have vast potential to provide much of the attitudinal support and knowledge from which can flow more motivated and informal vocational development. Many of the behavioral objectives for stu-dents cited in Chapter 3 and in the chapters dealing with the elementary school, junior high school, and senior high school can be met or facilitated within the instructional goals of curricula or training programs.

As has been indicated previously in this book, much of the existing research on the ingredients of vocational maturity at different developmental stages sug-gests that students (and by extrapolation older persons) need information and experiences which link what they are doing educationally at a particular point in time with future options in education and work which will be available to them. For some students this means relating academic disciplines to concrete vocational tasks, e.g. broadening the traditional conception of industrial arts and extending it to earlier periods in formal education, making the access to vocational education more flexible, and increasing work-study opportunities.

For other students, this means exploiting their natural curiosity about the world beyond the school, with systematic attention to the relationships between specific subject matter and specific task requirements in different occupational areas. For many of those described as disadvantaged, unemployable, or dis-abled, education or training will have to be more specifically tailored to indi-vidual characteristics than has been traditional. Educational experiences will need to be conceived in rather concrete terms and conducted under condi-tions that closely approximate the conditions of employment. Counseling, as a complement to such instruction, will need to take place in the physical presence of students occupied with their concrete tasks and will need to focus directly on their progress with actual work experiences: e.g. the acquisition of employment skills, relationships with supervisors and co-workers, work tolerance, the importance of getting to work on time, and the meaning of a paycheck (Bernstein, 1966).

In addition to structural changes in curricula, through the creative use of materials, films, displays, field trips, role playing, dramatizations, gaming and stimulation, teachers can introduce students at all educational levels to vocational development concepts that are accurate and pertinent to their future development and that will expand their awareness of available alternatives. Through themes and concepts woven into subject-matter areas (as examined in earlier chapters), teachers can reinforce the importance of exploration, of the student's exploiting his personal characteristics in shaping his future work life, of seeing himself in process as a value-determining agent. Such acquired insights can diminish the remote, outside-the-person focus which may inhibit students from sensing the vitality of the occupational world as they begin to gain a glimmer of themselves in it.

The themes and concepts used as examples here and earlier provide teachers the raw material to create, throughout the educational spectrum, experiences which spiral in complexity as students move through learning phases described variously as perceptualization, conceptualization, and generalization (Gysbers, 1969); fantasy, tentative, realistic (Ginzberg, Ginzburg, Axelrad, and Herma, 1951); and exploration, crystallization, choice and clarification (Tiedeman and O'Hara, 1963). Awareness by teachers of how individual students cope with such experiences could provide a schema to identify specific students—e.g. those potentially subject to long-term unemployment, who could be referred to counselors for follow-up and corrective action.

Essentially, all the thoughts in this section thus far have been expressed more fully in the separate chapters on specific educational levels. However, there is one point which has not had sufficient attention. This is the matter of teacher attitudes as reflected in the behavioral models students are required to emulate and the levels of encouragement students are provided. Research data exist (Watley, 1966) which suggest that teachers, and counselors also, sometimes de-emphasize factors that should be considered carefully in vocational development or, more important, encourage students who meet particular stereotypes of social desirability and withhold such encouragement from other students not so endowed even when these students have equal ability (Herr, 1965; Day, 1966).

Through preparation, supervision, and in-service experiences, every teacher must be helped to remain conscious of the fact that what he says and does will have significant influence on student behavior. The teacher must consider himself as a point of reference, a role model, for each student. How teachers respond to students will affect the attitude of the individual student to the educational process, to his own worth, to vocational attitudes, and to life itself. These attitudes foster in the student and also in the teacher a perception of education as either a series of hurdles over which the student must jump or a process of developing whatever talents he brings to the process. Herr (1968, p. 15) has described the latter teacher perception as a "can do" syndrome manifested by the teacher's

> expecting that each student can and will succeed if his developmental key can be found; by insuring that experiences in success exceed failures; by continuously reinforcing the attitude that it is all right to try, fail, and try again; by displaying enthusiasm for the importance of the learning that is taking place and its relevance to the real world; by making it plain that vocational education is not only an acceptable program but critical to the maintenance of our present technological as well as humanistic movement; and by developing problem-centered learning experiences to heighten student interest and make functionally visible the application of learning.

These are the elements of the psychological climate and the experiential bases which are at the heart of a teacher's contributions to vocational guidance. Concentrated efforts to increase each student's perception of himself as capable and worthy are directly attuned to helping him see himself as capable of becoming a successful something.

THE SCHOOL COUNSELOR

In view of the previous description of teacher involvement with vocational guidance, it is apparent that the school counselor must collaborate with teachers in accomplishing these mutual objectives. To do so, counselors must begin at a given student's level of development—as defined by his experiences, aspirations, values, capacities—to help him sort out his concept of occupations, of education, of self, and what mix of these interacting dimensions is of personal consequence. Because much of what teachers can contribute to vocational guidance is group oriented, the school counselor's task is to help individuals—to help them cast into bold relief those factors which are assets and those which may be self-limiting, whether they stem from lack of experience, lack of information, physical disability, learning dysfunction, lack of specific skill, or lack of decision-making competency.

Because students proceed at different rates through the acquisition of the attitudes and skills making up vocational guidance objectives, the counselor will need to monitor, diagnose, and prescribe to a greater degree than now seems typical. The outcome will be that given students will need to work on information or be exposed to experiences that are different from those of other students at any specific time. This will, in turn, require that school counselors work directly with teachers in identifying the goals of particular educational experiences for particular students, in making the access to certain courses or experiences more flexible for given students, and in broadening the curricular responses to individual characteristics. Such advocacy by the counselor of educational fare to broaden the range of exploratory or try-out experiences for students will immerse counselors and teachers in joint planning focusing upon where a given student is in acquiring those attitudes and competencies required by his goals, rather than upon fitting or forcing him into a preconceived mold.

Counselor-teacher collaboration on behalf of specific students is but one appropriate counselor function. Another is to serve as a resource for teachers in promoting the use of appropriate occupational and educational information or vocational development concepts in the classroom as a referral source for available community welfare, mental health, and employment opportunities.

But none of the collaborative and resource functions of the counselor negate his responsibility for providing individual and group counseling to students. Indeed, it is in counseling itself that the counselor's sensitivity to individual needs and his prescriptions for meeting these needs find their impetus. Chapter 9 speaks directly to these counselor functions, so they will not be discussed at length here. Suffice it to say that if many of the previously described teacher contributions to vocational guidance were systematically implemented, the counselor's efforts could be more effectively individualized than at present. Before a student's interests, aptitudes, goals, and other personal characteristics can be clearly identified and their implications examined, the individual needs reference points from which to evolve and relate these personal characteristics. Exposure to such reference points in curricula and other educational experiences would create a generalized base of information from which a more personalized counselor role could ensue.

Finally, the school counselor has a role in placement. If placement is viewed as a transition process as well as a point in time, the counselor can assist the student to prepare himself psychologically for placement. This role is in addition to providing information about how to contact employers, whom to contact, jobs available in the local setting, and appropriate educational opportunities, collegiate and noncollegiate.

Inherent in each of these functions is the need for the school counselor to evidence a research attitude. If counselors are going to succeed in persuading those charged with creating educational policy to broaden educational experiences for students and to join forces with community resources, they cannot rely on intuition and opinion. Instead, they will need such information as follow-up data on graduates and dropouts, data on the characteristics and aspirations of the student population, data on students who are successful in various course patterns and on those who are not. They will also need to put this information into forms which clearly communicate the problems and possible solutions (Cramer, Herr, Morris, and Frantz, 1970).

THE EMPLOYMENT SERVICE COUNSELOR

Much of what has been stated about the need for the school counselor to be concerned about the total vocational development of his clientele as shaped by myriad factors is also applicable to the Employment Service Counselor and the rehabilitation counselor, although important differences do prevail. Until recently, a counselor in the Employment Service, by definition, has been more concerned with direct placement than has the school counselor. His principal task has been to assist a client to become employed, optimally if possible, as quickly as he can. Such a circumstance led McGowan and Porter (1964, p. 17) to state that the Employment Service Counselor "is more concerned with the tangible or *product* aspects of counseling outcome than with reconstructing the emotive or *process* aspects of a counselee's personality." Where the latter was a necessity for employability, the Employment Service Counselor would typically rely upon referral to other community resources, e.g. rehabilitation counselors or welfare agencies, rather than accomplishing such behavioral changes himself. The United States Training and Employment Service has recognized, however, that simple job advising is inadequate to meet the new challenge it faces and has instituted concerted efforts to upgrade the educational standards and incentive system for Employment Service Counselors (Levine, 1965; Levine, 1965b).

The Employment Service Counselor has historically been responsible for a clientele broader in age and occupational history than has the school counselor, although his period of potential influence on the lives of such clients is more limited. Recent federal legislation has broadened even further the clientele to be served by the Employment Service and by implication has expanded the period of potential contact with these clients. For example, the testing and counseling responsibilities of the Employment Service now include all eighteen-year-old boys unable to meet the "mental" standards for induction into the Armed Forces, as well as those persons of all ages who need to be identified, recruited, trained, and guided into available training programs as provided by the Area Redevelopment Act of 1961 and the Manpower Development and Training Act of 1962. In addition, the Economic Opportunity Act of 1964 assigned to the Employment Service the task of interviewing and counseling youth for a variety of work-training programs. The Job Corps and the Youth Opportunity Centers together have broadened the responsibility of Employment Service Counselors in specific ways.

The point is that the Employment Service, as the most directly identified federal manpower agency, can no longer simply match with jobs those persons who come to the Employment Service Office for assistance. This agency is now required to identify, recruit, and provide appropriate training experiences for wider classifications of persons than ever before in the history of this agency. To accomplish this task in the terms of this paper requires greater emphasis upon professional counseling than upon job advising (Schantz and McGowan, 1965). It also demands greater articulation between school counselors and

Employment Service Counselors, as well as between Employment Service Counselors, teachers, rehabilitation persons, and industrial representatives.

As specified by the 1968 Amendments to the Vocational Education Act of 1963, school guidance and counseling personnel are encouraged to furnish to the Employment Service Counselor information regarding "the occupational qualifications of persons leaving or completing vocational education courses or schools, and toward consideration of such information by such offices in the occupational guidance and placement of such persons." In turn, such cooperative relations between schools and Employment Service Offices should include the latter's "making available to the State Board and local educational agencies occupational information regarding reasonable prospects of employment in the community and elsewhere, and toward consideration of such information by such board and agencies in providing vocational guidance and counseling to students and prospective students and in determining the occupations for which persons are to be trained" (Public Law 90-576, 1968, p. 12). Thus in particular cooperative arrangements there is nothing to preclude Employment Service Counselors' actually being housed in the school—as now happens in isolated urban situations—to help them provide better placement and information aid to school guidance and counseling personnel. Without such locus in the schools, however, a better understanding of the limits within which all these different counselors accomplish their essentially mutual objectives would produce greater breadth of cooperation between them.

One study of school counselor–Employment Service cooperation (Rossman and Prebonich, 1968) suggested that services provided by the Employment Service—such as aptitude testing, employment counseling, placement, proficiency testing, a source of local employment trends by industry and by occupation, information on MDTA classes, speakers at career days or in classes, a source of local wage rates, consultation on work-bound students, information on shortage occupations, consultation on potential dropouts—all could be of help to the school counselor although the first four were the most frequently used. The barriers cited to communication between counselors and the Employment Service included the area of General Aptitude Test Battery (GATB) information. More than half the school counselors felt that their knowledge of the content and use of the GATB was inadequate and over a third said that when the GATB was administered to their students by the Employment Service, no information was reported to them.

When asked how the relationship might be improved, over two-thirds of the school counselors (total N = 238) suggested increased consultation between the Employment Service and themselves; almost one-half would like to have more information about the role of the Employment Service; and approximately one-third felt the relationship could be improved by additional follow-up efforts by either the Employment Service or the high school. The barrier reported by Employment Service Counselors was the practice by high schools of restricting the amount of time Employment Service Counselors may spend with a student. Over half said their time was limited to twenty minutes. One of the thirty-one local offices responding to the question said they spent more than two interviews with the high school seniors they saw.

Such data, though limited, prompt several observations. If the GATB is a valuable tool to both the Employment Service Counselor and the school counselor, its use as a guidance instrument at the ninth or tenth grades in addition to its use as a placement instrument at the twelfth grade should become more pervasive in schools. Further, GATB information, as well as other information at the command of the Employment Service, should influence more directly the efforts of the school counselors and educators in assessing student proficiency, planning the vocational program, designing curricula, as well as placing individual students whether under the aegis of the school or the Employment Service. This is obviously the thrust of the Vocational Act Amendments of 1968. The point is that these two social agencies already have the potential for gaining a better understanding of the role each can play to complement vocational guidance, counseling, and placement as well as the strategies each can use to accomplish mutual goals, but such an outcome is possible only if comprehensive and mutual dialogue is created at all levels—local, state, and national (National Vocational Guidance Association, 1965).

THE REHABILITATION COUNSELOR

Like the Employment Service Counselor, the rehabilitation counselor is concerned with optimum vocational adjustment of clients. He may, in fact, receive referrals from Employment Service Counselors or school counselors, as well as from other sources. His principal, historic difference from his counterpart counselors in schools and Employment Services is that he is constantly working with clientele limited by physical disability. To the degree that such physical disabilities are modifiable, he coordinataes those services which will modify them, e.g. medical, training, prosthetic; when they are not modifiable, he assists the client to circumvent them and find employment within the limits prescribed by the disability.

The rehabilitation counselor typically has more latitude than the Employment Service Counselor in dealing with the emotional and psychological factors impeding the vocational development of a client. In part this is true not necessarily because the rehabilitation counselor works with these matters himself but because he can purchase or otherwise secure from private or other agencies the specific kind of assistance that a given client needs.

A major factor in the interaction of school counselors and state rehabilitation counselors is the broadening of definitions of the clients to be served, as well as the increasing importance to rehabilitation of the concept of habilitation. Legislation governing the Rehabilitation Services Administration has widened the scope of services significantly to embrace not only clients with simple physical disability but also those with emotional disturbance in its many manifestations, mental retardation, and social and educational dysfunctions as these impede vocational adjustment. Against this broadened clientele can be contrasted rehabilitation versus habilitation as goals for rehabilitation counselors working with different classes of clients. Rehabilitation is the restoring or re-educating of individuals to productive lives. In contrast, vocational habilitation (Bitter, 1967) is the educational process of developing the vocationally unsophisticated (i.e. individuals with little or no previous contact with the work world). Impetus has been given to the latter by the upsurge of job-training programs for the handicapped and the disadvantaged, as well as by state cooperative programs between special education and vocational rehabilitation.

Habilitation, like rehabilitation, rests at the outset upon evaluation of the fundamental work capabilities, knowledge, experiences, and attitudes which characterize the client. Then the counselor in cooperation with others prescribes a series of concrete transitional experiences, leading from sheltered workshop or cooperating employer job sites to community adjustment and employment. To accomplish such goals the rehabilitation or training counselor must break down into manageable increments the specific experiences that a particular client needs to move toward a productive life. In this sense, the client is responded to as a total being, not just a potential employee.

As vocational rehabilitation moves to an increasing emphasis on vocational habilitation, the line separating the mandate of the Employment Service and that of State Rehabilitation Agencies will become fuzzier. However, such a development reflects the need for comprehensive manpower policy and implementation less affected by specific descriptions of individuals to be served by a specific agency. Further, such a development will necessitate a more encompassing delivery of services to persons needing help with vocational planning and employment and will diminish the present splintered approach. There is no question that the services and expertise of rehabilitation counselors must be articulated more clearly with those of the Employment Service Counselor and the school counselor. This is needed not only to obtain earlier referrals of students or other clients eligible for rehabilitation assistance and to get feedback about the jobs in which persons with particular disabilities function most effectively. But it is also needed in order to increase the comprehensiveness of the processes of habilitation through use of other institutional and agency settings.

BUSINESS AND INDUSTRY PERSONNEL

While it is difficult to define specifically the contributions of personnel and/or training officers in business and industry to vocational guidance, counseling, and placement needs, it is possible to assert the need for greater communication between such persons and their counterparts in schools, Employment Services, and rehabilitation. As Kunze (1967, p. 138) has pointed out, industrial resources for counselors fall roughly into two categories: "those that serve primarily the counselor's client (the student or post-school adult) and those intended to inform and update the counselor." The spectrum of occupational information identified by Kunze as available for counselor and client use includes the following:

1. On-the-job try-out: part-time jobs, summer jobs, work-study programs

2. Directed exploratory experiences: work samples, work evaluation tasks

3. Direct observation: visits to work settings

4. Synthetically created work environments: simulation of work settings and occupational roles

5. Simulated situations: career games, role playing

6. Interviews with experts: questioning representatives of occupations, career days

7. Computer-based systems: computer systems which store, retrieve, and process occupational data in response to individual requests

8. Programmed instructional materials: books and workbooks

9. Audiovisual aids: films, tapes, slides, etc.

10. Publications: books, monographs, charts, etc.

One can only imagine the effect of *systematic* interaction between teachers or counselors, and representatives of business and industry in combining the resources and expertise available in these multiple settings to provide experiences geared to individual needs. Such communication might serve a further important purpose. In frequent cases, it is apparent that the educational and/or training requirements for specific jobs are unrealistically high. While this is partly a function of supply and demand, it may also be a ploy to keep certain "undesirables" out of a particular company. But such unrealistic requirements for access to employment cause psychological and economic handicaps in many who could perform the jobs and be motivated by such experience to achieve further growth in vocationally effective behavior.

Part of the benefits of close industry-education relationships could be a cracking of stereotypes about so-called "undesirables" or "unemployables." In frequent cases, personnel officers in industry seem not to understand the backgrounds and characteristics of minority-group members who come to them for jobs. It is easy to hire the qualified. It is quite another matter to devise training programs which break down a job into its basic skill components and then provide for the acquisition of these skills by those employees who need and can achieve job upgrading (Lloyd, 1968).

The above observation is not intended to be a categorical indictment of industry but rather to emphasize the continuing need for education-industry cooperation to increase the employability of certain segments of the population. Indeed, many industries are providing effective leadership in stay-in-school campaigns to raise the occupational sights of minority youth, in earn-and-learn programs, faculty summer internships, industry-education seminars, and vocational training for the unemployed (Carr and Young, 1967). The point is that while business and industry seek competent personnel and the school counselor and teachers seek personal competence, the band of overlap in these two objectives is sufficiently large to insure that increased cooperation between these groups would enhance the goals of all concerned.

A vehicle to help achieve these mutual goals is Section 553 of the Vocational Educational Amendments of 1968, which provides funding for various forms of exchange programs, institutes, and in-service education for vocational education personnel.

> Grants under this section may be used for projects and activities such as exchange of vocational education teachers and other staff members with skilled technicians or supervisors in industry (including mutual arrangements for preserving employment and retirement status, and other employment benefits during the period of exchange), and the development and operation of cooperative programs involving periods of teaching in schools providing vocational education and of experience in commercial, industrial, or other public or private employment relating to the subject matter taught in such schools. . . .

The professional literature has supported the importance of such exchange programs for teachers and counselors involved in the vocational aspects of guidance and education, but more about such cooperative endeavors has been said than done. Prototype experiences already exist in which school and Employment Service counselors exchange roles or work in industry (Gorman, 1966) and others in which teachers are exposed to institutes, workshops, and actual work experiences translating current developments in industry into operational concepts useful in improving education—and ultimately industry (Kelly, 1968).

Such cooperative endeavors between the various sectors of society need to be expanded dramatically. Given current legislative support, the task now is to develop with ingenuity the specific goals of such experiences, based on the effect those who are involved in cooperative exchange programs can have on the vocational behavior of their clientele.

THE GUIDANCE PARAPROFESSIONAL

The term "guidance paraprofessional" is typically used to identify persons who are employed in schools, under the supervision of school counselors, to perform technical and nontechnical duties which do not require the level of profesional preparation needed by the school counselor. Depending upon the requirements of a particular local setting, such persons might have a baccalaureate degree, some college, a high school diploma, or less than high school preparation.

Instead of the term "guidance paraprofessional," the official American Personnel and Guidance Association term is "support personnel" (American Personnel and Guidance Association, 1966). The role of support personnel as described by APGA includes direct helping relationships as well as indirect helping relationships. Although these are not identical nor qualitatively equivalent to those conducted by professional school counselors, nevertheless they enhance and facilitate the professional work of the counselor. The use of support personnel in guidance frees the school counselor from certain important guidance functions which do not require professional expertise but which need be accomplished so that a comprehensive range of guidance services can be provided to all students.

Among the activities of support personnel which have particular relevance to vocational guidance objectives are the following (APGA, 1966):

a. *Secure information from an interviewee by means of a semi-structured interview schedule. The information elicited would tend to be factual and limited in nature.*

b. *Give information prepared in advance and approved by the counselor for its appropriateness for the interviewee. Such information would usually be factual rather than interpretative.*

c. *Engage the counselee in informal, casual, colloquial discussion as a means of putting him at ease and establishing an openness to counseling. Such a dyadic activity may be especially important when performed by an interviewer who is making initial contact with potential counselees who are hostile toward or apprehensive of counseling.*

d. *In structured groups with a largely preplanned program, guide discussions as a discussion leader.*

e. *Administer, score, and profile routine standardized tests and other appraisal instruments (non-clinical type).*

f. *Obtain and maintain routine information on the scope and character of the world of work with current reference to employment trends, in accordance with instructions established by the counselor.*

g. *Prepare educational, occupational, and personal-social information for visual-auditory verbal and graphic presentation or transmittal to others for use, in accordance with instructions established by the counselor.*

h. *Initiate general contacts with specific referral agencies.*

i. *Through appropriate channels, establish and maintain working relationships with organized placement agencies in the community.*

j. *Maintain appropriate personnel and information records for the counselor.*

Some authors apparently prefer titles other than support or paraprofessional to describe the work of persons serving under the general supervision of school counselors. Goldman (1967, pp. 49–50), for example, describes a guidance information technician, whose primary responsibilities are to collate and transmit information. Specifically, the tasks of such a technician might include the following:

1. *Assists pupils to locate reference materials about occupations and about schools and colleges.*

2. *Places on cumulative and other records significant information such as test scores, teacher ratings, and anecdotal or health reports.*

3. *Conducts individual and group orientation conferences with incoming pupils. Informs pupils of school curricular offerings, extracurricular opportunities, study methods, and other aspects of adjustment and development in the school.*

4. *Assists pupils with the more routine aspects of scheduling.*

5. *Carries out routine statistical work in compiling data pertaining to pupils such as test-score distributions, occupational and educational preferences, and socioeconomic status. He may prepare local norms and experience tables.*

6. *Carries out prescribed activities in connection with studies such as surveys of job opportunities; surveys of referral possibilities in the community; follow-up studies of the school's graduates and dropouts.*

7. *Maintains an up-to-date collection of information materials concerning educational and occupational opportunities.*

8. *Administers paper-and-pencil tests in groups and individually as directed by the school counselor.*

Hoyt (1970, pp. 64–65) also discusses the use of guidance technicians. He classifies possible duties of such technicians in four categories, each supportive of vocational guidance programs.

1. *Outreach specialist—concerned primarily with contacting and recruiting disadvantaged students for vocational education.*

2. *Data gatherer—concerned with conducting local occupational surveys and in recording and updating information regarding full- and part-time job opportunities, labor unions, apprenticeship councils, and vocational training opportunities outside the public school setting.*

3. *Test operator—concerned with the development and operation of a wide variety of simulation activities that would produce a reliable sample of the student's ability to actually perform the kinds of tasks taught in a particular vocational education program.*

4. *Follow-up man—concerned with developing procedures and conducting studies of the outcomes of different phases of education and guidance.*

There are other perceptions of the duties of support personnel, technicians, paraprofessionals, or assistants in guidance. However, the job descriptions cited here are representative of the types of subprofessional tasks appropriate to such roles. As such individuals are more frequently incorporated into the personnel resource pool of vocational guidance, specific tasks for which they might assume responsibility will undoubtedly be refined.

On balance, the use of support personnel in vocational guidance, when combined with the other personnel resources identified in this chapter, permits the broadening of the perimeters of service of vocational guidance; supports the potential of differentiated staffing, by which many levels of expertise can be systematically related to student needs; and, most important, reaffirms the need for a master plan of objectives, strategies, and outcomes to which such personnel resources can be related.

SUMMARY

This chapter examines the dimensions of cooperative effort necessary in providing a systems approach to vocational guidance. Examples of the forms of contributions needed from state and local personnel both in education and in the larger society are described. The concept of differentiated staffing, which includes support or paraprofessional personnel, is discussed as an emerging, vital issue in vocational guidance and in education.

REFERENCES

*American Personnel and Guidance Association. *Support personnel for the counselor: Their technical and nontechnical roles and preparation.* A statement of policy. Washington, D. C.: Association, Nov., 1966.

Arnold, W. M. Vocational guidance and vocational education: The common goal. *Vocational Guidance Quarterly,* 1967, 16, 2–6.

Bernstein, S. Vocational rehabilitation and the war on poverty. *Vocational Guidance Quarterly,* 1966, 14, 175–178.

Bitter, J. A. The training counselor: An emerging professional. *Vocational Guidance Quarterly,* 1967, 15, 294–296.

Carr, H. C., and Young, N. A. Industry-education cooperation. *Vocational Guidance Quarterly,* 1967, 15, 203–304.

Cramer, S. H.; Herr, E. L.; Morris, C. N.; and Frantz, T. T. *Research and the school counselor.* Boston: Houghton Mifflin, 1970.

* Recommended for additional reading.

*Day, S. R.   Teacher influence on the occupational preference of high school students.   *Vocational Guidance Quarterly*, 1966, 14, 215–219.

Ginsberg, E.; Ginzburg, S. W.; Axelrad, S.; and Herma, J. L.   *Occupational choice: An approach to a general theory.*   New York: Columbia University Press, 1951.

Goldman, L.   Help for the counselor.   *Bulletin of the National Association of Secondary School Principals*, 1967, 51, 48–53.

Gorman, R. E.   *A guidance project to investigate characteristics, backgrounds, and job experiences of successful and unsuccessful entry workers in three selected industries.*   Helena: University of Montana and Montana State Department of Public Instruction, 1966.

Gysbers, N. C.   Elements of a model for promoting career development in elementary and junior high school.   Paper presented at the National Conference of Exemplary Programs and Projects Section of the 1968 Amendments to the Vocational Education Act, Atlanta, Ga., March, 1969.

Herr, E. L.   Differential perceptions of "environmental press" by high school students as related to their achievement and participation in activities.   *Personnel and Guidance Journal*, 1965, 43, 678–686.

Herr, E. L.   Implications for state vocational guidance program development from selected Office of Education supported conferences.   Paper presented at the National Conference on Vocational Guidance, Development of State Programs, Washington, D. C.: Jan., 1967.

*Herr, E. L.   Uniquely qualified to divert the dropout.   *American Vocational Journal*, 1968, 43, 13–15.

Herr, E. L.   What are the personnel and nonpersonnel resources available and needed to meet the vocational guidance, counseling, and placement needs of people?   In N. C. Gysbers and D. H. Pritchard (eds.) *Proceedings, National Conference on Guidance, Counseling, and Placement in Career Development and Educational–Occupational Decision-making.*   Columbia: University of Missouri, Oct., 1969, 31–51.

Hitchcock, A. A.   Counselors: Supply, demand, need.   In J. McGowan (ed.) *Counselor development in American society.*   Invitational Conference on Government-University Relations in the Professional Preparation and Employment of Counselors, Washington, D. C., June, 1965.

Hoyt, K. B.   The influence of the state supervisor on the future of vocational guidance.   In N. C. Gysbers (ed.) *Proceedings, National Seminar on Vocational Guidance.*   Marquette: Northern Michigan University, August, 1966, 8–13.

*Hoyt, K. B.   Vocational guidance for all: New kinds of personnel needed.   *American Vocational Journal*, 1970, 45, 62–65.

*Kelly, R. K. Experimental work-study programs for disadvantaged youth. *Educational Record,* 1968, 49, 214–220.

*Kunze, K. R. Industry resources available to counselors. *Vocational Guidance Quarterly,* 1967, 16, 137–142.

Levine, L. Comment. *Vocational Guidance Quarterly,* 1965, 13, 173–175 (a).

Levine, L. Implications of the antipoverty program for education and employment. *Vocational Guidance Quarterly,* 1965, 14, 8–15 (b).

Lloyd, G. A. The human side of industry. *Vocational Guidance Quarterly,* 1968, 16, 301–305.

McCully, C. H. Making a troika work. *Counselor Education and Supervision,* 1964, 3, 191–201.

*McGowan, J. F., and Porter, T. L. *An introduction to employment service counseling.* Columbia: University of Missouri, 1964.

*National Vocational Guidance Association. Suggested guidelines for further coordination of educational institutions and employment services. *Vocational Guidance Quarterly,* 1965, 13, 215–220.

Pritchard, D. H. Impact of government programs on the development and employment of counselors. *Vocational Guidance Quarterly,* 1965, 14, 36–40.

Rossman, J. E., and Prebonich, E. M. School counselor–employment service counselors in Missouri. *Vocational Guidance Association,* 1965, 13, 169–172.

Schantz, L., and McGowan, J. F. Upgrading employment service counselors in Missouri. *Vocational Guidance Quarterly,* 1965, 13, 169–172.

Shertzer, B., and Stone, S. C. *Fundamentals of guidance.* Boston: Houghton Mifflin, 1966.

Tiedeman, D. V., and O'Hara, R. P. *Career development: Choice and adjustment.* New York: College Entrance Examination Board, 1963.

*Watley, D. Student decisions influenced by counselors and teachers. *Vocational Guidance Quarterly,* 1966, 15, 36–40.

THIRTEEN

BRINGING ABOUT CHANGE IN THE SCHOOLS

Although there is a great deal of literature relating principles of the behavioral sciences to change in organizations and institutions, there is not presently a theory of change through which a practitioner can implement new programs or techniques with absolute assurance of success. Frequently, one encounters a semantic difficulty in the terms "strategy of change" and "theory of change." Lake (1968, p. 5) suggests, "When concepts are tied in with tactics of inducing those concepts and when time-phasing activities are suggested, then the theories become strategies of innovation." Much of what is written concerns business or industrial institutions rather than educational institutions; yet many principles that have been evolved specifically for offices and factories appear to have transfer value in education. The purpose of this chapter is, in general, to summarize briefly some of the appropriate principles of change and, in particular, to evolve a tentative plan for putting into effect a systems approach to vocational guidance in the schools.

CHANGE FROM WITHIN VERSUS CHANGE FROM WITHOUT

One must first make a distinction regarding the impetus for change. An organization, such as the school, may not be functioning well. It may be beset by stresses and strains, crises and conflicts, role incongruities and obfuscations, dissatisfactions and tensions, and/or general malaise. On the other hand, an organization may be operating smoothly, have high morale and cohesiveness, and generate great satisfaction on the part of all concerned individuals. Yet there may be a need within even that admirable setting for new programs or procedures. In either case—conflict or harmony—*planned change* is what is needed. Planned change is change that is "conscious, deliberate, and intended" (Chin and Benne, 1969). It implies a strategy encompassing a series of moves designed to achieve optimal functioning with minimal transitional woes.

The obverse of planned change is change that comes about typically during periods of high emotion. It is usually haphazard at best, inadequately thought through, and more often than not implemented in a hasty, disorganized way. Such change frequently emanates from sources external to the institution or from a nonmanagerial element in it. For example, a group of parents pressures the school for a course in Black Studies, a coterie of students demands that the institution provide a smoking lounge, or some local politicians push for student released time to work in elections. Such events are frequently enveloped in guarded hysteria, and too often the school is unprepared to cope with such demands for change.

In this chapter we address ourselves solely to planned change. The inauguration of a systems approach to vocational guidance indeed calls for "conscious, deliberate, and intended" change. Subsequent portions of this chapter deal with the problem of how best to implement a systems approach within an existing institutional structure.

GENERAL PRINCIPLES AND STRATEGIES OF CHANGE

Several years ago Kurt Lewin postulated that within any institutional setting there are forces operating in opposite directions. He termed these restraining forces and driving forces and hypothesized that change takes place when these two types of forces are in imbalance. In order to effect change, one must increase driving forces, decrease restraining forces, or combine the two approaches (see Chapter 9).

Working from Lewin's premise, Benne and Birnbaum (1969, p. 330) have suggested several principles of change:

1. To change a subsystem, relevant aspects of the environment must also be changed.

2. To change behavior on any one level of a hierarchical organization, it is necessary to achieve complementing and reinforcing changes in organization levels above and below that level.

3. The place to begin change is at those points in the system where some stress and strain exist. Stress may give rise to dissatisfaction with the status quo and thus become a motivating factor for change in the system.

4. In diagnosing the possibility of change in a given institution, it is necessary to assess the degree of stress and strain at points where change is sought. One would ordinarily avoid beginning change at the point of greatest stress.

5. If thoroughgoing changes in a hierarchical structure are desirable or necessary, change should ordinarily start with the policy-making body.

6. Both the formal and informal organizations of an institution must be considered in planning any process of change.

7. The effectiveness of a planned change is often directly related to the degree to which members at all levels of an institutional hierarchy take part in the fact-finding and the diagnosing of needed changes and in the formulating and reality testing of goals and programs of change.

Chin (1969) has echoed this concern in discussing the need to involve different "sizes" or "limits" of human interactions in change: the person, the group, the organization, and the community. In collaboration with Benne (1969), Chin has described the various types of strategies that have evolved for producing change.

First, there are so-called *empirical-rational* strategies. Here man is conceived as a rational animal. If, through research and education, he is allowed to see his rational self-interest, he will follow it. In this approach, then, systems analysts use knowledge as power to effect change. This method has been criticized as appropriate for thing technologies but inappropriate for people technologies.

A second strategy is termed *normative—re-educative*. Here we depart from the purely intellectual orientation of the empirical-rational approach and take cognizance of man as an active being in need of impulse gratification. Thus change must include an appeal to the habits and values of those being changed. If man is to be re-educated at all, then he must participate in his own re-education and must be aware of his own unconscious and preconscious bases for action. Therefore, change comes about by means of the direct intervention of change agents who emphasize client systems and involvement, because merely providing more adequate technical information is not sufficient. Power is equated with mastery of the noncognitive elements. Since people technology is as necessary as thing technology, values must be clarified and reconstructed. This approach, therefore, seeks to improve problem-solving capabilities and to release and foster growth in those persons who make up the system to be changed.

A third strategy for change is designated as *power-coercive*. Here political, economic, and moral sanctions are regarded as all-important. Applications of this system include strategies of nonviolence and civil disobedience, strikes, political institutions, and various manipulations of power élites. Etzioni (1961) has described three types of power: *coercive,* which uses pain, deformity, and death; *remunerative,* which promises rewards; and *normative,* which allocates esteem and prestige symbols.

Perhaps an example of the three main approaches to a single school problem will make their diversity clearer. Suppose we have a problem in a school that revolves about the wishes of a segment of the community to institute a Black Studies program. The empirical-rational approach might take the form of having nationally known Black leaders talk to the Board of Education, the professional staff, and the students, advancing arguments in favor of the program. The normative—re-educative approach might call for encounter-type groups, wherein Blacks and whites confront each other to determine if prejudices are hampering change. The power-coercive method might involve a boycott of classes by Black students and picketing of Board of Education offices. Obviously, these three approaches are not mutually exclusive.

Bennis (1966) has placed change strategies in a somewhat different context. Table 1 presents a paradigm of what he envisions to be the primary human problems confronting organizations, past attempts at solution, and newer factors that militate against the older methods.

Table 1   Human Problems Confronting Contemporary Organizations

Integration	The problem of how to integrate individual needs and management goals.	No solution because of no problem. Individual vastly oversimplified, regarded as passive instrument or disregarded.	Emergence of human sciences and understanding of man's complexity. Rising aspirations. Humanistic-democratic ethos.
Social Influence	The problem of the distribution of power and sources of power and authority.	An explicit reliance on legal-rational power but an implicit usage of coercive power. In any case, a confused, ambiguous, shifting complex of competence, coercion, and legal code.	Separation of management from ownership. Rise of trade unions and general education. Negative and unintended effects of authoritarian rule.
Collaboration	The problem of managing and resolving conflicts.	The "rule of hierarchy" to resolve conflicts between ranks and the "rule of coordination" to resolve conflict between horizontal groups. "Loyalty."	Specialization and professionalization and increased need for interdependence. Leadership too complex for one-man role of omniscience.
Adaptation	The problem of responding appropriately to changes induced by the environment of the firm.	Environment stable, simple, and predictable; tasks routine. Adapting to change occurs in haphazard and adventitious ways. Unanticipated consequences abound.	External environment of firm more "turbulent," less predictable. Unprecedented rate of technological change.
"Revitalization"	The problem of growth and decay.		Rapid changes in technologies, tasks, manpower, norms, and values of society, and in goals of enterprise and society all make constant attention to the process of revision imperative.

Reproduced by special permission from W. G. Bennis, Changing organizations, Journal of Applied Behavioral Science, 1966, 2, 250.

All these past failures are attributed to the fact that they failed to take into account three fundamentally valid concepts, concepts of recent vintage which are replacing the old and thus represent change: (1) a new concept of *man*, based on increased knowledge of his complex and shifting needs, which replaces the oversimplified, innocent, push-button idea of man; (2) a new concept of *power*, based on collaboration and reason, which replaces a model of power based on coercion and fear; (3) a new concept of *organizational values*, based on humanistic-democratic ideals, which replaces the depersonalized, mechanistic value system of bureaucracy. These assumptions are rather utopian and perhaps make more sense in the abstract as a description of what should be rather than as an accurate account of what actually is.

Walton (1965) further delineates the differences inherent in the power strategy of change versus the attitude strategy of change. The power strategy largely evolves from the work of game theorists, diplomatic strategists, and students of revolutions. Two tactical operations are necessary in order to build a power base and strategically manipulate that power "In order to establish a base for negotiation with the other and improve the probable outcome for itself, a group must [1] build its power vis-a-vis the other . . .[2] biasing the rival group's perceptions of the strength of the underlying preference functions" (pp. 168-169).

The tactics of the attitude strategy for change are different. Here emphasis is placed on increasing the trust between involved persons or groups, minimizing perceived differences, emphasizing mutual dependence, openness, acceptance, and empathy. In Walton's view, a third alternative is problem solving (usually subsumed as part of the attitude strategy). Walton sees this strategy as especially useful whenever the issue is such that both parties can gain, or one can gain without the other losing. This type of situation has been termed integrative.

Other studies have dealt with factors that facilitate change. Kolb, Winter, and Berlew (1968), for example, have demonstrated that change is most easily achieved when goal setting has been cooperatively achieved and specifically stated and when commitment to those goals has been high. Winn (1966, p. 172) has reported that attitude strategies for change which seek to provide members of an organization with insight are inadequate in and of themselves. Transfer of insight gained from "micro-cultural group experiences is a difficult but necessary condition for change." Finally, Davis (1967) has indicated several plateaus as necessary for effective problem solving in order to bring about change. These may be characterized as problem awareness, identification and freeing of key people within the organization, action-experimental steps stimulated by participation in various types of workshops, and development of an independent and self-supporting system.

Peter and Bennis (1966) suggest that any problem of planning change will contain six elements: a client system, behavioral change agents, a collaborative relationship between client system and the change agent, specification and selection of goals, methods and interventions, and feedback. Leavitt (1965) provides another way of characterizing methods of change. He suggests three approaches: *structural,* in which attempts are made to manipulate systems of communication, authority, and work flow; *technological,* in which problem solving is used to manipulate; and *people,* in which direct intervention with people and their values in organizations is necessary.

Dionne (1966), in addressing himself to school systems, has stated that a prerequisite to effective change is the understanding of a school district as a social system. He suggests that four problems must be solved (pp. 4-5):

> *The first problem is gaining commitment to a new set of values. The second is to produce environmental conditions conducive to their attainment. The third is to mobilize the resources to attain the goals. The fourth problem is that of guaranteeing harmony in inter-unit relationships following the introduction of change.*

What does all this literature relating to change say to us? How applicable for schools are strategies of organizational change which have been developed largely for business and industry?

Several points are helpful. First, it is clear that there are three possible strategies for change that may be used singly or in combination: (1) Information or knowledge may be employed to demonstrate rationally the sound nature of a proposed change. (2) Attitudes and values may be explored and related to problem-solving techniques. (3) Power in one form or another may be brought to bear.

In addition, change appears to be facilitated if several principles are recognized and followed: Change in any one aspect of a system frequently requires changes in other aspects of the system. Change evidently comes about most easily at points in an organization where stress and strain are at a minimum. There is a need to involve various elements of an organization in the planning and implementation of change. Commitment to democratically formulated goals enhances effective change possibilities. A systematic approach to effecting change is necessary. Finally, one must understand the total Gestalt of a system before change is attempted.

All the foregoing discussion has related to positive aspects of achieving planned change. There are obviously variables that work against achieving change—impediments that must be overcome if change is to take hold. The following section deals with these resistances to change.

OVERCOMING RESISTANCE TO CHANGE

Most notions of resistance to change speculate that individual reactions and group-induced forces militate against the occurrence of change and that these proclivities must be overcome. Watson (1966) has characterized these forces as

resistance in personality and resistance in social systems. His outline of resistance to change is reproduced below in adapted form.

A. Resistance in Personality

1. *Homeostasis.* It is hypothesized that there are stabilizing forces within
   an individual that cause him to return to a previous state.

2. *Habit.* Once a habit is established, its operation is often satisfying to
   the individual and is therefore difficult to change.

3. *Primacy.* The way in which an individual first successfully copes with
   a situation sets a pattern which is unusually persistent.

4. *Selective Perception and Retention.* Situations may be seen as reinforcing an original attitude when they actually are dissonant.

5. *Dependence.* Agreement with early authority figures may carry over
   into adult life.

6. *Superego.* In a dependence sort of way, the superego may act as a tradi-
   tion-serving agent.

7. *Self-distrust.* Individuals tend to distrust their own impulses and thus
   are fearful of change.

8. *Insecurity and Regression.* Individuals tend to seek security in the past
   and thus be cautious about the future.

B. Resistance to Change in Social Systems

1. *Conformity to Norms.* Norms are to a social system what habits are
   to an individual. Because norms are shared by many participants, they
   cannot easily be changed.

2. *Systematic and Cultural Coherence.* It is difficult to change one part of a
   system without affecting other parts of the system.

3. *Vested Interests.* Change is frequently perceived as a threat to the economic or prestige interests of individuals.

4. *The Sacrosanct.* It is easier to change technology than to change what
   people hold to be sacred.

5. *Rejection of "Outsiders."* Most changes come from the outside. Outsiders tend to be distrusted; hence change is difficult.

In general, when an environment removes expected rewards and changes
are instituted which tend to polarize values, structure, and practices, then the
members of that organization "[1] will perceive new demands as threatening
and feel resentful and unable to cope with these demands and . . . [2] will
behave defensively to resist these new demands . . ." (Greiner, 1967).

What can be done to overcome these resisting tendencies? First, it is clear that for change to have the greatest chance of success, it must come from *within* the system and must have the support of the policy-making and managerial portions of the system. Second, social psychology has demonstrated that in groups and organizations participation tends to produce high morale. Therefore, inclusion of all relevant elements of a system in planning and implementing a change should prove facilitative. Third, individuals within an organization must perceive the need for a change. Change must be viewed as reducing present difficulties, offering new experiences of interest, or enhancing goals—and at the same time it must be in accord with extant values. It must not be perceived as a threat either to the autonomy or the security of the participants.

To accomplish these counter-resistance steps, Watson (1966) suggests joint participation in dialogue, group decision making, alleviation of unnecessary fears, and provision for feedback of perceptions to avoid miscommunication and misunderstanding.

INAUGURATING A SYSTEMS APPROACH

The history of change in the schools suggests that two approaches have been utilized. The most common approach involves the direct change of work practices—new curricula, programmed-learning hardware, grouping practices, and electronic data-processing scheduling procedures, for example. The second approach, less common, is aimed at improving problem-solving capabilities. Here the aim is to invent or adapt new structures and work practices and, in general, to become more creative. The ultimate goal is increased organizational health (Benedict, et al., 1967).

One study (North Central Association, 1967) has demonstrated that specific, well-packaged curriculum materials have the greatest chance of being adopted by schools, while technological innovations are adopted less widely. Finally, changes in ways of organizing teaching practices are least readily adopted. In other words, it appears that thing technologies hold greater likelihood for change than do people technologies.

In terms of effecting a systems approach to vocational guidance in the schools, the problem of change can be viewed as relatively simple or relatively difficult, depending upon the magnitude of the change desired. Two types of implementation are possible. The first is merely to view a systems approach as a concrete, specific, well-packaged curriculum program to be implemented within the existing structure. Effecting a program conceived on this basis presents few major problems. On the other hand, one can view the inauguration and operation of a systems approach in broader perspective, arguing that it calls for attitude and expectation changes on the parts of participants and requires a different structure—a guidance period programmed weekly for each student, for example. This point of view presents a monumental change problem.

We do not know which of these two methods is the more sensible and realistic, because attempts to implement systematic approaches have been few and have not typically been intensively evaluated. In the absence of precedent, we would operate on the premise that if two approaches—a priori—seem to have differing chances for success, the one which offers the greater prospect of success should be tried. That would be the first approach—a thing technology strategy. The remainder of this chapter (drawing on preceding portions) proposes specific steps to inaugurate a systems approach to vocational guidance in the schools.

THE STEP-BY-STEP PROGRAM

1. We begin with the assumption that in this case the appropriate major strategy to be employed to effect change is an empirical-rational one. This strategy historically has been considered appropriate for the implementation of thing technologies. A systems approach to vocational guidance in the schools, although it obviously involves people, may be conceived as of nothing more nor less than an example of a thing technology. The task, then, is simply to convince appropriate others that a systems approach is a better method of providing vocational guidance than whatever other approach is currently employed.

Toward this end, *the innovator or change agent must first thoroughly ground himself in the precepts, concepts, and methodologies of the systems approach.* He needs to understand the goals-vocationalization-treatment-evaluation approach and how it is applied in a K–12 comprehensive vocational guidance program. He must know the characteristics of youth in general and the needs of the young people of his own community in particular. He should comprehend the difference between vocational guidance as vocationalization and vocational guidance as treatment. He ought to realize how the various helping strategies and the tools of vocational guidance are applied in a systems approach. In short, he should be able to demonstrate how a systematic approach to vocational guidance in the schools can provide for and give evidence of adequate student vocationalization and concommitant vocational decision making.

2. Planned change occurs most easily when those who will be affected by the change and those who represent the power structure of an organization are involved in the formulation of the goals of that change and subscribe to those goals. Therefore, it is imperative to secure the cooperation and endorsement of guidance counselors, administrators, teachers, and (at upper-grade levels) students. Large-group meetings are unwieldy and mitigate against active participation. One wants active advocates, not passive individuals who will go along. Hence each of these subgroups should be met with individually, at which time the change agent "sells" the program by indicating that everyone

involved can gain and no one can lose. The second step, then, in effecting a systems approach to vocational guidance in the schools is *securing commitment from the diverse elements of the institution.*

Possible approaches to securing commitment might include demonstrating to principals and superintendents the potential vocational development gains to students while at the same time showing that no great additional per-pupil expenditure is necessary; assuring them that continuous evaluation is built into a systematic program; persuading Boards of Education they will have evidence that guidance does have tangible behavioral goals and that they will be provided with measures of how closely these goals have been achieved; convincing all guidance counselors and other pupil personnel specialists that they will function more effectively as they operate within the structure of an integrated vocational guidance program rather than within what is perhaps a never-never land of slapdash, haphazard energy output; demonstrating to teachers that no great additional demands will be made on their time and energies and that enhanced vocationalization can enable students to see increased relevance in their course work; and motivating students by pointing out that a systematic approach to vocational guidance should help lessen anxieties and provide skills for future decision making. Informed enthusiasm is contagious; it is one disease worth spreading.

Hunt (1968) points out that instead of identifying with an organization as a whole, members tend to identify primarily, if not exclusively, with some subsystem close to their principal occupational interests or other salient interests. If members of the various subsystems can be marshaled in the pursuit of a common goal—a systematic approach to vocational guidance—they will tend to identify with that goal. What individuals identify with, they value more. What they value, they work for.

3. Taking into account the need to consider the institution as a social system, *representatives of each group should be involved in a steering or advisory committee,* responsible for overseeing the inauguration, implementation, and evaluation of the new approach. It has previously been indicated that a change in one segment of a social system frequently affects other elements of the system. Giving representatives from various parts of a system a feeling of participation and involvement often prevents future difficulties. A committee of teachers, administrators, students, and—especially in core area schools—community representatives provides an open channel of communication, opportunity for feedback, and valuable input regarding student needs.

4. The advisory committee should have as its initial task the *production of environmental conditions that will enhance the possibilities of successful implementation of the systems approach.* Since prior commitment has been secured from various important substrata, this task should not be overly difficult. Basically, it involves establishing a positive psychological set within those who perform various role functions in the institution. Teachers, administrators, students, the Board of Education, and the community should continually be in-

formed of progress. Success breeds success. Each interim goal that is achieved in the process of establishing a systematic program of vocational guidance in the schools paves the way for the attainment of the next goal.

5. The next task of the committee is to see that the *resources essential to goal achievement are available and mobilized*. Resources can be viewed in human terms, in space and time terms, and in material terms. Obviously, each of these three types will be necessary. There must be sufficient staff to implement the program; there must be appropriate physical places to serve as settings and sufficient time allocated; and there must be equipment available. In some cases, in-service training of the guidance staff may be necessary both prior to the implementation of the systematic program and during its operation. As more schools move to modular scheduling, time concerns are diminished. Purchases of new equipment (e.g. simulation devices, closed-circuit television, on-line computer time-sharing) can be justified in terms of product output per money expended.

6. The program is now ready for implementation. The groundwork has been laid; careful and comprehensive planning has preceded the change. During the operation of the program, the committee tries *to ensure that harmonious relationships among the inter-units continues*. One person (e.g. a head counselor or a pupil personnel director) bears general responsibility for coordination. He is careful to see that communication remains open, that all individuals involved in the program are given feedback on their roles and have access to additional input. He works to eliminate "noise" or "distortion" in the system. He sees to it that the partners join in dialogue efforts, that consensual group decisions remain the primary means of operation, that unnecessary fears are relieved. In short, he provides a climate that works against miscommunication and misunderstanding and removes any threats to the security and/or autonomy of the participants.

7. Finally, built into the systems approach is the *need for careful evaluation in relation to goals*. Demonstration of the effectiveness of a program by means of careful evaluation is the best impetus for continued enthusiasm and cooperation. The chapter in this volume dealing with measurement in vocational guidance suggests means and techniques for facilitating this evaluation.

Ralph W. Tyler (1967, p. 44) has summed up the basic premise of this book in a paragraph.

The education required for occupational competence involves much more than training in specific vocational skills. It begins in early childhood and continues throughout active occupational life. Its objectives include: increasing understanding of the world of work, knowledge of vocational opportunities, development of basic literary and work habits, development of ability to plan for a career, development of the abilities required in the general field of an occupation, and development of specific occupational skills as needed. Occupational education is a core responsibility of the

*schools when viewed in this larger context, but as such it should em-
phasize individual flexibility, broad general education, competence in
career planning and in developing more specific skills as needed. It involves not only experiences in the elementary and secondary schools
but also in colleges and other post–high school institutions. Opportunities should not be limited by age or previous schooling if the student
can be substantially aided in his educational development by further
school experiences.*

These are goals that have been held for some time. In the past, they have
not been satisfactorily translated into practice. The authors feel that a systems
approach can successfully implement these goals. It remains to get on with
the task.

REFERENCES

Benedict, Barbara A. et al.   The clinical-experimental approach to assessing
organizational change efforts.   *Journal of Applied Behavioral Science,* 1967,
3, 347–380.

*Benne, K. D., and Birnbaum, M.   Principles of changing.   In W. G. Bennis,
K. D. Benne, and R. Chin (eds.) *The planning of change.*   2nd ed.   New
York: Holt, Rinehart, and Winston, 1969, 328–335.

Bennis, W. G.   Changing organizations.   *Journal of Applied Behavioral Science,* 1966, 2, 247–263.

Chin, R.   The utility of systems models and developmental models for practitioners.   In W. G. Bennis, K. D. Benne, and R. Chin (eds.) *The planning
of change.*   2nd ed.   New York: Holt, Rinehart, and Winston, 1969, 297–312.

Chin, R., and Benne, K. D.   General strategies for effecting changes in human
systems.   In W. G. Bennes, K. D. Benne, and R. Chin (eds.) *The planning
of change.*   2nd ed.   New York: Holt, Rinehart, and Winston, 1969, 32–59.

Davis, S. A.   An organic problem-solving method of organizational change.
Journal of Applied Behavioral Science, 1967, 3, 3–4.

Dionne, J. L.   Organization for innovation.   Paper read at Curriculum Conference, Teachers College, Columbia University, New York, July, 1966.

Etzioni, A.   *A comparative analysis of complex organizations.*   New York:
Free Press, 1961.

Greiner, L. E.   Anecedants of planned organization change.   *Journal of Applied Behavioral Science,* 1967, 3, 51–85.

* Recommended for additional reading.

Hunt, R. G.   On the social and normative structure of the school and the problems of organizational effectiveness.   Speech given to Clinical Conference for School Personnel Administrators, State University of New York, Buffalo, July, 1968. Mimeographed.

Kolb, D. A.; Winter, Sara K.; and Berlew, D. E.   Self-directed change: Two studies.   *Journal of Applied Behavioral Science,* 1968, 4, 453–471.

Lake, D. G.   Concepts of change and innovations in 1966.   *Journal of Applied Behavioral Science,* 1968, 4, 3–24.

Leavitt, H. J.   Applied organizational change in industry: Structural, technological, and humanistic approaches.   In J. G. March (ed.) *Handbook of organizations.*   Chicago: Rand McNally, 1965, 1144–1170.

North Central Association.   Special issue of *Today,* Vol. 11, 1967.

Peter, H. W., and Bennis, W. G., eds.   *Comparative theories of social change.*   Ann Arbor, Mich.: Foundation for Research on Human Behavior, 1966.

Tyler, R. W.   Purposes, scope and organization of education.   In E. L. Morphet and C. O. Ryan (eds.) *Implications for education of prospective changes in society.*   Denver: Project for Designing Education for the Future, 1967, 34–46.

Walton, R. E.   Two strategies of social change and their dilemmas.   *Journal of Applied Behavioral Science,* 1965, 1, 167–179.

*Watson, G.   Resistance to change.   In G. Watson (ed.) *Concepts for Social change.*   Washington, D. C.: National Training Laboratories, 1966.

Winn, A.   Social change in industry: From insight to implementation.   *Journal of Applied Behavioral Science,* 1966, 2, 170–184.

INDEX

abilities, and vocational level, 33–34

Abington School District Project, 157–158

achievements: in high school, 195–196; of Negro adolescents, 42–43

actuarial approaches to guidance, 30–38

adjustment factors, 36–37

alienated youth, work-study program for, 202. See also dropouts

The American High School Student, 84

American occupational structure, 64–83

American Personnel and Guidance Association, 327–328

American Psychological Association, 259

American vs. Soviet guidance systems, 221–222

Ames, Louise, 104–106

Appalachian youth, 93–94

apprenticeship programs, 303

approaches to vocational guidance: actuarial, 30–38; and decision theory, 38–41; developmental emphases, 49–53; psychological emphases, 44–49; sociological emphases, 41–44; summarized, 53–55; trait-and-factor, 30–38

aptitude tests, 255–257, 260–263

assessment, 250–277: and discrimination, 265–268; for evaluation of guidance systems, 270–274; for monitoring, 268–270; for prediction, 261–265. See also evaluation; tests

assistance techniques for life-stage transitions, 227–228

Astin, Helen S., 92

Atlanta, Ga. Occupational Information Center, 213–215

Aubrey, R. F., 227

audio approaches to information, 286

audiotapes, 212

Ausubel, D. P., 88

Autocon, 178

automatic counseling systems, 178–181

Bank, I. M, 151

Beck, Carlton E., 252

behavior, vocationally related, 102–110

behavioral objectives: development of, 272–273; at different educational levels, 132–138; missing from elementary-school projects, 159–160; in occupational fields, 122; sample of, 130–138

behavioral style and vocational choice, 48

behavioral-reinforcement counseling, 210–211, 224

Benne, K. D., 334

Bennis, W. G., 335–337

Berenson, B. G., 224, 225

Bernstein, S., 319

Birnbaum, M., 334

Blacks: adolescents' achievement image, 42–43; counseling of, 86–90; vocational education for, 206–208; work future of, 65–68

Blocher, D. H., 117, 298

Bloom, B. S., 88, 89

Boocock, S. S., 288

Bordin, E. S., 8, 259

Bottoms, J. R., 216

Bowman, F. Q., Jr., 163

Boy, A. V., 230

Brammer, L. M., 229

Brough, J. R., 166

Buehler, Charlotte, 104–106

Bugg, C. A., 299

Burchill, G. W., 201, 203

Busacker, W. E., 163

business and industry: cooperative counseling efforts by, 325–327; employment by type of, 67–69; and work-study programs, 200–202

Byrne, R. H., 9

California Occupational Preference Survey, 268

Campbell, R. E., 194, 245

career conferences, 287

career development. See vocational development

Career Guidance Resources Center, 212–213

Career Information VIEW System, 181, 286

career model, 28–29

Career Pattern Study, 36, 51, 102, 110–113, 117

careers as related to school subjects, chart of, 172–173

Carey, E. Neil, 187

Carkhuff, R. R., 224, 225

Carr, H. C., 327

Census of Population Occupational Classification, 72–73

certification, 315

Champaign, Ill. program for handicapped, 203–206

Champion, G., 199

change: educational, 245–246; overcoming resistance to, 338–340; principles of, 334; strategies of, 335–338; systems approach to, 340–344

Cherryholmes, Cleo, 288

childhood: developmental tasks in, 109; experiences and personality differences, 46

Chin, R., 334

choice, vocational. See vocational choice

choice making. See decision making

Choosing a Vocation, 4, 5

Clarke, R., 226

class expectancies, 44

classification of occupations, 70–81: DOT, 6, 72, 78–81; field-level, 46–47, 76–78; listed, 70–71; psychological, 71–72; sociological, 72–76

clinical prediction, 254–255

cluster concept of vocational education, 185–186, 196, 199

Cody, J. J., 175

cognitive domain, 124

cognitive flexibility, 223

Coleman, J. S., 288

College Entrance Examination Board, Educational Guidance Information System, 289

college-bound students: counseling of, 84; and social-class factors, 43–44; vocational education for, 12–13, 209

college students' changing vocational interests, 76

community involvement: resource use, 212–214; in work-study program, 201–202

community size, effect on vocational choice, 36

Computer-Assisted Occupational Guidance Program, 178–179

Computerized Vocational Information System, 179–180

computers: sample print-out, 295–296; technology of, 178–181; use in vocational guidance, 178–181, 292–298

conferences: for individual counseling, 195; on vocational resources, 213–214

congruent interactions, 49

consumers of vocational guidance, 84–98: as heterogeneous, 84–86; minority groups, 86–95; summarized, 95–96

continuing education, 16–17

Cooley, W. W., 280

cooperative efforts in vocational guidance, 308–332: by business and industry, 200–202, 325–327; by Employment Service Counselor, 322–324; by guidance paraprofessional, 327–330; and master plan for vocational guidance, 310–311; by rehabilitation counselor, 324–325; by school counselor, 320–321; state-level leadership in, 311–318; by teachers, 318–320; work-study programs, 200–202

coordination of guidance efforts, 310–311, 317. See also cooperative efforts

correlation coefficient, use in testing, 252–253

counseling: by action vs. by insight, 225–226; broad view of, 229–230; and collaboration with vocational educators, 197;

of college-bound vs. non-college-bound, 84–85; by computers, 178–181; cooperative effort in, 320–321; for decision making, 175, 226–227, 230–236; defined, 222–236; diagnostic system for, 230–236; education of counselors, 315–316; Employment Service Counselors, 322–324; and environmental treatment, 242–246; for girls vs. boys, 90–93, 167–168; goals of, 221–248; group processes for, 236–242; individual, 195, 222–236; and job placement, 215; leadership in, 315; of minority groups, 86–96; paraprofessional use in, 327–330; and rehabilitation, 324–325; reinforcement, 210–211; relationship of counselor and counselee, 222–236; school, 320–321; and student's internal frame of reference, 232–236; supply of counselors, 309; teacher-counselor collaboration, 320–321; not therapy, 228–229. See also vocational guidance

Counts, G. S., 74–75

Cramer, Rosalind, 239

Cramer, S. H., 85, 195, 222, 237, 239, 280

Cranston, R.I. work-study program, 202

Crites, John O., 265, 269

culturally disadvantaged. See disadvantaged

curriculum: development of, 100–101; formal vocational, 290–291; personalized, 101; state supervision of, 316; zero-reject concept of, 199

Dailey Vocational Tests, 262

Dale, E., 290

DAT (Differential Aptitude Tests), 261–262

Davis, Allison, 88, 89

Davis, S.A., 337

decision making: counseling for, 226–227, 230–235; junior high school guidance on, 174–177; mastery standards for, 125; strategies to foster, 209–212; theory of, 38–41

Deeg, M. E., 74–75

definitions of: career development, 28–29; counseling, 222-223; developmental task, 103; group counseling, 239–240; vocational development, 28–29; vocational guidance, 3–4, 7–8, 233; vocational maturity, 101–102; vocationalization, 29

delivery systems for information, 285–298

Dennard, C. L., 206

Detroit's Developmental Career Guidance Project, 155–156

development of vocational behavior. See vocational development

Developmental Career Guidance Project, 155–156

developmental tasks, 102–110

Dictionary of Occupational Titles, 6, 72, 78–81

Differential Aptitude Tests, 261–262

differentiated staffing, 186–187, 327–330

Dilley, J. S., 175, 226

Dinkmeyer, D. C., 147

Dionne, J. L., 338

disadvantaged: how to help? 16; testing of, 263–264; vocational education for, 206–208; work-experience program for, 184

discriminant analysis, 265

discrimination, tests used for, 265–268

diversity among students, 84–86

DOT (Dictionary of Occupational Titles), 6, 72, 78–81

dramatization, 242

dropouts: junior high school, 168–170; placement of, 215–216; vocational guidance for, 300–303; work program for potential, 184

Drucker, Peter F., 26–27, 64–66, 230

Duncan's Sociometric Status Index, 74

Dunnette, Marvin D., 74–75

early school leaving. See dropouts

education: of counselors, 315–316; for disadvantaged, 206–208; elementary school, 127–138; 143–162, 298–300; general, 198–200; goals of, 13–14; for the handicapped, 203–206; interrelationship with vocational guidance, 10–17; junior high school, 127–136, 163–191; senior high school, 127–138, 192–220; and technology, 14–15; vocational, 10–14, 185–186

Educational and Career Exploration System, 180

Educational Guidance Information System, 289

effectiveness, human, 117

ego. See self-concept

elementary school: behavioral objectives for, 132–138; group counseling in, 241; occupational information in, 298–300; sample program showing objectives for, 132–134; vocational guidance in, 143–162; vocationalization in, 127–130

employment: of minority groups, 326; predictions on future changes in, 66–68

Employment Service Counselors, 322–327

environment: and development of elementary school children, 144–145; occupational, 48; school counselor's effect on, 242–246

Erikson, E. H., 105–107

Etzioni, A., 335

evaluation: of information, 280–284; need for objectives in, 120; and objectives at different educational levels, 132–138; sample of, 130–138; in a systems approach, 270–274

Evans, J. R.,175

expectations: occupational, 34–35; student, 19

family's effect on vocational behavior, 36, 47

federal legislation, 6–7, 11, 309, 317

Feldman, M. J., 207

Fibkins, W., 291

Fiedler, F. E., 225

field-level classification, 46–47, 76–78

field trips, 290

films: occupational, 283–284; use in vocational guidance, 210

Flanagan, John C., 84

Flum, Y., 231

forecasting of performance. See prediction

Forkner, H. L., 109

formulation of objectives, 99–142

Forsyth County, Ga. work program, 184

Fortner, Mildred L., 167

Froelich, C. P., 270

future, predictions on changes in, 64–68

Gambino, Thomas, 183

gaming techniques, use in vocational guidance, 287–290

GATB (General Aptitude Test Battery), 262, 263, 268, 323–324

Geis, H. J., 225

Gelatt, H. B., 226, 239

General Aptitude Test Battery, 262, 263, 268, 323–324

general education, 198–200, 208–209

Georgia State College, 213

Georgia's job-placement program, 216–217

Gesell, A., 104–106

Ghiselli, Edwin, 256

Ginzberg, E., 49–50, 104–106

girls, counseling of, 90–93, 166–168

goals: behaviorally stated, 272–273; for Black youths, 88; of guidance, 6; of vocational guidance, 221–222. See also objectives

Goff, W. H., 156

Goldman, Leo, 233, 239, 259–261, 329

Goodson, A., 299

Gordon, M. S., 288

gratification from work, 45

Greiner, L. E., 339

Gribbons, W. D., 115–118, 269

Gronlund, N. E., 121

Gross, E., 116–117, 154

group counseling, 174, 236–242

groups: characteristics of, 237–238; dynamics of, 238; information delivery to, 286

guidance: defined, 3; evaluation of, 120; goals of, 6; measurement in, 252. See also vocational guidance

guidance paraprofessional, 327–330

guidance teacher, 186–187

guidance technicians, 329–330

Gysbers, N. C., 146, 153, 193

habilitation, vocational, 325

Hackett, D. F., 153–154

Hagen, Elizabeth, 255–256

Hakel, Milton D., 74–75

Halpern, G., 284

Halverson, P. M., 145, 151

Hamilton, J. A., 288

handicapped: testing of, 264; vocational education for, 203–206

Hansen, J. C., 225, 237

Havighurst, R. J., 103, 105–109

Helmstadter, G. C., 258
helping strategies in vocational guidance, 221–249
Herr, E. L., 50–51, 85, 115, 195, 222, 236, 244, 280, 310, 313, 318–320
Hershenson, D. H., 85, 227–228
Hess, R., 88, 89
high schools: college-bound vs. non-college-bound in, 84-85; diversity of students in, 84–86; education in, 10–11; guidance in, 163–220; junior, 134–136, 163–191; senior, 127–132, 136–138, 192–220; student views on occupational prestige, 75; vocationalization in, 127–132, 136–138
Hill, G. E., 148
Hitchcock, A. A., 309
Holland, J. L., 48–49, 71–72, 289
Holland Vocational Preference Inventory, 268
Hollis, J. W., 15, 284
Hollis, Lucille V., 15, 284
Hollman, Thomas D., 74–75
Hosford, R. E., 211
Hoyt, K. B., 209, 303, 311, 329
Hull, W. L., 122–123
human effectiveness, 117
Hunt, Elizabeth E., 150, 153
Hunt, J. McV., 144
Hunt, R. G., 342

IBM Educational and Career Exploration System, 180
Ilg, Frances L., 104–106
imitative learning, 212
Indians, American, 94
individual, adapting the school to the, 242–246
individual counseling, 222–236
individualized instruction, 101
industrial arts in elementary school, 153
industry: cooperative counseling efforts of, 325-327; employment by type of, 67–69
information, 278–307; available for counselor-client use, 326; and computer technology, 292–298; delivery of, 285–298; for dropouts, 300–303; in the elementary school, 298–300; evaluated, 280–284;

listed, 326; retrieval at junior-high level, 181-183; uses of, 279–284
Information System for Vocational Decisions, 180
in-service training, 314–315
Interactive Learning Systems, 180
interests: counselee's, 236; inventories of, 265–268; vocational, 33–34, 265–268
interview approach to information, 286–287
inventories of interests, 265–268

Jenkins, D. H., 245
job classifications at Georgia center, 214
job clinics, 287
job placement, 214–217, 321
job training, 183–184
job-experience kits, 176
Johnson, Beverly, 213
Johnson, G. O., 205
Johnson, M., Jr., 163
Johnson, R. G., 176–177
Jones, B., 209
Jordaan, J. P., 110–111
junior high schools: group counseling in, 242; sample objectives for vocationalization in, 127–130; sample program for, 134–136; vocational guidance in, 163–191
juvenile delinquency prevention, 202

Kabak, Goldie R., 152, 159, 298, 299
Kansas City, Mo. work-study program, 202
Kaplon, Alice J., 288
Karlin, Muriel, 213
Kinnick, B. C., 174
kits, problem-solving, 176–177, 288
Kitson, H. D., 229
knowledge society, 64–66
Kovar, Lillian C., 91
Kraskow, B. S., 182
Krathwohl, D. R., 123
Krippner, S., 43–44
Krumboltz, J. D., 176, 209–212, 288
Kuder Preference Record-Vocational, 267
Kunze, K. R., 325–326

Lake, D. G., 333
Lathrop, R. L., 169
leadership skills for counselors, 315

learning theory, 40–41, 146
Leavitt, H. J., 338
legislation: federal, 6–7, 11, 309, 317; state, 312–314
Leonard, G. E., 155–156
Leonard, Rachel, 171
Levine, L. A., 226
Lewin, Kurt, 334
Lichter, S. O., 301, 302
Life Career Game, 178, 289
life-stage transitions, 227–228
Lister, James L., 265
Lloyd, G. A., 326
local occupational information, 180–182
Lockwood, Ozelma, 171, 242
Lohnes, P. R., 115–118, 269, 294
Longfellow, R. E., 204
Loughary, J. W., 294
Luchin's primacy effect, 144

McCauley, J. S., 16
McCourt, H., 240, 288
McGowan, J. F., 322
McKenzie, Donald H., 265
McKim, Margaret, 109

Mager, R. F., 120–122
Magoon, T. M., 176
Mahler, C. A., 239
Mangum, G. L., 207
Man-Machine Counseling System, 178
mass counseling, 238
master plan for vocational guidance, 310–311
mastery standards for careers, 125
Matheny, K., 216
Matlin, R., 110–111
maturation differences, 168
maturity, vocational: defined, 100–102; research on, 110–119
measurement in guidance, 252–253
Meehl, Paul E., 254
Merachnik, D., 203
Mexican Americans, 94–95
Meyer, J. B., 211
Miller, A. W., 40
Miller, J., 294

Minnesota Department of Education, 172
Minnesota Vocational Interest Inventory, 2, 268
minority groups: Appalachian youth, 93–94; Blacks, 42–43, 86–90; counseling of, 86–96; employment of, 326; girls, 90–93, 166–168; vocational education for, 206–208; work future of, 65–68
models: adult, for elementary-school children, 144, 151–152; occupational, 28–30; use in counseling, 210–212
monitoring tests, 268–270
Moore, G. D., 225, 226
Morse, Wayne, 243
Mosher, R. L., 223
motivation: of individual, 44–49; and information use, 279–280

Nachman, L. R., 302
National Conference on Guidance, Counseling, and Placement . . ., 163, 193
National Defense Education Act, 6
National Opinion Research Center, 73–74
National Vocational Guidance Association, 280–281, 283, 299
National Youth Administration, 6
needs: gratification of, 45; hierarchy of, 46; and vocational interests, 33–34
Negroes. See Blacks
Newton, Mass. Career Guidance Center, 212–213
non-college-bound students: counseling for, 183; specialty-oriented, 209, 303; tests for, 262; vocational guidance for, 301
NORC Scale of Occupational Prestige, 73–74
Norman, R. P., 286
Norris, Willa, 151, 284
NVGA (National Vocational Guidance Association), 280–281, 283, 299
NYA (National Youth Administration), 6

objectives, 99–142; behavioral, 159–160, 272–273; and developmental tasks, 102–110; and research on vocationalization, 110–119; sample objectives, 127–130,

132–138; as treatment, 131; and vocational maturity, 100–102; writing up of, 120–130

occupational information. See information

Occupational Information Center for Education-Industry, 213–215

Occupational Interest Survey, 267

occupational models, 28–30

Occupational Outlook Quarterly, 302

Occupational Outlook Service, 6

occupational preparation. See vocational guidance

occupations: and career development, 25–56; changing nature of, 64–68; classification systems for, 46–47, 70–81; computer systems to counsel on, 178–181; information on, 181–183; 278–307; listed, 70–71; prestige scale of, 73–76; psychology of, 30; sex-typing on, 166; structure of, 64–83. See also vocational guidance

O'Hara, R. P., 52–53, 149–151, 279

Ohio Vocational Interest Survey, 267–268

OIS (Occupational Interest Survey), 267

Olechowski, Nan, 157

organizational change, 333–345

others, significant, 35

OVIS (Ohio Vocational Interest Survey), 267–268

paraprofessionals, 187, 327–330

parents: and child's occupational choice, 36, 46–47; involvement in vocational development, 148–149

Parsons, Frank, 4–5, 7, 31

Passow, A. W., 109

Paterson, D. G., 74–75

Pearson, Richard, 238

personality theories, 45–49

personalized instruction, 101

personnel selection, tests for, 257–259

Peter, H. W., 337

Philadelphia public schools, 125

Pine, G. J., 230

placement: of high school students, 214–217; school counselor's role in, 321

planning: attitude towards, 118; for change, 337; for coordination and cooperation,

310–311; readiness for, 115; and Using Effective Methods of Work concept, 109

poor. See disadvantaged

Porter, T. L., 322

power, concepts of, 335–337

prediction: clinical vs. statistical, 254–255; of future occupational scene, 64–68; tests used for, 251–261; and validity of tests, 252–254; of vocational success, 31–32

preferences, vocational, 111–114

prestige scale for occupations, 73–76

Pritchard, D. H., 193

problem criteria, 8–9

problem solving: junior high school guidance on, 174–177; kits for, 176. See also decision making

program objectives, samples of, 130–138

programmed instruction, 20

Pruitt, W. A., 204

psychological approaches to vocational choice, 44–49

psychological classification of occupations, 71–72

psychology, vocational, 30

psychomotor domain, 123

Puerto Ricans, 94–95

racial differences, 87. See also Blacks

Readiness for Vocational Planning, 110, 115–116, 269–270

regression equations, 252–253

rehabilitation counselors, 324–325

Rehabilitation Services Administration, 324–325

reinforcement counseling, 210–211, 224

reliability coefficients, 252–253

research: current, 110–119; on specific traits, 33–37; state support of, 316–317; on vocational maturity, 110–119; on vocationalization, 110–119

residence's effect on vocational choice, 36; resource centers, vocational, 212–214

risk taking, and vocational choice, 37

Robinson, F. P., 9

Roe, Anne, 45–47, 77–78

Rogers, Carl, 7

Rosen, H., 301

Russia, vocational guidance in, 221–222
RVP (Readiness for Vocational Planning), 110, 115–116, 269–270

Samler, J., 226, 236
sample objectives for vocational guidance, 127–138
San Mateo School District, 199
Santa Barbara work-experience program, 201–202
Santa Cruz occupational information program, 181
scales of occupational status, 73–76
school dropouts. See dropouts
schools: bringing about change in, 333–345; elementary, 127–138, 143–162, 298–300; environment as altered by counselor, 242–246; junior high, 127–130, 134–136, 163–191; senior high, 127–132, 136–138, 199–220
Schroeder, W. W., 210
secondary education, 10–11
secondary schools. See high schools
self-concept, 13, 32; counselee's, 225–236; counselor as helping student to develop a, 232–236; and ego identity, 53; inner and outer influences upon, 231–233; need for, 117; of Negro adolescents, 43; and occupational environment, 48; role in vocational development, 49–53, 113–115
Self-Directed Search for Educational and Vocational Planning, 289
senior high schools: guidance in, 192–220; sample program showing objectives for, 132, 136–138; vocationalization in, 127–132, 136–138
sequencing vocational guidance, 151–159
sex differences: at junior high level, 166–168; and vocational development of girls, 90–93
Shane, H. G., 100–101
Shaw, M. C., 99
Sherman, Vivian, S., 168
Shostrom, E. L., 229
Silvern, L. C., 18
Simons, J. B., 235
simulation: use with occupational information, 287–290; as a vocational guidance

strategy, 177–181
skill-centered curriculum, 169
skill development, 169
Slocum, W. L., 54–55
Smith, D. B., 171
Smith, E. D., 147
Smith, R. E., 242
social roles: importance of, 153; knowledge of, 17; and vocational development, 42–44
sociological classification of occupations, 72–76
sociological factors in vocational guidance, 41–44
SOS project, 303
Soviet Union, vocational guidance in, 221–222
special education programs, 203–206
specialty-oriented students, 209, 303
Specialty-Oriented Student project, 303
specifying a vocational preference, 110–111
Sprinthall, N. A., 223
staff: counselors, 222–236, 309, 315–316, 320–325; differentiated, 186–187, 327–330; guidance technicians, 329–330; in-service training for, 314–315; paraprofessionals, 327–330; support personnel, 328; teachers, 35, 318–321
stages in vocational life, 227–228
standardized tests, 250–251
standards for career development, 125–126
Standards for Education and Psychological Tests and Manuals, 259
Starishevsky, R., 110–111
state supervisors, 311–318
state-level leadership in vocational guidance, 311–318
stating vocational objectives, 120–130
statistical vs. clinical prediction, 254–255
status level of occupations, 73–76
stereotypes of occupations, 34–35
Stewart, J. A., 226
stimulus materials, 211–212
stimulus variable, vocational guidance as a, 9–10, 99–100, 131
strategies of vocational guidance, 148–159, 221–249
Stratemeyer, Frances B., 109

Strong Vocational Interest Blank, 37, 266
Strowig, W., 211
structured stimulus materials, 211
subject-matter courses, chart on relationship to careers, 172–173
Super, Donald E., 7–8, 51–53, 101–118, 180, 230–234, 265, 269–270
supervisors of guidance, 311–318
support personnel, 328
SVIB (Strong Vocational Interest Blank), 37, 266
Swails, Richard, 69
symbolization, 150
systems approach, 18–20; assumptions on, 99; to change in the schools, 333–345; evaluation in a, 270–274; master plan for a, 310–311; to vocational guidance, 341–344

tasks, developmental, 102–110
teachers: cooperative effort in vocational guidance, 318–321; influence of, 35; in junior high occupational education, 172
Techdays, 216–217
technicians, guidance, 329–330
technology: and education, 14–15; and state-level guidance, 314–315; use in vocational guidance, 293–294
terminal students, 300–303. See also dropouts
tests: aptitude, 260–263; base rate on, 258; cutting score on, 258; for the disadvantaged, 263–264; for the handicapped, 264; of interests, 265–268; interpretation of, 264–265; for personnel selection, 257–259; for prediction, 251–265; selection of, 259–260; standardized, 250–251; uses of, 251; validity of, 252–257; of vocational maturity, 268–278; work value measures, 268–270. See also assessment
Thalleen, W., 216
therapeutic counseling, 224–225, 230
therapy models, 227–229
This, L. E., 177
Thompson, J. M., 147
Thoresen, C. E., 210–212
Thorndike, Robert L., 255–256
Tiedeman, D. V., 52–53, 104–106

tools, use in elementary-school guidance, 153
training programs for dropouts, 302–303
trait-and-factor approaches, 30–38
transitions in vocational life, 227–228
treatment: condition, 8–9; objectives for, 131; vs. stimulus, 99–100
Trezise, R., 171, 242
Truax, C. B., 224, 225
"true reasoning," 4–5
Tyler, Leona E., 226
Tyler, Ralph W., 120, 313

Unger, M. B., 213
United States Office of Education, 6, 10, 317
University City Science Center, 125
unskilled worker in a knowledge society, 65–66
Using Effective Methods of Work, 109

validity of occupational tests, 255–257
values, effect on vocational choice, 35–36
Varenhorst, Barbara, 212, 239
VIEW (Vocational Information for Education and Work), 181, 286
VMI and VMII, 101–102
vocational choice. See vocational development
vocational development, 25–56; and abilities, 33–34; approaches to, 29–55; and aspiration level, 37; classification of, 29–30; and decision theory, 38–41; defined, 28–29; in elementary school, 145–146; and expectations, 34–35; and family background, 36; ingredients of, 35–56; and interests, 33–34; mastery standards for, 125; and needs, 33–34; psychological approaches to, 44–49; and residence, 36; and self-concept, 49–53; sociological factors on, 41–44; and stereotypes of occupations, 35; theory of, 25–29; trait-and-factor approach to, 30–38; and values, 35–36; when does it begin? 149. See also vocationalization
Vocational Development Inventory, 269
vocational education: characteristics of, 10–11; cluster concept of, 185–186; for disadvantaged, 206–208; for handicapped,

203–206; in high school, 196–209; inferior image of, 197–198; for minority groups, 206–208; as partner of general education, 198–200. *See also* vocational guidance
Vocational Education Acts, 11, 323–324, 327
vocational evaluation, 204–205
vocational guidance: assessment in, 250–277; and career development, 25–56; consumers of, 84–98; cooperative efforts in, 308–332; and decision making, 209–212; definitions of, 3–4, 7–8, 233; in elementary schools, 143–162; and environmental treatment, 242–246; evaluation of, 270–274; goals of, 221–222; group counseling, 236–242; history of, 4–7; individual counseling, 222–236; information in, 278–307; interdependence with education, 10–14; interdependence with society, 14–17; in junior high school, 127–130, 134–136, 163–191, 242; master plan for, 310–311; objectives for, 99–142, 221–222; and the occupational structure, 64–83; problems classified, 8–9; in senior high school, 192–220; sequencing of, 151–159; Soviet vs. American, 221–222; state-level leadership in, 311–318; as stimulus variable, 9–10; strategies of, 149–159, 221–249; systems approach to, 18–20, 341–344; as treatment, 8–9, 99–100, 131. *See also* counseling
vocational habilitation, 325
Vocational Information for Education and Work, 181
vocational maturity: defined, 100–102; measures of, 268–270; research on, 110–119
vocational psychology, 30
vocational resource centers, 212–214
vocational resource conferences, 213–214
vocational schools, 216–217
vocationalization: concept of, 268; defined, 29; and general education, 208–209; ingredients of, 25–56; inputs to, 119; requirements of students, 84–86. *See also* vocational guidance

Walton, R. E., 337
Walz, R., 294
Warner, Richard, 69
Watley, Donivan, 254
Watson, G., 338–340
Weeks, C., 125–126
Wellington, J. A., 157
Wellman, Frank E., 270, 271
West, E. H., 89–90
Wherry-Doolittle Test Selection, 258
Whiteley, J. M., 223
Williamson, E. G., 8
Willowbrook High School, Ill., 179, 297
Wolfbein, S. L., 15, 66–67
women: career development for, 167; counseling of, 90–93; in future work force, 66, 68; and sex typing of occupations, 167
Woody, R. H., 212
work: automation to displace? 26; character of, 26–27; future of minority groups, 65–68; and people as irrevocably related, 150; using effective methods of, 109
work evaluation, 204–205
work experiences, 183–184, 291–292
work life, 154
work samples, 205
work-study programs, 169, 200–202
Work Values Inventory, 270
Wrenn, C. Gilbert, 27, 222, 230
writing up objectives, 120–130

Yabroff, W., 176
young workers, in future work force, 66, 68
youth, developmental tasks of, 109

Zaccaria, Joseph S., 103, 270
zero-reject concept, 199
Zytowski, D. G., 167